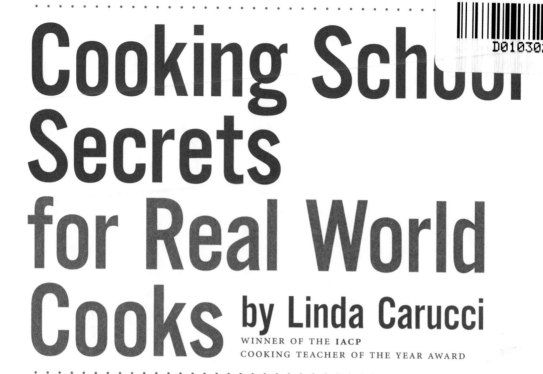

Cooking School Secrets for Real World Cooks

by Linda Carucci

WINNER OF THE **IACP**
COOKING TEACHER OF THE YEAR AWARD

CHRONICLE BOOKS
SAN FRANCISCO

Library of Congress Cataloging-in-Publication Data:

Carucci, Linda.
Cooking school secrets for real world cooks /
by Linda Carucci.
        p. cm.
Includes bibliographical references and index.
ISBN 0-8118-4243-6 (pbk.)
        1. Cookery. I. Title.
TX715.C325 2005
641.5—dc22
        2004023236

Manufactured in Canada.
Designed by Ed Anderson.

Distributed in Canada by Raincoast Books
9050 Shaughnessy Street
Vancouver, British Columbia V6P 6E5

10 9 8 7 6 5 4 3 2 1

Chronicle Books LLC
85 Second Street
San Francisco, California 94105

www.chroniclebooks.com

To my mother and father,
Florence Carucci and the late Leonard Carucci,

and to my late grandmother, Filomena Guglietta,
at whose side I took my first culinary apprenticeship.

ACKNOWLEDGMENTS

I appreciate the generosity of each person named in this book for sharing recipes, tips, techniques, anecdotes, and research with me. In cases where we have lost touch, may this book be a catalyst in our becoming reacquainted.

A big thank-you to everyone who served as a recipe tester for this book, which has been enhanced immeasurably by your significant contributions: Erin Alaimo, Daniele Amtmann, Kay Austin, Jamie Barnett, Howard Becker, Nancy Berglas and Ben Highton, Chris Brown and Dee Broglio, Mark Caballero and Janell McClish, Wendy Calia, Marilyn Callender, Paul Camic and Larry Wilson, Rose Carle, Katherine and Chris Carter, Florence Carucci, Paul Carucci, Allyson Cesario, Kata Chillag, Shawn Harris Chillag, Joan Cirillo, Don Clark and Jill Steinbruegge, Katherine Cordick, Bill and Liesel Cruise, Martha Curti, Gerald Daniels, Lynn Davis, Maureen Dellinger, Ken Durso, Robin Edwards, Joyce Ehrenberg, Michael Emanuel, Jen Engst, Karen Ewing, Lorraine Eyl, Martha Fanning, Suzy Farnworth, Cristina Frazier, Susan Galindo-Schnellbacher, Cindy Garcia, Steve Gere, Linda Gold, Robert Green, Victoria Green, Debra Hanavan, Chris Hanrahan, Mitcie Hanson, Teresa Harbottle, Barbara Hardacre and Mel Harrison, Connie Herman, Sarah Herringer, Mary Herrmann, Randall Hicks, Alvin Hom, Monica Inocencio, Donna Jackson, Karen Jang, Christina Johnson, Sarah Johnson, Stephanie Kay, Dara Kennedy and Rags Gupta, Kieran King, Lisa Lavagetto, Brenda Leppo, Barb Magee, Jan Makin, Denise and Pat Marshall, Matthew Martellari, Charlene McAulay, Tracey McKeown, David McKey, Maritza McMahon, Rachel Meserve, Christine Mohan, Joan Myers, Haruko Nagaishi, Colleen Nibler, Michael and Laura Nichols, Laura Pauli, Lynn Paxton, Susan Glowacki, Peggy Poole, Anu Prints-Seldin, Linda Reynolds, Ellen Robinson, Gail Roth, Dabney Sanders, Deanna Savant, Rita Schepergerdes, Gretchen Schmahl, Liane Scott, Pamela Scott, Naomi Seid-Cronkite, Patricia Shanks, Lisette Silva, Andrine Smith, Dawn Smith, Connie Standfield, Pam Stowe, Art Stremm, Kristen and Mark Taylor, Christina Terry, Amy Treadwell, Lynn Virgilio, Jean Vosti, Meghan Wallingford, Cal Walters, Janet Weisberg, Anne Willis, Michelle Winchester, Bill Wren, Linda Yoshino, and Lynn Zanardi.

I am indebted to my mentors and colleagues who have helped me with the humbling craft of writing: Antonia Allegra, John Birdsall, Joan Cirillo, Nancy Freeman, Deborah Grossman, Randy Milden, Joanne Robb, Jennie Schacht, Elizabeth Thomas, Thy Tran, Charlene Vojtilla, and Laura Werlin. I also want to acknowledge and thank the faculty, staff, and fellow students at Book Passage in Corte Madera, California; fellow members of the Food Writing and Publishing section of the International Association of Culinary Professionals; the San Francisco Professional Food Society writers' group; the 2002 Culinary Institute of America Food Media Conference; and the 2002 Symposium for Professional Food Writers at The Greenbrier.

Lorraine Eyl and Connie Gores were pivotal in helping me zero in on the title for this book. Rebecca Staffel and Doe Coover helped me fine-tune the book proposal and then found it the perfect home.

I am grateful to Chronicle Books for their willingness to take on this project. This book would not have come to fruition were it not for the careful advice, guidance, and shepherding provided by Bill LeBlond, Amy Treadwell, and Jan Hughes. I want to be the president of Sharon Silva's fan club. Her genius and sensitivity as copy editor have enhanced this book significantly. When this book was just a daydream, I fantasized that it would have an exemplary index. With mastery, Alexandra Nickerson has made my dream come true. Thanks also to Alice Harth for her clear and precise illustrations, Ed Anderson for design, and Jake Gardner for art direction.

As a cooking teacher, I feel lucky whenever I get to share my craft with enthusiastic students, either in my own kitchen in Oakland, California, in cooking schools around the country, or at COPIA: The American Center for Wine,

Food & the Arts in Napa, California, where, since writing this book, I have been invited to serve as the Julia Child Curator of Food Arts. Doralece Dullaghan got me started teaching home cooks by inviting me to develop and teach Tools for the Cook, a basic cooking series for Sur La Table customers and students in Berkeley, San Francisco, and Los Gatos, California. It was at Sur La Table where I met the incomparable Meghan Wallingford, my capable and fun-loving assistant, as well as several Sur La Table staff and students who have been involved in this cookbook project as recipe testers. For the past five years, I've had a ball teaching hands-on classes at Ramekins Sonoma Valley Culinary School and working with Bob Nemerovski and the terrific staff there. It's always a pleasure to teach at In Good Taste Cooking School in Portland, Oregon, where owner Barbara Dawson has become my fairy godsister. Teaching in such hospitable, warm surroundings and working with superior staff and volunteer assistants wherever I teach is a dream come true.

In 1983, I left my job as Associate Dean of Students at Occidental College in Los Angeles, moved to San Francisco, and enrolled at the California Culinary Academy. Twenty years have passed and there's no place I'd rather live than the San Francisco Bay Area. The food scene here is lively and dynamic and my professional life is rich, thanks to the support and friendship of many colleagues from near and far, among them Joey Altman, Mary Ayers, Lidia Bastianich, Paul Castrucci, Michael Chiarello, Elaine Corn, Rosetta Costantino, Carol Crawford, Lisa Ekus, Courtney Febbroriello, Janet Fletcher, Fran Gage, Linda Graebner, Patricia Healy, Linda Hillel, Ruta Kahate, Sam King, Susan Klugerman, the late Loni Kuhn, Karen MacKenzie, Rosemary Mark, Alice Medrich, Weezie Mott, Sheila Olaksen, Cindy Race, Karola Saekel, Marie Simmons, the late Barbara Tropp, Denise Vivaldo, Russ Zipkin, my chef-instructors at the California Culinary Academy, my colleagues in the San Francisco Professional Food Society recipe developers' group, the staff at KQED-TV in San Francisco and the production team for *Cooking at the Academy,* my wonderful friends and colleagues at COPIA, and the students, staff, and volunteers at the San Francisco Conquering Homelessness through Employment in Food Service (CHEFS) program.

Thank you to the following individuals and agencies who provided me with helpful information as I wrote this book: for her willingness to assist me with all things Spanish (including a fantastic recipe that space limitations prevented us from including in this book), Libby Creed, former manager of The Spanish Table in Berkeley, California; for the private tutoring session on olive oil, Darrell Corti; for sharing her research on butter, Fran Gage; for the lowdown on pomegranate molasses, Joyce Goldstein; for her wisdom about chocolate, Alice Medrich; for the skinny on fats, Fran McCullough; for lamb insights, Brenda Leppo; and for setting me straight on short ribs, Bruce Aidells. Also, thanks to the California Beef Council, Stephanie Lee and Susan Zieleniewicz of the University of California Cooperative Extension of Alameda County, Kristen Foley and the Pacific Coast Farmers' Market Association, and Jennifer Quermann of the California Walnut Marketing Board.

It's been fun traveling down memory lane with my mother as I've written this book, exchanging spurts of e-mail across the country about whether she added raw or sautéed onions to her meatball mixture and how long she cooks her escarole. I've done my best to get the facts straight for you.

My husband, Allen Rehmke, the significantly underpaid facilities manager of Linda Carucci's Kitchen, gets special commendation for all the support along the way, especially for keeping his Italian American wife stocked with delicious canned tomatoes, handpicked from the family farm. I appreciate his discerning palate, and I remain hopeful that he will one day forgive me my sin of adulterating his favorite white chocolate cheesecake by serving it with raspberry sauce.

CONTENTS

Introduction 10

PART ONE: COOKING BASICS 13
....

Equipment Matters 15

Knife Skills and Cuts 19

Mise en Place 22

Do No Harm: Food Safety 23

Cooking Methods 24

How Cooking Changes the Texture
and Flavor of Foods 35

Using Your Senses When You Cook 37

Understanding Your Palate 38

Cooking with the Seasons 40

Seasoning to Taste 42

Brining and Today's "New" Meats
and Poultry 45

Attentive Tasting 46

A Few Words about
Menu Planning 47

Creative Cooking 48

A Few Words about
Plate Presentation 49

PART TWO: RECIPES 51
....

Guidelines for Preparing the Recipes
in this Book 52

Stocks, Soups, and Salads 54
....

Secrets for Successful Stocks and Broths 56

Recipes that Use Homemade Chicken
Stock, Chicken Broth, or Vegetable Broth 59
Stock and Broth Recipes 60

Secrets for Successful Soups 65
Soup Recipes 66

Secrets for Successful Salads 78
Salad Recipes 81

Risottos and Pastas 93
....

Secrets for Successful Risotto 95
Risotto Recipes 98

Secrets for Cooking Perfect Pasta 107
Pasta Recipes 109

Seafood, Poultry, and Meat Main Dishes   131

Secrets for Preparing Fish and Shellfish
Successfully   134

Seafood Recipes   136

Secrets for Selecting and Cooking
Poultry Successfully   162

Poultry Recipes   168

Secrets for Preparing Meats Successfully   208

Meat Recipes   211

On the Side   247

Secrets for Pairing Side Dishes with
Main Dishes   249

Side Dish Recipes   250

Sweet Endings   285

Secrets for Choosing an Appropriate
Dessert   287

Secrets for Preparing Successful Desserts   288

Dessert Recipes   289

PART THREE: SEASONAL RECIPES,
MENUS, AND SOURCES   314

Seasonal Recipes   316

Twelve Seasonal Menus for Casual and
Special Occasions   319

Sources   326

Bibliography   327

Index   328

Table of Equivalents   352

INTRODUCTION

I got into trouble in high school chemistry. I never memorized the hallowed periodic table. Lacking that foundation, just as the teacher predicted, I was good for nothing for the rest of the term. I did, however, manage to enjoy myself (wasn't that the point?) on the days the class moved into the chemistry lab—perhaps a bit of foreshadowing for my future career.

It wasn't until I got to cooking school that, thanks to Robert Jorin, a patient and particularly effective chef-instructor, I began to grasp and appreciate some of the science I'd missed twelve years earlier. Indeed, many of the recipes in this book are based on principles, techniques, and secrets to success I learned from Chef Robert and his colleagues at the California Culinary Academy.

These days, as a cooking instructor and enthusiastic home cook, I read everything I can get my hands on about food chemistry. As the saying goes, there's no one more fervent than a convert. In fact, many years after graduating from cooking school, I married a chemical engineer, my own personal Mister Science, whose counsel I value tremendously in sleuthing out the hows and whys of chemistry as it applies to day-to-day cooking. After all, when we talk about cooking, or applying heat to change the physical properties of food, we're talking about chemistry.

So, what does all this have to do with the book you're holding in your hands right now? For starters, I think it's only fair that you know my frame of reference before we saunter into the kitchen together. The recipes and methods in this book are based on the foundation of classical French cooking that was drilled into my head in cooking school. I wasn't exactly a blank slate when I got there, however. Nor did I stop learning the day I graduated.

My first apprenticeship was cooking at my grandmother's side in the kitchen of my family's five-room ranch house in Massachusetts. We made *linguine aglio e olio* and pizza fritt' at the pink electric stove, and pulled loaves of soft, dense grandma bread from the pink oven. (Can you guess what my mother's favorite color was?) My grandmother made bread once a week, and ravioli once a summer. "I'll only make the ravioli if you promise to roll out the dough," she'd tease. When it came time to pull the big, wooden ravioli board out from under my parents' double bed, there was no way anyone could possibly grab the rolling pin out of her hands. She was on a mission, and, to her way of thinking, no one else was capable of rolling the dough as thin as she could. I was happy to sit and watch her work the smooth, delicate dough, treating her ravioli with more tenderness than she did her husband. She let me mix up the rigott' and eggs with our flimsy whisk, and grate the Romano cheese with the old metal Mouli that made an indentation in the side of my hand where I gripped it tight the way she showed me.

These early influences shaped my palate as well as my patience. I grew up eating simple, robust Italian American food, and I just assumed everyone else did, too. In my house, it was a foregone conclusion that it takes time to cook. Few activities (outside of working hard—it was New England, after all) were more important than food. Even when my mother got home late from work, she still managed to whip up a satisfying pot of chili (page 245) in the pressure cooker. I know some people find cooking to be a chore (sorry, but I must confess to feeling that way myself about rolling out a pie crust), but for me it's always been something I just lose myself in. The pleasure I get from cooking is as satisfying as eating great food.

I'd be remiss not to acknowledge how living in Northern California has helped shape the cook I am today. Living in the state that's often referred to as the nation's salad bowl has taught me a healthy respect for ingredients and the seasonality of foods. While I do admit to some strong opinions about this, I assure you I'm not one of those food snobs who brags about using "only-all-fresh-ingredients-all-the-time." Having been raised in New England, and being a practical cook with a southern Italian background, I know how dull my cooking would be if that were the case. If you don't believe me that good things come in cans, too, let me prove it through a nice bowl of Rigatoni with Sausage and Mushroom Ragù (page 118), with an unctuous sauce made from terrific canned tomatoes. Or how about Grilled Leg of Lamb with Pomegranate Marinade (page 221), which owes its assertive personality to a bottle of antioxidant-rich concentrated pomegranate molasses. Flavorful ingredients—both fresh and prepared—will always be welcome in my kitchen.

In this book, I'm on a mission to allay new cooks' apprehensions and answer experienced cooks' most vexing questions. It all starts with a substantial Cooking Basics section where you'll learn about the most appropriate equipment for the job; which cooking methods to use for which foods and why; how to cut, chop, dice, julienne, and chiffonade; and more. There's information on seasoning to taste and how to bring out the inherent flavors in certain foods, as well as pointers on creative cooking and menu planning.

Throughout the book you will find numerous drawings that illustrate everything from how to butterfly a chicken breast and strip leaves from a sprig of fresh thyme to how to remove the skin from a fish fillet. You'll also find twelve sample seasonal menus for casual and special-occasion dinners, a list of recipes arranged by season, and reliable internal-temperature doneness charts to ensure that your Rack of Lamb with Garlicky Bread Crumbs (page 224) will be cooked to perfection every time. One of my recipe testers calls *Cooking School Secrets for Real World Cooks* "the Talmud of cookbooks, the version with the commentary on the side."

The heart and soul of this cookbook are its 100 recipes. They run the gamut from Shortcut Chicken Broth with a Dividend (page 61) to Devil's Food Cake with Dark

Chocolate Ganache or Chocolate Fudge Frosting (page 298). Main dishes include both quick-fix weeknight recipes, such as Cracker-Crusted Nubble Point Scallops (page 142), and special main dishes to prepare when you have more time, such as Braised Short Ribs with Frizzled Leeks (page 237). Each recipe begins with "Secrets," where I offer guidelines on potential stumbling blocks, what steps can be prepared in advance, and tips on specific ingredients. It's as if you have your own personal kitchen buttinsky.

Most of the recipes in this book are my personal favorites that have withstood the test of time. But each and every recipe has also been prepared by at least three home cooks who live in small towns and big cities all across the United States, from Medway, Massachusetts (my hometown), to Atlanta, Georgia; from Glendora, California, to Seattle, Washington; from Magnolia, Texas, to Evanston, Illinois. The dedication of these recipe testers has been phenomenal; one even sent in testing reports from her temporary quarters in Botswana.

I am tremendously indebted to this posse of 116 home cooks, many of whom have been my students or assistants in the classes I've taught either in my home-based cooking school in Oakland, California, or around the country. Some of the recipe testers are friends. Several have become friends. A few are family. They range as much in cooking experience as they do in demographics. There is no question that the recipes are stronger than ever, thanks to their observations, suggestions, and occasional stumbles.

The recipes are divided into five sections: Stocks, Soups, and Salads; Risottos and Pastas; Seafood, Poultry, and Meat Main Dishes; On the Side; and Sweet Endings. Their titles are listed at the beginning of each section, along with indications of which are quick, vegetarian, and able to be made ahead. Many are appropriate for weeknights; others are more suitable for when you have plenty of time to enjoy the pleasures of cooking. This latter category includes such personal favorites as paella (page 158), crown roast of pork (page 219), and gumbo (page 138), all of which I particularly enjoy preparing for holidays and special occasions. Be sure not to miss the *timpano* (page 126), a spectacular pastry drum filled with pasta, cheeses, tender little meatballs, hard-cooked eggs, and more.

Among my weeknight favorites are Thai-Style Minced Chicken with Basil and Chiles (page 170) and Weeknight Green Salad (page 81); I've prepared the latter several times a week as far back as I can remember, as did my mother, and her mother. Chicken Cacciatore (page 202) and Spaghetti and Meatballs (page 114) are also dishes my mother made, and many testers found them to be as comforting as I still do. I occasionally prepare risotto for a weeknight supper or as a first course for a special dinner. The risotto recipes in this book have also withstood the test of time, serving as standard repertoire in my Hands-On Risotto Workshops.

Occasionally, you'll see a recipe such as Kalijira Rice Pilaw (page 277) or Lemon Marzipan Cake (page 301) that friends have shared with me and I have included to round out the collection. Finally, you'll notice several attributions, especially in cases where I felt a recipe would be enhanced by sharing the wisdom of a trusted colleague.

I wrote *Cooking School Secrets for Real World Cooks* because my students asked for a reliable kitchen go-to guide with more than just recipes. I hope you'll give this book a good workout and that, in the process, it will become your trusted kitchen companion. Please let me know what you think about it via my Web site, **www.LCKitchen.com**.

COOKING BASICS

PART ONE

"WHEN YOU COOK, YOU NEVER STOP LEARNING. THAT'S THE FASCINATION OF IT."

—JAMES BEARD

If you're an experienced cook, pat yourself on the back as you go through this section, secure in the knowledge that you already have the basics under your belt. Reading it will reinforce the skills you've already mastered and affirm that we're approaching the stove from the same perspective. You'll discover the hows and whys behind the techniques and methods you've picked up over time, just as I did in cooking school. Understanding cooking on this level is rewarding and gives you the surefooted confidence you need to cook with new ingredients and create new recipes.

If you're a less experienced cook, this section will provide you with an elementary understanding of cooking, including the hows and whys of twelve basic cooking methods, divided into two primary categories, moist heat and dry heat. Armed with this knowledge, you'll be able to figure out why your Chicken Cacciatore (page 202) could come out tender and moist one time and dry and tough another, or how to ensure that your flank steak always develops a flavorful crust when you grill.

Along with cooking techniques, in this section, you will find information on kitchen equipment, knife skills, how cooking affects the flavor and texture of foods, using your senses when you cook, seasoning to taste, and more.

EQUIPMENT MATTERS

I'm not exactly what you'd call an equipment junkie, but over the years a few favorite pots, pans, tools, and gadgets have found their way into my kitchen—and into my heart. Teaching in cookware stores, cooking schools, and private homes across the United States has provided me a terrific opportunity to test-drive other cooks' knives, colanders, and cutting boards. Here's my short list of basic equipment you'll need to prepare the recipes in this book.

COOKWARE

Sturdy, dependable pots and pans are a necessity, and just about every line of cookware can be purchased in a set. But, before you invest in someone else's idea of the perfect set, do two things: First, be sure you have plenty of room to store all the pieces. Second, ask yourself if you'd be better off buying just a few of the pieces you really need as open stock (single purchase) and putting any money saved toward something else.

How do you know what type of cookware to choose? Sometimes, as with glass-top ranges or high-BTU-output cooktops, the features of your particular stove dictate the type of cookware that will work best for you. Considering heat conduction alone, copper, cast iron, and aluminum all perform well. But each of these has drawbacks. As a surface on pots and pans, aluminum has fallen out of favor due to its link with health conditions such as hardening of the arteries. However, it's not unusual to find cookware with an aluminum core, where the metal is sandwiched between copper and/or stainless steel. Many cooks (count me among them) are enamored of copper and cast-iron pieces, but each requires a commitment to upkeep that some people aren't willing to make. Here are the specific sizes and brands of pots and pans I find particularly useful.

POTS

If you like the performance of cast iron, an all-purpose, porcelain-enameled, cast-iron 8-quart Le Creuset (pronounced luh crew-*zay*) Dutch oven can't be beat for braising or making soups. In fact, recipe testers who made the short ribs on page 237 in a Le Creuset Dutch oven unwittingly shaved off as much as a half hour of cooking time, thanks to its even heating and heat-retention properties. This line is easy to clean, too. On the downside, Le Creuset pots are superheavy, and I wouldn't recommend them to children or to people with weak wrists or arthritis in the arms or hands. One-third of their weight is in the lid, so it's possible to lighten the load significantly if you don't put the lid on until you get to your destination, be it the oven or storage cabinet.

For cooking pasta, nothing I have beats the old, thin, lightweight, copper-bottomed 6-quart Revere Ware pot I've been using since grad school. I'd never choose a heavier pot over this old friend for pasta, because the water takes so much longer to boil in those behemoths.

SAUCEPANS

All-Clad saucepans are both dependable and a cinch to clean. They're dishwasher safe, too, which comes in handy after you've melted sugar. I particularly love the curved bottom on All-Clad's saucier pans (see illustration, page 104), a shape ideal for risottos, sauces, and puddings, as there's no corner to trap food (see Sources for buying All-Clad seconds online). I constantly reach for my 5½-quart saucier. When it comes to saucepans, it's good to have a 1-quart pan for small jobs, such as poaching an egg or two, and at least one all-purpose 3- or 4-quart pan for cooking vegetables and the like.

STIR-FRY PAN

Urged on in an article in *Fine Cooking* magazine by the late Barbara Tropp, I bought a lightweight, nonstick, unlabeled 14-inch stir-fry pan at a restaurant supply warehouse (see Sources). I was won over before I even cooked in this pan once I saw how easy it is to wash, especially compared to my dear, old round-bottomed wok. Its flat bottom allows it to sit directly on the burner of my gas stove, in contact with the flame, and the pan is so light I can easily flip food as I sauté or stir-fry. (We'll get into this more fully in a few pages, but flipping is the most efficient way to sauté.) This inexpensive (less than twenty-five dollars) stir-fry pan is fun to use, too.

SKILLETS AND SAUTÉ PANS

Skillets have sloping sides and are usually sold without a lid. Sauté pans have straight sides and most come with a lid. I'm not a snob when it comes to skillets. You'll need two workhorse pans, one 6 or 8 inches and another 10 or 12 inches. (Skillets and sauté pans are measured across the top; baking pans are measured across the bottom.) When you're just starting out, stay away from anything larger than 12 inches, unless it's to supplement these two.

Choose a heavy-duty material, such as stainless steel on the outside and aluminum in the core, for a sauté pan. I like All-Clad's sauté pans. Since this pan is frequently used to brown foods, or to prepare an *à la minute* dish that includes a quick pan sauce (see Turkey Piccata, page 177), it's important to have even heat distribution, which the stainless steel and aluminum combination provides. Also, I prefer a conventional finish, rather than nonstick, on a sauté pan, so the flavorful pan drippings will stick to the bottom of the pan, developing the foundation for a flavorful sauce.

Nonstick skillets are great when it comes to easy cleanup, but spend your money on those made by a company specializing in nonstick cookware, such as Look or Scanpan. The other major cookware companies that sell both conventional and nonstick skillets emphasize the heavy-duty, solid construction of the pan, which means the pan is heavier in your hand. A heavy pan is less conducive to flipping, which is important when sautéing small foods. Keep in mind that you pay dearly for the heavy-duty core of those nonstick pans. I still swear by my little Wearever nonstick skillet. My hat's off to them for etching the pan size right into the bottom of the pan, too. If only the other cookware companies would follow suit.

Look, a cookware company from Iceland, uses the same material used in football helmets to make their moderately priced line of jet black nonstick pots and pans. The nonstick surface is on both the inside and outside, making for cookware that's particularly easy to clean. My 11-inch Look skillet has held up well for several years under the rigors of operating a cooking school in my home. Look nonstick cookware is completely ovenproof to 500 degrees F. I can also vouch for Scanpan from Denmark, which makes a sturdy, well-built line of nonstick saucepans, sauté pans, skillets, and braising pots (see Sources for buying seconds online).

INDOOR GRILLS AND GRILL PANS

If you're a fan of indoor grilling, as I am, consider investing in a cast-iron stove-top grill, either a flat model or one with raised sides to deflect splattering and a handle for easy maneuverability. If you go with the flat one, the rectangular double-burner size is more versatile than the square single-burner model. For small jobs, you could always heat just one end of the larger grill, but there's hardly enough room for a flank steak on the smaller one. Many home cooks who tested recipes for this book swear by their portable, electric countertop grills such as the George Foreman brand. I haven't tried one, only because my fairy godfather installed an indoor gas grill when I remodeled my kitchen. When I teach in other cooking schools, I rely heavily on the Le Creuset stove-top grill. One caveat: Don't even consider indoor grilling unless you have excellent ventilation.

BAKING PANS AND DISHES

Emile Henri has a terrific line of baking dishes made from a particular French clay that is prized for its heat retention properties. These pieces—some with lids—come in a range of sizes, shapes, and vibrant colors, and feature an easy-to-clean finish. I use these dishes for everything from lasagna to savory corn pudding to chocolate bread pudding. They're attractive enough to take right to the table. If money is a consideration, Pyrex tempered-glass baking dishes and ramekins do a respectable job, and have the advantage of being clear, so you can monitor how the outside edges of a crust are browning. For baking cakes, look for pans with straight sides, rather than slightly flared ones. They make frosting layer cakes a piece of, well, you know.

KNIVES

When it comes to knives, I'm as flexible as I am about cookware. More than with any other piece of equipment, knife selection is personal. Knives must be comfortable in *your* hand; you should feel safe and in control when using them. I prefer knives made of a carbon stainless steel alloy, as they hold an edge well and, as the name implies, are virtually stainless. The most important—and versatile—is your chef's knife. A good chef's knife is like an extension of your hand. The blade should be as long as you're comfortable wielding. Shop for knives at a cookware store where the staff is knowledgeable and will help you compare several different sizes and brands. If you know the store has a kitchen for cooking classes, bring along a few carrots and ask if they'll let you test the knife before you buy it. Look for a thin blade and a solid handle that's comfortable for you to grip or balance. People with smaller hands seem to like Japanese-made Global knives. They hold an edge well, but you must use a diamond steel to hone them. (The sharpening steel should be made of a surface that's harder than the blade material.)

Choose a paring knife you can comfortably cradle in your hand. It should be relatively lightweight, so as not to cause hand fatigue when you're trimming lots of vegetables. You don't have to spend a lot of money to get a good paring knife with a thin blade.

Other knives I reach for often include:

• A fillet knife for cutting paper-thin slices and removing fish skin.

• A cheese knife for cutting sticky cheeses such as Brie or Taleggio.

• A boning knife for boning—and carving—poultry and meats.

• A Granton edge carving knife identifiable by its dimpled blade, for cutting thin, even slices of meat.

• A sturdy serrated knife for cutting bread and tomatoes, shaving off the crusts of bread for fresh bread crumbs, and shaving chocolate for melting.

If you invest in good knives, be sure to keep them sharp and to give them a good home. Whether you choose an in-drawer knife rack, countertop knife block, or hanging magnetic bar, store your knives so the blades aren't touching.

CUTTING BOARDS

A good knife deserves a firm, solid cutting board or two. Ideally, it's good to have at least one plastic board you can put through the dishwasher, so you don't have to worry about cross contamination. Buy the largest board you can accommodate in your sink. This way, you can prep ingredients for a stir-fry in separate corners of the board, then transfer them with a metal bench scraper (another tool I find indispensable) to the stir-fry pan without dirtying lots of bowls. Trudeau makes plastic (polypropylene) boards with rubber gripper corners (see Sources). Otherwise, place a damp kitchen towel or a piece of skidproof plastic shelf liner underneath your cutting board to prevent it from sliding around as you chop.

THERMOMETERS

I couldn't function in the kitchen without an instant-read thermometer. These days, chef coats are even designed with two narrow pockets on the arm: one for a pen, the other for an instant-read thermometer. They come in digital and traditional dials; the latter are less expensive and seem to last longer. I use my instant-read thermometer most often to check the doneness of meat and poultry, but I also reach for it when I want to be sure a sorbet mixture is cool enough to pour into the ice-cream maker.

When roasting meats and poultry, nothing beats a probe-type instant thermometer. This device features a long probe, which you stick into the roast. The probe is attached to a wire-mesh cord, which gets inserted into a timer device that rests on the countertop (or sticks magnetically onto a nearby surface—great for outdoor grills). The oven door gets closed right on top of the cord, and you never have to open the door to check the internal temperature: the display window on the timer device tells you the exact temperature at all times.

A deep-frying thermometer is one of those single-use gadgets that makes a big difference to fine cooks, whether you're heating a couple of inches of oil for frizzled leeks or considerably less for eggplant parmigiana. Clipped on the inside of the pot, it lets you know just when the oil is ready, while also providing a constant indication of the oil temperature so you can regulate the heat promptly as you fry.

SMALL ELECTRICS

It's great to have a food processor with at least an 11-cup capacity. But if money is a consideration, you can make do with a stand blender. An immersion—or stick—blender works well for puréeing soups and sauces directly in the pan without dirtying another vessel or having to transfer hot liquids. For safety, I recommend the cordless, rechargeable immersion blender over the electric model with its long cord. A handheld or stand mixer is necessary for creaming butter and sugar for cakes, and makes easy work of whipping cream and egg whites.

SMALL WARES

You'll need a sturdy slotted spoon for transferring foods and stirring liquids (the holes prevent splashing). A bulb-shaped balloon whisk is useful for combining dry ingredients and for whipping air into heavy (whipping) cream and egg whites. Don't overlook measuring spoons, dry measuring cups, and a liquid measure or two. Measuring cups specifically designed for liquids have a pouring spout. It's nice to have them in 1-, 2-, and 4-cup increments. You'd be amazed at the versatility of both 4- and 8-cup Pyrex liquid measures. You can melt butter and chocolate in them in the microwave, then stir in the other ingredients for one-bowl brownies. I use the 8-cup measure for rising dough. It allows me to see precisely when the dough has doubled in size.

Other important kitchen equipment includes a set of three to six stainless-steel, glass, or plastic nesting bowls for mixing, washing produce, and even serving. Fine- and medium-mesh strainers are invaluable for straining and draining foods. I favor a hand-operated food mill for puréeing canned tomatoes and for making applesauce without having to peel, seed, or core the apples. A Microplane is unparalleled for its ability to zest citrus fruits without a trace of pith; it does double duty admirably as a grater for hard cheeses.

You'll see other, nonessential tools mentioned throughout this book, including a mandoline, Boerner Original V-slicer, or Benriner slicer; a Chinese strainer, or "spider"; a heatproof rubber spatula (actually made of silicone); and a Silpat (or other brand) silicone baking liner.

Among the favorite gifts I've received are spoons and utensils made of hardwoods such as olive, cherry, and maple. They feature smooth, rounded handles that are comfortable for long stirring sessions. Because these hardwood utensils are less porous than inexpensive softwood spoons, they tend not to absorb odors, which is particularly important if you reach for the same spoon to stir saffron risotto one day and chocolate pudding the next. I also find that the softwood spoons tend to splinter and break long before their smooth, hardwood cousins develop a patina from steady use.

A swivel-blade vegetable peeler is something I couldn't live without. You may be surprised at how reasonably priced these peelers are. Select one in a bright color that will be easy to spot in your equipment drawer.

Over the years I've come to the conclusion that, with cookware, you get what you pay for. Often it's worth waiting for what you really want to go on sale (or looking online for bargains on seconds), rather than buying a poor-quality alternative.

KNIFE SKILLS AND CUTS

Call me weird. When I look down at a plate and see meltingly soft, perfectly chopped onions in my tomato sauce, I know the person who made this sauce understands—and cares about—an important fundamental of cooking. This cook gets it.

We are not born with the knowledge of how to chop vegetables, particularly onions. Out of cooking school for more than twenty years, I still watch closely when people chop onions, and I'm still learning little tricks. Onions reveal the sophistication—or innocence—of the cook. Whether you're a television chef, an author promoting your latest cookbook, a cooking-school assistant, or a fine home cook, nothing says more about your level of expertise than your knife skills. If no one ever taught you how to chop an onion, you've just hit the jackpot. That's next on our agenda here.

HOW TO CHOP AN ONION

Certainly, there are many legitimate ways to chop an onion. If the way you've been doing it for years works for you, you needn't change a thing. Before you even reach for your knife, figure out how you will use the onions; this determines their size and shape. If they're for something like red pepper bisque (page 66) that's going to be blended or passed through a food mill, the size and shape is immaterial. However, for even cooking, all the pieces should be about the same size. Here's one way to chop an onion:

- First, put down a damp kitchen towel between the countertop and your cutting board. This keeps the board anchored.

/continued

- Select a chef's knife, one with a sharp 8-, 10-, or 12-inch blade, or another size that you're comfortable with.

- Cut off the hairy root end of the onion and remove the skin. Do this in some far corner of the cutting board so the root doesn't leave dirt in the center of the board. Designate that corner as your discard pile, or use a bowl for discards.

- Cut the onion in half lengthwise, that is, through the stem and root ends. Place the halves flat side down on the cutting board.

- Make a series of long, parallel cuts, lengthwise from the stem end to the root end, starting just below the stem so that the onion half holds together. For roughly chopped—rather than precisely diced—onions, it's not important how far apart the cuts are. If you want to end up with neatly diced onion, however, space the cuts uniformly. Repeat with the other onion half.

- With the knife blade parallel to the cutting board, and with your other hand resting flat on top of the onion to keep it together, make another series of parallel cuts from root end to stem end. Repeat with the other onion half.

- Hold the knife perpendicular to the board, and compress the onion half with your other hand so it stays in a neat package. Starting at the root end, cut the onion crosswise. These final cuts will sever the onion into chopped pieces. When you get close to the stem, grab it and turn the remaining unchopped piece on its side, chopping around the stem before tossing the stem in the discard pile. Repeat with the other onion half. Gather the chopped onion into a big pile and, if necessary, chop until the pieces are all about the same size.

- To dice—rather than roughly chop—onions, each time you make the cuts described above, make them at ¼-inch intervals for ¼-inch dice, ½-inch intervals for ½-inch dice, and so on.

All of this by-hand detail may seem picayune. In fact, many students often ask if it's okay to whip out a food processor and pulse the onion until it's roughly chopped. When I need lots of chopped onions, say for turkey stuffing, that is precisely what I do. But before you add onions to a food processor, you must first cut them into roughly 1-inch chunks. In most food processors, you can only pulse a handful of chunks at a time; if you overload the processor, you'll get uneven pieces. It's important to pulse several times, rather than let the motor rip. Otherwise, that is just what the onions will be: ripped up into a juicy mush.

MIREPOIX

The next vegetables to prep for the red pepper bisque are carrots and celery. Onions, carrots, and celery comprise the holy trinity of vegetables known by the French term *mirepoix* (pronounced meer-*pwah*). Italian cooks call a similar mixture *soffrito* (pronounced soh-*freet*-toh), which would be *sofrito* in Spain.

The standard ratio for mirepoix is four parts onions to two parts carrots to one part celery. This doesn't mean 4 onions to 2 carrots to 1 celery stalk. Think instead in terms of volume, such as 1 pound onions to ½ pound carrots to ¼ pound celery. Of course, this ratio can vary some, depending on many factors, including how sweet your carrots are, how vegetal your celery tastes, and what the flavor profile is in the dish. For example, I would add no carrots at all to a mirepoix for asparagus soup, because the red color and sweet flavor would compete with the fresh, herbaceous green purée I'm striving for.

For the puréed red pepper bisque, you'd chop the carrots and celery for the mirepoix into pieces roughly the same size as the onions. If, however, you were making Herb-Crusted Chicken Potpies (page 198), where the vegetable pieces make up a collection of solids that are bound together in a sauce along with chunks of chicken, you would chop them more precisely into large dice. These vegetable and chicken chunks in the potpies are called the *garniture*.

BATONNET

In order to cut a rounded vegetable such as a carrot into dice for garniture, start by making squared-off sticks known by the French term *batonnet* (pronounced bah-tone-*nay*). First, cut a large, thick unpeeled carrot crosswise into 2-inch lengths. Square off each piece by cutting off the rounded edges (save the trim for mirepoix). Cut the squared-off carrot blocks into slabs ½ inch wide by 2 inches long. Cut the slabs into batonnet, or sticks ½ inch wide by ½ inch thick by 2 inches long. Besides being the precursor to diced and julienned carrots, you could use these sticks in Pot Roast and Gravy with Peas and Carrots (page 241), Chicken Cacciatore (page 202), or in a stir-fry.

DICE

To achieve perfectly cubed vegetables, as in a pair of dice, cut the batonnet into ½-inch cubes.

JULIENNE

To achieve a julienne cut, start with 1½-inch-long squared-off pieces of carrot and cut lengthwise into ⅛-inch-thick slices. Stack the slices, then cut into ⅛-inch-wide pieces, the size of matchsticks.

PAYSANNE

The French term *paysanne* (pronounced pay-*zahn*) refers to roll-cut vegetables. They are often used in stocks where it is desirable to expose as much of the inside surface area of a vegetable as possible. To cut long, dense vegetables such as carrots or parsnips into paysanne cut, first cut off the end at a 45-degree angle. Roll the vegetable over 180 degrees (onto its "back") and make another crosswise, diagonal cut at a 45-degree angle about 2 inches down. You should end up with roughly triangular pieces that are broad at the base and have a narrower, flat top (see illustration, right).

CHIFFONADE

The final cutting technique you'll need for preparing the recipes in this book is yet another French term, *chiffonade* (pronounced shif-on-*ahd*). Basil, spinach, and sorrel have delicate leaves that bruise easily when chopped vigorously. To keep them green, the leaves are cut into ribbons, or chiffonade. Stack several leaves on top of one another, aligning the stems (see illustration, page 86). Roll the stack from a long side into a cigar-shaped cylinder. Using one hand, hold the cylinder tight at the stem end. Then, with a chef's knife, start cutting crosswise at the tip end of the leaves, continuing to cut across the cylinder until you get to the stem end. Discard the stems and fluff up the ribbons with your fingers.

HOW TO CHOP BASIL

I use a fair amount of chopped basil in my cooking. The best way to chop it is first to cut it into chiffonade. Toss the chiffonade with your fingers to separate the ribbons. Make just a few contacts with the front part of your blade as you chop the chiffonade into small pieces. Use chopped basil or chiffonade immediately, or place in a dry bowl and cover with a damp paper towel to prevent moisture loss and discoloration. It will keep this way for a few hours.

Paysanne-cut carrot

Mince: ⅛- to ¼-inch pieces.

Chop: ¼- to ½-inch pieces.

Dice: precise squared-off pieces of a specific size, commonly used for carrots, parsnips, turnips, or similar vegetables.

Batonnet: squared-off sticks roughly 2 to 3 inches long by ½ inch wide by ½ inch thick.

Julienne: matchstick-sized pieces, about 1½ inches long by ⅛ inch wide by ⅛ inch thick.

Paysanne: 2-inch-long pieces of vegetables that have been cut on a sharp diagonal to yield roughly triangular pieces that are broader on the bottom and flat and narrower on top.

Chiffonade: ribbons of delicate herbs or leafy greens, such as basil, spinach, or chard.

MISE EN PLACE

The term *mise en place* (pronounced *meez*-ahn-plahss) describes the preparations made by a cook before approaching the stove. For example, to complete the mise en place for the red pepper bisque recipe I referred to in the previous discussion about chopping an onion, you'd chop all the mirepoix ingredients, prep and measure out all the remaining items in the ingredient list, and gather together all the equipment needed to cook the soup.

In cooking school, students are graded every day on the neatness, timeliness, and precision of their mise en place. I'd be pulling your leg if I told you I always follow the rules of mise en place when I'm cooking supper for two, although it's the only way to go when a stir-fry is on the menu. Whether you're a beginner or an experienced cook, it's a great habit to get into. Indeed, a cooking teacher would be sunk without having done a thorough mise en place before every class. Here's why:

• When I take the time to do a complete mise en place before I get to the stove, I can really focus on what's happening inside the pots and pans. When my focus is more attentive, my cooking becomes more finely tuned. When I don't take the time to do a mise en place before starting to cook, I find myself reacting, instead of cooking. I might let the garlic get too brown because the herbs I'm supposed to add a minute later aren't chopped—or even washed—yet. Has this ever happened to you?

• I feel more relaxed and in control when I've prepped all my ingredients before starting to cook. It's no accident or coincidence that when my mind is uncluttered and I'm focused on what's cooking, I've had my most inspirational, creative moments as a cook. Consider mise en place a giant step forward toward achieving a new level of fun and satisfaction in cooking.

DO NO HARM: FOOD SAFETY

One of the first courses you're taught in cooking school is some version of Safety and Sanitation. Right up front, before you even get into the kitchen, they drill into you that if you're going to cook for other people, you're obligated not to make them sick. The same imperative applies to home cooks, and the basic guidelines can be summed up in four simple points:

1. Wash your hands—early and often.

2. To prevent cross contamination (page 163), wash everything—including hands—that comes in contact with raw meat, poultry, and eggs in hot, soapy water.

3. When in doubt, throw it out.

4. Keep food out of the danger zone (see below).

DANGER ZONE
. . . .

What's this about a so-called danger zone in the kitchen? Protein-rich food that languishes in temperatures between 40 degrees and 140 degrees F for more than four hours is in the danger zone. In other words, it is in the perfect setting for nasty microorganisms and polysyllabic food-borne pathogens to multiply. At a minimum, these invisible bugs can cause you all sorts of gastrointestinal distress, the symptoms of which I will spare you.

One caveat: Call me supervigilant, but if it's warmer than about 70 degrees F in the kitchen, I recommend getting food out of the danger zone after *two* hours. Why take chances?

ABOUT SALMONELLA

Salmonella (pronounced sal-mah-*nell*-ah) are bacteria that may be present on raw meat, poultry, and eggs. Salmonella poisoning causes stomach upset and flulike symptoms, but rarely kills humans. It can develop as quickly as six hours after exposure, or up to three days later. If present on meat and poultry, salmonella are killed during cooking. To be safe, discard eggs that have cracked shells.

COOKING METHODS

There's nothing quite as satisfying to me as perfectly braised meats and poultry. Through my teaching, I've discovered that, for some reason, braising can be confusing to inexperienced cooks. I'll never forget how a young man I was interviewing once for a cook's job unwittingly made our selection process a little easier. I asked about what he liked to cook at home. He mentioned that over the past weekend he had braised some pork tenderloin. At the time of the interview, he was working in a pastry kitchen. As far as I was concerned, that was where he should stay. What drew me to such a conclusion?

Pork tenderloin is a relatively small, lean cut of meat, best suited to quick dry-heat cooking methods such as grilling, broiling, sautéing, or even roasting. Braising, or slow cooking the meat in liquid, just doesn't play to the strengths of that particular cut of meat.

When you understand how and why each cooking method works, it's easy to figure out the optimal way to bring out the best in whatever you're cooking. Just as it's true that not all foods lend themselves to all cooking methods, the right cooking methods can actually enhance the taste and texture of any food.

Cooking methods fall into two main categories: dry heat and moist heat. Broiling, grilling, roasting, baking, sautéing, stir-frying, and deep-frying are dry-heat methods. Moist-heat methods include braising, steaming, poaching, blanching, and boiling. (Technically, blanching is more a technique than a cooking method, but you'll see as you read on why I've chosen to include it in this section.)

DRY-HEAT COOKING METHODS

This type of cooking happens under a broiler, on a grill, in an oven, or in a deep-fryer, wok, skillet, or sauté pan on the stove top. These methods serve to caramelize both natural and added sugars in food as it cooks, resulting in great flavor, texture, and appearance. Generally, foods prepared using dry-heat methods have a crusty surface and call for a minimum of additional liquid.

UNIVERSAL SECRETS TO SUCCESS FOR ALL DRY-HEAT COOKING METHODS

- To ensure even cooking, bring food to room temperature before cooking.

- Blot up excess marinade or moisture before cooking to enhance caramelization and prevent steaming and sticking. When appropriate, wait until the surface has been caramelized before brushing on any basting sauces.

- Don't crowd items in the pan or on the grill. Leave plenty of room for steam to escape as food cooks, or the food will steam instead of caramelize. Cook in batches if necessary to avoid crowding.

- For tender and moist results, cook foods to the appropriate internal temperature (see pages 164 and 209).

BROILING

In broiling, the heat source is above the food being cooked. Generally, it's best to broil on a raised, perforated tray or rack nested inside a larger pan. The rack allows the juices released during cooking to drip down to the bottom, so the food doesn't stew in them. You can make your own broiler pan with a wire cooling rack placed on top of a sturdy, rimmed baking sheet. In certain instances, such as with crème brûlée, broiling is used to finish a baked or sautéed dish by browning it on top to create caramelization. This technique is called gratinée. When gratinéeing, be sure to use a baking dish that's durable enough to withstand the intense heat of the broiler. Tempered-glass baking dishes, such as Pyrex, will crack. Porcelain, clay, copper, and other metal pans are a better alternative.

SECRETS FOR SUCCESSFUL BROILING

- To prevent undesirable flavors, odors, and flare-ups, don't broil items that will burn easily, such as minced garlic or meat with lots of external fat.

- Parchment paper and excess alcohol can ignite under the broiler, so use caution when broiling with these. Aluminum foil is a good substitute for parchment.

- Before preheating the broiler, adjust the rack to 4 to 6 inches from the broiler element, depending on the thickness of the food.

- Preheat the broiler for 15 to 20 minutes, or according to the manufacturer's instructions.

- If your oven allows it, broil with the oven door ajar. This will allow any steam that builds up to escape, ensuring the best caramelization.

GRILLING

In grilling, the heat source is below the food being cooked. Grills can be fueled by electricity, gas, or charcoal. Stove-top grill pans with raised ridges are terrific if you don't have a freestanding or built-in grill. These are usually made of cast iron or heavy aluminum. You need good ventilation for grilling, as a fair amount of smoke is produced when moisture from the food drips onto the briquettes, heating coil, or bottom of the grill pan.

SECRETS FOR SUCCESSFUL GRILLING

- Grill foods that have a relatively short cooking time.

- If foods are small enough to slip through the cooking grate, place them on a perforated grill rack, which rests directly on the grate.

- Be sure the fire and grate are hot before placing the food on to cook. Rub the hot grate and/or the food with a little cooking oil before you begin to grill.

- Be sure food isn't overly wet from marinades or the like before placing on the grill. If food sticks, it means that it hasn't finished searing yet. Don't try to move it until it releases easily—you'll be rewarded with bold grill marks.

- To create the characteristic cross-hatching on grilled foods such as steaks and chops, about two-thirds of the way through the cooking time on each side, lift and rotate the food 45 degrees.

- For easiest cleanup, rub the hot grate with a sturdy wire grill brush right after you take the food off.

ROASTING

Roasting is the way to cook most savory—as opposed to sweet—foods in a gas or electric oven. Roasting is done without a cover or lid. Generally, large, tender cuts of meat, such as beef tenderloin, pork rib roast, and whole chickens and other birds are roasted. Potatoes and other root vegetables are good roasting candidates, too. Pan-roasting is a two-step process in which you first brown, say, a duck breast in a sauté pan on top of the stove, and then transfer the pan to the oven to finish cooking. This method is usually reserved for dense foods that would burn on the stove top before they are cooked through, such as thick chops, filets mignons, and quail. Baked savory foods, such as eggplant parmigiana, are typically distinguished from their roasted counterparts by the addition of a small amount of fat, liquid, or sauce; these foods are sometimes covered with aluminum foil during cooking.

Roasting temperatures can range from 250 degrees F for slow-roasted salmon to 500 degrees F for high-temperature roasting of chicken or meats. Be advised that with high-temperature roasting, if the food has much external fat, it will splatter all over the oven—not recommended, unless you have a self-cleaning feature.

Be sure to keep the inside of your oven clean. This will help ensure an accurate temperature, and you won't have to worry about the odor of burned-on foods wafting through the kitchen whenever you use the oven. If you suspect that your oven thermostat isn't accurate, consider purchasing an oven thermometer to test its accuracy. If there is a discrepancy, have the oven calibrated professionally.

SECRETS FOR SUCCESSFUL ROASTING

- Unless specified otherwise, arrange one oven rack in the middle (and another in the bottom-third) of the oven before preheating.

- Most roasting pans come with high sides, but you get the best caramelization—and flavor—when the greatest surface area is exposed to the heat. Consider using a rimmed baking sheet to roast small items such as vegetables and chicken pieces.

- To roast large cuts of meat or whole poultry, set them on a rack inside the roasting pan so they won't stew in their own juices.

- For easiest cleanup, before adding food, coat the pan with vegetable oil spray, or grease lightly with oil or butter. I find that parchment paper and silicone baking liners impede caramelization, so I don't use them when roasting.

- To develop a dark crust or crispy skin on large cuts of meat or whole poultry, roast at 425 or 450 degrees F for the first 20 to 30 minutes, then reduce heat to 350 or 325 degrees F, depending on size.

- Foods roasted on the bone, such as a whole chicken, have better flavor than smaller, boneless pieces.

- To ensure even cooking when roasting vegetables, cut them into same-sized pieces before cooking.

- To roast several types of vegetables in the same pan, give the denser ones a head start, so they will all be done at the same time.

BAKING

Baking is the dry-heat method used to cook sweet—and some savory—dishes in the oven. In convection baking, a fan blows the hot air around inside the oven, resulting in food that's evenly browned and crusty. Convection baking is great for drying bread for bruschetta or bread crumbs and for baking cookies, cakes, and tart shells. To preheat the oven faster for roasting or conventional baking, use the convection setting. If necessary, turn the dial back to conventional bake once the oven is preheated.

Baking temperatures generally range from 300 degrees F for a dense cake in a dark Bundt pan to 400 degrees F for quick breads and muffins. To prevent them from drying out, bake most layer cakes and cookies, as well as casseroles and chicken and fish pieces, at temperatures between 325 and 375 degrees F.

SECRETS FOR SUCCESSFUL BAKING

- If you use nonstick or other dark metal baking pans, food will brown faster on all surfaces that come in contact with the pan. To prevent overcooking, check for doneness sooner than the recipe suggests.

- If you use tempered glass, such as Pyrex, which holds heat more efficiently, lower the suggested oven temperature by 25 degrees F and bake for 10 percent less time.

- If your recipe gives a standard baking temperature and time for baking cookies and you prefer to use convection baking, follow this rule: Reduce the regular baking temperature by 25 degrees F and reduce the baking time by 10 percent. So, if a recipe says to bake cookies at 350 degrees F for 10 minutes, set the oven to 325 degrees F convection bake and check at 9 minutes.

- A bain-marie (pronounced *ben*-mah-*ree*), or hot-water bath, is used when baking delicate custards, puddings, and other egg-based dishes. The baking dish sits inside a larger roasting pan that contains hot water. Since the temperature of the water never rises above 212 degrees F, it provides a buffering, protective moat around the pudding or custard, preventing the eggs in the dish from curdling or scrambling. And as the oven temperature naturally fluctuates, the dish cooks evenly. To avoid walking across the kitchen with a full bain-marie, place the filled baking dish in the empty bain-marie on the oven rack, then add the water to reach halfway up the sides of the baking dish. I like to line the bottom of the roasting pan with paper towels to prevent the baking dish from sliding around when removing the bain-marie from the oven.

SAUTÉING

Sautéing is a stove-top cooking method in which food is cooked in a small amount of fat, but not enough to cover the food. The term is derived from the French verb *sauter*, which means "to jump." Sautéing is perfect for delicate, thin foods that cook quickly, such as vegetables, fish fillets, or chicken breasts. Frying is similar to sautéing, but typically more fat is used when frying.

Two types of pans are commonly used for sautéing, sauté pans and skillets (see page 16). Use a straight-sided sauté pan if you plan to use the same pan to make a sauce that requires liquid—wine, cream, or stock—to be reduced or stirred. The sides help to contain the liquid; they also make the pan more suitable for cooking thicker cuts of meat and chops. While its short sides tend to create more of a mess when sautéing, a lighter-weight skillet is great for browning meats before braising. Its sloping sides allow steam to dissipate, encouraging caramelization. A skillet is also the better choice for sautéing foods such as onions or mushrooms, because it lends itself nicely to flipping.

Flipping, rather than using a spatula, is the most efficient way to turn small pieces of food while sautéing. It's a technique that requires practice to be well executed. First, try it with an empty, unheated pan: With the bottom of the pan parallel to the floor at all times, quickly move the pan like a Ferris wheel in a circle from about waist high to about chest high. Add a few lightweight items, such as two or three wine corks. When you get to the top Ferris wheel position, flick your wrist toward you as you quickly lower the pan, allowing the corks to become airborne before they land back inside the pan. As you gain confidence, practice outdoors with dried beans or popped popcorn. Before long, you'll get the hang of it. (Until you do, you might want to position an old kitchen rug in front of the stove to absorb any spills and catch the occasional escaping vegetable.) You'll know you're a master flipper when you don't need a utensil to turn small pieces of food.

SECRETS FOR SUCCESSFUL SAUTÉING

- Always heat the dry pan first over medium heat. Then add the fat (oil or butter) and allow it to get hot before adding the food. This prevents the food from sticking and absorbing the fat. When food absorbs fat, it becomes sodden.

- Test the heat of the fat by dropping in a tiny piece of the food you want to sauté. If it sizzles, the fat is at the correct temperature for sautéing.

- If smoking occurs before you add the food, the fat is too hot and has gone beyond its smoke point (see page 30). If this happens, wipe out the pan with a paper towel and start again.

- To prevent butter or oil from burning when you sauté, add enough food to the pan so that it covers most of the bottom without crowding. (Crowding creates steam, which prevents caramelization.) When necessary, cook in batches.

- If the food is not of even thickness, such as with a chicken breast, it will not cook evenly. Before sautéing, pound uneven pieces gently with a meat mallet to create an even thickness.

- Breading delicate foods before sautéing helps prevent them from drying out or overcooking, while adding desirable texture and flavor (see page 147).

- Be sure food is dry before placing it in the pan. Usually when food sticks to the pan, it means it hasn't finished searing yet. If you wait until it releases easily (assuming there's enough fat in the pan), you'll be rewarded with exemplary caramelization.

STIR-FRYING

Stir-frying is traditionally done in a wok or stir-fry pan on top of the stove. It is similar to sautéing, but with stir-frying, emphasis is placed on cutting the food into uniform, bite-sized pieces before cooking. In stir-fries, the food and sauce are ultimately cooked together in the same pan. Foods suitable for stir-frying must be tender, or, if not particularly tender, must be sliced thinly prior to stir-frying (as with flank steak, for example). Because stir-frying is done over very high heat, good ventilation and a cooking oil with a high smoke point (see page 30), such as peanut oil or grapeseed oil, are essential.

SECRETS FOR SUCCESSFUL STIR-FRYING

- Always heat the dry wok over high heat before adding the oil. When the wok is hot, add the oil, drizzling it down the sides of the pan as you pour it in.

- Stir-frying is a very quick cooking technique, so mise en place (see page 22) is critical: be sure to have all ingredients washed, cut, and ready to cook before you heat the wok.

- Flip the ingredients or use a stir-fry spatula to turn them as they cook, but don't start flipping or stirring until you see steam rise, which means the food has begun to caramelize on the bottom. If you stir too soon after adding large pieces of meat or vegetables, you'll create steam, which impedes caramelization. On the other hand, when you add tiny items, such as minced garlic or ginger, that will burn readily in the hot oil, start stirring as soon as they hit the oil, and don't stop.

DEEP-FRYING

In deep-frying, food is submerged in very hot oil, typically resulting in a crisp outside and delicate inside. To ensure this delectable texture, the oil has to be hot enough to seal off the edges of the food, and the food must be sizzling the entire time it's in the oil. If the food isn't sizzling, or expelling moisture, chances are good it's absorbing oil. This results in sodden foods that can be hard to digest.

Use a heavy pot, such as cast iron, to maintain a constant oil temperature, and fill it with oil to a depth of at least 2½ inches. A wok is also a good choice for deep-frying, as the shape allows you to use a smaller volume of oil than another pan with the same diameter. Portable electric deep-fryers are a dependable alternative. Whatever vessel you use, you need excellent ventilation to prevent frying odors from lingering in the air.

For accuracy, use a deep-frying thermometer to test the oil temperature. Or, drop a cube of bread or stick the end of a wooden chopstick into the hot oil. If it sizzles on contact, cook a piece of the food you wish to deep-fry. If the outside browns before the inside gets hot, the oil is too hot. If the item tastes greasy, it's likely that the oil isn't hot enough. Adjust the temperature before continuing, and regulate the heat as necessary to keep the food sizzling as it cooks.

SECRETS FOR SUCCESSFUL DEEP-FRYING

- Make sure foods are of uniform size so they will cook evenly.

- To prevent the temperature of the oil from plummeting, don't add too many pieces of cold food all at once to the hot oil.

- Since salt breaks down cooking oil, never salt the outside surfaces of foods before deep-frying them.

- Always serve deep-fried food while it's hot, but not immediately out of the fryer. Let it cool enough to prevent burned tongues.

ABOUT REFINED OILS

Refined oils are cooking or condiment oils that have been extruded at a high temperature and/or with chemicals, as opposed to cold-pressed oils, which are extracted at low temperatures and with no chemicals. Refined oils are more shelf stable, less likely to turn rancid, and have a higher smoke point (see below). However, they have fewer nutritional benefits and some fats experts, such as Fran McCullough, author of *The Good Fat Cookbook,* see refined oils as virtual time bombs. Because certain of these highly refined oils, such as the ubiquitous canola oil, have an offensive odor after they are extracted, they are treated with a chemical deodorizer that also prevents the human nose or palate from detecting rancidity in the oil. (Rancid oil is cause for all sorts of concerns, including the development of free radicals, which are linked to cancer, not to mention the undesirable flavor that rancid oil imparts to food.) For health reasons, use refined oils with care and in moderation.

ABOUT SMOKE POINT

The smoke point of a cooking fat or oil is the temperature at which the fat begins to give off smoke and unpleasant odors and imbue food with an unpleasant taste. Smoke points of unrefined fats and oils are at the low end of the range; refined or highly processed oils can tolerate higher temperatures. Following are smoke points of common cooking fats and oils, moving from lowest to highest: butter, 350 degrees F (higher for clarified, page 155; higher still for ghee); extra-virgin olive oil, 375 degrees F; refined corn oil or olive oil, 410 degrees F; refined canola oil, 435 degrees F (lower for cold-pressed); refined grapeseed oil, 445 degrees F (lower for cold-pressed); refined peanut oil, 450 degrees F (lower for cold-pressed).

MOIST-HEAT COOKING METHODS

Generally, moist-heat cooking is done on the stove top, usually in a covered pot. Braising can be done in the oven as well, just as long as you check periodically to be sure the braising liquid never reaches a steady boil. Foods cooked by moist-heat methods do not have the characteristic crisp surface of foods prepared by dry-heat methods.

THERE'S ONE MAIN UNIVERSAL SECRET TO SUCCESS FOR ALL MOIST-HEAT COOKING TECHNIQUES:

FOR GOOD HEAT TRANSFER, BE SURE THE POT IS LARGE ENOUGH FOR STEAM AND/OR LIQUID TO SURROUND THE FOOD.

BRAISING

During braising, meats, poultry, fish, or vegetables are cooked in a flavorful liquid such as wine, tomato sauce, or broth. Braised dishes include pot roasts, curries, and anything that is cooked in a sauce, such as meatballs in tomato sauce or chili with beans. Braising and stewing are similar, but in stewing, the food is completely submerged in liquid. Less liquid is used in braising—typically just enough to reach the top of the food. In this book, I use the term *braising* to describe any dish that is cooked in a copious amount of flavored liquid, with the liquid ultimately becoming part of the finished recipe.

Ideal for tougher, fattier cuts of meat or larger muscles with connective tissue, braising calls for long simmering to break down the tough fibers and melt the connective tissue, collagen, and fat into the liquid. These actions create viscous, rich pan juices, which are degreased, if necessary, and served as a sauce. This type of rich sauce is said to have a lot of body.

Braising is often done in a Dutch oven, a tall-sided, round or oval pot with two handles and, preferably, a concave lid. The dimensions allow you first to brown the food without splattering fat all over the stove, and then to braise in the same pot, either on the stove top or in the oven.

Browning causes the surface of foods to darken, or caramelize, which intensifies their flavor before they are simmered in the seasoned liquid. To brown nearly any food, season it with salt and pepper, dredge in flour, and then tamp off the excess flour so it doesn't burn before the food is browned. Then, sauté the food in hot oil or butter over medium-high heat, just until it's dark brown on each side. It should not be cooked through, just browned on the surface.

SECRETS FOR SUCCESSFUL BRAISING

- Always braise with a lid, preferably one that is concave, rather than flat. During braising, steam forms and is trapped as condensation on the underside of the lid. When you remove a concave lid, you can trap the steam before it can slide off into the sauce, unlike with a flat lid. The secret is to lift the lid and immediately turn it upside down, then shake off the condensation in the sink.

- To eliminate splattering fat when browning meat for braising, season the meat with salt and pepper (but no flour) and broil it in the oven, rather than browning it on the stove top.

- Proteins, which shrink during cooking, should always be braised at a steady but gentle simmer. When protein fibers tighten, moisture is squeezed out and meat becomes dry and tough. To keep meat tender during braising, once the liquid comes to a good, robust boil, cover the pot and reduce the heat to a steady simmer for the duration of the cooking time. It's critical to bring the liquid up to an initial boil to be sure it achieves a sufficient temperature to sustain a good simmer throughout the cooking time. A good simmer means that bubbles break progressively on the surface, not as quickly as they do in boiling, but in steady succession.

- Because tenderness is not an issue, it's okay to braise vegetables, such as zucchini in tomato sauce, at a higher temperature.

- Thanks to a process called "reverse osmosis," salting and seasoning meats and poultry up to 24 hours before braising actually helps keep them moist and flavorful.

- If you don't have a Dutch oven, brown your food in a heavy skillet. (It's actually more efficient because the short, sloping sides dissipate the steam better.) Deglaze the pan by adding liquid to loosen the caramelized bits, which are called *fond*. Then transfer everything to a roasting pan with high sides and a lid (or cover with aluminum foil), bring to a boil, and reduce the heat so the food can braise at a steady simmer, either in the oven or on the stove top.

- You can braise on the stove top over low heat, or in the oven preheated to 325 degrees F. Be sure to maintain a steady simmer, but not a rollicking boil, and stir every so often to be sure you have sufficient liquid (if not, stir in broth or hot water) and that the food is cooking evenly. If braising on top of the stove, some burners with a high BTU output may require the use of a Flame-Tamer or other heat deflector to keep the heat low enough to prevent boiling.

- Braised foods often taste better the next day, after the flavors have a chance to meld. Let cool to room temperature, cover, and refrigerate. If any fat rises to the surface and solidifies during refrigeration, remove it before reheating. If necessary, stir in some broth or water to thin the liquid. Reheat, covered, in a preheated 325 degrees F oven, or on the stove top.

- If starchy ingredients, such as turnips or potatoes, are in the braise, they will absorb liquid as the dish cools, resulting in less sauce overall and potatoes that are saturated with flavor. Add more broth if a looser sauce is desired.

STEATING

For steaming, food is placed on a rack above boiling water, covered tightly, and cooked in very moist, hot air. Steaming can be done in layers, with different foods placed on metal, bamboo, or wire racks, then stacked tightly, one on top of the other, above a cauldron of boiling water. The top layer is always covered. Because no added cooking oil or fat is required, steaming is an inherently low-fat way to cook. For added flavor, drizzle plain steamed foods with a bit of flavored oil or sauce, such as Asian toasted sesame oil or pesto, before serving.

The best foods for steaming are tender, fresh items that cook relatively quickly and have plenty of flavor on their own, such as impeccably fresh fish, vegetables, and so on. Chicken and fish steamed on the bone are particularly flavorful. To ensure that dishes in an all-steamed menu are done at the same time, begin steaming the densest foods first, adding more delicate foods that take less time later.

SECRETS FOR SUCCESSFUL STEAMING

- Always tightly cover the pot when steaming. If there is no lid available, use a sauté pan or baking sheet large enough to completely cover the food being steamed.

- To be sure you don't run out of water in the base of the steamer, put a coin in the water. If you hear the coin start to rattle, the pan is dry. This is particularly important when using a bamboo steamer inside a wok, as the bamboo will start to smolder if the wok is empty. If you smell something strange coming from the stove, check the water level right away.

- To prevent steam burns, always open the lid away from you.

- Cut food for steaming into same-sized pieces for even cooking.

- To prevent comingling of flavors and possible cross contamination, steam fish, meat, and poultry on the first level of the steamer, directly above the water, with other foods such as potatoes and vegetables on racks above the protein-rich foods. If denser foods are already on the bottom, be sure to put the proteins directly on a plate, then on the steamer rack, to prevent juices from dripping down.

- When steaming moist food, such as fish, directly on the steamer rack (not on a plate), place it on a large lettuce leaf. The lettuce will absorb any drips from the food as it cooks. After steaming, remove the piece of food with the lettuce, then discard the lettuce before serving.

- To prevent cruciferous vegetables such as broccoli or cauliflower from giving off their well-known sulfurous odor during cooking, steam them for less than 7 minutes.

- Before you store a bamboo steamer, let it air-dry for 24 hours, or until you are certain it is completely dry. Otherwise, it may become moldy during storage.

POACHING

In poaching, such proteins as meats, eggs, poultry, fish, and shellfish are completely submerged in liquid during cooking. The liquid can be as simple as salted water or as flavorful as a broth or court bouillon. When poaching large items, such as a side of salmon or a whole chicken, both the food and the poaching liquid should be at room temperature when added to the pot. With smaller items, such as shellfish and eggs, the liquid is brought to a boil before adding the food. It is critical, in both cases, to maintain a temperature no higher than a bare simmer in order to keep the food tender. If the liquid comes to a boil, the protein fibers shorten and tighten rapidly, resulting in toughness.

Poaching is done on top of the stove in a pan large enough for the food to be completely submerged in liquid. You can buy a special fish poaching pan, but it's simple to poach large sides of salmon in a roasting pan straddled over two adjacent burners. Use a rack to prevent the food from sticking to the bottom of the pan, and to make it easy to lift a large item out of the hot liquid the moment it's done. To be sure that meat, fish, or poultry is fully cooked, test with an instant-read thermometer. See page 134 and the charts on pages 164 and 209 for the internal temperatures of these cooked foods.

SECRETS FOR SUCCESSFUL POACHING

- When poaching eggs, add a teaspoon or so of white vinegar to the water. It helps the white of the egg to coagulate more quickly, and the egg keeps its shape better.

- To flavor the liquid when poaching meat, poultry, fish, or seafood, add a mirepoix (page 20) along with aromatic spices and herbs such as a bay leaf, black peppercorns, and the like.

- To ensure even cooking, bring food to room temperature before poaching.

BLANCHING

Blanching is the process of briefly dipping a vegetable, fruit, nut, or legume into a pot of boiling water, then immediately stopping the cooking by immersing or rinsing the food in cold water. In fact, blanching is not as much a cooking method as it is a technique. However, because it is often the first step before employing another cooking method, I've included it here. Foods such as fresh fava beans, tomatoes, peaches, pearl onions, and almonds are blanched so that their skins can be more easily removed.

In another application, vegetables such as carrots or asparagus are blanched before they are cooked further by a dry-heat cooking method, such as sautéing or grilling. (Some recipes call for leaving them in the water until they are half cooked; technically, this is parboiling, rather than blanching.) In this case, blanching ensures that these vegetables will ultimately cook more evenly and retain their bright color when cooked later with less-dense vegetables.

SECRETS FOR SUCCESSFUL BLANCHED VEGETABLES

- Salt the blanching liquid before adding food. This will lightly flavor the food.

- Likewise, salt an ice-water bath before immersing blanched vegetables in it.

- To prevent them from becoming waterlogged, remove vegetables from an ice-water bath as soon as they are cool to the touch.

BOILING

Boiling, which calls for submerging foods completely in liquid, most often salted water, is primarily used for cooking vegetables, pasta, and other starches. Boiling is done in a pot on the stove top, with or without a lid, at a temperature higher than that used for poaching. Always use plenty of water—at least enough to cover the food completely.

To boil root vegetables, such as potatoes, turnips, and carrots, start them in cold, salted water and bring the vegetables and water to a boil together. This helps them to cook evenly, preventing mushy outside edges and hard centers. To boil pasta, or vegetables that grow above ground such as green beans, asparagus, and corn, bring the water to a boil first, add some salt, and then add the food. Again, this ensures even cooking.

To prevent chlorophyll from leaching out of noncruciferous green vegetables, boil them uncovered or with the lid ajar. Otherwise, they will lose their vibrant hue. Keep a lid on cruciferous vegetables, such as cauliflower, broccoli, and cabbage, to keep their undesirable sulfurous odor from escaping, and boil these nutritionally dense and pungent vegetables for 7 minutes or less to prevent the reaction that causes the odor to develop.

SECRETS FOR SUCCESSFUL BOILING

- Unlike for poaching, it's not necessary to bring vegetables to room temperature before boiling.

- Add plenty of salt to the water if you want your vegetables or starches to be flavorful. The water should be salty enough to taste like the ocean.

- To make cleanup easier, soak pots used to boil starchy foods—rice, pasta, and potatoes—in cold, soapy water. Hot water makes the starch gluey.

HOW COOKING CHANGES THE TEXTURE AND FLAVOR OF FOODS

As you can see, these twelve cooking methods present all sorts of options for preparing raw ingredients. But how do you know which method to use when? To answer this question, let's begin by looking at how each method affects the texture and flavor of food. To illustrate this point when I teach, I serve the class a rather cavalier offering: an all-zucchini tasting menu. Intended more as a teaching device than a zucchini degustation, this menu allows us to observe how seven different cooking techniques bring out a variety of sensations in something as pedestrian as zucchini. As you read along, try to imagine the textures and flavors as I describe them. Or better still, buy some medium-sized zucchini, go into the kitchen, and cook up a comparative tasting of your own.

First, it's important to taste some zucchini *raw*. Slice a zucchini into a few ½-inch-thick coins and bite into a slice. You'll discern all sorts of vital information about its age, freshness, and flavor. In zucchini, ripeness registers on the palate as sweetness and freshness manifests as firmness. Fresh zucchini resist light pressure if you squeeze them a bit. An underripe zucchini could be described as "vegetal" or overly "herbaceous." An overripe zucchini can be tough and bitter, thanks to seeds. Given this bitter flavor, fine cooks prefer younger, more tender zucchini, also called fancy zucchini.

Next, taste the zucchini slices prepared by three different moist-heat cooking methods. When *steamed,* the texture of zucchini feels different on the tongue. It's less spongy than the raw zucchini and considerably more damp. There's more contrast in texture between its skin and flesh, too. The skins of steamed zucchini are a bit tougher than the center pulp. Flavorwise, steaming brings out a zucchini's sweetness.

When you bite into *boiled* zucchini, the skin softens and yields easily to the flesh. Also, the boiled slices, which soften evenly as they cook, pick up the pleasant flavor of the salt that was added to the cooking water. Nutritionwise, boiling vegetables has fallen out of favor because nutrients are leached out into the cooking water. If you opt to boil mild-flavored vegetables such as zucchini, save the cooking water to use in place of stock when making soups.

It's unnecessary to taste zucchini that are poached or blanched; *poached* are similar to boiled and *blanched* resemble lightly steamed zucchini.

Next, taste zucchini slices cooked by dry-heat cooking methods. We can assume that *broiled* zucchini are similar to grilled, *stir-fried* are like sautéed, and *baked* are comparable to roasted.

Roasting is the cooking method of choice for preparing stuffed zucchini. The dry heat of the oven dries out the skin, creating a nice, firm shell for a savory meat or rice filling. The tougher skin supports the weight of the stuffing, and the layer of spongy flesh just inside the skin absorbs the juices and flavors of the stuffing as it softens during roasting. To protect the skin from becoming leathery, brush some olive oil on the outside before roasting or baking. Flavorwise, the natural sugars in the zucchini caramelize a bit in the intense heat of the oven, which is why roasted zucchini tastes richer than the steamed or boiled version. Zucchini cut up before roasting develop a rich flavor, thanks to both the olive oil they are tossed with before they go into the oven and the caramelization that occurs during roasting. The roasted slices also have a creamy, softer texture than the roasted halves for stuffing.

Of all the various cooking methods included in this little research project, *sautéed* zucchini are consistently the students' least favorite. Their flavor is rather bland, and the texture can be described as flabby or crisp-tender, depending on how long the vegetable is cooked.

Often, before **deep-frying**, vegetables are coated in a batter that cooks into a crispy coating and locks in the food's natural moisture. For this experiment, in order to focus on the flavor of the cooked squash, I suggest that you deep-fry both some plain zucchini slices and some dredged in seasoned flour. You'll discover that neither treatment enhances the texture nor brings out the naturally sweet, fresh flavor of the deep-fried vegetable. Simply put, deep-frying actually masks the true flavor of zucchini.

The last dry-heat cooking technique in this experiment is **grilling**. For this test, slice raw zucchini lengthwise into ¼-inch-thick slices and brush all surfaces with olive oil. Grilling gives zucchini a rich, complex taste. The characteristic seared or charred exterior imparts a distinctive flavor that is associated with a sense of satiety, or fullness. Indeed, don't be surprised if grilled zucchini seem more filling than steamed zucchini. Zucchini grilled with perfectly seared outsides and a soft, creamy flesh are succulent and tender, with the caramelized char marks enhancing the vegetable's natural sweetness.

If I had to choose my favorite method for cooking zucchini, without a doubt, it would be **braising**. In class, I save this moist-heat technique for last for two reasons: It delivers the most complex flavor, and I don't want to confuse the palate, because, by definition, all the other samples are relatively plain. Similarly, by definition, braised food is cooked in a flavorful liquid that contributes to its taste. In fact, I think zucchini were put on the earth to sponge up other flavors. As noted earlier, raw zucchini have both a bland flavor and spongy texture; both attributes make the squash a logical candidate for braising—or stewing—in a flavorful liquid. Braised Summer Squash with Sweet Peppers, Tomatoes, and Basil (page 262) is a good example.

First, sauté some onions and bell peppers with some sliced zucchini in a little olive oil. Add a little salt to draw out some of the moisture and concentrate the flavors. When the vegetables are glistening all over and starting to brown on both sides, add some tomatoes, enough to almost cover the zucchini. Next, bring all to a rolling boil, then reduce the heat so the mixture simmers steadily. Partially cover the pan and simmer the zucchini until the edges flop when you pick up a slice with a fork. At this point, the zucchini will have absorbed some flavor from the tomatoes. A final seasoning with salt is all that's needed.

Braising breaks down the fibers of the zucchini, resulting in tender slices that readily absorb the flavors of not only the tomatoes, onions, and peppers, but also the olive oil and salt. Simply put, the overall flavor of the braised zucchini is greater than the sum of its parts.

This zucchini exercise gives you an indication of how both the flavor and texture of a simple vegetable are transformed by each of the twelve dry- and moist-heat cooking methods. As you prepare the recipes in Part Two of this book, you'll gain even more insight as to which methods bring out the best inherent qualities in which foods.

USING YOUR SENSES WHEN YOU COOK

Part One of this book began with all sorts of objective information about what to look for in pots and pans, how to cut an onion, and how to keep food out of the danger zone. A discussion about how various cooking methods work their respective magic (or not) on zucchini took us into more subjective territory. Next, we'll consider taste, the most subjective aspect of cooking.

What's appealing about the specific flavors or textures in a dish is different for everyone. As a cook it's important to understand what endears us to certain flavors, textures, and combinations, and how to maximize those elements in our cooking. Memory plays a key role in our likes and dislikes about food, as well as in how we develop skills as cooks.

Scientists offer us a fascinating nugget about memory retention: the more senses we engage when we're learning something new, the better we retain the new information. One of the most prudent things you can do if you want to learn how to make a white sauce (page 110), for example, is to march into the kitchen and cook up a batch. As you begin, the scent of flour toasting in melted butter will beckon you to start adding milk, making an imprint on your brain. Just a couple of minutes later, the sensation of sweet, barely warm milk and gritty, uncooked flour will etch a memory on your taste buds. The temperature and texture will give you a sense of when the sauce should begin to boil. Then, finally, comes the unforgettable sight and sound of the first big, steamy geyserlike bubble exploding on the surface, heaving its way up from the thick mass below.

It was almost twenty years ago that I made my first official béchamel sauce, and as I write this, I can still conjure the sound of that first bubble breaking as the sauce came to a boil. The sights, smells, tastes, textures, and sounds I experienced then are still imprinted in my brain. Likewise, I urge you to experience cooking with all of your senses. Becoming aware is the first step to becoming a fine cook.

Take a moment to think about one of your favorite comfort foods, perhaps something you crave when you're feeling sad and blue. Name the food. When did you first taste it? What did it sound like as you ate it or as someone prepared it for you? How did it feel in your mouth? Was it slippery, cold, or chewy? Spicy, salty, or sweet? How did it smell? Was it on a plate or in a bowl? You've just reinforced a taste memory. For a fine cook, this is money in the bank.

UNDERSTANDING YOUR PALATE

For years, scientists have told us that we detect four tastes on different parts of our tongue: salty, sweet, bitter, and sour. Recently, however, taste experts have discredited the notion that certain regions of our tongue are exclusively devoted to a single taste sensation.

These days, the experts are zeroing in on the subject of volatility, or how certain ingredients come alive, or awaken, in the presence of others. There is much research yet to be done in the field of the volatility of flavors, but what's been discovered thus far has significant implications for cooks.

VOLATILIZING FLAVORS

Whenever you swirl a glass of wine, you're allowing the esters in the wine to mix with air, making the components in the wine more noticeable to your nose and, in turn, to your palate. Similarly, a splash of water added to a glass of scotch brings out new components in the scotch by releasing some of the flavors that were "trapped" in the liquor. How does this relate to cooking?

While air and water awaken the flavors in wine and scotch, respectively, fat and alcohol play a similar role in cooking. The nose acts as a chimney to aerate what's on the tongue, allowing us to identify foods beyond the sweet, salty, sour, or bitter flavors that the tongue can detect. When more of a food's flavors are awakened, the food tastes more complex.

Across the world, cooks have known this for centuries. Indian cooks awaken flavors by frying spices in ghee, a type of clarified butter, before adding braising liquid to a curry. Likewise, Thai cooks melt fat-rich coconut milk solids to sauté curry paste before adding the remaining watery part of the coconut milk. In both examples, the flavor and aroma of the spices are enhanced when the spices are

volatilized in fat, more so than if the spices were simply added to the liquid in either recipe. If you've ever noticed a difference in flavor between a soup made from just dumping a bunch of vegetables into a pot with some stock and a soup made from roasted, caramelized vegetables, you understand how fat can awaken and carry flavors.

THE ROLE OF ACID IN COOKING

Alcohol, when used in cooking in the form of wine, also volatilizes flavors, adding exponential complexity when it's used as a deglazing ingredient to coax flavorful caramelized bits of food off the bottom of a pan. Wine further enhances complexity by introducing acid. Acid has almost incredible control over our salivary glands—it causes us to salivate. On a most rudimentary level, this makes a case for serving wine with food. Cooking with acid ingredients such as tomatoes, citrus, and vinegars introduces a powerful dynamic. Try seasoning a pot of freshly puréed black bean soup with a splash of vinegar and you'll see what I mean.

UMAMI

In addition to the four fundamental tastes of bitter, salty, sweet, and sour, a fifth taste, the sensation of savoriness, known as umami (pronounced ooh-mah-mee), has rapidly been gaining recognition and acceptance among scientists and fine cooks around the world.

In 1907, a Japanese chemist named Kikunae Ikeda coined the word *umami* (based on *umai*, Japanese for "delicious" or "tasty") to describe the distinctive meatiness or brothiness he discerned in certain foods. He managed to extract the essence of umami from kombu seaweed, which he found had a remarkable ability to balance and enhance flavors when added to a soup. Professor Ikeda determined that umami comes from glutamates, which are naturally present in many common foods. (You may be familiar with Dr. Ikeda's related, more notorious contribution to the food world, Ac'cent, or monosodium glutamate.)

Ingredients as diverse as cooked mushrooms, certain Parmesan cheeses, fermented soy sauce (not all soy sauces are fermented), meats, asparagus, anchovies, Asian fish sauce (which is made from fermented anchovies), olives, and bottled clam juice are all naturally rich in umami. When a melon, tomato, or ear of corn is perfectly ripe and full of flavor, it's said to be high in umami. A Caesar salad packs a double punch of umami thanks to anchovies and Parmigiano-Reggiano cheese.

If you have trouble recognizing or identifying umami, try to recall a bland vegan dish you might have been served at one time. Without a baseline sensation of savoriness, or umami, which otherwise might be contributed by animal fat, vegan recipes can seem one-dimensional in flavor. To get rid of the blahs and make the dish more "tasty," you only have to go as far as your pantry. There you're likely to find an arsenal of umami-rich glutamates ready to come to the rescue. For example, the flat vegan dish could be punched up with any of these umami-rich vegan ingredients: cooked potatoes, nori (dried seaweed used in sushi), aged balsamic vinegar, sautéed shiitake mushrooms, grapefruit, or green tea. In addition, omnivores will find plenty of umami in dry-aged steaks, scallops, lobsters, clams, and in such cheeses as Danish blue, Gruyere, Roquefort, and Parmigiano-Reggiano.

There's a final bit of good news about umami: Not only does it add remarkable depth of flavor and complexity to cooking, it also contributes to our sense of satiety, or satisfaction. Umami rules!

HOW FATS ENHANCE FLAVOR

When I was dean at the California Culinary Academy, my husband and I were fortunate to be invited for dinner one night to the home of our Introduction to Wines instructor, Steve Eliot. As we sat relaxing over wine and nibbles before dinner, every so often one of us couldn't resist remarking on the seductive fragrances wafting over from the stove. After a while, Steve pushed his chair back, cocked his head toward the stove, and announced, "It's time for me to start throwing butter into things." I winked, knowing full well what he was up to. I was certainly well aware that Steve knew plenty about wines, but now I was confident that the guy could cook, too. I suspected we were in for a treat. The first taste of his pork and chanterelles braised in Chardonnay confirmed my suspicions. What made Steve's food taste so fine?

One of the time-honored French flavor enhancement secrets you learn in cooking school is a classical technique called *monter au beurre* (pronounced *mohn*-tay oh *burr*), literally "to mount with butter." As a finishing step, after a sauce, soup, or stew has cooked and reduced sufficiently, the cook whisks in a nugget of unsalted butter, enriching the sauce by emulsifying all the ingredients, binding them to the fat molecules in the butter. If you've ever marveled at the distinctive gloss and rich mouth-feel of French sauces, this is how they do it. It's a great trick to have up your sleeve if the stock you used was a bit bland, the vegetables in your puréed soup weren't at their peak of flavor, or you want to limit the addition of any fat to the most critical point in a recipe's preparation. Likewise, a judicious drizzle of extra-virgin olive oil over a bowl of braised cannellini beans or a crème fraîche garnish on a soup can provide not only the eye appeal, but the same "finished" quality you'd achieve with a skillful *monter au beurre*.

This last-minute gilding with butter—or your fat of choice—also provides exponential dividends when the food hits your tongue. While the tongue does a good job of

COOKING WITH THE SEASONS

detecting salt, sweet, bitter, and sour, when coated with fat, the tongue becomes a hypersensitive flavor receptor. As the fat molecules coat your tongue, the chimney that is your nose aerates your mouth, and the fat distributes the flavors all across the surface of your tongue, not just where your spoon deposited them. The old cooking-school adage, "Fat is flavor," can be extended. In fact, fat also magnifies flavor.

THE CHALLENGE OF LOW-FAT COOKING

Herein lies the inherent challenge in low-fat cooking. Without the tongue-coating benefits of fatty ingredients, the cook has to rely on bursts of flavor from the raw ingredients themselves. If you're used to deriving a sense of satiety, or fullness, from fat-rich foods, you have to find other stimuli for satisfaction. What a case for cooking with the seasons, when fresh foods are at their peak.

With every change in season, new seafoods, fruits, and vegetables enter or, more accurately, re-enter the marketplace as others fade away. This dynamic aspect of cooking is particularly fun for fine cooks.

When you cook with the seasons, you don't have to tinker much to make food sparkle with flavor. Typically, simple preparations bring out the best in seasonal foods, and with some solid cooking skills under your belt, cooking fresh foods at their peak of flavor will make you look like a genius. Utilize the particular dry- or moist-heat cooking methods that bring out the best in seasonal foodstuffs, and you'll be amazed at how effortless it can be to create food that's vibrant and compelling.

When it comes to produce, once you figure out what's in season, chances are good you'll have a choice between organic and conventionally grown fruits and vegetables. Does it matter which you choose?

ORGANIC VERSUS CONVENTIONAL PRODUCE

Not that long ago, choosing organic produce over conventionally grown fruits and vegetables seemed more about taking a stand against pesticides, commercial fertilizers, factory farms, and hormone- and antibiotics-fed poultry and meats than it was an affirmation of the actual produce and foods that were produced organically. In fact, as recently as the late 1990s, the considerably more expensive, organically grown lettuce, carrots, and corn—often bug-eaten, puny, or wormy—were pushed off into a dark corner of the market.

When I began cooking professionally in the late 1980s, early supporters of organic foods were quick to point out the considerable trade-offs for these cosmetic inconveniences: Because they are produced without harmful chemicals, organically grown foods are better for farmworkers, the soil, air, rivers, streams, and "the planet" in general—not at all insignificant. Besides, it feels good to support small farmers and encourage biodiversity, which helps bring forth a wider variety of plant species.

"Organic foods taste better," Kathy Farrell-Kingsley cites as the number one reason to buy organic in *The Complete Vegetarian Handbook,* published in 2003. When we're talking about produce, I'd say organic foods have come a long way from those puny carrots. Today, many organic foods actually *do* taste better.

While for years I supported the organic movement in theory, when it came to buying my own groceries, I just wasn't willing to spend that much more money on holey spinach, especially for my catering business or cooking classes. As I learned about pesticide residue on conventionally grown produce, I became more vigilant about washing my conventional produce more thoroughly. I still wasn't convinced it was worth the switch to organics, so I just scrubbed harder.

But I've slowly been changing my ways about buying organic produce. It started with strawberries. Only twenty years ago, I would have been run out of the California Culinary Academy pastry kitchen if I even suggested rinsing off a strawberry. "You'd absolutely ruin it and besides, it would bleed all over the cream," the chef warned. Yet, on the list of fruits and vegetables most likely to have pesticide residue, strawberries are at the top. In the lists shown here you can see which items retain the most pesticide residue, as well as the twelve least-likely candidates. The good news is that if you eat only organic versions of the top "dirty dozen," you can reduce your pesticide exposure by 90 percent.

CONVENTIONALLY GROWN PRODUCE MOST LIKELY TO HAVE PESTICIDE RESIDUE

(in order of worst to best)

Strawberries	Peaches	Imported grapes
Raspberries	Nectarines	Spinach
Apples	Pears	Celery
Peppers	Cherries	Potatoes

CONVENTIONALLY GROWN PRODUCE LEAST LIKELY TO HAVE PESTICIDE RESIDUE

Corn	Onions	Mangoes
Avocados	Peas	Bananas
Cauliflower	Broccoli	Kiwifruits
Asparagus	Pineapples	Papayas

SEASONING
TO TASTE

Still, until a conversation with Berkeley, California nutritionist Laura Knoff, I continued to see organic produce as more of a default option than a first choice. Knoff explains that organic produce has more nutrients than conventionally grown produce, thanks to the more nutrient-rich soil in which it is grown. This stands to reason, since we know that pesticides deplete the soil—and in turn, the plant—of nutrients. So, nutritionally, you get less bang for the buck with conventionally grown produce.

Further, Knoff cites a study reported in the *Journal of Agriculture and Food Chemistry* that looks at two crops of corn, marionberries, and strawberries, one organically grown and one conventionally grown, on the same Oregon farm. The organically grown crop far exceeded the conventional crop in polyphenols, the powerhouse antioxidants that help slow aging and ward off cancer, heart disease, and diabetes. Perhaps not surprising, polyphenols also assist the plants in staving off pests and resisting bacteria and fungus.

Experts predict that as the volume and variety of organic produce increase to meet consumer demand, both quality and prices will become more competitive with conventionally grown produce. I must admit, even armed with all the data, I still catch myself hesitating to spend fifteen cents more for a gorgeous head of organic lettuce. When that happens, I remember something Kim Severson, author of *The Trans-Fat Solution,* said on the subject: just think of what a drop in the bucket that ten or fifteen cents is compared to what you're willing to pay for a cappuccino at Starbucks. That works for me.

Until I started teaching, I never really thought about the simple expression, "season to taste." In cooking school, it's drummed into you that salt brings out flavor. When you cook without printed recipes (as is the case in many professional chef training programs) seasoning to taste becomes instinctive. Even before I went to cooking school, when my grandmother and mother were teaching me how to cook, tasting, then adjusting the seasoning was simply how you cooked. As a teacher, I recognize that not everyone has had the good fortune of similar tutelage.

To teach this concept in class, I demonstrate seasoning soup to taste by adding salt and tasting, then continuing to add more salt until all the flavors in the soup sing in harmony. After each small addition of salt, I report to the class what new flavors I detect. Here's how a typical exercise, with a pot of bell pepper bisque (page 66), goes: Before any salt is added, the soup tastes flat. As you stir in more and more salt, a little at a time, the various ingredients reveal themselves: onions and celery at first, then carrots, bell peppers, and even the chicken stock. I'm not satisfied until I finally tease out a hint of cayenne pepper, a compelling baseline that adds complexity (or a spicy kick, if you use more cayenne) to the rich bisque. Not once do I report picking up the flavor of salt, even though that is the one and only variable I change as I go through the seasoning demonstration.

One night in class, as I was in the midst of this exercise, a particularly forthright middle-aged woman tentatively raised her hand and offered a telling confession: In all her years of cooking, whenever she had seen "add salt to taste" in a recipe, she thought it meant to add salt until you could taste it. That night she had an epiphany. And so did I.

I realized that fine cooks season this way by rote, while other good scouts cook food, following a recipe or their own muse, and serve it forth without fine-tuning the seasoning. Like putting new tires on a car and driving off without aligning them, the job hasn't been completed.

SODIUM CONTENT OF COMMONLY USED SALTS

		Teaspoon Measurement	Weight Measurement	Milligrams of Sodium	Ingredients
Kosher Salts	Diamond Crystal kosher salt	¼ teaspoon	.7 grams	280 mg	Salt
	Morton kosher salt	¼ teaspoon	1.2 grams	480 mg	Salt, yellow prussiate of soda (a water-soluble, anti-caking agent)
	North American Salt Company kosher salt	¼ teaspoon	1.2 grams	480 mg	Salt
Sea Salts	Lima French Atlantic sea salt	¼ teaspoon	1 gram	330 mg	Salt
	La Baleine sea salt, fine crystals	¼ teaspoon	1.5 grams	580 mg	Sea salt, magnesium oxide (an anti-caking agent)
Table Salt	Morton table salt	¼ teaspoon	1.5 grams	590 mg	Salt, calcium silicate (dextrose and potassium iodide are also added to Morton iodized salt)

Bringing the flavors into alignment makes the difference between good cooking and fine cooking, and using salt judiciously is the best way I know to accomplish this.

THREE BASIC SALTS

When I teach seasoning to taste, I start by conducting a salt tasting in class. To keep it simple, we taste three salts that are widely available in Northern California, where I most often teach: Diamond Crystal kosher salt, table salt, and a finely ground sea salt. Why a specific brand of kosher salt? As explained in great detail in her excellent book *CookWise*, food scientist Shirley Corriher tells us that Diamond Crystal salt crystals are actually pyramids—as opposed to grains—which are much more likely to adhere to food. In fact, these hollow pyramids, or crystals, also dissolve twice as fast as granular salts, including Morton kosher salt.

Fine cooks often cite another reason for preferring Diamond Crystal kosher salt: measure for measure, because the "grains" are bigger, thereby taking up more room in the measuring spoon, Diamond Crystal kosher salt has about

half the sodium of table salt or fine sea salt. As the accompanying chart illustrates, it takes 2 teaspoons of Diamond Crystal kosher salt to contribute the amount of sodium found in 1 teaspoon of common table salt. When you're seasoning to taste, you have more play with the kosher salt than table salt because the grains are bigger. It's harder to overseason with salt that tastes half as salty, measure for measure. Another reason fine cooks eschew table salt is that it's treated with calcium silicate to make it flow freely. To many, including me, this gives salt a metallic aftertaste.

ARE ALL KOSHER SALTS CREATED EQUAL?

Kosher salt is so named because it is the salt used in koshering, the process of purifying meat and poultry by drawing out its blood. As I mentioned briefly, Morton also makes kosher salt, but to keep it free flowing, it relies on yellow prussiate of soda, which, to my taste, lends the same metallic aftertaste as the calcium silicate Morton uses in their table salt. To complicate things further, because of the difference in the size of the salt grains, 1 teaspoon of Diamond Crystal kosher salt has the same amount of sodium as about ½ teaspoon of Morton kosher salt.

When I taught in Boulder, Colorado, I discovered a Canadian kosher salt with a distinctive appearance. North American Salt Company's kosher salt has the largest crystals I've ever seen. They remind me of the clumps of salt you see on soft pretzels sold at the ballpark. My recipes for the Colorado class had been developed and tested using the smaller grains of Diamond Crystal brand, so the students used a mortar and pestle to crush the North American Salt Company crystals to about the same size as other kosher salts before measuring them for the recipes.

SEA SALT

In the comparative tasting of salts I conduct in class, sea salt is the most variable in flavor, texture, and appearance. Much like the role *terroir* (pronounced tair-*rwah*) plays in wine, sea salt's flavor and color depend on the specific region where it's harvested. You'll find sea salts ranging in color from gray-tinged French salt to a vibrant red variety from Hawaii. Gray sea salts tend to be less refined than those that are pure white, and, in general, sea salts are less refined than kosher or table salts. Both table salt and kosher salt come from salt mines, and, as the name implies, sea salt comes from the sea. Because of the laborious process of raking off the salt deposits as seawater evaporates, sea salt is more expensive.

Personally, I like to use distinctive sea salts like French *fleur de sel* when I can taste their delicate nuances, such as on an ear of corn or with fried potatoes. I cook with Diamond Crystal kosher salt. And I bake with fine sea salt. In case you're wondering what I do with Morton table salt, I keep it in the pantry for impromptu salt tastings for the uninitiated. Then I put it right back in the pantry.

If everyone's palate is different, why not just let people season their own food to taste at the table? Certainly, if you're cooking for someone who has a health or medical reason for limiting salt intake, this might be the best approach. But, as you'll see soon, *when* you add the salt makes a significant difference in overall flavor.

A TALE OF TWO STEAKS

While we're on the subject of seasoning, I want to tell you about a master class I took in Chicago several years ago with meat expert Bruce Aidells. I was one of about a hundred culinary professionals assembled in a large hotel meeting room at eight-thirty on a Thursday morning. Aidells pan-seared copious amounts of New York steaks in well-seasoned cast-iron pans. We tasted two samples, both medium-rare. The first was cooked "nude," then seasoned with salt. The second was sprinkled with salt before cooking. The difference between the two steaks was nothing short of remarkable.

When I ate the first steak, I initially tasted salt on my tongue, then meaty, juicy steak. As I chewed, the saltiness dissipated and the steak tasted flat. An orchestra metaphor explains it best: the first steak was a decent solo. The second steak, revved up by spending a little more time with the salt before searing, was a symphony of flavors. This tasty number had a savory crust that yielded to rich-tasting, chewy meat. The salt grains had had a chance to melt during cooking, enhancing the meat and the inherent umami, or savoriness.

Aidells's demonstration left an indelible impression on me. Several years later, I was thrilled to learn more about the technique of early seasoning in Judy Rodgers's long-awaited *The Zuni Café Cookbook*. In this award-winning volume, the chef-owner of San Francisco's legendary restaurant explains her technique of seasoning meats, poultry, and fish up to a day or two ahead. Rodgers uses about a scant ¾ teaspoon sea salt per pound of beef, and recommends seasoning about four hours ahead for very thin skirt steak, or up to one day ahead for a chuck roast. When I make hamburgers, I salt the ground beef about three hours ahead.

For those of us who, for all our cooking lives, have dutifully abided by the iron-fisted caveat not to salt meat too early for fear that it would draw out the moisture, this early seasoning concept sounds blasphemous. In fact, it is true that salt draws out moisture. But then, in time, through the magic of reverse osmosis, the meat reabsorbs the salty fluid. Not only that, this process causes the internal protein fibers to open up and become saturated with the salty liquid.

Normally during cooking, protein fibers shrink, squeezing out moisture. When reverse osmosis has a chance to work its magic before cooking, the seasoned, moist protein cells actually retain some of the newly absorbed moisture, resulting in tenderer, moister, more flavorful meat through and through.

BRINING AND TODAY'S "NEW" MEATS AND POULTRY

If a little salt sprinkled on the surface of meat plus a little resting time can transform meats, poultry, and fish as significantly as early seasoning does, you can only imagine how these proteins are affected when they're brined, or completely submerged in a vat of salted water, for several hours. Furthermore, when aromatic ingredients such as ginger, garlic, peppercorns, orange zest, and red pepper flakes are added to a simple brine, it's easy to see how both the tenderness and flavor of a roasted turkey or pork roast can be enhanced exponentially. Other flavor enhancements for brines include sugar, maple syrup, brown sugar, and the like.

Brining has become particularly popular and important in the past fifteen years or so as a response to mass-market changes that have brought us free-range poultry and leaner "new white meat" pork. Strange bedfellows, perhaps, but as I see it, in both examples, we are now faced with tougher, less flavorful meat.

I started brining turkeys in about 1994, when I became fed up, literally and figuratively, with tough, dry free-range birds that cost too much to deliver such disappointment. If I'm going to preorder a free-range turkey, put down a deposit, take time off from work to stand in line two days before Thanksgiving, and give up a big chunk of change for

a fancy bird, it had better be pretty terrific. Having had good luck brining turkeys (see page 188), I began experimenting brining my annual Christmas crown roast of pork, tinkering with the aromatics in the brine (as suggested above) until I was satisfied. It was very tasty, and incomparably tender, but, honestly, what a pain—especially during the holidays. As I hope you will agree when you make the crown roast of pork (page 219) in this book, I have now zeroed in on how to make a tender, juicy, flavorful pork roast without brining. Two things make this possible: First, producers such as Niman Ranch (see Sources) are now bringing to market good, old-fashioned marbled pork, which renders brining unnecessary. Also, through my own trial and error, I've discovered that the rib end is the best cut to use for a crown (or smaller) pork roast, regardless of whose pork I buy.

I only wish I could say the same for turkeys. I'm still brining turkeys, but as much as I'd love to love them, I've given up on tough free-range birds. (Yes, I've ended up with tough free-range turkeys even after brining.) Instead, I spend less money, with no money down, on a nonpedigreed fresh turkey from my local grocery store. (If we could just do something about those long grocery-store lines at Thanksgiving.)

ATTENTIVE TASTING

SALT-TO-WATER RATIOS FOR BRINING CHICKEN AND TURKEY

The standard brine solution for a whole chicken is 1 part (½ cup) Diamond Crystal kosher salt to 8 parts (4 cups) water for 1 hour. If desired, the same tenderness and flavor can be achieved by using half as much salt and extending the brining time to 4 hours for a chicken. To brine a turkey, use a 1-to-8 ratio for 24 to 36 hours, depending on size.

AROMATIC BRINES

Ingredients that give fragrance and flavor are called aromatics. Aromatics used in brining can help define the flavor profile of the finished dish. For example, a Mediterranean flavor profile might include aromatics such as bay leaves, fennel seeds, garlic, lemon zest, peppercorns, red pepper flakes, and herbs such as basil and parsley. For a Chinese profile, consider using garlic, ginger, green onions, chiles, Sichuan peppercorns, star anise, and herbs such as Chinese parsley (also known as cilantro or coriander).

All this talk about umami, volatilizing esters, seasoning to taste, and brining makes it clear that if you want to take your cooking to another level, you must focus on flavor and texture. One way to explore the interplay of flavors and textures is to engage in a guided tasting of a lively, bold dish, such as Broiled Swordfish with Mango Salsa (page 155). Here are the key elements to be aware of as you taste attentively:

• The first sensation you may experience is refreshment from the vivid flavors of the tropical salsa.

• Next, the savory, umami-rich flavors of the broiled fish kick in—both texture and flavor can be described as meaty.

• This meatiness is enhanced by a caramelized surface, the result of the intense, direct heat of the broiler. Yet the fish has been kept moist thanks to a protective *glaçage* (see page 135). Here's a case where the cooking method complements the food, playing to the inherent strengths in both the flavor and texture of the fish.

• The texture of the red onion and diced jalapeños in the salsa are crunchy, perfect foils for the meaty texture of the fish.

• In the next bite, the oil from the fish coats your tongue, making the palate particularly sensitive to the bitter, sweet, salty, sour, and umami flavors in the salsa. Fat is a powerful force in making us perceive that certain combinations are greater than the sum of their parts. When the tongue is coated with fatty ingredients, it becomes a hypersensitive flavor sensor, making the other flavors on your tongue sing.

A FEW WORDS ABOUT MENU PLANNING

- Finally, the acid from the lime juice in the salsa puts the whole process in motion again, and makes the experience of eating it even more compelling. As the acid causes us to salivate, it cleanses the palate from the rich fish, and we're ready for the next bite. Dessert, anyone?

You don't have to taste fine food to practice attentive tasting. The next time you're at a ballgame, try a hot dog or sausage with a few different condiments. Notice how mustard, relish, and ketchup each have a different effect on your perception of the meat's saltiness and overall flavor. Do you prefer the texture of the bun steamed or grilled? Do you like the pop of the skin on a hot dog or do you prefer a skinless frank?

As you taste attentively, focus on what you like and ask yourself why. Besides flavor and texture, notice the temperature of both the food and your environment and what else is going on around you. Emotions, the people you're with, and your surroundings all contribute significantly to your overall enjoyment of a meal. There's nothing like the taste of a ballpark hot dog when your team is winning.

Presenting different textures on the same plate makes the overall eating experience interesting and compelling. When planning a menu, it's important to keep in mind complementary flavors, textures, and colors; even temperatures are important. For example, if you are serving the rich broiled fish with the tangy mango salsa (page 155) from the previous exercise, a pilaf made with wild rice (page 276) will add another welcome contrasting element. In other words, contrasts on the same plate are desirable. But, especially in time-honored combinations, similar characteristics can work well, too: Imagine a soft, hot open-faced turkey sandwich with gravy and creamy mashed potatoes and peas on the side. On the other hand, a hot fudge sundae illustrates perfectly how variety can be a winning combination with hot, cold, creamy, crunchy, smooth, sticky, bitter, and sweet all in one bowl.

HOW TO IMPROVE YOUR COOKING

Improving your cooking should be enjoyable, whether cooking is your hobby or your career. If reading appeals to you, books and periodicals about food and cooking are one place to begin. When you find a book that resonates with you, look through its bibliography, too. It's fun and insightful to see who and what inspires and shapes the opinions of a mentor. If you're not a reader, watch cooking shows on television. Better still, take classes to fill in your knowledge gaps in knife skills, cooking techniques, or information about a single subject, such as sauces, risotto, or pie making. Classes are a great way to develop confidence. Finally, I implore you to practice what you learn from books, cooking shows, and classes, to both reinforce the new knowledge and test out how the new recipes and techniques work for you, particularly while they're fresh in your mind. Each week I send off students in my Cooking Basics classes with homework: Cook something. And pay attention. It's really that simple.

CREATIVE COOKING

I expect you'll discover, as I have, that the more you cook, the more confident you feel in creating dishes that incorporate ingredients, cooking methods, and flavor profiles that you find satisfying. It's rewarding to be able to see a cut of meat or piece of fish in the market and know which cooking methods will bring out its best attributes.

There are many ways to become inspired as a cook: Shop in ethnic markets. Eat in ethnic restaurants. Pay attention to how the raw foods you see in one are transformed into cuisine in the other. Try new varieties of your favorite produce at the farmers' market, and ask the growers for cooking tips. Add new foods and condiments to your larder and cook with them in different combinations. Always keep in mind, however, that exercising restraint is critical to success.

PUTTING YOUR CREATIVITY TO WORK

Here are some tips and guidelines, along with examples of each, to guide you as you try your hand at inventing "new" recipes.

Tip: Pay attention to regional and ethnic variations on the classics, especially when you travel.
Example: BLT with avocado.

Tip: Observe the Rule of Threes when coming up with new combinations.
Example: Parmesan-Stuffed Eggs with Toasted Walnuts (by Marie Simmons in her award-winning book, *The Good Egg*).

Tip: Notice how food stylists and chefs reframe classic recipes with new presentations.
Example: Lettuce and tomato salad, in which dressed individual lettuce leaves are gathered into a bunch and inserted into a whole, hollowed-out tomato (by former California Culinary Academy chef-instructor Don Woods).

Tip: Practice restraint.
Example: Just because there are six varieties of decent-quality vegetables languishing in the fridge, you need not add them all to your cream-of-the-vegetable-drawer soup.

Tip: Finesse is often more important than your original plan.
Example: Turn the salmon you bought for three eaters into an impromptu dinner for six by cutting and cooking it differently and using it as an accompaniment instead of the star (page 102).

Tip: Cheat with style by using shortcut ingredients to add pizzazz to your cooking.
Example: Pan-sear prepared duck confit (available at Whole Foods Markets) and serve on arugula that's been tossed with toasted walnut oil and champagne vinegar; garnish with dried sour cherries and crumbled walnuts.

Tip: Use "new" ingredients in "old" ways.
Example: Traditional Caprese salad combines sliced tomatoes, mozzarella, and basil. Re-create it with "new" heirloom tomatoes cut into wedges, small balls of mozzarella, and white balsamic vinegar (which won't stain the cheese like red vinegar does), tossed together in a bowl and served family style (page 86).

Tip: Use classic flavor profiles to put a new spin on an old favorite.
Example: Flat bread topped with Chinese barbecued pork, green onions, and hoisin sauce (found in pizzerias across the United States).

A FEW WORDS ABOUT PLATE PRESENTATION

The Rule of Threes applies to plate presentation, too. Three contrasting colors of food—roasted red peppers, grilled stuffed chicken breast on herb-flecked orzo, and a drizzle of green pesto on a single plate—are guaranteed to dazzle. The look is classic, elegant, and vibrant, and reflects a strong respect for simplicity. It has integrity, too—in this case, a bold Italian flavor profile with nothing extraneous to confuse the diner. It shows restraint in not introducing unrelated elements, such as a sprig of rosemary or watercress, and it can be put together on the plate with little fussing, so the chicken doesn't get cold and the pesto doesn't start to run before it reaches the table.

To keep presentations simple, start by imagining the plate as the face of a clock. Place your pork chop, or whatever needs to be cut, in the six o'clock position. This way, the person eating doesn't have to drag his or her sleeve across the plate to cut the meat. Place the side dishes wherever they look best in relation to the chop. In so doing, think like a florist: Odd numbers rule. Three or five wedges of roasted root vegetables nestled against a perfectly grilled pork chop are more appealing to the eye than two or four pieces, just as five or seven tulips in a vase make a more striking statement than four or six. When you set the plates down at the table, make sure each pork chop is in the six o'clock position in front of each guest. Likewise, be sure the point end of a wedge of pie or cake is at six o'clock when serving dessert.

Keep in mind that, as in cooking, tasteful plate presentation often has as much to do with what you *don't* put on the plate as with what you do. Let the food speak for itself. Make the little extra effort to char cross-hatching onto the pork chops (it enhances the flavor of the chops, too), and slip some red apple skins and a squeeze of lemon into some homemade applesauce to stain it rosy pink. When the food looks terrific, the hot food is served hot, and the cold food arrives cold, you're well on your way to creating a memorable presentation. Wipe off any smudges on the rims, and bring forth your plates with pride. Your mood and expression are really what sets the tone at the table, after all.

RECIPES

PART TWO

GUIDELINES FOR PREPARING THE RECIPES IN THIS BOOK

Following are the guidelines that were followed by the 116 home cooks who tested the recipes in this book. At their urging, I'm including them here for you. If you aren't sure about an ingredient, utensil, or term in a recipe, consult the index to find out where you can read more about it.

- *Read completely through the recipe* before beginning to cook, and preferably before shopping for ingredients.

- I've tried to avoid repetition, so before you prepare a recipe, please *reread the general secrets* for that type of recipe at the beginning of its section. For example, before you make White Corn Chowder (page 68), reread "Secrets for Successful Soups" on page 65. This way, you'll refresh your memory.

- When a recipe calls for *kosher salt,* it refers to Diamond Crystal kosher salt (page 43). If unavailable, substitute ½ teaspoon table salt, ½ teaspoon fine sea salt, or ½ teaspoon Morton kosher salt for each 1 teaspoon Diamond Crystal kosher salt.

- In cases where the coarseness of ground *black pepper* makes a difference in the flavor of the dish, I have specified either "fine, freshly ground black pepper" or "coarse, freshly ground black pepper." If the coarseness is not specified, use whichever grind you prefer.

- When a recipe calls for "3 tablespoons *oil, divided,*" it means that you'll use some of the oil at one point in the recipe, and more later. It doesn't necessarily mean you should divide the oil in half.

MEASURE ACCURATELY

- **For liquids:** Use measuring spoons or glass or clear plastic liquid measuring cups (with a spout and handle). Hold the measuring cup with the ingredient at eye level to check accuracy.

- **For dry ingredients:** Use measuring spoons, or spoon the ingredient into a dry measuring cup (nesting set of cups with no spouts, usually stainless steel or sturdy plastic) and level off with a straight edge, such as the blunt edge of a knife blade.

- To measure 1 cup **sifted flour:** Sift some flour into a bowl. Spoon the sifted flour into a 1-cup dry measuring cup, heaping it over the top. Use a straight edge to level off the flour. Use only what's in the cup.

- To measure 1 cup **flour, sifted:** Spoon some flour into a 1-cup dry measuring cup, heaping it over the top. Use a straight edge to level off the flour. Sift what's in the cup and use only that flour in the recipe.

- **Do not fill the measuring cup by dipping** it into sifted or unsifted flour to scoop it up. This compacts the flour and you won't get an accurate measurement. Instead, use a spoon to add the flour to the cup.

- **Do not sift** flour unless the recipe specifies it.

- If you use the rasp-style **Microplane** grater to grate cheese, pack down the grated cheese when you measure it. This type of grater yields a fluffier result than a box grater does. Likewise, to measure citrus zest removed with a Microplane, pack it down, too.

- **Measure** sauté pans and skillets across the top (for diameter). Measure baking pans across the bottom. If you must use a different-sized pan than what is specified in a recipe, it may be necessary to adjust the cooking time.

- If you use **glass baking dishes** instead of metal, porcelain, or clay, reduce the oven temperature by 25 degrees and reduce the baking time by 10 percent.

- Use **shiny metal pans** for baking. If you must use nonstick pans or other dark metal pans, the items will brown faster on the bottom, and you may have to shorten the baking time.

- When an **internal temperature** is specified as a test for doneness, insert an instant-read thermometer into the thickest or densest part of the item. If the food is equally dense or thick, insert the thermometer in the center. Do not allow it to touch bone or fat, if present, as they can skew the temperature.

- **Room temperature** is about 68 degrees F. A **warm oven** is about 180 degrees F.

STOCKS, SOUPS, AND SALADS

STOCKS, SOUPS, AND SALADS
RECIPES

Recipe	Q	MA	V	Page
Classic Chicken Stock		●		60
Shortcut Chicken Broth with a Dividend		●		61
Vegetable Broth		●	●	63
Red Bell Pepper Bisque with Crème Fraîche		●	●	66
White Corn Chowder		●	●	68
Chicken Soup with Glass Noodles	●	●		70
Tomato-Cheddar Soup	●	●	●	72
French Onion Soup Gratinée		●	●	73
Three-Bean Minestrone with Sausage		●	●	75
Weeknight Green Salad	●		●	81
Butter Lettuce with Ruby Grapefruit, Avocado, and Glazed Walnuts		●	●	82
Heirloom Tomatoes with Bocconcini, Basil, and White Balsamic Vinaigrette	●		●	86
Shaved Celery with Medjool Dates, Feta, and Walnuts	●	●	●	88
Figs and Arugula with Creamy Goat Cheese and Toasted Pecans	●		●	90
Baby Greens, Roasted Chicken, Stilton, and Hazelnuts with Raspberry Vinaigrette		●	●	91

Q = Quick—prep to table in 45 minutes.
MA = Make ahead—part or all of the recipe can or must be made ahead.
V = Vegetarian—no meat, chicken, fish, or, with minor adjustments, such as substituting vegetable broth for chicken stock, can be prepared as a vegetarian recipe.

SECRETS FOR SUCCESSFUL STOCKS AND BROTHS

The beginning of this section includes recipes for Classic Chicken Stock, Shortcut Chicken Broth with a Dividend, and Vegetable Broth, followed by several soup recipes that utilize them. Each recipe features "Secrets" that pertain to the ingredients and techniques in that recipe. In addition, here are some general tips that apply whenever you are making stocks and broths, along with answers to some frequently asked questions about stocks and soups. The chart on page 59 lists all the recipes in this book that call for stock or broth.

INGREDIENTS

- Be sure to use impeccable, fresh (not wilted or rotting) vegetables. The same adage uttered by software engineers applies to making stocks: garbage in, garbage out.

- Mirepoix (page 20), the holy trinity of onions, carrots, and celery, is the basis for most stocks and many soups.

- There's no need to peel onions when making stock. Their skin will lend a pleasant brown hue to the liquid. Simply wash well and trim off any dirty roots.

- Cut carrots and celery on a sharp diagonal to expose as much surface area of the vegetables as possible. This also prevents the carrots from rolling around as you cut.

- Leeks are like sand traps. Trim off the root ends, then make a pair of perpendicular cuts down the entire length of the dark green leaves, but not all the way through to the white part. Swish leeks in a bowl of warm water (cold water makes the sand cling), separating the dark green leaves to expose any sand. Use both green and white parts in stocks and broths.

- When I was in cooking school, my first chef-instructor, an amiable Dane by the name of Lars Kronmark, taught the class his secret ingredient for great chicken stock: rutabaga. While you don't taste the flavor of rutabaga, the often-maligned root vegetable does add a level of complexity and depth of flavor. Twenty years later, I wouldn't think of making stock without a rutabaga. If all you can find is a huge one, use just a 1-pound piece here (and roast the rest). Peel off any waxy coating first.

CLARITY

- Clarity is of paramount importance in stocks and broths. The secret to a clear stock is twofold: First, never let the stock get hotter than a gentle simmer. Boiling agitates the impurities, which will cloud the stock. Second, it's virtually impossible to skim a stock too much. The most critical skimming time is before you add the vegetables, when the bones are heating up and releasing impurities, such as blood, into the liquid. Use a fine-mesh skimmer or a ladle, and skim early and often.

- Be sure to use a strainer, such as a chinois, with very fine mesh to strain the stock at the end. Alternatively, line a medium-mesh strainer with dampened cheesecloth—the dampening helps the cheesecloth adhere to the sides of the strainer.

COOKING TIME

- In the old days, cooks would leave chicken stock simmering gently on the back burner for 8 to 12 hours. Modern research shows that the chicken bones and aromatic vegetables have contributed just about all their goodness to a stock in 3 to 4 hours.

FLAVOR

- Typically, salt is not added to meat, poultry, or fish stock. A small amount is sometimes added to broths to season the meat, as in the broth on page 61. Some vegetable broth recipes, including mine, call for a little salt to bring out the flavor of the vegetables, but not actually to season the broth.

- Stock is not supposed to taste like soup. Because stocks and broths are the foundation on which recipes are built, they are intentionally mild—or bland—on their own. For a richer stock or broth, concentrate flavors by reducing, or boiling rapidly in a wide pot, until you reach a desirable flavor.

ABOUT BOUQUET GARNI

This aromatic seasoning package is used to perfume and flavor stocks and other liquids. The most common bouquet garni includes fresh parsley stems, fresh thyme sprigs, peppercorns, and imported bay leaf, either wrapped in cheesecloth and tied into a bundle or packed into a tea ball. Once the ingredients have lent their fragrance and flavor to a pot of stock, they are discarded.

FREQUENTLY ASKED QUESTIONS ABOUT STOCKS AND BROTHS

What's the difference between chicken broth and chicken stock?

Opinions abound, but here's how I distinguish broth from stock: In addition to aromatics such as onions, carrots, and/or celery, which flavor the water, *broth* is made from whole or large pieces of poultry, meat, or fish. Think of broth as a by-product of cooking meat or chicken. *Stock*, on the other hand, is made from bony chicken parts, such as necks and backs, plus feet and giblets, which are rich in minerals and collagen. Broth has a higher meat-to-bone ratio. Stock is cooked longer than broth, and you'll rarely see salt in a stock recipe. This is because stocks are often reduced, or cooked down, to concentrate their flavor when making sauces. Any salt added to the stock would also become concentrated, and the reduced stock would taste too salty. However, a small amount of salt is commonly added to meat or chicken broth to boost the flavor of the liquid, which in turn seasons the meat. Except when making stock-based reduction sauces, I use broth and stock interchangeably. The recipes in this book have been tested with homemade chicken broth, homemade chicken stock, and purchased reduced-sodium chicken broth. In the following questions, the word "stock" is used as a shortcut term for stock and broth.

What's the safest way to cool stock?

To prevent stock from developing a sour flavor, and to keep it from languishing in the danger zone (page 23), cool it promptly to room temperature and then refrigerate or freeze. Set a pot of hot stock, uncovered, on a sturdy rack to allow good air circulation.

/continued

To hasten the cooling process, put the stock-filled container in an ice bath: Fill the sink with ice water to reach about two-thirds up the sides of the container. Occasionally stir the stock in a figure-8 pattern with a slotted spoon until it cools to about 70 degrees F. Stir continuously for quicker cooling. (The figure-8 pattern covers a broad surface area and the slotted spoon minimizes splashing.)

. . . .

What's the best way to store stock?
. . . .

Refrigerate or freeze stock, depending on when you intend to use it. If you don't use refrigerated stock within 3 days, skim off any fat and impurities that have risen to the surface and boil the stock for 3 minutes. Let cool to room temperature and refrigerate again. Reboil every 3 days as necessary.

To freeze stock, transfer to wide-mouthed containers (preferably not glass), allowing plenty of headroom for expansion. Or pour into "dedicated" ice cube trays (stock tends to imbue plastic with a savory smell, which isn't terrific if you're planning to reuse the trays to make ice cubes). Freeze for up to 3 months and thaw overnight in the refrigerator.

Fellow cooking teacher Charlene Vojtilla passed on this great tip for freezing precise measurements of stock that also stack nicely in the freezer: Pour cool stock into rinsed, empty milk cartons (either quart or half-gallon), staple or tape shut, and freeze upright. Once frozen solid, if desired, peel off the cartons and store the blocks of stock in zip-top plastic bags.

ABOUT BAY LEAVES

The native Mediterranean bay laurel plant, *Laurus nobilis,* produces bitter, but subtle-flavored leaves that are dried and used as a culinary herb. Many fine cooks prefer these imported bay leaves, often called Turkish bay leaves, for their relatively delicate flavor. They are not to be confused with the more narrow-leaved Angustifolia variety of *Laurus nobilis,* also called willow-leaf or California bay laurel (see illustration). To some (including me), California bay has an undesirable turpentine-like flavor. The preferred imported leaves are a duller color and are shorter, wider, and often more brittle. Bay leaves are typically used whole, sometimes crumbled into a few pieces and added to marinades or brines, but never chopped. They are not meant to be eaten and should be removed and discarded from a dish before serving. Look for bay leaves in Middle Eastern markets, natural-foods stores, and supermarkets.

Turkish bay leaf, *Laurus nobilis*

Willow-leaf bay, *Laurus nobilis* Angustifolia

RECIPES THAT USE HOMEMADE CHICKEN STOCK, CHICKEN BROTH, OR VEGETABLE BROTH

	Recipe	Amount Used	Page
Soups	Red Bell Pepper Bisque with Crème Fraîche	4 cups	66
	White Corn Chowder	6 cups	68
	Chicken Soup with Glass Noodles	5 cups	70
	Tomato-Cheddar Soup	2 cups	72
	French Onion Soup Gratinée	6 cups	73
Risottos	Risotto Milanese	6 to 8 cups	98
	Butternut Squash Risotto with Parmigiano-Reggiano Rinds and Balsamic Drizzle	8 cups	99
	Risotto Primavera with Wild Salmon	4 to 6 cups	102
Main Dishes	California Crab Gumbo with Chicken and Sausage	8 cups	138
	Paella with Shellfish, Sausage, and Chicken	3 cups	158
	Chicken Salad Véronique with Whole Toasted Almonds	6 cups	168
	Stir-Fried Velvet Chicken with Cashews	¼ cup	174
	Roasted Stuffed Turkey with Pan Gravy	3 cups	188
	Maple-Glazed Quail Stuffed with Wild Mushrooms, Sausage, and Sour Cherries	1 cup	194
	Herb-Crusted Chicken Potpies	4 cups	198
	Slow-Roasted Beef Sirloin Tip with Pan Gravy	2 cups	232
	Osso Buco with Sweet Red Peppers and Gremolata	1 cup	234
On the Side	Braised Greens with Sausage and Onions	2 cups	266
	Creamy, Soft Polenta	6 to 7 cups	274
	Wild Rice Pilaf	2 cups	276

RECIPE SECRETS

While big pieces of chicken fat have a tendency to make a stock greasy, they also contribute great flavor. Many fine cooks add pieces of chicken fat to the stockpot, then degrease the stock completely after it's chilled.

Chicken skin and feet are loaded with collagen, which provides rich body and gelatinous viscosity, both desirable qualities in stock.

To ensure that you'll end up with the yield indicated, use a 16-quart stockpot. If unavailable, use the same amount of ingredients in a smaller pot, filling the pot two-thirds full of water, as directed.

Fine-mesh skimmer

Chinese strainer, or "spider"

CLASSIC CHICKEN STOCK

Use this all-purpose stock in soups, sauces, and in any recipe that calls for chicken stock or broth, such as risottos, paellas, pilafs, and stir-fries (see page 59 for recipes in this book that call for chicken stock). To use this stock as a base for a simple chicken soup, strain and degrease as directed, then boil until reduced in volume by half. This will concentrate the flavors, making a suitable base to which you can add your favorite soup ingredients and seasonings.

Makes about 7 quarts

6 pounds chicken backs, necks, and/or feet (some skin is okay)

½ pound chicken gizzards and hearts (optional)

6 whole cloves

6 large yellow onions, unpeeled, washed

5 large carrots, unpeeled, cut on a sharp diagonal into 3-inch pieces

3 celery stalks, cut on a sharp diagonal into 3-inch pieces

3 leeks, roots trimmed and cleaned (page 56)

1 rutabaga, about 1 pound, unpeeled, cut into quarters

5 fresh thyme sprigs

4 fresh parsley stems

1 bay leaf, preferably imported

8 black peppercorns

---

1. Rinse the chicken parts and the gizzards and hearts, if using, under cold water and place in a 16-quart stockpot. Fill the pot two-thirds full with cold water. Bring just to a boil over high heat. Reduce the heat to a low simmer. With a fine-mesh skimmer or ladle, skim off the white foam and all impurities that rise to the surface. Skim until the foam subsides and the liquid is clear, about 15 minutes total.

2. Stick a whole clove into each onion to keep the onions intact and prevent the cloves from floating to the top and being skimmed off. Add the studded onions, carrots, celery, leeks, and rutabaga to the pot.

3. To prepare a bouquet garni, place the thyme, parsley stems, bay leaf, and peppercorns on a double-thick piece of cheesecloth, bring the corners together, and tie with one end of a 12-inch piece of kitchen string. Tie the other end of the string to the handle of the pot and immerse the bouquet garni in the liquid. Alternatively, place the ingredients in a small mesh bag or tea ball and immerse in the pot.

4. Add cold water to come to within an inch of the rim of the pot. Bring the liquid to a simmer over low heat and simmer gently, uncovered, skimming occasionally, for 2 to 4 hours. You'll have a respectable stock if it simmers for 2 hours, but it will be richer tasting if you simmer it 4 hours.

5. Remove from the heat. (You can let the stock sit for up to 2 hours at this point before straining.) With a Chinese strainer (see illustration) or large slotted spoon, remove and discard the large solids and the bouquet garni (retrieving the tea ball if necessary). Strain the stock into 2 or 3 clean, large pots, pouring it through a chinois (see illustration) or fine-mesh strainer lined with a double-thickness of dampened cheesecloth. Discard the solids.

6. Place the pots on racks and let cool to room temperature. Cover and refrigerate until the stock is cold enough for the fat to rise to the surface and solidify. This will take several hours, or leave overnight. Use a slotted spoon or large serving fork to remove the solidified fat. For storage guidelines, see page 58.

Chinois

SHORTCUT CHICKEN BROTH
WITH A DIVIDEND

When you make this shortcut broth, in addition to saving time, you'll end up with an incomparably moist and flavorful whole chicken as a dividend. (See page 162 for information on buying chickens.) Use the chicken meat in your favorite enchiladas or salad recipes, in Chicken Salad Véronique (page 168), or in Herb-Crusted Chicken Potpies (page 198). This respectable broth can stand in for chicken stock in Wild Rice Pilaf (page 276), Risotto Milanese (page 98), Creamy, Soft Polenta (page 274), or any soup recipe that calls for chicken stock. See page 59 for recipes in this book that call for chicken broth or stock.

> **Makes about 3 quarts broth, plus 3 to 4 cups cooked, shredded chicken**
>
> | | |
> |---|---|
> | 1 chicken, 3 to 4 pounds | 3 fresh thyme sprigs |
> | 3 green onions, roots removed | 2 teaspoons kosher salt, divided |

/continued

RECIPE SECRETS

This recipe is actually the Cantonese method of preparing steeped—or poached— chicken, which I learned from veteran California Culinary Academy Chinese cooking instructor Rhoda Yee. Use a natural chicken (page 162), if possible. To keep the chicken tender, don't bring the liquid to a rolling boil. Boiling toughens protein fibers.

For great flavor, if there's a bag of giblets stashed inside the chicken, use everything except the liver. Clarity is one hallmark of a good broth, and the liver would cloud the broth and give it an undesirably strong flavor (see page 56).

RECIPE SECRETS

As the chicken steeps, its juices flow to the source of the heat, outward toward the skin. To immediately stop the cooking and force the chicken juices to retract back into the meat, once the chicken reaches the proper temperature, plunge it into an ice water bath that's been seasoned with a little salt. You'll be rewarded with a moist chicken, rather than one that squirts out its flavorful juices onto the cutting board when you cut into it.

For the silkiest texture, shred the chicken meat by hand. Use a knife to dice only the largest pieces of breast and thigh meat. To keep the meat juicy and moist if not using right away, place the meat in a 1-quart bowl and add just enough strained, room-temperature broth to cover it. Cover and refrigerate for up to 3 days, straining—and saving—the broth before using the meat.

Fresh thyme branch

Fresh thyme sprig

1. Remove the giblet package, if present, from the cavity of the chicken. Rinse the chicken and the giblets under cold water. Discard the liver, or reserve for another use. Place the chicken, gizzard, heart, and neck in a 6-quart lightweight pot. Add enough cold water to cover the chicken, about 3 quarts. Bring the water to a steady simmer over high heat, then reduce the heat to low. With a fine-mesh skimmer, or ladle, skim off the white foam and all the impurities that rise to the surface. Skim until the foam subsides and the liquid is clear, 5 to 10 minutes. Add the green onions, thyme, and 1 teaspoon of the salt. Cover the pot and simmer over the lowest heat setting for 10 minutes. Turn off the heat, keep covered, and let the chicken steep on the same burner for 30 minutes. Insert an instant-read thermometer into the deepest part of each thigh (one may be denser than the other); it should register 180 degrees F. If not, cover and continue steeping until the temperature is reached.

2. Fill a large bowl half-full with ice cubes. Add cold water to cover the ice. Stir in the remaining 1 teaspoon salt. Transfer the steeped chicken to the ice-water bath, reserving the pot of broth. If necessary, add more cold water just to cover the chicken. Turn the chicken in the ice water until cool enough to handle, about 10 minutes. Remove, drain, and pat dry.

3. Break or cut the chicken into pieces, and remove the skin, bones, and fat. Pulling the meat along the grain, shred the chicken by hand. Cut the larger pieces of breast and thigh meat with a sharp knife before shredding. Cover and refrigerate the chicken for up to 3 days (see Secret for keeping meat moist). Strain the broth into a clean 4-quart pot, pouring it through a chinois or fine-mesh strainer.

4. Place the pot on a rack and let cool to room temperature. Cover and refrigerate until the broth is cool enough for the fat to rise to the surface and solidify. This will take several hours, or leave overnight. Use a slotted spoon or large serving fork to remove the solidified fat, and discard it or reserve it for another use. (Chicken fat is great for sautéing potatoes.) For storage guidelines, see page 58.

VEGETABLE BROTH

I've always been disappointed with store-bought vegetable broth. Whether it comes in a can or a box, to me it tastes artificial and watered down. Beware, too, of those jars of vegetable broth base and their cousins, the MSG-laden salt licks passed off as vegetable bouillon cubes. Fortunately, it's both simple and quick to whip up a pot of homemade vegetable broth, especially if you've squirrelled away bits of vegetable scraps and trim. But remember, broths and stocks are not a repository for the detritus you might find languishing in the far reaches of the vegetable drawer. (Yes, I, too, have been known to discover unintentional science projects in my fridge.) As with chicken stock and broth, it's particularly important here to avoid using limp or mangy vegetables that have lost a good percentage of their nutrients. In my kitchen, I'm likely to generate broth-worthy mushroom stems and mirepoix trimmings at a pretty quick clip. To keep them fresh until I'm ready to make a pot of this broth, I seal the scraps in FoodSaver vacuum sealed bags. I find these bags to be much more effective than zip-top bags because they suck out—and keep out—more of the air and dampness that can cause deterioration. The vacuum seal method is also a great way to store fresh herbs such as parsley or thyme.

Whenever we make this vegetable broth in class, the students marvel at the flavor that can be coaxed out of just a handful of common vegetables. Few vegetables are off-limits in this broth, but use strong-flavored cruciferous vegetables, such as cabbage or broccoli rabe, sparingly. This all-purpose broth is suitable for soups, sauces, and any recipe that calls for stock or broth, such as risottos, paellas, pilafs, and stir-fries. (See page 59 for recipes in this book that call for vegetable broth.) Specific vegetables are listed here, but they are only suggestions. Regardless of the vegetables you choose, for the best body or viscosity, use a vegetables-to-water ratio of 2 to 1.

/continued

RECIPE SECRETS

For a richer-tasting broth, first roast the chopped onions, carrots, rutabaga, mushrooms, and garlic at 375 degrees F until they brown and caramelize, 45 to 60 minutes. (Stir every 15 minutes or so to caramelize all sides.) Use roasted vegetable broth in French Onion Soup Gratinée (page 73) or Kalijira Rice Pilaw (page 277).

For a sweeter broth, add a couple of corncobs, and use the broth as a base for White Corn Chowder (page 68).

The unexpected chamomile teabag adds a dimension of complexity, but it is not essential. I learned this teabag trick from chef Thomas Marconi, one of my former students at the California Culinary Academy.

RECIPE SECRETS

By the time the broth is done, the vegetables are spent, having given up their nutrients, flavor, and other goodness to the broth. If you feel uncomfortable discarding them, you might consider feeding them to the dog or adding them as ballast (don't rely on them for flavor) to a puréed vegetable soup.

To ensure that you'll end up with the yield indicated, use an 8-quart stockpot. If unavailable, use the same amount of ingredients in a smaller pot, covering the vegetables with water as directed.

Makes about 4 quarts

6 large yellow onions, unpeeled, washed	6 cloves garlic, smashed gently with the side of a chef's knife
5 carrots, unpeeled	1 bunch fresh flat-leaf parsley
3 celery stalks	10 fresh thyme sprigs
3 leeks, roots trimmed and cleaned (page 56)	8 black peppercorns
1 rutabaga, about 1 pound, unpeeled, chopped	1 chamomile teabag
	2 teaspoons kosher salt
½ pound fresh mushroom stems or fresh whole mushrooms, chopped	1 bay leaf, preferably imported

1. Roughly chop or slice the onions, carrots, celery, and leeks. (It may be easier to slice the onions with a serrated knife.) Place in an 8-quart stockpot. Add the rutabaga, mushrooms, garlic, parsley, thyme, peppercorns, teabag, salt, and bay leaf. Add enough cold water just to cover the vegetables. Bring to a boil over high heat. Cover, reduce the heat to low, and simmer for 30 minutes.

2. Uncover and simmer for an additional 30 minutes. Taste the broth to see if the flavor is to your liking. If you'd prefer a stronger broth, simmer, uncovered, for another 30 minutes.

3. Remove from the heat. Strain the broth into a large, clean pot, pouring it through a chinois or fine-mesh strainer lined with a double thickness of dampened cheesecloth. Discard the solids. For storage guidelines, see page 58.

SECRETS FOR SUCCESSFUL SOUPS

Each soup recipe in this chapter includes Secrets that talk about ingredients and explain the cooking techniques for that particular recipe. Here are some general guidelines that can be applied when making the soups in this book and those of your own creation.

CONSISTENCY

• To ensure the best texture and prevent a soup from becoming too watery or too thick, use enough stock or other liquid just to cover the vegetables.

• For chunky soups, such as minestrone (page 75), cut vegetables small enough so that several different types will fit into each spoonful of soup, but be sure the pieces are large enough not to disintegrate after considerable simmering.

CREAM SUBSTITUTE

• To reduce the fat grams in a recipe that calls for heavy (whipping) cream without sacrificing the creamy texture, substitute canned evaporated low-fat or nonfat milk.

FLAVOR

• Most soups taste better the next day. If you prepare soup a day ahead, season with salt and pepper, but wait until you reheat the soup to add any cream or butter (*monter au beurre,* page 39) to finish the soup.

SEASONING TO TASTE

• The final adjustment of seasonings is the step that can elevate a soup from good to great. Here's the way it's done in cooking school: Ladle about ½ cup soup into a small bowl and taste it. Observe what flavors you taste. Add kosher salt a bit at a time, tasting after each addition and noting how different flavors begin to come to the forefront. Continue until you can taste all the vegetables in the soup, such as onions, leeks, carrots, celery, and the like. Then push the limit a little by adding a few more grains of kosher salt. You may find that the flavors become even brighter. Keep adding more salt until you think you've coaxed out all the flavors. In so doing, you've just added a taste to your memory bank of flavors. If your sample gets too salty in the process, no harm done; just add it back to the bigger pot or discard it. Now season the entire pot of soup, bringing it to the perfect level of flavor you just stored in your memory bank.

FREQUENTLY ASKED QUESTIONS ABOUT SOUPS

What's the best way to purée a soup?

For the smoothest soups, purée in a stand blender. An immersion blender or food mill does a respectable job, too, but neither one aerates the soup or pulverizes the chunks the way a stand blender does. A food processor is my last choice, as it doesn't measure up in the smoothness department.

To purée soup in a stand blender, fill the jar only half to two-thirds full and hold the lid down with a kitchen towel as you increase and then decrease the speed. For safety, gradually increase and decrease the speeds, rather than going from off to high in one increment.

When is it necessary to strain a puréed soup?

It's your choice whether or not to strain. For a more refined soup—or if small pieces of skin or vegetable fiber bother you—strain it through a medium-mesh strainer. It's better not to strain soup if all you have is a fine-mesh strainer, as this would trap too much soup pulp, resulting in watery soup and a smaller yield. If you don't have a medium-mesh strainer, try a colander.

RECIPE SECRETS

This recipe calls for ¼ to ½ teaspoon cayenne pepper. The smaller amount will simply add a note of complexity without the heat. The larger quantity adds a spicy kick.

If you double a recipe that calls for cayenne pepper or other hot peppers, don't double the pepper. Capsaicin, which gives peppers their heat, increases exponentially as you add more pepper. Start with the same amount of cayenne, and, if desired, add more when you season the soup at the end.

An eye-catching garnish of a drizzle of crème fraîche or dollop of sour cream also serves to mitigate the spicy heat of the cayenne.

The soup can be prepared through straining and then refrigerated for up to 2 days. Just before serving, reheat slowly over low heat and add the cream and seasonings.

RED BELL PEPPER BISQUE
WITH CRÈME FRAÎCHE

For the past several years, this has been the workhorse recipe I use in my Cooking Basics classes to teach the concept of seasoning to taste (page 42). It's a fairly simple recipe for beginner cooks to replicate at home (this teacher loves to give homework to reinforce the lessons learned in class), and its unusual flavor is distinctive without being weird. A bisque (pronounced *bisk*) is a smooth, puréed soup, often made with seafood, and usually enriched with cream. When made with lobster or shrimp, it is sometimes thickened—or enriched—by adding a tablespoon or so of raw white rice when the stock is added. The rice disintegrates as the soup cooks, releasing its starch and thickening the soup in the process. To enhance the satisfying sensation of umami (see page 38), this vegetable bisque is prepared with chicken stock. If you prefer a vegetarian soup, simply substitute commercial or homemade vegetable broth (page 63) for the chicken stock. The amount of salt you'll need when seasoning to taste depends on the saltiness of your stock.

**Serves 4
(or more as a first course)**

3 tablespoons extra-virgin olive oil

1 large carrot, peeled and chopped

1 yellow onion, peeled and chopped

1 celery stalk, peeled if you don't plan to strain the soup, then chopped

¼ to ½ teaspoon cayenne pepper

4 red bell peppers, about 1¾ pounds total, seeded, deribbed, and chopped into 1-inch pieces

About 4 cups homemade chicken stock or broth (page 60 or 61) or purchased reduced-sodium broth

¼ cup heavy (whipping) cream

Kosher salt and fine, freshly ground black pepper

About ⅔ cup crème fraîche (page 67) or sour cream, stirred to a smooth consistency, for garnish

1. Heat a heavy 4-quart pot over medium-high heat. Add the olive oil. When the oil is hot enough to sizzle a piece of carrot, add the carrot, onion, and celery. Sauté until the carrot turns bright orange and the onion becomes translucent, about 8 minutes. Stir in ¼ teaspoon of the cayenne pepper and add the bell peppers. Cook, stirring occasionally, until the peppers start to soften, about 5 minutes. Add enough stock just to cover the vegetables and bring to a rolling boil. Reduce the heat to low, cover partially, and simmer until the carrot and peppers are soft, about 30 minutes.

2. Remove from the heat and use an immersion blender to purée the soup until very smooth. Alternatively, use a stand blender to purée the soup until smooth, blending just 2 cups at a time and holding down the blender lid as you gradually increase and decrease the speed. If desired, strain the puréed soup through a medium-mesh strainer into a clean pot. As you strain the soup, extract as much pulp as possible from the solids by pressing on them with the bottom of a ladle.

3. Stir in the cream and season to taste with salt, pepper, and additional cayenne pepper, if desired. If necessary, gently reheat the soup over low heat, stirring constantly. Ladle into warmed bowls and drizzle with crème fraîche or garnish with a dollop of sour cream.

VARIATION

. . . .

Substitute unseasoned Roasted Peppers (page 254)—red, yellow, or green—for the raw bell peppers. If you plan to strain the soup, there's no need to peel the peppers after roasting them.

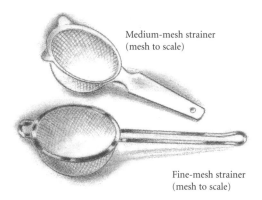

Medium-mesh strainer
(mesh to scale)

Fine-mesh strainer
(mesh to scale)

HOMEMADE CRÈME FRAÎCHE

Crème fraîche (pronounced *crem fresh*) is a rich-tasting, thick French sour cream that's used to garnish everything from hors d'oeuvre to soups to desserts. In her well-documented book *Nourishing Traditions,* nutrition researcher Sally Fallon cites a variety of health benefits from eating cultured dairy products such as crème fraîche. Look for crème fraîche in the dairy case of well-stocked supermarkets, or for a less expensive alternative, make your own. Be sure to plan ahead, as it takes up to 48 hours to thicken sufficiently.

Combine 1 cup heavy (whipping) cream (preferably additive free and not ultrapasteurized) with 2 tablespoons cultured whole (or low-fat) buttermilk in a clean crock or glass jar. Stir, cover, and let sit at room temperature until mixture is no longer runny, 24 to 48 hours. It should be thick enough to fall from a spoon in a clump, rather than in a ribbon. Store in the refrigerator for up to 2 weeks.

RECIPE SECRETS

To extract even more flavor from the corn after removing the kernels, simmer the stripped cobs with the soup, then remove them before blending the chowder.

. . . .

To save time—or if you're making more than one batch of this recipe—bring the stock to a simmer on the back burner (or in the microwave) while you sauté the leeks. Turn off the heat when the stock reaches a bare simmer to prevent it from reducing.

. . . .

The finished soup can be refrigerated for up to 3 days before serving. Reheat slowly over low heat, stirring often.

HOW TO STRIP OFF THYME LEAVES

To strip the leaves off a woody thyme sprig, hold the sprig at the thin end with your thumb and index finger. Drag your other thumb and index finger down the length of the sprig, pulling off the leaves as you go. Pinch off the tender tip, discard the stems, and chop the leaves and tip together. If using younger thyme leaves that are attached to a light, wispy stem, you can chop the entire sprig without removing the leaves first.

WHITE CORN CHOWDER

Chowder, named after the French fisherman's *chaudière* pot, is a thick, chunky soup, usually made with fish or shellfish and enriched with heavy cream. This lighter version calls for sweet white corn instead of seafood and a combination of half-and-half and stock stands in for the heavy cream. If you prefer a richer chowder, use heavy cream in place of the half-and-half and all or part of the stock. I serve this hearty soup year-round, and when flavorful fresh corn isn't available, I substitute thawed frozen petite white corn kernels. In New England, where chowder is king, steaming hot bowls of chowder are traditionally served with oyster crackers, which stay afloat on the surface of the soup and add a delightful, crunchy texture.

**Serves 6
(or more as a first course)**

4 tablespoons unsalted butter

2 leeks, white part only, roots trimmed, cut into ¼-inch rounds, swished clean in a bowl of warm water, and drained

1 large russet potato, peeled and cut into ½-inch dice

Leaves from 3 fresh thyme sprigs, or 1 teaspoon dried leaf thyme, crumbled between your fingers

2 teaspoons kosher salt

¼ teaspoon fine, freshly ground white pepper or a few shakes of Tabasco sauce

6 cups homemade chicken or vegetable stock or broth (page 60, 61, or 63) or purchased reduced-sodium broth, heated

About 6 cups white corn kernels (from 5 large ears of corn), divided, plus corncobs

1 cup half-and-half

10 fresh chives, minced

Oyster crackers, for garnish

1. Heat a heavy 6-quart pot over medium-high heat. Add the butter. When the butter is hot enough to sizzle a piece of leek, add the leeks and sauté until translucent and soft, but not brown, 5 to 8 minutes. Add the potato, thyme, salt, white pepper or Tabasco, stock, and 3 cups of the corn kernels. Break the corncobs in half and add to the pot. Bring to a boil, reduce the heat to medium-low, cover, and simmer until the potato is tender, about 15 minutes.

2. Turn off the heat. With tongs, carefully transfer the corncobs to a colander placed in a bowl. Discard the cobs and pour any drained liquid back into the soup. Transfer about half of the soup (equal parts solids and liquid) to a 4-quart saucepan and set aside. Add the half-and-half and the remaining 3 cups corn kernels to the original pot of soup and bring to a gentle simmer over low heat, stirring occasionally.

3. Meanwhile, off the heat, use an immersion blender to purée the soup in the new saucepan until it is creamy and smooth. Alternatively, use a stand blender to purée the soup in 2 batches until creamy and smooth, holding down the blender lid as you gradually increase and decrease the speed. Transfer the blended soup to the original pot, stirring it into the balance of the chowder.

4. Raise the heat to medium-high and bring the chowder to a gentle simmer, stirring constantly. Reduce the heat to the lowest setting. Taste and adjust the seasoning with salt and white pepper or Tabasco, if necessary. If you'd like the corn kernels to remain crunchy, serve as is. Otherwise, continue simmering until the kernels are tender, another 5 minutes or so. Ladle the chowder into warmed bowls and garnish with the chives and a few oyster crackers. Pass a bowl of oyster crackers at the table.

HOW TO REMOVE CORN KERNELS FROM THE COB

Here are two ways to prevent corn kernels from spraying all over when cutting them off the cob: Lay the cob horizontally on the cutting board to cut off the kernels. Or, hold the cob vertically and cut off the kernels from the bottom half first, then turn the cob so you're holding onto the opposite end as you shave off the remaining kernels. Whichever method you use, be sure to run the blunt side of the knife blade down the cob to coax out the flavorful "milk."

HOW TO MINCE CHIVES

The most efficient way I know to mince fresh chives is to use a pair of kitchen shears and snip the chives into ⅛- to ½-inch pieces directly into each bowl of soup. Alternatively, gather a bunch of chives on a cutting board and cut into equal pieces with a very sharp chef's knife.

RECIPE SECRETS

Silky, smooth glass noodles, also called bean thread, cellophane, or mung bean noodles, contribute a distinctive texture and glistening appearance here. Look for these cellophane-wrapped dried noodles in Asian markets. Soak in water (and, if desired, cut once they're softened) before adding to soup. Because they expand dramatically once they're immersed in hot liquid, don't add them more than 10 minutes before you serve the soup. Otherwise, they'll melt and disappear into the broth.

In Western cooking, it's understood that complexity and depth of flavor in nearly any soup are more pronounced the second day, after the flavors have a chance to meld. What I find so compelling about this soup is how complex the flavor is as soon as it's done, particularly in light of its relatively short preparation time. Don't get me wrong: this soup is certainly good the next day (wait to add the glass noodles), but you won't miss its deep flavors if you eat it right away. What gives this soup such savoriness? In a word, it's umami (page 38). Both mushrooms and Asian fish sauce contain substantial amounts of glutamates, nature's flavor enhancers, which exponentially increase a dish's savoriness.

CHICKEN SOUP WITH GLASS NOODLES

This recipe was inspired by my favorite quick soup in Mai Pham's terrific *Pleasures of the Vietnamese Table.* One day I had a craving for this restorative combination of savory broth, tender chicken, and silky cellophane noodles, but I couldn't get to the store to buy the bok choy and wood-ear mushrooms in Mai's recipe. So I substituted ribbons of romaine lettuce and dried porcini mushrooms, respectively. A new star was born.

**Serves 4
(or more as a first course)**

2 ounces cellophane noodles	2 cups cold water
¾ ounce dried porcini or other wild mushrooms	1 pound bone-in chicken breasts (2 large or 3 small breast halves)
1 cup hot water	2 to 3 tablespoons Asian fish sauce
1 small head romaine lettuce	2 teaspoons sugar
1 tablespoon mild-tasting extra-virgin olive oil	2 green onions, green and white parts, cut into thin rings
1 shallot, thinly sliced	3 tablespoons chopped fresh cilantro (okay to use some stems)
1 clove garlic, thinly sliced	Freshly ground black pepper
5 cups homemade chicken stock or broth (page 60 or 61) or purchased reduced-sodium broth	

---

1. Place the noodles in a bowl and add enough room-temperature water to cover. Let soak for 30 minutes. Drain the noodles and cut with clean kitchen shears into roughly 8-inch pieces. Set aside. (This can be done up to 8 hours in advance. Set aside, covered, at room temperature.)

2. In a small bowl, combine the mushrooms with the hot water. Let soak for 30 minutes. If necessary, float a small plate or saucer on top of the water to keep the mushrooms submerged. Once they have softened, lift them out with your fingers into a strainer, reserving the soaking liquid, and rinse off any remaining sand or grit. Strain the soaking liquid through a fine-mesh strainer and set aside. If the mushrooms are too large to fit into a soup spoon, cut them smaller and set aside. (This can be done up to 8 hours in advance. Set aside, covered, at room temperature.)

3. Trim off the core of the lettuce and cut the leaves crosswise into ribbons ½ inch wide. Swish around in a bowl of water, drain, and set aside. (This can be done up to 8 hours in advance. Cover and refrigerate.)

4. *Prepare the soup:* Heat a heavy 6-quart soup pot over medium heat. Add the olive oil. When the oil is hot enough to sizzle a piece of shallot, add the shallot and garlic and sauté for 20 seconds. Add the stock and cold water, raise the heat to high, and bring to a boil. Add the chicken, reduce the heat to low, cover, and cook at a gentle, steady simmer until the chicken is no longer pink at the center (145 degrees F internal temperature) or until the juices run clear when the densest part of the chicken is pricked with a meat fork, about 15 minutes. Using a Chinese strainer or slotted spoon, remove the chicken and let stand until cool enough to handle. Shred by hand into bite-sized pieces, discarding the skin and bones (or save them for stock).

5. Add the reserved mushrooms and their soaking liquid, 2 tablespoons of the fish sauce, and the sugar to the soup and simmer gently, uncovered, for 5 minutes. (The recipe can be prepared to this point up to 8 hours ahead. Cover and set aside off the heat. Cover and refrigerate the chicken.)

6. Add the lettuce (it will wilt and soften as it gets hot), chicken, green onions, cilantro, and a few grinds of pepper, and adjust heat as necessary to maintain a gentle simmer. Ten minutes before serving, stir in the soaked noodles. Taste and add more fish sauce if the soup isn't salty enough.

7. To serve, use tongs or a pronged spaghetti server to divide the noodles and solids among warmed bowls, then ladle the broth and other ingredients on top. Serve with soup spoons and chopsticks or forks.

RECICE SECRETS

RECIPE SECRETS

For the best flavor and value, use bone-in, skin-on chicken. Also, don't let the liquid get hotter than a steady simmer when cooking the chicken. Boiling will make the chicken tough.

To prevent green onion pieces from rolling all over the cutting board as you cut them into rings, cut them on a slight diagonal, rather than into perfect rounds.

ABOUT ASIAN FISH SAUCE

Made from salted, fermented anchovies, fish sauce has a powerful scent. Look for it in the Asian section of well-stocked grocery stores and in Asian markets. If you have a choice of brands, look for one in a glass bottle. To compare quality, turn the bottles upside down. The best fish sauces won't cling to the bottleneck when you right the bottle. Store fish sauce, tightly covered, in a cool, dark pantry. If you don't use it frequently, store it in the refrigerator, where it will keep for months. You can substitute kosher salt, to taste, for Asian fish sauce in this recipe, but the flavor of the soup will not be as complex.

RECIPE SECRETS

Add a little baking soda to neutralize the acid in the tomatoes, which prevents the milk from curdling in this dairy-enriched tomato soup. When you add it, the mixture should foam up a bit and then subside, which proves that the soda is active.

. . . .

Be sure to sauté the onion until it's translucent and very soft before adding the other ingredients. Otherwise, the acid in the tomatoes will impede further softening of the onion.

. . . .

When adding cheese to a hot soup, remove it from the heat to prevent the cheese from becoming rubbery. Stir in the cheese a little at a time. Wait until it melts before stirring in another handful.

TOMATO-CHEDDAR SOUP

My father-in-law grew up on a three-hundred-acre farm in Dixon, California, outside of Sacramento. He and his sister still own the farm, and lease it to a grower who plants fields and fields of great canning tomatoes. One of our annual summer highlights is gathering the family together to visit the farm and pick tomatoes. The plants are so prolific—and we've gotten our picking down to such an efficient routine—that it doesn't take much more than half an hour for my husband and me to pick two hundred pounds of tomatoes. Good thing, because some years the temperature out in the sun-drenched fields hovers around 100 degrees F. We spend the next several days canning the tomatoes for 20-Minute Tomato Sauce (page 114) and for making soups such as this gem. This recipe comes from my mother-in-law, who taught me the secret of adding baking soda to tomato soup. When fresh, juicy tomatoes aren't in season, and you don't have a cellar filled with canned tomatoes, substitute a 26.5-ounce box of imported Italian Pomi brand chopped tomatoes, in distinctive red packaging and additive free, or use a 28-ounce can of your favorite diced tomatoes. For a vegetarian version, substitute Vegetable Broth (page 63) for the chicken stock. Serve this soup hot or cold, with a dollop of crème fraîche.

Serves 4 to 6

4 tablespoons unsalted butter	¼ teaspoon baking soda
1 yellow onion, finely chopped	5 shakes of Tabasco sauce
2 pounds very ripe Roma tomatoes, cores removed and cut into 1-inch chunks	1 cup milk (low-fat is okay)
2 cups homemade chicken stock or broth (page 60 or 61) or purchased reduced-sodium broth	½ pound Cheddar cheese, coarsely shredded on the large holes of a box grater to yield 2 cups
2 fresh thyme sprigs, or ½ teaspoon dried leaf thyme, crumbled between your fingers	About ⅓ cup crème fraîche, homemade (page 67) or purchased, or sour cream, for garnish
1 teaspoon kosher salt	About 3 tablespoons minced fresh chives, for garnish

---

1. Heat a heavy 4-quart pot over medium heat. Add the butter. When the butter is hot enough to sizzle a piece of onion, add the onion and sauté until translucent and very soft but not brown, about 10 minutes.

2. Add the tomatoes, stock, thyme, salt, baking soda, and Tabasco sauce. Bring to a boil, stir in the milk, reduce the heat to low, cover, and simmer until the mixture thickens and the tomatoes break down and are tender, 10 to 15 minutes.

3. Remove from the heat and remove and discard the thyme sprigs, if used. Stir in the cheese one handful at a time, stirring to melt before adding more. Use an immersion blender to purée the soup in the pot until it is creamy and smooth. Alternatively, use a stand blender to purée the soup until creamy and smooth, blending just 2 cups at a time and holding down the blender lid as you gradually increase and decrease the speed. Transfer the puréed soup to a clean 4-quart saucepan. If necessary, gently reheat the soup over low heat to serving temperature. Taste and adjust the seasoning with salt and Tabasco sauce, if necessary. Ladle into warmed bowls, top with a drizzle of crème fraîche or a dollop of sour cream, sprinkle with the chives, and serve.

FRENCH ONION SOUP GRATINÉE

While I was in college in Massachusetts, one of my friends spent her junior year living with a family in France. The summer she returned she made us this soup, the same recipe her French family prepared the night she arrived to live with them. We felt so sophisticated buying wine that was actually intended for cooking. The use of chicken stock and white wine here, instead of the traditional beef broth, makes for a soup that's light in both color and flavor. If you prefer, substitute beef broth and red wine. Set the table with knives and forks, as well as soup spoons, to make it easier to eat the toasted baguette croutons covered with melted Gruyère. Serve with Butter Lettuce with Ruby Grapefruit, Avocado, and Glazed Walnuts (page 82), and you've got a complete supper.

/continued

RECIPE SECRETS

The secret to memorable onion soup with big flavor is to spend plenty of time caramelizing the natural sugars in the onions. Don't rush this step, because the acid in the wine will impede the further softening of the onions.

The Dutch oven (see page 15), which is broad, rather than tall, is the perfect pot for sautéing the large volume of sliced onions called for in this recipe. If using a Le Creuset Dutch oven, be sure to uncover it before lifting, as a third of the weight of a Le Creuset pot is in its lid.

For incomparable flavor, use organic or European-style unsalted butter. If you prefer, substitute extra-virgin olive oil.

This recipe requires that you very thinly slice a huge pile of onions. For such volume, my preferred tool is a food processor fitted with the slicing disk. To keep the strong onion fumes at bay, discard the peels in a closed trash container and cover up the onions you've already sliced. See page 74 for additional tips on preventing tears when cutting onions.

For ease in cutting and eating the crusts of the croutons, cut the baguette slices on the diagonal.

Some people swear they don't cry when chopping lots of onions because they buy shorter, squatter onions, instead of longer ones—it's true that squat, red Italian onions are called "sweet" red onions. Others hold a slice of bread between their teeth to deflect the fumes from reaching their nose. My mother-in-law once confided that she stores onions in the refrigerator and doesn't have a problem with tears. In fact, Robert L. Wolke, professor emeritus of chemistry and author of *What Einstein Told His Cook,* reports that an onion at refrigerator temperature causes tearing only 25 percent as quickly as an onion at room temperature. When a friend had a catering business, he wore ski goggles whenever he prepped lots of onions. Myself, I just let the tears flow, although I must admit, it's a bit odd standing in front of a class, crying. As a cooking teacher, I figure it just comes with the territory.

STORING ONIONS

Store onions in a cool, dark place, preferably in a basket or other ventilated container. Be sure to keep onions and potatoes separate, as one gives off a gas that causes the other to rot.

Serves 6

4 tablespoons unsalted butter

5 pounds large yellow onions, sliced 1/16 inch thick

1/4 cup all-purpose flour

1 cup dry white wine or vermouth

6 cups homemade chicken stock or broth (pages 60 or 61) or purchased reduced-sodium broth

3 fresh thyme sprigs

1 bay leaf, preferably imported

1 teaspoon kosher salt

Freshly ground black pepper

12 baguette slices (not sour-dough), each 3/4 inch thick and cut on the diagonal

6 ounces Gruyère cheese, coarsely shredded on the large holes of a box grater to yield 1 1/2 cups

1. Heat a heavy 8-quart pot over medium-high heat. Add the butter. When the butter is hot enough to sizzle a piece of onion, add the onions and sauté, stirring only occasionally, until they wilt and lose their moisture, about 10 minutes. Reduce the heat to the lowest setting and cook, stirring occasionally, until the onions are caramelized, about 15 minutes. At this stage they should be sticky and clinging together in a mass. Sprinkle with the flour and cook for another 5 minutes, stirring frequently. Add the wine all at once. When the wine evaporates, add the stock, thyme, bay leaf, salt, and a few grinds of pepper. Bring to a boil, reduce the heat so the soup is at a steady simmer, cover partially, and cook, stirring occasionally, for 30 minutes.

2. Meanwhile, preheat the broiler. Place the rack about 6 inches from the broiler element. Line a sturdy, rimmed baking sheet with a silicone baking liner or aluminum foil (to ease cleanup). Arrange 6 deep, ovenproof soup bowls or 1 1/2-cup ramekins on the lined baking sheet and set aside.

3. Place the baguette slices on another baking sheet and lightly toast both sides under the broiler. They will need only 2 to 3 minutes on each side. Set aside. Leave the broiler on.

4. When the soup is done, taste and adjust the seasoning with salt and pepper. Remove and discard the thyme sprigs and bay leaf. Ladle the soup into the bowls and top each with 2 toasted baguette slices placed side by side. Top the baguette slices with the cheese, dividing it evenly.

5. Place the baking sheet with the soup bowls under the broiler and watch closely, moving the pan as needed to expose all the bowls to the broiler element so the cheese melts evenly. Remove from the oven as soon as the cheese has melted, about 1 minute. Place each bowl on a plate lined with a napkin (to prevent the bowls from sliding around as you carry them to the table) and serve immediately.

THREE-BEAN MINESTRONE WITH SAUSAGE

In Italy, any "big" soup thick with beans, lots of vegetables, and sometimes pasta is called minestrone. (Please pronounce it min-eh-*strohn*-eh—or min-eh-*strohn*, as in Neapolitan dialect—not min-eh-*strohn*-nee.) For a sensational, creamy addition to this big soup, stir in a few pieces of rind from Parmigiano-Reggiano or *pecorino romano* cheese. The rind can be added in large pieces or cut into small dice, depending on personal preference. Left whole, the rind melts into the soup, adding a distinctive creaminess to the broth; if cut into small pieces and added just before serving, the cheesy nuggets remain intact and can be savored in every spoonful. Next time you finish grating a wedge of Parmigiano-Reggiano or *pecorino romano* cheese, store the rind in a zip-top plastic bag in the freezer. It'll keep for months. Minestrone is a country-style soup with no rules or restrictions about ingredients, so feel free to experiment by preparing it with your favorite beans, vegetables, and seasonings.

/continued

RECIPE SECRETS

This minestrone is flavored with pancetta (pronounced pahn-*cheh*-tah), which is rolled, cured—but not smoked—Italian bacon. Look for pancetta at Italian delicatessens. If you prefer a vegetarian minestrone, omit the pancetta and sausage and add more salt.

Cannellini (pronounced kan-el-*lee*-nee) are white kidney-shaped beans. The canned beans are often mushy, so I prefer to cook my own. Start with dried beans and soak in cold water to cover overnight. Use about 2 quarts water to soak 1 cup beans. If time is short, place the beans and 6 cups cold water in a heavy pot over high heat. Bring to a boil and boil for 2 minutes. Turn off the heat, cover the pot, and let the beans sit for 1 hour before adding the pancetta. Proceed with the recipe as directed.

To thicken this soup, some of the beans and the pancetta are puréed with a little cooking liquid in a food processor or blender.

For tenderness and a sweet flavor, use savoy cabbage, a ruffle-leaved cousin of the standard round green cabbage. Choose a firm, tight head that feels heavy for its size. If unavailable, substitute regular cabbage.

Serves 8
(or more as a first course)

1 cup dried cannellini or other white beans, picked over and soaked overnight in water to cover

6 cups water

1 slice pancetta, about ¼ inch thick

1 can (15½ ounces) garbanzo beans, rinsed and drained

1 can (15½ ounces) kidney beans, rinsed and drained

1 large carrot, peeled and chopped into ¼-inch dice

1 celery stalk, chopped into ¼-inch dice

3 cloves garlic, minced

½ head Savoy cabbage, cut into thirds lengthwise, core portions removed, and then cut crosswise into ½-inch-wide pieces

1 zucchini, quartered lengthwise and cut crosswise into ½-inch pieces

1 yellow squash, quartered lengthwise and cut crosswise into ½-inch pieces

1 tablespoon extra-virgin olive oil

1 large yellow onion, diced

4 fresh (not smoked) mild Italian sausages, casings removed

1½ teaspoons fennel seeds

1 teaspoon dried leaf oregano, crumbled between your fingers

¼ teaspoon red pepper flakes

1 can (28 ounces) diced tomatoes with juice

¾ cup water

2 pieces Parmigiano-Reggiano or *pecorino romano* cheese rind, each 3 by 2 inches, left whole or cut into ¼-inch dice

3 tablespoons chopped fresh flat-leaf parsley, divided

3 tablespoons chopped fresh basil, divided

1 bay leaf, preferably imported

2 teaspoons kosher salt

½ teaspoon freshly ground black pepper

½ cup fresh English or frozen petite peas

1 cup freshly grated *pecorino romano* or Parmigiano-Reggiano cheese, for serving

1. Combine the soaked cannellini beans, the 6 cups water, and the pancetta in a heavy 8-quart pot and place over high heat. Bring to a boil, reduce the heat to low, cover, and simmer until the beans are tender, about 1 hour. In a food processor or blender, combine about 1½ cups of the cooked beans and the pancetta with about ½ cup of the cooking liquid and purée until the beans and pancetta are smooth. Return the purée to the pot.

2. Add the garbanzo beans, kidney beans, carrot, celery, garlic, cabbage, zucchini, and yellow squash. Add enough water to cover all the vegetables (about 8 cups). Bring to a boil over high heat, stirring occasionally. Reduce the heat to a simmer, cover partially, and simmer the soup while you cook the sausages.

3. Heat a 10-inch nonstick sauté pan or skillet over medium-high heat. Add the olive oil. When the oil is hot enough to sizzle a piece of onion, add the onion and sauté, stirring occasionally, until it softens, about 8 minutes. Scrape the onion to the sides of the pan and add the sausages. Using a flat-bottomed wooden spatula, break up the sausages into roughly ½-inch chunks and sauté until they are no longer pink, about 5 minutes. Regulate the heat as necessary to prevent the onions from browning. Stir in the fennel seeds, oregano, and red pepper flakes and sauté for 1 minute. Add the tomatoes and their juice. Add the ¾ cup water to the tomato can, swish to clean the inside of the can, and add to the sausage mixture.

4. When the sausage mixture starts to simmer, carefully add it to the simmering pot of soup. Add the cheese rinds, 2 tablespoons of the parsley, 2 tablespoons of the basil, the bay leaf, salt, and pepper. Continue to simmer the soup, partially covered, until all the vegetables are cooked through, about 1 hour. Stir occasionally, tasting the vegetables to check for doneness every so often. When the carrots are very tender and the cabbage is soft, add the peas and the remaining 1 tablespoon each parsley and basil. Simmer the soup until the peas are tender, about 5 minutes. Taste. If the soup tastes flat or dull, add salt ½ teaspoon at a time until the vegetables taste bright and the broth tastes rich. This is a big pot of soup; don't be shy with the salt.

5. Remove and discard the bay leaf. Ladle the soup into warmed bowls. If any large pieces of cheese rind are still visible, leave them in the pot as you serve the soup. If diced rinds are still visible, serve a few nuggets in each bowl. Sprinkle each serving with a little of the grated cheese and pass the rest in a bowl at the table.

SECRETS FOR SUCCESSFUL SALADS

Each salad recipe in this chapter features Secrets for how to bring out the best in specific ingredients. In addition, here, in alphabetical order, are a few general tips for working with some common salad ingredients.

CELERY

- To remove the strong vegetal flavor that's sometimes present in celery, peel the rounded side of the outer stalks with a swivel-blade vegetable peeler before slicing. This way, the strings won't get caught in your teeth and the vegetal-tasting outside stalks will have a more delicate flavor.

CHEESE

- To keep white cheeses white in salads, prepare salad dressings with citrus juice or white vinegar such as white balsamic, champagne, or other white wine vinegar. White vinegar or citrus juice won't stain creamy cheeses an unsavory dark brown the way red vinegars do.

- Add creamy cheeses, such as goat cheese and feta, with the final ingredients (or use as a garnish on top) so they'll stay fluffy and light and won't get mashed down when you toss the salad.

CITRUS

- Remove any inked-on brand stamps *before* washing citrus fruits. Rub the dry fruit with a dry kitchen towel until the ink is gone.

CUTTING ROUND VEGETABLES

- Cut carrots and other round vegetables such as cucumbers and green onions on the diagonal so they don't roll all over—or off—the cutting board as you chop.

NUTS AND SEEDS

- For the best flavor and texture, toast—and cool—nuts and seeds (see page 89) before adding to salads. It's not necessary to heat up a big gas or electric oven to toast a few nuts or seeds for salad. Instead, you can use a toaster oven or a microwave oven.

RED ONION

- Use a mandoline, V-slicer, or your sharpest knife with the thinnest blade to shave red onions as thinly as possible. If your red onion smells strong when you first cut into it, soak the cut pieces in cold water for 5 or 10 minutes, then drain and blot dry before adding to a salad. The cold water leaches out the harshness and crisps the onion a bit, too.

SALT

- Among its legendary attributes, the unique shape of Diamond Crystal kosher salt crystals (page 43) helps prevent lettuce from wilting in a salad. Unfortunately, other kosher salts cannot claim this virtue.

TOMATOES

- To preserve the delicate texture of fresh tomatoes, store in a cool area of the kitchen, not in the refrigerator.

- For easy serving and eating, cut cherry tomatoes (and other round fruits such as grapes) in half before adding to salads. Cut them lengthwise, through the blemish where the stem was attached.

FREQUENTLY ASKED QUESTIONS ABOUT MAKING SALADS

What's so great about wooden salad bowls?

Good question. It's rare to find a wooden salad bowl in a professional kitchen. My mother used to drag one out when we had company for dinner and rub it with a clove of garlic before adding the lettuce. It baffles me why most of these bowls are so deep—maybe to take up less room on the table. I dislike deep bowls because dressing and smaller ingredients, such as nuts, seeds, avocado, and cherry tomatoes, sink to the bottom. Personally, for tossing, I prefer a lightweight, inordinately-large-for-the-job, stainless-steel bowl, such as one of the larger ones from a set of shallow, broad nesting bowls. These bowls are light enough to grab with one hand if the other is full of vinaigrette—I like to toss with my hands—or when portioning out tossed salad from the bowl onto plates. If serving salad on a buffet or for family-style eating, toss in a big bowl, then transfer to a large, shallow pasta serving bowl.

Is it always necessary to make a separate vinaigrette to dress a salad?

For a classic French vinaigrette made with minced shallots, it's prudent to let the shallots and vinegar comingle in a bowl before whisking in the other seasonings and oil. This softens the sharpness of the shallots and infuses them with flavor. But, for many salads with simple dressings, there's no need to dirty an extra bowl and whisk by making a separate vinaigrette. Starting with the oil (it helps the acid stick to the leaves), simply drizzle and sprinkle the dressing ingredients evenly over the salad greens and toss well each time you add something new (see Weeknight Green Salad, page 81). For creamy dressings such as Caesar, it's preferable to mix the dressing in a bowl to be sure ingredients are completely combined before adding the lettuce.

How do you know how much dressing to use?

Toss salad greens with enough dressing to coat them lightly, but not so much that there's a pool of dressing remaining at the bottom of the bowl. Tossing salads with your (clean) hands gives you a good feeling (literally and figuratively) for how well the dressing coats the greens.

ABOUT OLIVE OIL

A cooking fat and condiment made from the "juice" of olives, olive oil is considered to be the most healthful of all oils, so much so that extra-virgin olive oil is often the first food given to Italian babies. *Extra-virgin* olive oil is the premium grade, which comes from the first pressing of the olives. It must be extracted by mechanical means, without heat or chemicals, and must have an acidity level of less than 1 percent. The experts seem to use a variety of different names (pure, virgin, and rectified among them) for the next grades of olive oil, but suffice to say these oils have less flavor than extra-virgin olive oil and can be both refined and blended. They are extracted by means of heat and/or chemicals, yielding a higher smoke point (page 30) that makes them acceptable for frying at higher temperatures. Light olive oil, a relatively recent American marketing creation, most accurately describes the color and flavor of the oil, rather than any reduction in fat grams or calories. Pomace is from the dregs of the olive oil, extracted with solvents, and is typically sold in tins to high-volume restaurants and institutions. Given the health benefits of extra-virgin olive oil, I use it almost exclusively.

For most recipes in this book, I call for one of two types of extra-virgin olive oil: mild tasting or bold tasting. In some cases, no particular type is specified; either type would work well in those recipes, so it boils down to personal preference. Pesto (page 186), for example, calls for mild-tasting extra-virgin olive oil. If a bold-tasting oil were used instead, the sauce would taste too strong and the olive oil would overpower the delicate basil. Typically, mild-tasting oils are produced from ripe olives that are harvested relatively late. They come from areas such as Liguria and Provence, where the climate is more temperate, and there is no risk of frost damage to the olives. Bold-tasting oils are produced from olives that are harvested green, when barely ripe, from places such as Chianti, where frost comes earlier and would harm the olives if they were left on the trees to ripen further. As such, a greener, more peppery olive oil is produced from these olives. Store all olive oils in a cool, dark place in tightly sealed glass bottles, with minimal headroom, for up to 6 months.

ABOUT VINEGAR

Vinegar is made from a fermented liquid, such as wine or apple cider, or from fermented rice, barley, sugarcane, or other foods. It adds a tart component to dressings, soups, pickles, potato salads, and more. The sourness of vinegar is determined by the percentage of acetic acid used to make it. Mild-flavored rice vinegar has about 4 percent acidity, while more pronounced red and white wine vinegars contain up to 6 percent. Balsamic vinegar, made from Trebbiano grape juice, is regulated by the Italian government and is aged over many years in a sequence of casks made from different woods. Aged balsamic vinegar is considered more of a finishing condiment (page 101), than an ingredient for a salad dressing or marinade. Bulk balsamic vinegars are more appropriate for the latter uses. When using vinegar with white or pale ingredients, use a white vinegar to prevent food from turning gray. When adding vinegar to chlorophyll-rich vegetables, such as green beans, do so right before serving, as vinegar turns vivid greens an unappetizing shade of army green.

> ## "IT TAKES FOUR MEN TO DRESS A SALAD:
>
> A WISE MAN FOR THE SALT, A MADMAN FOR THE PEPPER, A MISER FOR THE VINEGAR, AND A SPENDTHRIFT FOR THE OIL."
>
> —Unknown. Quote of the day, March 16, 2004, from the welcome placard at the Culinary Institute of America, Greystone

WEEKNIGHT GREEN SALAD

It feels strange to write up this simple salad recipe, but whenever I mindlessly throw this salad together on the spur of the moment in a cooking class, people start asking questions and taking notes. This is how my mother made salad every night of the week, except she used iceberg lettuce, table salt, and what seemed like a copious amount of vinegar. The salad came to the supper table as we all sat down, and it remained untouched while we ate our main course. Whoever finished the main course first would "start the salad." Dessert wasn't served until the salad bowl was empty and we'd all had a chance to dip our crusts of bread into the vinegary dressing at the bottom. Today, unless I'm making a special composed salad, this is still my recipe for our standard weeknight salad. Like my mother, I don't measure anything. Once you get the hang of it, leave your measuring spoons in the drawer, and just drizzle, sprinkle, and toss your favorite seasonal ingredients together in one big bowl.

Serves 4 to 6

1 head romaine or butter lettuce

1 large, ripe tomato, cut into wedges; large handful cherry tomatoes, cut in half through the stem end; or a few red radishes, cut into thin slices (use what's in season)

1 small handful red onion rings or crescents

2 small celery stalks, preferably from the heart, or 1 large outside stalk, peeled and sliced crosswise

1 small carrot, peeled and cut into thin coins

1 small cucumber or 4-inch section of a large cucumber, peeled and cut into slices

About 3 tablespoons bold-tasting extra-virgin olive oil

About 1 teaspoon kosher salt

About ¼ teaspoon dried leaf oregano, crumbled between your fingers (optional)

About ¼ teaspoon granulated garlic powder (optional)

About ⅛ teaspoon fine, freshly ground black pepper

2 to 3 teaspoons red wine vinegar or balsamic vinegar

1. Remove any discolored or wilted outer leaves from the lettuce. If using romaine, place on a cutting board and cut crosswise into ¾-inch ribbons. For butter lettuce, break off the leaves and tear the larger ones in half. Swish the lettuce around in a large bowl of cool water. Let stand to rehydrate a bit while you prepare the other salad ingredients.

/continued

RECIPE SECRETS

In cooking school, salad was an important part of the *garde manger* (pronounced *gard* mahn-*zhay*), or cold kitchen, curriculum. We were even taught how to clean and prep each variety of lettuce in the standard seven-green *salade verte*. It was considered acceptable to use a knife to cut romaine into ribbons, but all other lettuces had to be torn by hand so as not to bruise the leaves. I still use these as guiding principles, but I must confess that sometimes I prefer crunchy chunks of butter (Boston) lettuce hearts, instead of more delicate, separate leaves. Try cutting a head of butter lettuce into quarters or eighths—the texture is excellent.

Several recipes in this book call for granulated garlic powder, by which I mean top-quality granulated garlic powder (not garlic salt) with discernible, smooth grains that are not so powdery that they become airborne when the container is shaken (see Sources). I realize I'm an anomaly among fine cooks who always prefer fresh garlic, but I think of granulated garlic powder in the same way I think of sun-dried tomatoes: the dehydrated version of a seasonal ingredient can quickly add distinctive flavor and complexity to raw or cooked foods. In the case of granulated garlic powder, the dividend is that it coats foods evenly and won't burn or doesn't have to be scraped off when used in marinades and rubs (typically, fresh garlic burns before the marinated item is cooked through). Also, good-quality granulated garlic powder, which is made from fresh cloves that are dehydrated, crushed, and granulated, contributes the characteristic sweet garlic flavor without cooking, unlike raw garlic. For example, I would not add chopped raw garlic to a salad, but I do add a light sprinkling of granulated garlic powder to lightly dressed greens, as in the salad here. If desired, fresh garlic may be used in place of granulated garlic powder in the recipes in this book.

2. Lift the lettuce out of the water, allowing any sediment to fall to the bottom. If the lettuce feels sandy, or there's a lot of dirt at the bottom of the bowl, repeat the rinsing. Transfer the lettuce to a salad spinner and spin dry. If you don't have a salad spinner, transfer to a strainer and shake off the excess water, dump into the center of a clean, dry kitchen towel, fold in the sides of the towel, roll, and squeeze gently to blot up any remaining moisture. (If preparing the lettuce in advance, place this roll in a plastic bag and refrigerate for up to 8 hours.) Transfer lettuce to a large, shallow bowl, such as a pasta serving bowl.

3. Add the tomatoes or radishes, onion, celery, carrot, and cucumber. Drizzle with the olive oil and toss with 2 large, flat spoons or your clean hands to distribute the oil evenly among the ingredients.

4. Sprinkle lightly all over with salt, oregano, garlic powder (if using), and pepper and toss. Drizzle with 2 teaspoons vinegar and toss. Taste a piece of lettuce and adjust the oil, vinegar, and seasonings to your preference. If the salad tastes flat, bitter, or acidic from the vinegar, add salt. (Salt mitigates bitterness and brings out the other flavors.) Often this step of correcting the seasoning takes a few trials, depending on the individual ingredients and the type of oil and vinegar you use. Taking the time to correct the seasoning can make the difference between an average salad and a compelling one.

BUTTER LETTUCE WITH RUBY GRAPEFRUIT, AVOCADO, AND GLAZED WALNUTS

For years I searched for a recipe for the perfect glazed walnuts. I wanted something not too sweet, and certainly not greasy. The nut had to be versatile enough to garnish a variety of composed salads, and respectable enough to stand alone as a nibble with drinks before dinner. One day, I found what I was looking for while having lunch with friends in a Chinese restaurant. The technique here is the same method used for a popular Chinese dish of shrimp and walnuts in a mayonnaise sauce. Serve this refreshing winter salad before—or after—a hearty main course such as California Crab Gumbo with Chicken and Sausage (page 138) or French Onion Soup Gratinée (page 73). Or top it with strips of Garlicky Chicken Breasts (page 176) for a main-course salad. During the December holidays, when pomegranates are in season, sprinkle the salad with a handful of fresh seeds for a burst of color and flavor. This recipe works well for dinner parties all winter long because everything can be prepped ahead and the salads assembled at the last minute. Just keep the glazed walnuts out of sight—they are addictive.

Serves 8

Citrus Dressing

Finely chopped zest of 1 orange

1 teaspoon sugar

1 tablespoon seasoned rice vinegar

1 tablespoon freshly squeezed orange juice

1½ teaspoons freshly squeezed lemon juice, preferably Meyer lemon

1½ teaspoons freshly squeezed lime juice

½ teaspoon kosher salt

¼ teaspoon granulated garlic powder

⅛ teaspoon fine, freshly ground black pepper

¼ cup mild-tasting extra-virgin olive oil

Walnuts

¼ cup superfine sugar

2 quarts water

2 cups (6 ounces) walnut halves

About 2 cups light-tasting vegetable oil, for frying

Salad

2 large, firm heads butter (Boston) lettuce

½ small red onion, ends cut off and cut lengthwise into thin crescents

2 large, ripe Hass avocados, halved, pitted, peeled, and cut into ¾-inch cubes

4 large, sweet Ruby grapefruits, cut into segments

RECIPE SECRETS

To ensure that everyone gets some leafy greens and some crunchy hearts, I cut the lettuce heads lengthwise into about 8 pieces. For the biggest hearts, select firm, compact heads.

If you're fortunate enough to have a choice of red grapefruits, ask the produce manager which are the sweetest in the market that day. This salad depends on them.

The walnuts come out best when you use superfine sugar. Buy it or make your own by processing ¼ cup granulated sugar in an impeccably clean and dry food processor for 15 seconds.

Be sure to have ingredients measured and equipment in place before beginning to prepare the walnuts. The process goes quickly and its success depends on timing. A slotted spoon works fine for transferring nuts to and from the hot oil, but a larger-capacity Chinese strainer is more efficient.

Briefly boiling the walnuts removes any bitterness, if present, in their skins. After boiling and rinsing with hot tap water, make haste as you transfer them to the sugar so the residual heat will melt the sugar.

1. *Prepare the dressing:* In a small bowl, combine the orange zest and sugar and stir to combine. Add the rice vinegar, orange juice, lemon juice, lime juice, salt, garlic powder, and pepper. Whisk to combine. While whisking continuously, drizzle in the oil. Taste and adjust the seasoning, if necessary. Stir well before tossing with the salad. (The dressing can be prepared up to 8 hours before serving. Cover and set aside in a cool place.)

2. *Prepare the walnuts:* Place the sugar in a bowl large enough to hold the walnuts eventually and have a heatproof rubber spatula ready. Place a strainer in the sink for the walnuts. Nest a clean, dry wire-mesh strainer inside a bowl and place near the stove. Coat the bottom of a rimmed baking sheet lightly with vegetable oil spray. Set aside.

/continued

Here's how to cut any citrus fruit into perfect, pith-free segments: Slice off the top and bottom ends. Place on a cutting board with a cut side up. With a very sharp chef's knife, cut off the skin in pieces, working from the top to the bottom, following the curve of the fruit. If necessary, trim off any remaining pith—the bitter white part under the skin—before continuing. Cradle the peeled fruit in one hand held over a bowl, and, using a sharp, thin-bladed fillet knife, slice toward the center on either side of each membrane that separates the segments. As you work your way around the fruit, allow the segments—and any juice that escapes—to fall into the bowl. Remove any seeds before using the segments, and keep the segments immersed in the juice until you're ready to drain and use them. Don't discard the juice—it's the cook's reward.

3. Pour the water into a 4-quart saucepan and bring to a rolling boil over high heat. Add the walnuts and cook for 1 minute. Drain the walnuts in the strainer in the sink, then rinse well with hot tap water. Shake to drain well. Immediately transfer the hot nuts to the bowl with the sugar and toss with the spatula until the sugar melts and evenly coats the nuts.

4. Pour the vegetable oil into a clean 1½-quart saucepan. It should be about 1 inch deep. Place over medium-high heat and heat to 350 degrees F on a deep-frying thermometer. Using a Chinese strainer or slotted spoon, carefully transfer half of the sugared walnuts to the hot oil. Fry until the walnuts are golden brown, 3 to 4 minutes. Remove the pan from the heat and, using the Chinese strainer or slotted spoon, immediately transfer the fried walnuts to the strainer nested in the bowl. Shake the strainer to drain off excess oil and separate the nuts. Immediately transfer the nuts to the prepared baking sheet. Quickly and carefully (they're very hot), spread out the nuts so they aren't touching. Keep them separate as they cool.

5. Reheat the oil to 350 degrees F and repeat the process with the remaining nuts. Be aware that the second batch may brown more quickly. Let the nuts cool completely before eating them or garnishing the salad. (The nuts can be prepared up to several days in advance, transferred to an airtight container with very little headroom, and stored in a cool, dark place.)

6. *Prepare the salad:* Remove any tough outer leaves from the heads of lettuce. Cut each head lengthwise into quarters, cut out the core portions, and then cut each quarter into halves or thirds, depending on the size. Swish the pieces in a bowl of cold water and spin dry.

7. In a large bowl, toss together the lettuce and red onion. Just before serving, stir the dressing, pour over the salad, and toss. Add the avocado cubes and toss gently. Taste a piece of lettuce and add more salt and pepper, if necessary. Divide the salad evenly among large plates. Tuck the grapefruit segments into the folds of lettuce, dividing them evenly among the salads. Break the walnuts into pieces and divide among the salads. Serve at once.

STORE WALNUT HALVES AND PIECES —AND OTHER SHELLED NUTS—IN THE FREEZER TO KEEP THEM FRESH.

AVOCADO SECRETS

For the first twenty years of my life, until I moved away from New England, I had never even *seen*—let alone tasted—an avocado. Now I can't take my hands off them. Imagine my delight when the bungalow I lived in for a year in Los Angeles had a prolific avocado tree in the backyard. When ripe, avocados will yield slightly to pressure and their skin turns dark greenish black. I prefer the Hass variety, which has bumpy skin and comes in many sizes.

The easiest way to dice an avocado is to first cut around the perimeter lengthwise, keeping in mind the large, round pit in the center of the bulbous part. Grab a half with each hand and rotate them in opposite directions to separate them. Thrust the heel end of a chef's knife into the pit and twist the knife slightly, pulling the pit free of the avocado at the same time. Use a dull butter knife to score the flesh of each avocado half into a grid pattern, creating roughly ¾-inch cubes. With a wooden spoon, scoop out the cubes, letting them fall into the salad bowl. If possible, wait until the last minute to cut the avocado, as the flesh will turn brown when exposed to air. Or, if prepping in advance, place the cubes, still stuck to one another, in a small bowl with no extra headroom, place a piece of plastic wrap on the avocado, pressing it directly onto the surface, and then immediately cover with a lid.

NUTS FOR NIBBLING

If you plan to nibble on these glazed walnuts and *not* use them in the salad, salt lightly—and/or toss with a little *pimentón* (page 138), cayenne pepper, cinnamon, or your favorite spice—right after frying.

STORING NUTS

Store shelled nuts, halves, and pieces in the freezer in lock-top plastic bags to keep them fresh.

RECIEPE SECRETS

. . . .

Heirloom tomatoes are grown from
seeds culled from old varieties of non-
hybridized plants. While they may not
be as uniform in appearance or as
hardy as what is readily available in
the supermarket, heirloom tomatoes
can't be beat for old-fashioned tomato
flavor. Look for them in a rainbow of
colors and various sizes. Buy one of
each and see which you like best. To
determine ripeness, smell the tomato
at the stem end. The most fragrant
tomatoes taste best.

. . . .

Toybox tomatoes are assorted cherry
tomatoes in various shapes and colors
(see illustration, page 284). Unless your
cherry tomatoes are tiny, cut them in
half so their juices will blend with the
other ingredients. I find them easier to
serve and eat when cut in half, too.

HEIRLOOM TOMATOES WITH BOCCONCINI, BASIL, AND WHITE BALSAMIC VINAIGRETTE

. . . .

Serve this vibrant, tossed variation of the classic Italian Caprese salad as a side
dish with Grilled Stuffed Chicken Breasts with Prosciutto, Taleggio, and Pesto
(page 183), Grilled Pork Chops with Garlic and Fennel Rub (page 211), or
Italian Sausage Contadina with Roasted Sweet Peppers, Potatoes, and Onions
(page 215) as part of a summertime buffet. For the best flavor, use the freshest,
ripest heirloom tomatoes from the garden or your local farmers' market or specialty-produce market. Be sure to serve plenty of crusty Italian bread to mop
up every last drop at the bottom of the bowl.

Serves 8

1 large clove garlic, cut in
half crosswise

4 large or 6 medium-sized
heirloom tomatoes, preferably
assorted colors and varieties

1 basket Sweet 100, Sungold,
or Toybox tomatoes

½ pound *bocconcini,* cut in half

½ red onion, ends cut off and cut
lengthwise into crescents

3 tablespoons fresh basil
chiffonade

½ cup bold-tasting extra-virgin
olive oil

2 tablespoons white balsamic or
Pinot Grigio vinegar

1 teaspoon dried leaf oregano,
crumbled between your fingers

1 teaspoon kosher salt

¼ teaspoon fine, freshly ground
black pepper

Steps for basil chiffonade

1. Rub the cut sides of the garlic all over the inside of a large, shallow serving bowl, then lightly crush the garlic with the side of a chef's knife and place in the bowl. Core and cut the heirloom tomatoes into wedges and add to the bowl. Cut the cherry tomatoes in half lengthwise (through the stem end) and add to the bowl. Add the *bocconcini,* onion, and basil. Drizzle with the olive oil and vinegar, and sprinkle with the oregano, salt, and pepper. Toss well. Let stand for about 10 minutes for the flavors to mingle.

2. Before serving, remove the garlic, toss the salad again, taste, and adjust the seasoning, if necessary. If not serving right away, keep the salad in a cool place, but do not refrigerate.

ABOUT COLD-PRESSED AND EXPELLER-PRESSED OILS

Cold-pressed oils are cooking or condiment oils that are produced at low temperatures (some reportedly as high as 180 degrees F, others only as high as 120 degrees F) by mechanical means, which preserves more nutrients (such as omega-3 fatty acids) than higher-heat processing or refining. Expeller-pressed oils, such as canola oil, are produced with extreme pressure, which can produce temperatures up to 300 degrees F. Expeller-pressed oils are also considered more healthful than refined oils, which can be produced with solvents. While cold- and expeller-pressed oils are more healthful, they also have a lower smoke point (page 30) and are more fragile, and therefore more susceptible to turning rancid. Rancidity, detected by smell and taste, not only gives food an offensive flavor, but is also a prime condition for the development of free radicals, which are linked to cancer. High-heat processing helps preserve oils, while admittedly causing another set of concerns (see About Refined Oils, page 30). Cold-pressed and expeller-pressed oils are becoming more widely available. Typically, they cost more than their highly refined counterparts. Purchase them in sizes that can be consumed within a month or two, and store in a cool, dry place, preferably in tightly sealed, dark bottles with little headroom (air is the enemy here). Refrigerate for longer storage.

RECIPE SECRETS

Bocconcini (pronounced boh-con-*chee*-nee) are 1-inch balls of soft, creamy, fresh whole-milk mozzarella cheese, often packed in brine. If your *bocconcini* are larger, cut into ¾-inch pieces. If unavailable, substitute regular-sized balls of whole-milk mozzarella, preferably fresh (not low moisture) and cut into ¾-inch pieces. In this salad, the cheese absorbs the flavorful juices from both the tomatoes and the vinaigrette, which is why a soft, fresh cheese is best.

The vibrant color contrast of the brilliant-hued tomatoes, white cheese, and green basil make this particularly appealing. Keep the colors "clean" with a white vinegar.

RECIPE SECRETS

Native to the Middle East, dates are the fruit of the prehistoric date palm tree. The Medjool variety, originally from Morocco, now grown in California and Arizona, yields fruits up to 2 inches long. Look for dried, pitted Medjool (or Medjul) dates in the bulk-produce section of your grocery store. Select ones that are soft and plump, and avoid any with shriveled, dry, or crystallized skins. Store them, wrapped, in a cool place; refrigerate in hot weather to prevent molding. Besides their characteristically sweet flesh, dates contribute protein and vitamins to this salad.

Use a mandoline, a V-slicer, or a sharp knife with a very thin blade to shave the celery on the diagonal into thin slices.

If your bunch of celery doesn't have many leaves on the outside stalks, don't fret. You're sure to find tender, sweet yellow leaves on the inner stalks.

SHAVED CELERY WITH MEDJOOL DATES, FETA, AND WALNUTS

The ingredients in this delightfully refreshing salad can be tossed together and served family style or as part of a buffet, or arranged on individual plates as a distinctive composed salad to serve before—or after—a rich or hearty main course. I once took this salad to a potluck lunch on a hot summer day, and kept it chilled until the last minute. Everyone welcomed the cool, yet complex refreshment it provided. Look for incomparably lusty and creamy Medjool dates at farmers' markets and in specialty-produce stores. I credit chef Jim Moffat for introducing me to this salad at his now-defunct San Francisco restaurant, 42 Degrees. The walnuts and feta are my additions.

Serves 6 to 8

6 large celery stalks, peeled and cut very thinly on the diagonal to yield 4 cups

1 cup loosely packed celery leaves, very coarsely chopped

1 cup loosely packed fresh flat-leaf parsley leaves, very coarsely chopped

4 teaspoons white balsamic vinegar

¾ teaspoon kosher salt

Freshly ground black pepper

¼ cup bold-tasting extra-virgin olive oil

6 ounces feta cheese, preferably French, crumbled to yield 1½ cups

18 pitted Medjool dates, cut into quarters (or into eighths if longer than 1½ inches)

¾ cup chopped walnuts, toasted (see opposite page)

---

1. In a medium bowl, combine the sliced celery, celery leaves, and parsley. In a small bowl, combine the vinegar, salt, and a few grinds of black pepper. Whisk in the olive oil. Pour the dressing over the celery mixture and toss to combine. Add the feta and toss lightly.

2. To serve family style, add dates and walnuts, reserving a few nuts. Toss together and sprinkle with the reserved nuts. Serve at once.

3. To serve as individual composed salads, arrange a few date and walnut pieces in the center of each salad plate. Divide the celery-feta mixture evenly among the plates, mounding it on top of the dates and walnuts. Scatter the remaining dates and walnuts on and around the salads. Serve at once.

HOW TO TOAST NUTS

Toasting nuts magnifies their flavor by releasing their volatile oils. For the best crunch, be sure to toast nuts ahead of time, so they have a chance to cool completely before you chop them or add them to a recipe.

There's more than one way to toast nuts. While some people swear by using a sauté pan on top of the stove, I'm consistently disappointed with this method. I always seem to end up with undertoasted nuts (because I'm afraid they're going to burn), or unevenly toasted nuts with some edges almost burned, while other sides are barely bronzed. I prefer to use an oven, toaster oven, or microwave.

Preheat the oven or toaster oven to 350 degrees F. Place the nuts in a single layer on a rimmed baking sheet. Toast, stirring occasionally, until golden brown and fragrant, 6 to 10 minutes, depending on the size and type of nut. Transfer the toasted nuts to a plate and set aside to cool completely.

Or, toast nuts in a single layer on a rimmed plate in the microwave on high for 3 to 5 minutes, depending on the size and type of nut. Be sure to stop the microwave to stir the nuts at 1-minute intervals, and remember that the microwave cooks foods from the inside out. If the nuts smell fragrant, but they're not quite brown enough on the surface, set them on the counter for a minute or two before you determine whether they need more time.

See also "How to Toast and Skin Whole Hazelnuts," page 92.

RECIPE SECRETS

In her definitive book, *Fig Heaven,* my friend and fellow cooking teacher Marie Simmons notes that figs have two seasons in California: May–June and August–September. For this salad, look for dark purple Black Mission figs at your local farmers' market. Figs do not ripen further once they are picked, so select figs that yield to gentle pressure and feel heavy for their size. Ideally, they should have a bead of moisture, called a teardrop, on the bottom. Figure on about 12 medium-sized Black Mission figs to the pound. Once home, take them out of the box and place on a plate to prevent them from becoming moldy. In particularly hot or humid climates, refrigerate ripe figs. Use as soon as possible after purchase.

FIGS AND ARUGULA WITH CREAMY GOAT CHEESE AND TOASTED PECANS

This refreshing salad is perfect before or after the main course at an early- or late-summer dinner party, just when fresh figs are ripe and flavorful. The combination of toasted pecans and creamy goat cheese works well with juicy, fragrant figs and a few delicate rings of red onion. Baby spinach is a good substitute for the arugula. Serve with a crusty loaf of Italian bread.

Serves 4 to 6

½ pound arugula or mixed baby salad greens

8 ripe Black Mission figs, about 10 ounces total, stems trimmed and cut lengthwise into quarters

1 small handful very thin red onion rings

3 to 4 tablespoons walnut or bold-tasting extra-virgin olive oil

2 teaspoons white balsamic vinegar or white wine vinegar

½ teaspoon kosher salt

⅛ teaspoon fine, freshly ground black pepper

⅔ cup pecan halves, toasted (page 89)

3 ounces creamy, mild fresh goat cheese

---

1. Swish the arugula or salad greens in a bowl of cold water and spin dry. Place in a large bowl along with the figs and onions. Drizzle with 3 tablespoons of the walnut or olive oil and the vinegar and toss well. Sprinkle with the salt and pepper and toss again. Taste and add more oil, if necessary. Crumble the pecans, if desired (save a few nice halves for garnish), add to the salad, and toss again. Crumble the goat cheese into small clumps as you add it to the salad. Toss gently. Taste and adjust the seasoning, if necessary. Divide evenly among salad plates and garnish with the reserved pecans. Serve at once.

BABY GREENS, ROASTED CHICKEN, STILTON, AND HAZELNUTS WITH RASPBERRY VINAIGRETTE

Once, during an interview, a reporter asked for my signature dish. It would have to be this salad. Hands down, this is consistently mentioned as the students' favorite recipe in my Roasting Techniques classes. In class we use a freshly roasted bird and it's sublime, but you can also use leftover roasted chicken or, when time is short, a purchased rotisserie chicken. Just be sure not to buy one that's lemon or barbecue flavored, as the flavors would compete with the dressing. Accompanied by some crusty artisanal bread, this big, rich salad makes an impressive luncheon main course or light supper. Or, as we do in hands-on teambuilding cooking classes, serve this—with or without the chicken—before a main course of My Grandmother's Baked Stuffed Manicotti (page 120).

Serves 4 to 6 as a main-course salad, or 12 as a first course

Raspberry Vinaigrette	Salad
1 large shallot	Classic Herb-Roasted Chicken (page 187) or a purchased rotisserie chicken
1 teaspoon Dijon mustard, preferably imported	
1 tablespoon fresh thyme leaves	1 pound mixed baby salad greens, rinsed and spun dry
2 teaspoons kosher salt	1 small red onion, very thinly sliced
1 teaspoon sugar	
½ teaspoon fine, freshly ground black pepper	½ pound Red Flame or other red seedless grapes, halved
¼ cup raspberry vinegar	¾ cup hazelnuts, toasted and skinned (page 92), coarsely chopped, divided
1 to 2 tablespoons red wine vinegar (not balsamic)	½ pound Stilton cheese, crumbled
⅔ cup toasted walnut oil	

RECIPE SECRETS

For the best flavor, use a freshly roasted, still-warm chicken. If using leftover chicken, bring it to room temperature (or warm it in the oven) before adding to the salad.

There's something special about hand-shredded chicken. Cutting chicken into uniform pieces with a knife changes the texture and gives it a less silky mouth-feel.

Walnut oil imparts a subtle but haunting richness to this dressing. For flavor and for better health, use cold-pressed (page 87) toasted walnut oil, if possible. Because walnut oil easily turns rancid, store it in the refrigerator. If you can find toasted hazelnut oil, it's also outstanding in this salad.

When my cooking school was rather young, I was fortunate to have a terrific intern, Sam King, from the California Culinary Academy. Sam taught me an invaluable trick to prevent Stilton and other soft cheeses from "melting" on your fingers when you break them into pieces: Place the cold cheese on a plate and crumble with a fork.

/continued

To remove the bitter pellicle, or skin, from shelled whole hazelnuts (also known as filberts), preheat the oven to 350 degrees F and spread the nuts on a rimmed baking sheet. Toast the nuts in the oven until they are fragrant and the skins turn brown and start to flake off, 10 to 12 minutes. Transfer to the center of a clean, old (the nuts stain) kitchen towel (not terrycloth), gather up the corners and sides, and rub the hazelnuts together through the towel. As they release their skins, remove the nuts from the towel and shake out the towel (if doing so outside, be sure your back is to the wind), discarding the loose skins. No matter what you do, some stubborn hazelnuts just won't give up their skins. But don't worry if this happens. In most recipes, it's okay to use a few nuts with skins. To get the full flavor and texture benefits from roasting, let the hazelnuts cool completely before chopping and proceeding with any recipe.

1. *Prepare the vinaigrette:* With the motor running, drop the shallot into a food processor and mince. (Alternatively, cut it into a few pieces and drop into a blender with the motor running.) Stop and scrape down the sides of the bowl. Add the mustard, thyme, salt, sugar, and pepper. Add the raspberry vinegar and 1 tablespoon of the red wine vinegar and process until blended. Scrape down the bowl. With the motor running, slowly drizzle in the walnut oil. Taste and add more red wine vinegar, if necessary. The dressing should be acidic enough to balance the natural richness in the chicken and Stilton. Set aside for at least 15 minutes for the flavors to develop. (The dressing can be made up to 24 hours in advance. Cover and refrigerate; let sit at room temperature for about 30 minutes before using.)

2. *Prepare the salad:* Remove the skin and bones (save for stock or discard) from the chicken and shred the meat by hand into large bite-sized pieces. You should have 3 to 4 cups shredded chicken. In a very large bowl, toss the chicken with about half of the vinaigrette. Add half of the greens, all of the red onion, and most of the remaining vinaigrette and toss well. Toss in the remaining greens, the grapes, and all but about 3 tablespoons of the hazelnuts. Taste a piece of lettuce and add more dressing, salt, and pepper, if necessary. Add the Stilton and toss to combine. Divide the salad evenly among plates and garnish with the reserved hazelnuts.

RISOTTOS
AND PASTAS

RISOTTO AND PASTA RECIPES

Risottos	Q	MA	V	Page
Risotto Milanese	●		●	98
Butternut Squash Risotto with Parmigiano-Reggiano Rinds and Balsamic Drizzle			●	99
Risotto Primavera with Wild Salmon			●	102
Savory Baked Risotto Cake		●	●	105
Pastas				
Linguine Aglio e Olio	●		●	109
Baked Macaroni with White Cheddar and Buttered Bread Crumbs		●	●	110
Macaroni and Cheese Variation	●		●	112
Fettuccine Alfredo with Baby Shrimp and Peas	●		●	113
Spaghetti and Meatballs with 20-Minute Tomato Sauce		●	●	114
Rigatoni with Sausage and Mushroom Ragù; Baked Rigatoni with Sausage, and Mushrooms Variation			●	118
My Grandmother's Baked Stuffed Manicotti		●	●	120
Lasagna Bolognese			●	122
"Bolognese" Sauce			●	124
Double-Crusted Timpano with Fusilli, Ricotta, and Tender Little Meatballs		●	●	126

Q = Quick—prep to table in 45 minutes.
MA = Make ahead—part or all of the recipe can or must be made ahead.
V = Vegetarian—no meat, chicken, fish, or, with minor adjustments, such as substituting
vegetable broth for chicken stock, can be prepared as a vegetarian recipe.

SECRETS FOR SUCCESSFUL RISOTTO

I never realized I had a particular knack for making risotto until I overheard my husband, Al, report it to someone he'd just met at a party. The new acquaintance had asked Al about my cooking specialties and risotto was at the top of his list. To tell the truth, I rarely make risotto at home (although I must confess to preparing it more often since that party), because I teach it frequently in classes. I do believe, however, I could eat it every night of the week. When I see risotto on a restaurant menu, I almost always order it. Maybe I'm trying to make up for lost time, since growing up in a family of southern Italians, I never ate anything that resembled risotto—or even rice.

I was taught the intricacies of risotto in cooking school by my esteemed chef-instructor Biba Caggiano. Biba was born and raised in Bologna, Italy, and now owns and operates Biba restaurant in Sacramento, California. Her risotto Milanese was love at first sight—and bite. Taught by a master, I learned that risotto is mostly all about technique, not to mention a few important ingredients. When you follow the proper guidelines, it's hard to go wrong.

Each risotto recipe in this chapter features its own particular Secrets. In addition, here are some general tips and some answers to frequently asked questions about preparing risotto.

INGREDIENTS

- Risotto requires the cook's attention. For smooth sailing, have all ingredients prepped before you start to cook. And don't answer the door unless it's someone from the Reader's Digest Sweepstakes.

- For best flavor, use European-style or organic unsalted butter. It's okay to substitute mild-tasting extra-virgin olive oil to start the risotto, but you'll be rewarded exponentially if you do the final emulsification with a knob of good butter.

- Be sure to mince onions into small pieces, no larger than half the size of your small fingernail. Onions should fade into the background, and barely be noticeable in the finished risotto.

- Use the right rice. Traditionally risotto is prepared with one of three imported Italian *superfino* rices: Arborio, Carnaroli, or Vialone Nano. Arborio is the most widely available and commonly used in the United States, although a new domestic short-grain rice called Cal-Riso and an Argentinean Carnaroli have been introduced here to positive reviews. All these short-grain rices contain the ideal starch content to create characteristically creamy risotto, and any one of them can be used in the following recipes. Avoid buying rice from self-serve bulk containers, as you often end up with broken grains. Store packaged rice tightly closed, in a cool, dark pantry. The older the rice, the dryer it becomes, and the longer it takes to cook.

- Use dry white wine, such as Pinot Grigio or a not-too-grassy Sauvignon Blanc, or substitute dry white vermouth. Don't use "cooking wine," to which salt has been added. Alcohol volatilizes certain flavors and adds a balancing acid component to creamy, rich risotto, but if it is verboten in your diet, simply omit it.

- Good stock or broth, preferably homemade (page 60, 61, or 63), is key. In Italy, risotto is often made with capon broth, which resembles turkey broth in depth of flavor. If you must use purchased broth, use a reduced-sodium one. I find Health Valley Fat-Free Chicken Broth and Pacific Free-Range Chicken Broth, both packaged in aseptic boxes, to be acceptable substitutes for homemade broth in making risotto.

- If it looks as if you're going to run out of hot stock during cooking, add some water to stretch what remains in the pot. As necessary, regulate the heat to keep the stock hot, but not simmering.

- In Italy, freshly grated Parmigiano-Reggiano is traditionally used to finish and garnish risottos, except those made with seafood. Because it's more of a staple in my house, I sometimes substitute saltier *pecorino romano* cheese. The way I see it, you have two choices: whether to use Parmesan or Romano, and whether to use either cheese in a seafood risotto. Whichever cheese you choose, grate it fresh, or when time is short, buy it freshly grated from a reputable shop with high turnover. Anything in a green cardboard container does not qualify. If using a Microplane to grate the cheese, be sure to pack it into the measuring cup for accuracy. As I have noted, a Microplane yields a fluffier result than other graters.

TECHNIQUES

- Bring stock to a boil in a separate pan, then reduce the heat to the lowest setting to keep the stock hot. Do not allow it to simmer, or it will reduce in volume and its flavor will concentrate. It's important to add hot stock to risotto to keep the temperature of the risotto constant. For ease and safety, use a ladle with a wooden or plastic handle so you can leave it in the hot stock without risking burning your hand. A wooden-handled wok "spoon" works well.

- Instead of heating stock in a pot on the stove, I sometimes bring it to a boil in a 2-quart liquid measure in the microwave, and simply pour in about ⅔ cup at a time. If microwaved stock cools too much while the risotto is cooking, reheat it.

- For best results, cook risotto in a broad pan, rather than a deep one. The sloping sides of an All-Clad saucier pan are ideal. Also, I find that risotto cooked in a Le Creuset Dutch oven cooks evenly. The risotto also stays hot in the pot for serving.

- Cook onions until soft, without letting them brown. Once you add wine, the acid will impede the onions from softening further, which can result in crunchy onions—undesirable in risotto.

- To prevent rice grains from sticking to one another and becoming gummy, gently sauté the rice with the onions over low heat, so the grains don't harden. They should be coated with butter and sparkle like jewels.

- Add wine all at once. If you dribble it in, it will evaporate on contact with the hot pan.

- Add stock about ⅔ cup at a time, waiting until each addition is absorbed before adding more.

- Stir the risotto constantly and regulate the heat as necessary to cook at a steady, brisk simmer. If risotto cooks too fast, the rice grains will cook unevenly; too slowly, and they'll become mushy.

- I prefer to stir with a heatproof rubber spatula. The rice doesn't stick to it and it's easy to scrape the sides of the pot, which are just as important as the bottom. A flat-bottomed wooden spatula works okay; just be sure to scrape the sides carefully.

- Anna del Conte, in *Gastronomy of Italy,* says it best: "At the end, the risotto must be *all'onda,* which means that the grains should be separate yet bound together in a creamy consistency."

- Once the rice is done, finish the risotto off the heat. Quickly add cheese and butter, cover, and let sit for 2 to 3 minutes, then stir vigorously to emulsify. Serve immediately (or sooner!).

SERVING

- I hate to be redundant, but risotto that isn't piping hot is hardly worth eating. (You can imagine what a nemesis this is in cooking classes.) To help keep risotto hot while you eat, always serve it in warmed shallow bowls or plates. Be sure everyone is seated before you start to serve. And don't waste precious time with fancy garnishes—a little sprinkle of cheese, where appropriate, is all you need. Italians have a saying about serving risotto: Risotto does not wait for people. People wait for risotto.

FREQUENTLY ASKED QUESTIONS ABOUT RISOTTO

How do I know when it's time to add more stock?

Add stock when the spatula leaves a track that exposes the bottom of the pot and you have to pull the spatula through the risotto.

Why do my onions end up crunchy?

Chances are they were not chopped finely enough and/or not sautéed long enough before adding the rice.

When is risotto done?

This is the most frequently asked question in risotto classes. In fact, the most common mistake I observe is when people assume risotto isn't done until all the stock has been used. The only way to know when risotto is done is to taste. Taste early, taste often. Cooking time depends on countless factors: type and dimensions of the pot, level of heat, temperature of the stock, and the age, type, and amount of rice, to name a few. When risotto is done, the rice grains should be tender but firm when you bite into one, with no chalkiness inside. The rice may be ready before you have used all the stock, or you may need to thin the remaining stock with a little water. Before you take risotto off the heat for the final addition of butter and cheese, it should be loose, but not runny. Keep in mind that the cheese will firm it up once the risotto is exposed to the air as it's being served.

Is risotto a side dish or a first course?

Risotto Milanese (page 98) is one of the few risottos that is served as a side dish, traditionally with osso buco (page 234). In Italy, other risottos are served as a first course. But in the United States, dishes such as Risotto Primavera with Wild Salmon (page 102) would certainly qualify as a main course, accompanied by only a simple salad.

How can I make risotto in advance for company? How do restaurants do it?

The only way I know to prepare a risotto dish completely ahead is to make *risotto al forno*, or baked risotto (page 105). However, you *can* get a headstart when serving a traditional risotto:

- If making up to 6 hours ahead, you can complete each of these steps: Sauté the onions; sauté the rice; add and reduce the wine; and add the first few ladles of stock. When the stock is absorbed, spread the risotto in a single layer in a nonreactive (or parchment-lined) baking pan and let cool to room temperature. Cover and refrigerate. At serving time, reheat the stock and add a ladle or two to an empty heavy, broad pot over medium-high heat. Add the cold risotto and stir constantly with a heatproof rubber spatula. The mixture should simmer briskly. When the stock is absorbed, continue adding more hot stock, a ladleful or two at a time, until the rice is done. Emulsify and serve.

- If making up to 1 hour ahead, you can complete each of these steps: In a heavy pot with a lid, such as a Dutch oven, sauté the onions; sauté the rice; add and reduce the wine; and add the first few ladles of hot stock. When the stock is absorbed, add about 3 cups hot stock, stir well, cover quickly, and turn off the heat (leave the pan on the same burner). Just before serving, stir in a ladleful or two of hot stock and reheat the risotto over medium heat, stirring constantly. Cook until the rice is done, adding hot stock as needed. Emulsify and serve.

RECIPE SECRETS

Before adding saffron to risotto, steep the threads in a little hot stock or broth to leach out some of their brilliant color. If you don't want to see the threads, strain them out as you add the saffron-infused broth to the risotto. I think they add a distinctive—and authentic—touch, so I leave them in.

RISOTTO MILANESE

In *Gastronomy of Italy,* Anna del Conte shares one legend on the origin of risotto Milanese (pronounced mill-ah-*nay*-zeh) that dates back to the sixteenth century. As the story goes, this risotto was a wedding gift for the daughter of a stained-glass craftsman who was working on the windows of the Duomo in Milan. One of his apprentices, who had a penchant for adding saffron to the molten glass, slipped some of the coveted filaments to the innkeeper where the wedding dinner was to be held, and asked him to mix the saffron into the risotto. Since it was fashionable then in Milan to "give a dish a semblance of containing gold, as it was believed to have health-giving properties," the saffron-stained risotto was fitting. This risotto is the traditional accompaniment to osso buco (page 234). Or use this risotto chilled (or left over) to make Savory Baked Risotto Cake (page 105).

Serves 6 to 8

6 to 8 cups homemade chicken stock or broth (page 60 or 61) or purchased reduced-sodium broth

1 heaping teaspoon saffron threads

6 tablespoons unsalted butter, divided

1 yellow onion, minced

2 cups Arborio rice

1 cup dry white wine

1 cup freshly grated Parmigiano-Reggiano cheese

Kosher salt

---

1. Bring the stock to a boil in a 3-quart saucepan over high heat. Reduce the heat to the lowest setting. In a small bowl, combine the saffron with a little of the hot stock; set aside.

2. Heat a heavy, broad 4-quart pot or saucier over medium heat. Add 4 tablespoons of the butter. When the butter is hot enough to sizzle a piece of onion, add the onion and sauté until very soft and translucent, 6 to 8 minutes. Adjust the heat as necessary to prevent the onion from browning. Stir in the rice and continue to stir until the grains are evenly coated with butter and begin to sparkle, about 2 minutes.

3. Add the wine all at once. Stir constantly until the liquid has been absorbed and the rice is very moist, about 2 minutes.

4. Add 1 cup of the hot stock and stir constantly with a heatproof rubber spatula or flat-bottomed wooden spatula until almost all of the liquid is absorbed. Adjust the heat to maintain a steady, lively simmer throughout the cooking process. As the liquid is absorbed, continue adding and stirring in more stock, about ⅔ cup at a time, for another 15 to 20 minutes, adding the reserved saffron and its soaking liquid after about 10 minutes.

5. Taste the rice for doneness. It should be tender, but firm to the tooth, and the risotto should be moist and creamy, but not runny. Continue cooking as necessary, tasting the rice frequently, until it's done. You may not need all of the stock.

6. Remove the risotto from the heat. Add the remaining 2 tablespoons butter and ¾ cup of the cheese. Stir quickly—it's not necessary to mix well—and cover the pot. Let sit for 2 to 3 minutes. Uncover, stir briefly, and taste for seasoning; add salt, if necessary. Spoon into warmed shallow soup plates. Sprinkle each portion with a little of the remaining grated cheese and serve immediately.

7. If using the Risotto Milanese—or other leftover risotto—for Savory Baked Risotto Cake (page 105), stir in the remaining ¼ cup cheese and spread the risotto in a thin layer on a rimmed baking sheet lined with parchment or a silicone baking liner. Let cool to room temperature. Cover and refrigerate if not using within 2 hours; bring to room temperature before making the cake.

BUTTERNUT SQUASH RISOTTO WITH PARMIGIANO-REGGIANO RINDS AND BALSAMIC DRIZZLE

For a distinctive addition to this saucy, squash-infused risotto, chop some Parmigiano-Reggiano cheese rind into small dice and stir the pieces into the risotto at the end. To gild the lily and provide a counterpoint to the rich, creamy risotto, drizzle each portion with aged balsamic vinegar just before serving. (For an alternative—and much less expensive—balsamic condiment suitable for drizzling, see page 101.) If you prefer, anoint each serving with a few splashes of white truffle oil, and if you're feeling extravagant, add a little of each. Serve Weeknight Green Salad (page 81) on the side, before or after this special main-dish risotto.

/continued

It takes some ten thousand hand-harvested stigmas from the crocus flower to produce a single ounce of saffron filaments, or threads. After harvest, the stigmas are spread between fine-mesh screens and baked in the sun to dry. The world's most expensive spice, saffron adds a distinctive, musky flavor to rice dishes throughout the world. It stains not only food, but also other porous materials it comes in contact with, including skin.

For the best quality, always buy saffron from a reputable source (see Sources). Often, it is steeped in hot liquid for a few minutes to help it "bloom," or release its vivid yellow color. Some cooks strain the liquid before adding it to a dish; others feel that the filaments add a distinctive look to the finished dish. (Count me in the latter camp.) Store saffron in a dark, cool pantry; stored properly, it keeps for up to a few years. Every so often, a student asks about substituting turmeric for saffron to stain a dish yellow. If you don't have an affinity for, access to, or the budget for this cherished spice, I suggest you leave it out and enjoy all the other flavors in the dish.

RECIPE SECRETS

The way you prep the squash has a definite effect on the creaminess of this risotto. I find it easiest—and least wasteful—to peel butternut squash with a swivel-blade vegetable peeler. Continue peeling until no more green "threads" are visible on the flesh, then cut off the ends, cut the squash lengthwise into quarters, scoop out the seeds and fibers, and cut crosswise into ⅛-inch-thick slices with a mandoline, V-slicer, food processor fitted with the slicing disk, or sharp knife with a very thin blade. Be sure to cut the squash into uniform pieces so they will cook evenly, then collapse and "melt" into the risotto as the rice cooks.

As explained in the recipe for minestrone (page 75), you can store the rinds from Parmigiano-Reggiano cheese in the freezer. About 2 ounces rind yields about ¼ cup diced pieces. Sometimes, depending on how old the rinds are and how soon they're added to the risotto, the rind pieces will melt completely, enriching the dish and giving it a subtle creaminess. If you prefer chewy bits, as in this recipe, add them at the end of cooking.

Serves 4 to 6 as a main course, or 8 as a side dish

About 8 cups homemade chicken stock or broth (page 60 or 61) or canned reduced-sodium broth

5 tablespoons unsalted butter, divided

1 yellow onion, minced

1 pound butternut squash, peeled, quartered lengthwise, seeds discarded, and thinly sliced crosswise to yield about 2½ cups

1 tablespoon chopped fresh thyme or sage

1 teaspoon kosher salt

1½ cups Arborio or Carnaroli rice

¼ cup ¼-inch-diced Parmigiano-Reggiano cheese rinds

¾ cup freshly grated Parmigiano-Reggiano cheese

½ teaspoon fine, freshly ground black pepper

1 tablespoon aged balsamic vinegar, for serving

---

1. Bring the stock to a boil in a 3-quart saucepan over high heat. Reduce the heat to the lowest setting.

2. Heat a heavy, broad 4-quart pot or saucier over medium heat. Add 4 tablespoons of the butter. When the butter is hot enough to sizzle a piece of onion, add the onion and sauté until very soft and translucent, 6 to 8 minutes. Adjust the heat as necessary to prevent the onion from browning. Stir in the butternut squash, thyme or sage, and salt and cook over medium heat until squash turns bright orange and the onions start to get sticky, about 2 minutes. Add enough hot stock just to cover the squash, about 2 cups. Raise the heat to high and bring to a boil. Reduce the heat to low, cover, and simmer steadily until the squash is soft and breaks apart easily with a fork, 15 to 20 minutes.

3. Raise the heat to medium and add the rice and about 1 cup of the hot stock. Stir constantly with a heatproof rubber spatula or flat-bottomed wooden spatula until almost all the liquid is absorbed. Adjust the heat to maintain a steady, lively simmer throughout the cooking process. As the liquid is absorbed, continue adding and stirring in more stock, about ⅔ cup at a time, for another 15 to 20 minutes.

4. Taste the rice for doneness. It should be tender, but firm to the tooth, and the risotto should be moist and creamy, but not runny. Continue cooking as necessary, tasting the rice frequently, until it's done. You may not need all of the stock.

5. Remove the risotto from the heat. Add the remaining 1 tablespoon butter, the cheese rinds, grated cheese, and pepper. Stir quickly—it's not necessary to mix well—and cover the pot. Let sit for 2 to 3 minutes. Uncover, stir briefly, and taste for seasoning; add enough salt and pepper to bring out the flavor of the thyme, cheese, and butternut squash. Spoon into warmed shallow soup plates. Drizzle each portion in a random pattern with the balsamic vinegar and serve immediately.

NOT ALL BALSAMIC VINEGARS ARE CREATED EQUAL

Aceto balsamico tradizionale di Modena is an incomparably rich, inky, sweet-tart vinegar made in Modena, Italy. It is aged over the course of several years in a series of casks made from different woods. The word *tradizionale* indicates the authentic product, and it may be aged from a few years to decades. Curiously, the amount of balsamic vinegar sold around the globe each year is more than twice the amount legally produced in Modena. In order to preserve and protect this unique condiment, a consortium has been established to monitor its production and distribution. Chances are excellent that the comparatively thin, reddish brown, sweet vinegar labeled balsamic sold in grocery stores across the United States is not the real deal. Look for authentic balsamic vinegar in specialty-food stores or Italian delicatessens. For a lively splash of flavor and a distinctive presentation, drizzle the authentic balsamic vinegar over creamy risottos just before serving.

If the real thing is not available, here's a simple way to create a respectable condiment for drizzling, using the everyday balsamic vinegar available in most grocery stores. To make enough of this balsamic syrup for 4 to 6 servings, pour 1 cup of the vinegar into a 1-quart saucepan. Bring to a simmer over low heat and boil gently until it reduces in volume to a syrupy consistency, about 10 minutes. You'll know it's ready by tilting the pan. If it coats the bottom, it's thick enough to use as a drizzling condiment. The residual heat in the pan will cause the vinegar to continue to thicken as it sits, so don't reduce it too much. If it becomes too thick, thin it down with a little more vinegar.

RECIPE SECRETS

To keep asparagus bright green, blanch it before adding to risotto. Immediately rinse with cold water to stop the cooking and set the color.

. . . .

Ecology and politics notwithstanding, there's nothing like the clean, vibrant flavor and firm, toothsome texture of fresh wild salmon. It happens to be in season at the same time as many springtime—and summer—vegetables, making it a natural addition to *risotto primavera*.

. . . .

When you have very thin fillets of fish, such as salmon, rub them with oil and broil them on one side only, undercooking slightly (the residual heat will firm them up nicely). Tent with aluminum foil and let rest a bit after removing from the oven so they'll firm up enough to be propped up against a bed of risotto or mashed potatoes.

. . . .

Use your choice of fresh English peas or fava beans, or fresh or thawed, shelled edamame (pronounced ed-ah-mom-eh, which is Japanese for soybeans). Each contributes a vibrant green color and subtle texture to the finished risotto. For information on how to remove the skins from fava beans, see page 253.

RISOTTO PRIMAVERA with **WILD SALMON**

One June night, at the last minute, I realized we had four people coming for supper and only three freshly caught wild salmon fillets. Instead of grilling the fillets as I usually do, I cut each fillet lengthwise into three ½-inch-thick slices and broiled them on one side only, just until they were firm. Rather than serving *risotto primavera* as a separate first course as originally intended, I mounded some risotto in the center of each main-course plate and crisscrossed a pair of broiled pieces of salmon on top of the risotto. I ended up with an extra slice of salmon for lunch the next day and the fresh wild salmon gave new meaning to *risotto primavera*, or "springtime risotto." Use whatever colorful combination of springtime vegetables you have on hand, and be sure to include the cherry tomatoes—they make the dish sing.

Serves 6

Salmon

. . . .

4 skinless salmon fillets, preferably wild, ½ pound each

1 teaspoon kosher salt, divided

½ teaspoon fine, freshly ground black pepper, divided

½ teaspoon granulated garlic powder, divided

Extra-virgin olive oil for brushing on salmon

Risotto

. . . .

6 cups homemade chicken stock or broth (page 60 or 61), Vegetable Broth (page 63), or purchased reduced-sodium broth

Kosher salt

¾ pound medium-thick asparagus, tough ends removed and cut on the diagonal into 1-inch pieces

5 tablespoons unsalted butter, divided

1 yellow onion, minced

1½ cups Arborio rice

¾ cup dry white wine or dry white vermouth

½ cup fresh shelled English peas or fava beans, or thawed, frozen shelled peas or edamame

1 cup Sungold, Sweet 100, or other flavorful red or orange cherry tomatoes, cut in half through the stem end

1 cup freshly grated Parmigiano-Reggiano cheese

2 tablespoons minced fresh chives, divided

1. *Prepare the salmon:* Cut each salmon fillet lengthwise into three ½-inch-wide slices (see illustration) and place on their sides on a broiler pan. You should have a total of 12 pieces. Sprinkle lightly with half of the salt, pepper, and granulated garlic powder. Turn, brush the tops lightly with olive oil, and sprinkle with the remaining salt, pepper, and granulated garlic powder. Set aside at room temperature. Position a rack 6 inches below the broiler element and preheat the broiler.

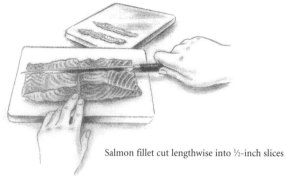

Salmon fillet cut lengthwise into ½-inch slices

2. *Prepare the risotto:* Bring the stock to a boil in a 2½-quart saucepan over high heat. Reduce the heat to the lowest setting.

3. Bring a saucepan three-fourths full of water to a rolling boil and salt the water. Add the asparagus and blanch for 1 minute. Drain and rinse immediately under cold water until they are cool to the touch. Drain and set aside.

4. Heat a heavy, broad pot or saucier over medium heat. Add 3 tablespoons of the butter. When the butter is hot enough to sizzle a piece of onion, add the onion and sauté until very soft and translucent, 6 to 8 minutes. Adjust the heat as necessary to prevent the onion from browning. Stir in the rice and continue to stir until the grains are evenly coated with butter and begin to sparkle, about 2 minutes.

5. Add the wine all at once. Stir constantly until the liquid has been absorbed and the rice is very moist, about 2 minutes.

6. Add about 1 cup of the hot stock and stir constantly with a heatproof rubber spatula or flat-bottomed wooden spatula until almost all of the stock is absorbed. Adjust the heat to maintain a steady, lively simmer throughout the cooking process. As the liquid is absorbed, continue adding and stirring in more stock, about ⅔ cup at a time, for about 15 minutes.

/continued

RECIPE SECRETS

. . . .

The tomatoes contribute an invaluable acid component here, as well as vibrant color and flavor. Cut them in half through the stem end, so that the brown spot where the stem was won't appear as a blemish. (If you don't cut them, when you bite into one, you'll get an unexpected hot explosion in your mouth.)

. . . .

Traditionally in Italy, you won't find cheese in a risotto or pasta made with fish or shellfish. But this isn't a traditional Italian risotto. Here, the Parmigiano-Reggiano plays a significant role in the overall flavor of the dish, balancing the acid in the tomatoes and bridging the sensation of umami (page 38) from the salmon to the risotto.

7. *Cook the salmon:* While the risotto is cooking, broil the salmon, on one side only, just until almost cooked through, 4 to 5 minutes. It's okay if there isn't much browning on the surface of the fish. Transfer the broiler pan to a cooling rack and tent with aluminum foil until ready to serve.

8. Add the asparagus, peas, and tomatoes to the risotto, then continue adding and stirring in stock, ⅔ cup at a time, until the rice is done. Taste the rice for doneness. It should be tender, but firm to the tooth, and the risotto should be moist and creamy, but not runny. Continue cooking as necessary, tasting the rice frequently, until it's done. You may not need all of the stock.

9. Remove the risotto from the heat. Add the remaining 2 tablespoons butter, the cheese, and 1 tablespoon of the chives. Stir quickly—it's not necessary to mix well—and cover the pot. Let sit for 2 to 3 minutes. Uncover, stir briefly, and taste for seasoning; add salt, if necessary. Spoon risotto into warmed shallow soup plates. Crisscross 2 pieces of salmon on each mound of risotto. Sprinkle evenly with the remaining 1 tablespoon chives and serve immediately.

Saucier pan with sloping sides and no hard-to-reach corners where risotto or polenta might stick

SAVORY BAKED RISOTTO CAKE

A terrific use for leftover Risotto Milanese (page 98) or Butternut Squash Risotto (page 99), this *risotto al forno* (from the oven) is baked in a springform pan with buttered fresh bread crumbs and grated cheese. It's a great make-ahead way to serve risotto, and makes an elegant presentation when cut into bread crumb–encrusted wedges. This serves 8 generously as a side dish, and is rich enough to serve 18 as part of a large buffet (see illustration, page 106). Serve with Garlicky Chicken Breasts (page 176) and bitter greens such as braised escarole (page 263) or Garlic Spinach with Currants, Pine Nuts, and Pecorino (page 265).

Serves 8

Buttered Bread Crumbs

½ pound Pugliese or other dense Italian or French bread (not sour-dough), preferably day-old

3 tablespoons unsalted butter

Kosher salt

Risotto Cake

1 tablespoon unsalted butter, at room temperature, for pan

About 5 cups Risotto Milanese (page 98) or other risotto, at room temperature

½ cup freshly grated Parmigiano-Reggiano or *pecorino romano* cheese

---

RECIPE SECRETS

The ideal risotto cake is about 1 inch high. For a 10-inch springform pan, you'll need about 5 cups of leftover risotto; if you have less risotto, use a smaller pan.

For serving ease, before you butter the springform pan, invert the bottom piece so the lip faces downward (see illustration). It might be a bit trickier to lock the springform in place, but later on it's much easier to slide a cake server onto the pan bottom as you remove each wedge.

1. Preheat the oven to 400 degrees F.

2. *Prepare the bread crumbs:* Using a serrated knife, remove and discard the crusts from the bread and tear the bread into roughly 1-inch pieces. Place in a food processor or blender and grind into crumbs no larger than ¼ inch. For best results, you may have to do this in batches. Melt the butter in a 10-inch nonstick skillet over medium-high heat. When the butter is hot enough to siz-zle a bread crumb on contact, add the bread crumbs and stir constantly until they turn a very pale golden brown, 5 to 7 minutes. Transfer to a bowl (to pre-vent crumbs from browning further). Sprinkle lightly with salt, toss, and set aside. You should have about 2 cups.

/continued

3. *Prepare the risotto cake:* Generously butter the bottom and 1 inch up the sides of a 10-inch springform pan. Using about one-third of the crumbs, cover the bottom of the pan as thoroughly as possible with an even layer of the buttered bread crumbs. Use half of the remaining crumbs to coat the sides of the pan, extending them about 1 inch up from the bottom. It's okay if they don't all stick to the sides. Set aside the remaining crumbs.

4. Using a large, damp spoon, gently transfer the risotto to the bottom of the springform pan, being careful not to disturb the bread crumbs. If you inadvertently dislodge any crumbs from the bottom or sides, fill in the holes with some of the reserved bread crumbs. Dip the bottom of a drinking glass into cold water and press the top of the risotto to form an even, compact cake. Sprinkle the surface with the cheese and cover evenly with the remaining bread crumbs.

5. Place the pan on a baking sheet and bake until the crumbs on top are golden brown and the tip of a paring knife inserted in the center comes out hot, 15 to 20 minutes. Let stand for 5 minutes. Run a knife along the inside edge of the pan before removing the sides of the pan. Place the risotto cake on a serving platter (with pan bottom intact), cut into wedges (or see illustration), and serve immediately.

To serve 18 elegantly, use what's called a catering cut (named for the way caterers cut wedding cakes): Cut a 3-inch circle into the center, then cut the outside ring into 16 pieces. Cut the center circle into 2 pieces.

It's easier to cut and serve from a springform pan bottom if you turn the bottom upside down before locking it in place and filling.

SECRETS FOR COOKING PERFECT PASTA

Each pasta recipe in this chapter features its own particular Secrets. In addition, here are some general tips and answers to some common questions about cooking pasta.

- For the recipes in this book, except where fresh pasta is specified, I recommend using good-quality, imported Italian dried pasta. Typically, Italian pasta is made with just semolina, which is harder than some of the wheat used to make domestic pastas. All-semolina pasta absorbs less water when cooking, which accounts for its characteristic suppleness and distinctive toothsome quality when cooked al dente. I find Italian pastas to be more forgiving during cooking, and more difficult to overcook. American pastas can become gummy or waterlogged if overcooked the slightest bit. Resilient chewiness is the hallmark of properly cooked, or al dente, pasta. For everyday cooking, I recommend Barilla and DeCecco brands. For special occasions, or when I'm feeling flush, I indulge in artisanal imports such as Latini or Rustichella d'Abruzzo brands.

- Always start with fresh water from the cold water tap when cooking pasta. Water from the hot water faucet isn't as fresh because it's been sitting in the hot-water heater.

- Pasta manufacturer Rustichella d'Abruzzo recommends using 1 quart of water to cook every ¼ pound of pasta. Bring the water to a rolling boil in a large pot. For 1 pound of pasta, use a 6-quart pot. A lightweight pot is best because it takes less time for the water to come to the initial boil and to return to a boil after adding the pasta. Add enough salt to flavor the water; it should taste like the ocean. Use 1½ teaspoons fine sea salt or 1 tablespoon Diamond Crystal kosher salt per quart of water. If your pot is stainless steel, it's okay to add the salt as you're heating the water. Salt can leave spotty deposits, known as pitting, on the surface of pans made of other materials. Because salt changes the boiling temperature of water, some chefs and fine cooks wait until the water comes to a boil before adding the salt. This way, they're sure the water is at a true 212 degrees F, which will require less time to return to a boil after the pasta is added. The bottom line is that it's okay to add the salt before the water comes to a boil, as long as the water is at a steady, ferocious rumble when you add the pasta.

- Don't add oil to the pasta water, or the pasta will become slick and repel your sauce. Pasta and sauce should stick together like good partners.

- Stir the pasta into the boiling, salted water with a wooden fork or spoon to prevent it from sticking. When cooking long pasta such as spaghetti, slowly push it down into the water as it collapses—don't break it! (I would consider making an exception about breaking pasta for very small children, but at an early age my mother taught me how to twirl my spaghetti—shouldn't every parent? For me, twirling is still part of the fun of eating the long pastas.)

/continued

- Stir pasta often during cooking and regulate the heat to maintain a steady boil.

- Set a timer for a few minutes less than the cooking time suggested on the pasta package. Taste the pasta every minute after the timer rings until the texture is chewy, without a trace of chalkiness on the inside. Save a cup or so of pasta cooking water to thin the sauce when tossing, if desired. To stop the cooking, pour a glass of cold water into the pot (particularly important if using domestic pasta). Drain the pasta into a colander and shake a few times to dislodge excess water.

- Unless you're cooking pasta ahead for good ol' American macaroni salad or macaroni and cheese, don't rinse it. The starch that clings to the pasta is what makes the sauce adhere to it.

FREQUENTLY ASKED QUESTIONS ABOUT COOKING PASTA

. . . .

Why do restaurant pasta dishes taste so flavorful?

. . . .

First, restaurant chefs use plenty of salt in the water, so the pasta picks up flavor as it cooks. Then, they transfer the pasta to a sauté pan with the hot sauce and both are tossed together over high heat, melding the flavors. There is no question that the open pores of hot pasta absorb flavor better than cold or room-temperature pasta. This is true whether you're tossing pasta with a robust hot sausage and mushroom ragù (page 118) or a delicate room-temperature olive oil dressing, as in Orzo with Toybox Tomatoes and Fresh Mint (page 283).

. . . .

Why is it important to use nonreactive cookware when making pasta dishes with tomato sauce?

. . . .

The term *nonreactive* describes a pot, pan, or dish that is lined with or made of a material that will not react with acids in foods such as tomatoes and lemons. Reactive materials include nonanodized aluminum, cast iron, and unlined copper, while nonreactive materials include—but are not limited to—porcelain, glass, enamel, and stainless steel. Such reaction can cause the food to take on a metallic flavor, and can result in pitting, or the development of small spots on the surface of the vessel.

. . . .

Why does aluminum foil get little holes in it when I use it to cover baked lasagna?

. . . .

The acid in tomatoes causes pitting in aluminum foil, as well as in reactive cookware. If using foil to cover reactive foods, cover first with parchment paper, waxed paper, or plastic wrap, to prevent the foil from pitting. Also, when baking, if the food is high enough in the baking dish to come in contact with foil used as a lid, place a sheet of parchment or waxed paper directly on the food before covering with foil. Use plastic wrap when storing cooked tomato-based dishes.

LINGUINE AGLIO E OLIO

Whenever my grandmother Guglietta served linguine or spaghettini with olive oil and garlic, she had us kids tuck a napkin inside our collars before we were allowed to start twirling the slick strands. She often made *linguine aglio e olio* (pronounced lin-*gwee*-neh *ahl*-yo eh *ol*-yo) on Fridays as an accompaniment to calamari in red sauce (page 144) or other fish dishes, mercifully omitting the red pepper flakes from the kids' servings. I loved this chewy, garlicky pasta so much that "eye-yo oh-yo" was the first lunch I cooked without a recipe as a kid. Somewhere along the line, I mastered the pronunciation and came to appreciate those chile flakes.

Serves 3 or 4 as a side dish	¼ to ½ teaspoon red pepper flakes, divided
⅓ cup bold-tasting extra-virgin olive oil	Kosher salt
3 to 5 large cloves garlic, cut crosswise into thin slices	½ pound dried linguine, vermicelli, or spaghettini

1. Bring a 4-quart pot of water to a boil for the pasta.

2. Set aside a small, fine-mesh strainer on top of a tempered glass or heat-resistant bowl for straining the hot garlic oil.

3. *Prepare the garlic oil:* Place the olive oil and sliced garlic in a heavy 1-quart saucepan or 6-inch skillet. Place over the lowest heat and heat the oil until the garlic starts to turn from golden to dark brown, about 5 minutes. Immediately strain the oil into the reserved bowl and add ¼ teaspoon red pepper flakes to the oil. Discard the garlic chips, or chop and set aside to add to the pasta before serving. Set aside the garlic oil.

4. *Cook the pasta:* Add enough salt to the boiling water to make it taste like the ocean. Cook the pasta according to package directions, stirring occasionally, until al dente. Drain the pasta.

5. Return the empty pasta pot to the turned-off burner. Reserve about 2 tablespoons of the garlic oil. Add the remaining garlic oil to the hot pot. Add 1 teaspoon salt and swirl to blend. Add the hot pasta and toss with tongs to coat evenly with the oil. Taste and add more garlic oil, salt, or red pepper flakes, if necessary. (If there's leftover garlic oil, cover and refrigerate for up to a few days. Use in a stir-fry or to season steamed vegetables.) If desired, add the reserved chopped garlic. Serve immediately in warmed bowls.

RECIPE SECRETS

The secret to bringing out the sweet flavor in garlic when making garlic oil is to heat the sliced cloves as slowly as possible in the oil. As soon as the garlic starts to change from golden to dark brown, take the pan off the heat and strain the oil. Garlic oil is perishable and must be stored in the refrigerator.

Don't underestimate the importance of salt here, in both seasoning the pasta cooking water and bringing out the garlic flavor in the finished dish.

The amount of garlic you use in this dish depends on personal preference. If you find the finished dish isn't strong enough, first add a little salt to bring up the flavors. If desired, toss in the chopped, fried garlic slices from the garlic oil. Or, supplement with a sprinkling of good-quality granulated garlic powder and make a note to use more fresh garlic next time.

Be sure your red pepper flakes aren't left over from the last millennium. This simple preparation depends on their full flavor for a bold, vibrant kick.

ABOUT GARLIC

A member of the lily family, garlic is a summer crop related to chives, shallots, leeks, and onions. White-skinned bulbs of American garlic have the strongest flavor, while mauve-skinned Italian or Mexican garlic tends to be milder. If you notice a green germ, or shoot, growing inside a clove (individual piece) of garlic, remove and discard it. The green germ is part of the natural life cycle of the garlic plant, and appears in garlic that has been stored over the winter. It is not toxic, but has a bitter taste and can cause indigestion. Like chiles, the more you cut garlic, the stronger it tastes. Garlic that is minced in a garlic press can be particularly strong. For mild garlic flavor, gently crush the clove with the side of a knife, or slice. To remove the strong smell of garlic from your hands, rub them over something made of stainless steel, such as a faucet, sink, or bowl.

ABOUT AL DENTE

In Italian, *al dente* (pronounced ahl *den*-teh) means "to the tooth," and is the term used to describe the firm texture of cooked pasta or rice that is resilient when chewed, with no chalkiness or dryness inside. Tasting is the only way to determine whether something is cooked al dente.

BAKED MACARONI WITH WHITE CHEDDAR AND BUTTERED BREAD CRUMBS

When I teach Sauces classes, this adult version of good ol' mac and cheese is the recipe I use to demonstrate the distinctions between béchamel (pronounced *bay*-shah-mel) and Mornay sauces. In béchamel, a white sauce is thickened with roux (pronounced roo), or butter and flour cooked together until the flour loses its raw flavor and the starch grains are coated in fat, making them less likely to become lumpy when milk is ultimately added. Béchamel is one of the classic French "mother," or primary, sauces. (There are four or six mother sauces, depending on whom you listen to.) Mornay sauce is a derivative of béchamel and is made by adding cheese. It was drilled into us in cooking school that in order to make a smooth béchamel, the roux and the milk couldn't both be hot or cold. One had to be the opposite temperature of the other. Since we always scalded the milk first, we were taught to cook the roux, then thinly spread it on a baking sheet, and place it in the freezer to chill quickly. We'd end up breaking off pieces of frozen roux and whisking them with scalded milk. It seemed too complicated for such a simple sauce, so I did some sleuthing and discovered that scalding the milk was a vestige from prepasteurization days. You'll see how simple it is, instead, to add cold pasteurized milk to a hot roux. Voilà! For a quicker, nonbaked version of this recipe, try the Macaroni and Cheese variation that follows.

Serves 6

Mornay Sauce
. . . .

6 tablespoons unsalted butter

5 tablespoons all-purpose flour

3 cups milk (low fat is okay)

2 teaspoons kosher salt

A few shakes of Tabasco sauce or
¼ teaspoon cayenne pepper

2 cups (½ pound) coarsely
shredded sharp white Cheddar
cheese, divided

Macaroni
. . . .

Kosher salt

¾ pound shell macaroni or
other pasta shape

Buttered Bread Crumbs
. . . .

½ pound Pugliese or other dense
Italian or French bread (not sourdough), preferably day old

2 tablespoons unsalted butter

½ teaspoon kosher salt

1. *Prepare the Mornay sauce:* In a heavy 4-quart saucier or saucepan, melt the butter over medium heat. When the foam subsides, whisk in the flour. Cook for 2 minutes, whisking constantly. Add the milk, ¼ cup at a time, whisking constantly. Have faith and continue to whisk as you blend more milk into the lumpy mass. As each addition of milk is absorbed, add more. Once the mixture is smooth, add the remaining milk all at once. Switch to a slotted wooden spoon and stir in a figure-8 pattern over medium heat until the sauce thickens and begins to simmer, 8 to 10 minutes. Drag your finger over the back of the spoon. If the track remains for a bit, rather than filling in immediately, the sauce is done. (At this stage, the sauce is said to be at *nape;* see page 112.) Remove from the heat and stir in the salt and Tabasco or cayenne. To transform this béchamel sauce into Mornay sauce, add 1 cup of the cheese, a little at a time, stirring as you add each handful. Stir until the cheese is melted. Taste and add more salt or Tabasco, if desired. Cover and set aside.

2. Preheat the oven to 375 degrees F. Butter a 9-inch square baking dish with 2-inch sides or other 10-cup baking dish with a large surface area. Set aside.

/continued

RECIPE SECRETS
. . . .

The best pastas for saucy dishes such as this are macaroni shapes that have built-in pockets that allow the sauce to wend its way inside. Elbow macaroni are traditional in mac and cheese, but I like medium-sized shells, penne, *mostaccioli,* or even *gemelli.* Since this recipe calls for only ¾ pound pasta, if you're buying a 1-pound box, choose a shape whose leftovers you're likely to use in a soup or side dish.

. . . .

Here's how to keep pasta firm when preparing dishes that call for boiling the pasta and then baking it in a sauce: Boil it to just before the al dente stage, or about two-thirds of the time specified on the package. The pasta should be firm and chewy, but not hard inside. To stop the cooking immediately, dump a glass of cold water into the pot as soon as the pasta is ready. Then drain into a colander.

. . . .

A flat whisk (see illustration, page 123) is my preferred tool for making roux-based sauces such as béchamel, Mornay, and pan gravy. Its distinctive shape allows all the tines to come in contact with the surface of the saucepan.

. . . .

Use the large holes of a box grater to shred semisoft cheeses such as Cheddar. If you prefer a more traditional orange-tinged mac and cheese, substitute orange Cheddar for the white.

3. *Cook the pasta:* Bring a 4-quart pot of water to a boil. Add enough salt to the boiling water to make it taste like the ocean. Cook the pasta for about two-thirds of the time indicated on the package, stirring occasionally. Drain the pasta, add to the pot of Mornay sauce, and stir to combine. Transfer to the prepared baking dish. Top with the remaining 1 cup cheese and set aside.

4. *Prepare the buttered bread crumbs:* Using a serrated knife, remove and discard the crusts from the bread (see page 106). Tear the bread into roughly 1-inch pieces. Process in a food processor or blender, grinding into crumbs no larger than ½ inch. Melt the butter in a 10-inch nonstick skillet over medium-high heat. When the butter is hot enough to sizzle a bread crumb on contact, add the bread crumbs and stir constantly until they turn a very pale golden brown, 5 to 7 minutes. Sprinkle with salt and toss. Strew the crumbs evenly over the cheese-topped pasta.

5. Bake, uncovered, until the casserole is piping hot throughout (insert a butter knife in the center and touch the knife blade to see if it's hot enough) and the crumbs are golden brown, about 30 minutes. Let rest for 5 minutes to set up a bit before serving.

MACARONI AND CHEESE VARIATION
. . . .

Omit the bread crumbs. Proceed as directed for cooking the pasta and making the Mornay sauce, adding all the cheese to the sauce. After combining the pasta and sauce, reheat over medium heat, stirring constantly with a heatproof rubber spatula until the pasta is piping hot.

FETTUCCINE ALFREDO WITH BABY SHRIMP AND PEAS

Pasta doesn't get much richer than fettuccine Alfredo. This cream sauce was first prepared in Rome by Alfredo di Lelio in the early 1900s using triple-rich heavy (whipping) cream, known in the United States as manufacturing cream. You can buy manufacturing cream at Smart and Final or other stores frequented by restaurateurs and caterers. If you use manufacturing cream, the sauce will be thick enough that you can omit the egg yolks. If serving the fettuccine as a main course, accompany with Weeknight Green Salad (page 81), lightly dressed with robust olive oil and good vinegar. If serving as a first course, omit the shrimp and peas and follow the pasta with a light main dish, such as grilled fish or Garlicky Chicken Breasts (page 176) and braised escarole (page 263). Be sure to have all the ingredients prepped, the serving plates warming in the oven, and your guests seated when you start the Alfredo sauce, as this recipe comes together quickly at the end and is best served piping hot before the eggs have a chance to scramble. For a colorful variation, fold in a big handful of steamed small broccoli florets just before adding the eggs.

Serves 8 as a first course, or 4 to 6 as a main course

Kosher salt	½ pound (2 cups) cooked bay (salad-sized) shrimp
1 pound dried fettuccine	1 cup fresh English peas, cooked, or thawed, frozen petite peas
½ cup (1 stick) unsalted butter	
3 cups heavy (whipping) cream	3 large egg yolks, lightly beaten
Coarse, freshly ground black pepper	1 cup freshly grated Parmigiano-Reggiano cheese, plus more for garnish

---

1. Bring a 6-quart pot of water to a boil. Add enough salt to the boiling water to make it taste like the ocean. Cook the pasta according to the package directions, stirring occasionally, until al dente.

/continued

RECIPE SECRETS

Good-quality butter and cream make a difference here. Look for European-style or organic butter and pure heavy (whipping) cream with no additives.

Because egg yolks serve as a liaison to thicken and bind the sauce, and they are not fully cooked in this recipe, use pasteurized eggs if you're planning to serve this to young children, the elderly, or people with compromised immune systems.

If using fresh English peas, figure on 1 pound peas in the shell to yield about 1 cup shelled peas. Before adding the peas to the sauce, cook them in salted boiling water until tender, a couple of minutes, and then drain and shock them in an ice-water bath to set the color (page 33).

Pronged pasta serving spoon

2. While the pasta cooks, in a 12-inch or larger sauté pan or Dutch oven large enough to hold the cooked pasta and sauce, melt the butter over low heat. Just before the butter is completely melted, add the cream, raise the heat to medium-high, and bring to a boil, swirling the pan to incorporate the ingredients. By adding the cream before the butter melts completely and separates, you ensure that the sauce will stay emulsified. Watch carefully, and reduce the heat as soon as the cream boils to prevent it from boiling over. Season the sauce with salt and pepper to taste.

3. As soon as the pasta is done, use a pasta serving spoon (with "teeth" to grab the pasta; see illustration, left) and a Chinese strainer to drain and transfer the pasta from the water to the sauce. If the pasta is done before the cream comes to a boil, reserve about 1 cup of the pasta cooking liquid and let the pasta drain in a colander in the sink.

4. Use tongs to toss the pasta with the sauce, then bring to a boil over medium heat, reduce the heat to low, and cook until the sauce is just thick enough to lightly coat the pasta, just 1 minute or so. The sauce will thicken more once you add the egg yolks and cheese. Add the shrimp and peas.

5. Add a spoonful of the sauce to the egg yolks to temper them and stir to combine. Using a heatproof rubber spatula, stir the egg yolks into the pasta over the lowest heat. If the sauce is too thick, thin it with a little of the reserved pasta cooking water. Remove from the heat, sprinkle in the 1 cup cheese, and toss with the tongs. Divide immediately among warmed shallow bowls and sprinkle each serving with additional cheese and pepper. Serve at once.

SPAGHETTI AND MEATBALLS WITH 20-MINUTE TOMATO SAUCE

I've never actually taught a recipe for spaghetti and meatballs in a cooking class. But when I make *timpano* (page 126), it's not uncommon for people to remark about the unusual tenderness of the meatballs. So here it is, my version of the Italian American favorite, adapted from my mother's and grandmother's recipes. When I was a child, we ate either spaghetti or macaroni and meatballs once a week for supper. Whoever set the table or grated the cheese got to choose which shape we'd have: spaghetti, which included any variety of long pasta such as long *fusilli,* linguine, capellini, and so on, or short shapes of macaroni such as *ziti,* rigatoni, *farfalle, mostaccioli,* or the like. We never called it pasta in those days; it was either spaghetti or macaroni. Whichever you choose, for the authentic comingling of flavors and to keep the pasta pieces separate, toss it with a little sauce and grated cheese before serving. You'll most likely have some leftover sauce, which you can put to good use in Weeknight Chili (page 245), Eggplant Parmigiana (page 259), Chicken Thighs Parmigiana (page 180), Braised Calamari in Red Sauce (page 144), or Pot Roast and Gravy with Peas and Carrots (page 241). Or just freeze it for a rainy day. You'll be glad you did.

RECIPE SECRETS

For the best texture, purée the tomatoes in a food mill, food processor, or blender. Your sauce will be so thick and smooth you won't need to add tomato paste.

. . . .

The secret to tender meatballs is twofold: don't squeeze the meat mixture too much, and simmer—don't boil—the meatballs gently in the sauce. As is the case with any braised dish, boiling toughens protein fibers.

. . . .

Be sure to mince the onions no larger than ¼ inch for the meatballs and the sauce. Then, for the sauce, be sure the onions are soft, tender, and translucent before you add the tomatoes. The acid in the tomatoes would impede their softening further, and you don't want crunchy onions in your tomato sauce.

Serves 4 to 6

20-Minute Tomato Sauce
. . . .

3 cans (28 ounces each) imported San Marzano tomatoes with juice

2 tablespoons mild-tasting extra-virgin olive oil

1 yellow onion, chopped into ¼-inch pieces

½ teaspoon dried leaf oregano, crumbled between your fingers

2 cloves garlic, crushed with the side of a chef's knife or minced

1 bay leaf, preferably imported

2 teaspoons kosher salt

¼ teaspoon freshly ground pepper

2 tablespoons chopped fresh flat-leaf parsley, divided

1 fresh basil sprig

1 teaspoon sugar (optional)

Meatballs
. . . .

3 slices day-old Italian or French bread (not sourdough), ½ inch thick, crusts removed

3 to 4 tablespoons milk (nonfat or low fat okay)

4 tablespoons mild-tasting extra-virgin olive oil, divided

½ cup finely chopped yellow onion

1 ¼ teaspoons kosher salt, divided

1 large egg

¼ cup freshly grated Romano cheese

1 tablespoon finely chopped fresh flat-leaf parsley

¼ teaspoon granulated garlic powder

⅛ teaspoon fine, freshly ground black pepper

1¼ pounds ground beef chuck

Pasta
. . . .

Kosher salt

1 pound spaghetti or other dried pasta shape of choice

¾ cup freshly grated Romano or Parmesan cheese, preferably imported

/continued

1. *Prepare the tomato sauce:* Pass the tomatoes and their packing juices through a food mill fitted with the medium disk into a bowl. Use a rubber spatula to scrape the underside of the food mill, capturing all of the purée. Discard the seeds and cores. Alternatively, remove the cores by hand and purée the tomatoes and packing juices in a food processor or blender, then pass through a medium-mesh strainer. Set aside.

2. Heat a heavy 6-quart pot over medium heat. Add the olive oil. When the oil is hot enough to sizzle a piece of onion, add the onion and sauté until soft and translucent, but not brown, 6 to 8 minutes. Add the oregano and garlic and sauté for 1 minute, stirring often so the garlic doesn't brown.

3. Add the puréed tomatoes, bay leaf, salt, and pepper, raise the heat to high, and bring to a boil. Reduce the heat to low and add half of the parsley and the basil sprig. Cover partially and simmer until the sauce no longer has a watery consistency, about 15 minutes. Taste and add the sugar, if necessary, to reduce acidity, and more salt and pepper, if necessary. (The sauce can be prepared up to 48 hours ahead. Let cool completely, then cover and refrigerate if making more than 4 hours ahead. Reheat to a gentle simmer before continuing.)

4. *Prepare the meatballs:* Tear the bread into roughly 1-inch pieces and place in a medium bowl. Pour 3 tablespoons milk over the bread and let stand until the bread is moistened, about 10 minutes. Squeeze the bread with your fingers; if it feels dry, add the remaining 1 tablespoon milk. Shred the bread into roughly ¼- to ½-inch pieces and set aside in the bowl.

5. Heat a 12-inch sauté pan or skillet over medium heat. Add 1 tablespoon of the oil. When oil is hot enough to sizzle a piece of onion, add the onion and sauté, stirring occasionally, until soft and translucent, but not brown, 6 to 8 minutes. Reduce the heat to low, sprinkle the onion with about ¼ teaspoon of the salt, and continue cooking until the onion begins to get sticky, about 5 more minutes. Remove the pan from the heat and set aside.

6. In a small bowl, mix the egg lightly with a fork. Add the cheese, parsley, the remaining 1 teaspoon salt, the garlic powder, and pepper and stir with the fork to combine. Transfer to the bowl holding the bread and stir to combine. Add the ground beef and sautéed onion and mix with a fork or your hands until all the ingredients are evenly incorporated.

7. Shape a little of the mixture into a small patty and fry (or microwave) to test for seasoning. Taste and add more cheese, salt, pepper, and/or garlic powder, if necessary, to bring the flavors into balance.

8. Using a 2-inch or smaller ice-cream scoop, form the meatball mixture into 12 to 16 meatballs, depending on preferred size. As they are formed, place them on a plate. Dip your hands in a bowl of cold water to prevent the mixture from sticking as you gently compress and shape the balls between your palms. (The meatballs can be prepared up to 24 hours ahead. If preparing more than 1 hour in advance, cover tightly with plastic wrap and refrigerate.)

9. Return the pan used for cooking the onions to medium heat. Add the remaining 3 tablespoons oil. When the oil is hot, add the meatballs and sauté until nicely browned on all sides, about 15 minutes total. Use a splatter guard or cover adjacent burners with aluminum foil to make cleanup easier. Do not crowd the meatballs in the pan; instead, brown them in batches if necessary. To preserve the crusty exterior, use a fork or thin metal spatula to turn the meatballs, first loosening them on the bottom before turning. Transfer to a plate (it's okay to use the same plate you used for the raw meatballs).

10. Bring the sauce to a steady simmer over medium heat and add the meatballs one by one. To keep them tender, regulate the heat as necessary to maintain a steady simmer. Simmer gently, stirring occasionally, until the meatballs are cooked through and steaming hot inside, about 10 minutes. Stir in the remaining 1 tablespoon parsley. Keep warm.

11. *Prepare the pasta:* Bring a 6-quart pot of water to a boil for the pasta. Add enough salt to the boiling water to make it taste like the ocean. Cook the pasta according to package directions, stirring occasionally, until al dente. Drain the pasta and return it to the pot. Place on a turned-off burner.

12. Remove and discard the bay leaf, basil sprig, and the crushed garlic, if used, from the tomato sauce. Add about 1 cup of the sauce and ¼ cup of the cheese to the pasta and toss well with a spoon or tongs. Transfer to a heated shallow pasta serving bowl, top with a ladle or two of sauce, and sprinkle with a tablespoon or so of the remaining cheese. Arrange the meatballs on top. Fill a warmed bowl with the remaining sauce and put the remaining grated cheese in another bowl. Pass the sauce and cheese at the table for each diner to add as desired.

ABOUT FLAT-LEAF PARSLEY

Also called Italian parsley, this herb has a distinctive, fresh, vibrant flavor, especially in contrast to its ubiquitous, far milder curly-leaf cousin. The leaves of flat-leaf parsley are sturdy and can withstand rather vigorous chopping without turning brown; the stems are used in bouquets garnis. Parsley imbues cooked and raw foods with a characteristic fresh flavor; a sprig, or individual stem, is sometimes eaten as a palate or breath freshener after eating garlic. To store a bunch of parsley, shake off any moisture, wrap in a paper towel, place in a plastic bag, squeeze out as much air as possible, and refrigerate for up to 2 weeks. The leaves from 3 large parsley sprigs yield about 1 tablespoon chopped.

RECIPE SECRETS

To prevent mushrooms from absorbing oil when you sauté them, be sure to heat the pan, then add the oil, and wait until the oil is hot before adding the mushrooms. Once you add the mushrooms, let them sit, undisturbed, so they can brown. Don't start stirring until they brown on the bottom, unless you want them to steam instead of caramelize. Follow these directions and you'll end up with flavorful mushrooms and nice *fond*—or caramelization—in the bottom of the pan.

To keep the sausage tender and juicy, don't let the sauce boil. A steady simmer is all it takes to cook down the tomatoes and marry the flavors.

To remove the casing from a fresh sausage, slit it lengthwise with a paring knife and slip it off in one piece, as if you're taking off a baby's jacket.

Be sure the onion is soft before adding the tomatoes. Otherwise, the acid in the tomatoes will impede the onions from softening further and you'll end up with crunchy onions.

RIGATONI with SAUSAGE and MUSHROOM RAGÙ

This hardy tomato, sausage, and mushroom ragù is a versatile sauce that works well with any sturdy macaroni shape such as *ziti, mostaccioli,* penne, or even frozen cheese ravioli. Any leftover sauce makes a respectable topping for home-made or purchased pizza crust, especially a cornmeal crust with a few roasted peppers and provolone layered on top. Serve with simple Weeknight Green Salad (page 81), or make the Baked Rigatoni with Sausage and Mushrooms variation that follows and take a rib-sticking casserole to your next potluck supper. To make the casserole ahead, cook the sauce and pasta, transfer to a baking dish, and refrigerate for up to 24 hours. Reheat, covered, in an oven preheated to 325 degrees F until piping hot in the center, then top with mozzarella as directed in the variation and return to the oven just long enough to melt the cheese.

Serves 8 to 10

3 tablespoons extra-virgin olive oil, divided

½ pound fresh white or brown mushrooms, sliced ½ inch thick

1 pound fresh (not smoked) sweet or hot Italian sausages, casings removed

1 cup water, divided

1 small yellow onion, chopped

1 clove garlic, green germ removed if present, minced

1 teaspoon dried leaf oregano, crumbled between your fingers

Pinch of red pepper flakes

½ cup tomato paste

1 can (28 ounces) crushed tomatoes with juice

3 tablespoons chopped fresh flat-leaf parsley, divided

Kosher salt

½ teaspoon freshly ground black pepper

¼ to ½ teaspoon sugar (optional)

1 pound rigatoni or other macaroni

½ cup freshly grated Romano or Parmesan cheese, preferably imported, divided

---

1. Heat a 6-quart Dutch oven or heavy 12-inch sauté pan over medium-high heat. Add 2 tablespoons of the olive oil. When the oil is hot enough to sizzle a mushroom slice, add the mushrooms and sauté until browned on both sides, about 8 minutes total. Transfer the mushrooms to a small bowl and set aside.

2. Add the sausages and ½ cup of the water to the pan and, using a flat-bottomed wooden spatula, break them into small pieces. Cook over medium-high heat, stirring occasionally, until the water evaporates, about 5 minutes. Add the remaining 1 tablespoon olive oil and the onion and sauté until the onion is soft and translucent and beginning to brown at the edges, about 10 minutes. Add the garlic, oregano, and red pepper flakes and sauté for 1 minute, stirring frequently to prevent the garlic from browning. Add the tomato paste and stir, dislodging any browned bits from the bottom of the pan. Add the tomatoes, reserved mushrooms and any mushroom juices, 1 table-spoon of the parsley, 1 teaspoon salt, and the pepper. Rinse the tomato can with the remaining ½ cup water and add to the pan. Bring to a boil, reduce the heat to a steady simmer, cover partially, and cook, stirring occasionally, for 15 minutes. Add 1 tablespoon of the remaining parsley. Taste the sauce and adjust the seasoning, adding salt if the tomatoes taste bitter or if the sauce tastes flat. Add ¼ teaspoon sugar if the tomatoes taste acidic, and then add more if necessary. Add black pepper or red pepper flakes if you want a spicier sauce. If the sauce seems too thin, continue to simmer, uncovered, until you achieve the desired consistency, usually about 5 more minutes. Reduce the heat to the lowest setting.

3. Bring a 6-quart pot of water to boil for the pasta. Add enough salt to the boiling water to make it taste like the ocean. Cook the pasta according to package directions, stirring occasionally, until al dente. Reserve about ½ cup of the pasta cooking liquid. Drain the pasta.

4. Add the pasta to the sauce and toss to combine. If the mixture seems too thick, thin with some of the reserved pasta water. Add ¼ cup of the cheese, toss, and transfer to a warmed serving bowl or individual shallow bowls. Garnish with the remaining ¼ cup cheese and 1 tablespoon parsley. Serve immediately.

BAKED RIGATONI WITH SAUSAGE AND MUSHROOMS VARIATION
. . . .

Prepare as directed, but transfer the sauced pasta to a 9-by-13-inch baking dish. Top evenly with ½ pound low-moisture mozzarella, coarsely shredded, and then sprinkle with the remaining ¼ cup grated cheese. Bake in an oven preheated to 325 degrees F just until the mozzarella melts and begins to bubble, about 5 minutes. Sprinkle with the remaining 1 tablespoon parsley and serve piping hot.

HOW TO CLEAN MUSHROOMS

There's a bit of controversy about how to clean mushrooms. Some chefs claim that mushrooms become waterlogged if immersed in water, while others swear that notion is a myth. Personally, if I can wipe them sufficiently clean with a quick swipe of a paper towel or soft-bristled brush, I'm satisfied. If they're really schmutzy, I give them a quick swish in a bowl of lukewarm water (cold water seems to make the dirt cling), lift them out with my fingers into a strainer, and quickly wipe them dry with an old kitchen towel or paper towels.

TOMATO PASTE IN A TUBE

You can't beat tomato paste in a tube for vibrant tomato flavor and convenience. Squeeze out what you need, screw the cap back on tightly, and refrigerate. Imported from Italy, the tubes are packaged in long cardboard boxes. Look for them beside the canned tomato paste in specialty food markets and Italian delicatessens. Don't mistake the saltier, sun-dried tomato paste for plain tomato paste.

BAKED STUFFED MANICOTTI

This recipe was created by my beloved grandmother Guglietta using the ricotta and mozzarella cheeses that my grandfather made in his commercial dairy in Hartford, Connecticut. These ricotta-filled crepes are incomparably light and delicate, and nothing at all like the thick, cardboardlike tubes of dried pasta you can buy in a box labeled manicotti. While these are terrific when eaten the day they're made, they're even better after the flavors have had a chance to meld. Reheat, covered, in a 325 degree F oven until they are piping hot in the center, 30 to 45 minutes. To make this recipe ahead, cover and refrigerate the stuffed crepes up to 24 hours before topping them with sauce and baking. Over the years, these manicotti have been served at all sorts of important family events. I hope your family and friends enjoy them as much as we do.

**Makes 15 to 18 manicotti;
serves 6 to 8 as a main course,
or 15 to 18 as a first course**

Crepes

1 cup water

3 large eggs

1 teaspoon mild-tasting extra-virgin olive oil, plus more for pan

1 cup all-purpose flour

Pinch of salt

1 tablespoon chopped fresh flat-leaf parsley

½ teaspoon kosher salt

¼ teaspoon fine, freshly ground black pepper

¼ teaspoon sugar

2 large eggs, lightly beaten

2 teaspoons unsalted butter, for baking dishes

Filling

1½ pounds (about 3 cups) whole-milk ricotta cheese, any excess liquid at top of carton drained off

½ pound fresh whole-milk mozzarella cheese, cut into roughly ½-inch dice

3 tablespoons freshly grated Romano cheese, or more if needed

Assembly

About 6 cups 20-Minute Tomato Sauce (page 114)

Freshly grated Romano cheese, for garnish

1 tablespoon chopped fresh flat-leaf parsley, for garnish

1. *Prepare the crepe batter:* Place the water, eggs, 1 teaspoon oil, flour, and salt in a blender and blend at medium speed until mixed thoroughly. Scrape down the sides of the blender and blend for a few more seconds. Strain through a fine-mesh strainer into a 1-quart liquid measure or medium bowl, cover, and refrigerate for at least 1 hour, or until all bubbles disappear. (It's okay to refrigerate the batter overnight; stir it if it separates.)

2. *Prepare the crepes:* Place a 2-foot length of waxed paper on a flat surface near the stove. Keep the roll of waxed paper handy. Heat a 6-inch crepe pan or skillet over medium-high heat. Using a paper towel, rub about ¼ teaspoon oil over the surface of the pan. When the pan is hot, pour in a scant ¼ cup crepe batter while simultaneously lifting and tilting the pan to distribute the batter evenly over the entire surface. Don't worry if there are spots where the batter doesn't cover the bottom of the pan. For delicate crepes, it's better to have too little batter than too much. Return the pan to the burner and cook just until the edges of the crepe start to curl and the center is dry to the touch, 30 to 45 seconds. Do not let the crepe brown. Run the tines of a fork between the edges of the crepe and the pan to release the crepe. With your fingers, turn the crepe and cook on the second side just until dry, about 10 seconds. Slide the crepe onto the waxed paper and straighten it out, if necessary. It's not unusual for the first crepe to be too dark or too thick, so that you have to discard it. Cook the remaining crepe batter in the same manner, placing the crepes in a single layer on as many sheets of waxed paper as needed. Once the crepes are cool, it's okay to stack the sheets of crepes. You should end up with 15 to 18 usable crepes. They can be made up to 24 hours ahead, covered, and kept in a cool, dry place.

3. *Prepare the filling:* In a bowl, stir together the ricotta, mozzarella, 3 tablespoons Romano cheese, the parsley, salt, pepper, and sugar. Taste and adjust the seasoning, adding more grated cheese, if necessary, to heighten the flavor. Add the eggs and mix to blend completely. The filling can be made up to 24 hours ahead, covered, and refrigerated.

4. *Assemble the manicotti:* Preheat the oven to 325 degrees F. Butter 2 baking dishes, one 9 by 13 inches and the other 8 or 9 inches square. (Porcelain or clay baking dishes retain heat best.)

/continued

RECIPE SECRETS

Make the crepe batter an hour ahead so the gluten in the flour can relax. This keeps the crepes tender.

For the lightest manicotti, make the crepes very thin by using as little batter as possible for each one. Each crepe should be so thin that you can see your fingers through it when you hold it up to the light.

The best-tasting manicotti are made with fresh, creamy whole-milk ricotta cheese. I find part-skim ricotta to be too grainy. Look for top-quality ricotta at specialty-cheese shops and Italian markets. It's rather perishable once opened, so buy just as much as you'll use in a few days. In this recipe, I prefer the more widely available cow's milk ricotta over the drier, artisanal sheep's milk cheese that is sometimes available.

5. Check to be sure that each crepe separates easily from the waxed paper. Use a blunt table knife, if necessary, to free them. Divide the filling equally among the crepes, placing about 2 heaping tablespoons in a strip down the center of each. Lift one side of a crepe and fold it loosely over the filling. Repeat with the other side, forming a cylinder with two open ends. Do not roll the crepes or tuck the ends underneath; they should stay open for the filling to expand as it bakes. Shape the remaining manicotti in the same way. Transfer, seam side down, to the buttered baking dishes. Turn the outside edges of the ends down into the pan as you place the manicotti closely beside one another. (The recipe can be made to this point up to 24 hours in advance. Cover and refrigerate. Bring to room temperature before continuing.)

6. Top the manicotti with a very light layer of about 2 cups of the tomato sauce, saving some sauce for serving. Cover with aluminum foil and bake until bubbles appear in the center and around the edges of the baking dishes and the manicotti are puffy and piping hot inside, 30 to 35 minutes.

7. Let the manicotti stand for 5 minutes for the filling to set before serving. Reheat the remaining tomato sauce. Use an offset spatula (a narrow icing spatula works well) to remove the manicotti from the baking dishes. Serve 1 or 2 manicotti per person, topped with a spoonful of hot sauce, a light sprinkling of grated cheese, and some chopped parsley.

LASAGNA BOLOGNESE

. . . .

The first time I ever tasted true Italian lasagna made with fresh pasta, béchamel, and meaty, rich ragù like this, I was stunned by how different it was from the towering school-cafeteria versions made with curly dried noodles, cottage cheese, and lots of stringy mozzarella. My mother never made lasagna until I was in high school; instead, for holidays and special occasions, we ate manicotti. I've made this Italian classic with both fresh spinach and "plain" fresh pasta sheets. You don't necessarily taste the spinach, but the finished dish is exponentially better when made with spinach pasta. If you have access to fresh egg pasta, spinach or not, use it. If you don't, use dried lasagna noodles made with semolina. I often prepare this lasagna for friends who don't eat red meat by omitting the pancetta and substituting ground dark-meat chicken for the sausage in my version of Bolognese sauce. It gets rave reviews. This lasagna is particularly tasty when prepared and baked up to 2 days ahead, then reheated before serving. If you do so, cool the lasagna to room temperature, cover, and refrigerate. Be sure to remove it from the refrigerator at least 1 hour before reheating. Cut it into serving portions while it is still cold, then cover and bake in a preheated 400 degree F oven until piping hot in the center. Serve with Weeknight Green Salad (page 81) and open a bottle of Zinfandel.

Serves 6

Béchamel Sauce
. . . .

6 tablespoons unsalted butter

5 tablespoons all-purpose flour

3 cups milk (low fat is okay)

1 teaspoon kosher salt

⅛ teaspoon white pepper or dash of Tabasco sauce

Lasagna
. . . .

About 1 tablespoon unsalted butter, for baking dish

Kosher salt

4 sheets (about 1 pound) fresh spinach or egg pasta, or ½ pound dried lasagna noodles

About 3 cups "Bolognese" Sauce (page 124)

1 cup freshly grated Parmigiano-Reggiano cheese

RECIPE SECRETS

. . . .

For lump-free béchamel sauce, add cold milk to hot roux. A flat whisk is my preferred tool for making béchamel sauce and pan gravies.

. . . .

I've been teaching this recipe in my Classic Italian Comfort Foods classes for years. As is traditional, this recipe calls for stirring together the creamy white béchamel sauce with the chunky, red, meaty Bolognese ragù before layering the pasta and sauce. Every so often, the class decides they'd rather layer the two distinct sauces separately. To be honest, I love both versions.

1. *Prepare the béchamel sauce:* In a heavy 2-quart saucier or saucepan, melt the butter over medium heat. When the foam subsides, whisk in the flour. Cook for 2 minutes, whisking constantly. Add the milk, ¼ cup at a time, whisking constantly. Have faith and continue whisking as you blend more milk into the lumpy mass. As each addition of milk is absorbed, add more. Once the mixture is smooth, add the remaining milk all at once. Switch to a slotted wooden spoon and stir in a figure-8 pattern over medium heat until the sauce thickens and begins to simmer, 8 to 10 minutes. Drag your finger over the back of the spoon. If the track remains for a bit, rather than filling in immediately, the sauce is done. (At this stage, the sauce is considered to have reached *napé.*) Add the salt and white pepper. Place a piece of parchment or waxed paper directly on the surface of the béchamel and set aside.

2. *Prepare the lasagna:* Position a rack in the top third of the oven and preheat to 400 degrees F. Generously butter the bottom and sides of a 9-by-13-inch or 11-by-13-inch baking dish. Set aside.

3. Bring a 6-quart pot of water to a boil for the pasta. Add enough salt to the boiling water to make it taste like the ocean. Set a large bowl of cold water on the counter near the stove to rinse excess starch off the pasta after it cooks. Have ready several clean, dry kitchen towels (not terrycloth) on which to dry the pasta. If using fresh pasta sheets, cut in half lengthwise before boiling.

Flat whisk

/continued

4. Cook half of the pasta in the boiling, salted water until just before the al dente stage, about 3 minutes for fresh pasta and about two-thirds the time indicated on the package for dried pasta, stirring occasionally. Use a Chinese strainer to transfer the cooked pasta to the bowl of cold water, separating the pieces with your fingers. When the pasta is cool to the touch, lay each piece flat on a kitchen towel. Repeat cooking, cooling, and drying the remaining pasta.

5. In a bowl, stir together the béchamel and Bolognese sauces. You should have about 8 cups sauce.

6. Spread a couple of tablespoons of sauce on the bottom of the buttered baking dish (to make serving easier). Arrange a single layer of cooked pasta in the dish. You may have to cut the pasta to fit; don't overlap the pieces by more than ¼ inch. Gently spread about 2 cups of the sauce mixture over the pasta, covering it with a thin layer. Sprinkle with ¼ cup of the cheese. Repeat layering the remaining pasta, sauce, and cheese, ending with sauce and grated cheese. There should be 4 layers.

7. Bake the lasagna until it is piping hot in the center and bubbling around the edges, 20 to 30 minutes. The tip of a paring knife inserted into the center should come out hot when the lasagna is done. If your lasagna comes right up to the top of the dish, you may want to place a baking sheet on the oven rack beneath it during baking to catch any drips as it bubbles. Let sit for 10 minutes before cutting; the lasagna will "set up" and be easier to cut and serve.

"BOLOGNESE" SAUCE

Versatile and bold, Bolognese (pronounced bow-lohn-*yay*-seh) sauce is named after Italy's culinary capital, Bologna. Typically, this rich meat, tomato, and vegetable ragù is served with broad tagliatelle pasta, over a bed of soft polenta (page 274), or layered with fresh pasta sheets and béchamel sauce in a classic Lasagna Bolognese (page 122). My version calls for Italian sausage, rather than the traditional ground veal or beef. Feel free to use either kind of meat, or a combination, or use ground dark-meat chicken and omit the pancetta for non-red-meat eaters. As a further departure from tradition, I add garlic, herbs, and spices, so technically, this isn't an authentic Bolognese sauce (thus the quotation marks). If you're lucky enough to have any sauce left over, freeze it to use as a quick and hardy topping for homemade pizza.

**Makes about 3 cups sauce
(enough for 1 pound of pasta)**

1 can (28 ounces) imported San
Marzano tomatoes with juice

2 tablespoons extra-virgin
olive oil

1 yellow onion, finely chopped

1 slice pancetta, ¼ inch thick,
cut into julienne

1 carrot, peeled and finely
chopped

1 celery stalk, peeled and finely
chopped

1 pound fresh (not smoked)
sweet or hot Italian sausages,
casings removed

3 cloves garlic, green germ
removed if present, minced

2 tablespoons chopped fresh
flat-leaf parsley, divided

1 teaspoon dried leaf oregano,
crumbled between your fingers

¼ teaspoon fennel seeds

¼ to ½ teaspoon red pepper
flakes

Kosher salt and freshly ground
black pepper

½ cup dry white wine

1 fresh basil sprig

½ teaspoon sugar (optional)

1. Pass the tomatoes and their packing juices through a food mill fitted with
the medium disk into a bowl. Use a rubber spatula to scrape the underside of
the food mill, capturing all the purée. Discard the seeds and cores. Alternatively,
remove the cores by hand and purée the tomatoes and packing juices in a food
processor or blender, then pass through a medium-mesh strainer. Set aside.

2. Heat a heavy 4-quart pot over medium-high heat. Add the olive oil. When
the oil is hot enough to sizzle a piece of onion, add the onion, pancetta, carrot,
and celery and sauté until the onion is soft and translucent, about 8 minutes.

3. Add the sausages and, using a flat-bottomed wooden spatula, break them up
into small pieces. Cook over medium-high heat just until the meat is no longer
pink, 3 to 5 minutes.

4. Add the garlic, 1 tablespoon of the parsley, the oregano, fennel seeds, red
pepper flakes, 1 teaspoon salt, and ¼ teaspoon black pepper. Sauté for
1 minute, stirring to prevent the garlic from burning. Raise the heat to high
and add the wine all at once. Cook, stirring to deglaze the pan, until the wine
evaporates, about 3 minutes.

/continued

RECIPE SECRETS

For the most tender, succulent meat
sauce, simmer the sauce gently, as boiling toughens proteins.

Pancetta is cured, but not smoked,
Italian bacon. Look for pancetta in fine
delicatessens and ask the clerk to cut it
into ¼-inch-thick slices. To julienne
pancetta, unroll the slice and cut crosswise into matchstick-sized pieces.

To soften the prominent vegetal flavor
of celery, use a swivel-blade vegetable
peeler to remove the outside layer of
strings from the rounded side of the
stalk.

Be sure the onions are very soft before
you add the wine. The acid in both the
wine and tomatoes will impede further
softening.

To achieve a smooth, thick tomato
purée without the addition of tomato
paste, pass the tomatoes through a food
mill or purée in a food processor or
blender.

To remove the casing from a fresh
sausage, slit it lengthwise with a paring
knife and slip it off in one piece, as if
you're taking off a baby's jacket.

5. Add the puréed tomatoes and basil and bring to a boil. Reduce the heat to low, cover partially, and cook at a steady, gentle simmer, stirring occasionally, until a saucelike consistency is achieved, 35 to 45 minutes. Add the remaining 1 tablespoon parsley during final few minutes of cooking. Taste and adjust the seasoning, if necessary. If the tomatoes taste acidic, stir in the optional sugar. If they taste bitter, stir in some salt. Remove and discard the basil sprig before serving.

RECIPE SECRETS

. . . .

The first sturdy *pasta frolla*–type crust I tried when developing this recipe called for ½ cup sugar, which seemed odd in a savory recipe, but I tried it anyway. Much to my surprise, the sweetness balanced quite nicely with the acid in the tomato sauce. I've since cut back to ¼ cup sugar, but if you dislike the idea of a sweet note in the crust, omit the sugar entirely.

. . . .

If you cannot find canned San Marzano tomatoes (see page 116), substitute three 26½-ounce boxes Pomi brand chopped tomatoes or, to save time, use 3 quarts top-quality prepared tomato sauce.

. . . .

In this recipe, the meatballs are shaped into walnut-sized balls and dropped into simmering tomato sauce without frying them first. Use a small ice-cream scoop to create balls of uniform size. The secret to tender meatballs is twofold: do not handle the mixture any more than necessary to blend the ingredients together, and simmer the meatballs gently in the sauce.

DOUBLE-CRUSTED TIMPANO WITH FUSILLI, RICOTTA, AND TENDER LITTLE MEATBALLS

. . . .

I figure I've made at least a hundred *timpani* since I started offering classes based on the 1990s cult film *Big Night*. Inspired by the pièce de résistance in the movie, I developed this recipe with the assistance of a few esteemed colleagues, including fellow cooking teachers Nelly Capra, David McKey, and Weezie Mott. In this foolproof version, a savory pastry drum constructed in a springform pan encases macaroni, meatballs, three cheeses, peas, hard-cooked eggs, and tomato sauce. The recipe works well in a hands-on cooking class because there are many components for people to get involved in, and the results are spectacular. Likewise, I encourage you to gather a group of friends or family members, put on some Italian music, open a bottle of wine, and spend a few hours preparing your very own *timpano*. You'll be rewarded with a mouth-watering masterpiece, and you'll have lots of fun—and create new memories—in the process.

Serves 10 to 12

Pastry Dough

2 large whole eggs

3 large egg yolks (reserve 2 egg whites for making meatballs)

Scant 3 cups all-purpose flour

¼ cup sugar

1½ teaspoons kosher salt

1 cup cold unsalted butter, plus more for pan

Meatballs

3 day-old slices Italian or French bread (not sourdough), ½ inch thick, crusts removed

3 to 4 tablespoons milk (nonfat or low fat okay)

2 egg whites reserved from pastry recipe or 1 large whole egg

¼ cup freshly grated Romano cheese

Heaping 1 tablespoon chopped fresh flat-leaf parsley

1 teaspoon kosher salt

¼ teaspoon granulated garlic powder

⅛ teaspoon fine, freshly ground black pepper

¾ pound extra-lean ground beef

½ cup very finely chopped yellow onion

Tomato Sauce

3 cans (28 ounces each) imported San Marzano tomatoes with juice

2 tablespoons mild-tasting extra-virgin olive oil

1 large yellow onion, finely chopped

½ teaspoon dried leaf oregano, crumbled between your fingers

3 cloves garlic, green germ removed if present, minced

2 teaspoons kosher salt

¼ teaspoon fine, freshly ground black pepper

2 tablespoons chopped fresh flat-leaf parsley, divided

1 fresh basil sprig

1 teaspoon sugar (optional)

Assembly

½ pound long *fusilli* pasta

Kosher salt

1 cup freshly grated Romano cheese, divided

1 pound top-quality whole cow's milk ricotta cheese (15-ounce container is okay)

2 hard-cooked eggs, peeled and cut lengthwise into quarters (see page 129)

½ pound fresh whole-milk mozzarella cheese, cut into ¾-inch dice

1 cup fresh English peas, cooked, or thawed frozen petite peas

RECIPE SECRETS

I use spaghetti-length curly *fusilli* pasta here, called *fusilli col buco*. It's sturdy enough to maintain its shape under the weight of all the other ingredients in the *timpano*, yet it's not too bulky. If unavailable, use shorter *fusilli* or *rotini*.

While it's lots of fun to make a *timpano* with a group of friends, it certainly is possible to prepare one on your own. Here's what you can do in advance: Make the sauce. Cook the pasta and toss with the sauce and some of the grated cheese. Hard-cook the eggs. Cut up the mozzarella. Butter the springform pan and press the dough into the bottom and sides. Roll out the top crust between waxed paper. Prepare the egg wash.

To prepare the *timpano* a day ahead for a party, bake as directed, then let cool for 30 minutes before releasing it from the springform pan. Once the sides are removed, let cool completely, cover, and refrigerate for up to 2 days. Slice the *timpano* into wedges while cold, and bring to room temperature before reheating individual pieces on a parchment-lined baking sheet in a preheated 400-degree-F oven. Bake until a paring knife inserted deep into the center of each piece comes out piping hot.

/continued

1. *Prepare the pastry dough:* Lightly beat the whole eggs and yolks in a small bowl. Measure out a scant 1 tablespoon of this egg mixture, cover, and refrigerate to use as egg wash for the top crust of the *timpano*. Set aside the remaining beaten eggs. Place the flour, sugar, and salt in a food processor (or the bowl of a stand mixer) and pulse a few times (or mix) just to combine. Cut the butter into ½-inch pieces and add to the processor (or bowl). Pulse (or mix) until the butter pieces are the size of peas. Add the beaten eggs and process (or mix) just until ingredients are combined. If necessary, mix in a few drops of cold water—or add a bit more flour—so that dough is moist enough to hold together when you press together a handful. Transfer to a clean work surface and knead together by hand just until the mixture is smooth. Shape into a log about 9 inches long. Cut off one-third and flatten into a disk for the top crust. Shape the remaining dough into a larger disk for the bottom crust. Wrap the disks separately in plastic wrap and refrigerate for 1 hour. (The dough can be prepared up to 48 hours ahead.)

2. *Prepare the meatballs:* Tear the bread into roughly 1-inch pieces and place in a medium bowl. Pour 3 tablespoons milk over the bread and let stand until the bread is moistened, about 10 minutes. Squeeze the bread with your fingers; if it feels dry, add the remaining 1 tablespoon milk. Shred the bread into ¼- to ½-inch pieces. In a small bowl, combine the egg whites or whole egg, cheese, parsley, salt, garlic powder, and pepper. Add the ground beef, onion, and egg mixture to the bowl with the bread. Mix with your hands until combined, but don't overmix.

3. Shape a little of the mixture into a small patty and fry (or microwave) to test for seasoning. Taste and add more cheese, salt, pepper, and/or garlic powder, if necessary, to bring the flavors into balance.

4. Using a small ice-cream scoop or melon baller, shape the meatball mixture into 24 walnut-sized balls. Place on a waxed paper–lined rimmed baking sheet. Dip your hands in a bowl of cold water to prevent the mixture from sticking as you gently compress and shape the balls between your palms. Loosely cover with waxed paper and refrigerate for at least 15 minutes. (The meatballs can be mixed and shaped up to 24 hours in advance. Cover tightly with plastic wrap if preparing more than 1 hour in advance and refrigerate.)

5. *Prepare the tomato sauce:* Pass the tomatoes and their packing juices through a food mill fitted with the medium disk into a bowl. Use a rubber spatula to scrape the underside of the food mill, capturing all the purée. Alternatively, remove the tomato cores by hand and purée the tomatoes and packing juices in a food processor or blender, then pass through a medium-mesh strainer. Set aside.

6. Heat a heavy 6-quart pot over medium heat. Add the olive oil. When the oil is hot enough to sizzle a piece of onion, add the onion and sauté just until soft and translucent, 6 to 8 minutes. Add the oregano and garlic and sauté for 1 minute, stirring often so the garlic doesn't brown.

7. Add the puréed tomatoes, salt, and pepper, raise the heat to high, and bring to a boil. Reduce the heat to low and add half of the parsley and the basil sprig. Cover partially and simmer until the sauce no longer has a watery consistency, 15 to 20 minutes. Taste and add the sugar, if necessary, to reduce acidity, and more salt and pepper, if necessary. Stir in the remaining chopped parsley. (The sauce can be prepared up to 48 hours in advance. Let cool completely, then cover and refrigerate if making more than 4 hours ahead. Reheat to a gentle simmer before continuing.)

8. Carefully drop the meatballs into the simmering tomato sauce. To keep them tender, regulate the heat as necessary to keep the sauce at a steady simmer. Simmer gently, stirring occasionally, until the meatballs are cooked through and steaming hot inside, about 10 minutes. Turn off the heat.

9. *Assemble the timpano:* Remove the disks of pastry dough from the refrigerator to soften a bit. Bring a 6-quart pot of water to a boil for the pasta. Preheat the oven to 400 degrees F (or 375 degrees F if using the convection setting). Generously butter the bottom and sides of a 9½-inch springform pan.

10. Place the larger disk of dough in the buttered pan. With your fingers, press the dough evenly onto the bottom and all the way up the sides—extending a bit above the rim—of the pan. Place the smaller dough disk between two 10-inch lengths of waxed (not parchment) paper, flatten a bit with a rolling pin, and roll between the paper into a 10-inch circle. Stop and adjust the paper as needed to prevent it from becoming imbedded in the dough as you roll. Refrigerate this top crust, still sandwiched between waxed paper, until firm, about 20 minutes.

11. When the pasta water comes to a boil, add enough salt to it to make it taste like the ocean. Cook the pasta according to package directions until almost al dente, about two-thirds of the time specified on the package (it will cook more in the oven). Drain well.

12. Discard the basil sprig from the tomato sauce. Place 1 cup of the sauce (without any meatballs), the drained pasta, and ¼ cup of the Romano cheese in the empty pasta pot. Toss well.

/continued

SECRETS FOR SUCCESSFUL HARD-COOKED EGGS

"Hard-boiled" is actually a misnomer. Perfect hard-cooked eggs are achieved by steeping eggs in very hot water. If boiled, eggs are likely to have tough, not tender, whites, and an unsightly blue ring around the yolk. Not true of hard-cooked eggs.

Start with eggs that are about a week old or older. (The fresher the egg, the harder it is to peel off the thin white membrane underneath the shell.) Place them in a saucepan large enough to hold them in one layer. Add enough cold water to cover the eggs by an inch or so. Bring to a boil, uncovered, over high heat. Cover, turn off heat, leaving the pan on the burner, and set a timer for 10 minutes. When the timer rings, place the pan of eggs in the sink and run cold water into the pan until the eggs feel cool to the touch. Let the eggs sit in the cold water for 5 minutes. To peel, tap and roll the eggs on a hard, flat surface, cracking the shell into many small pieces. Starting at one end, peel off the shell in circular strips. Dip each peeled egg in cold water and rub gently to remove any small bits of shell.

13. Place half of the pasta mixture in the springform pan. Press down gently with a spoon to compact the pasta as much as possible. Spread all the ricotta on top of the pasta. Randomly scatter 12 of the meatballs (drained of excess sauce) on top of the ricotta. Fill in the spaces with pieces of hard-cooked egg, mozzarella, and peas, in that order. Cover with 1½ cups of the tomato sauce (without any more meatballs) and sprinkle with another ¼ cup of the Romano cheese. Cover with the remaining pasta and press to compact the ingredients. Top with 1 cup of the tomato sauce (without any more meatballs) and the remaining ½ cup Romano cheese.

14. Carefully peel off the top sheet of paper from the reserved pastry circle. Invert the circle (still attached to bottom sheet of paper) onto the *timpano* so that the paper is on top. Center the crust over the pan and carefully peel off the paper. With a paring knife, trim around the edges of the top crust so it meets the sides. With your fingers, press together the side and top crusts completely, all around the perimeter. If you have any cracks, use the dough scraps to make patches.

15. Brush the top lightly with some of the reserved egg wash (from making the pastry dough), stopping within ½ inch of the edges. If you brush farther, the egg may drip and bake onto the pan, making it difficult to remove the springform. Place the *timpano* on a parchment-lined rimmed baking sheet and bake until golden brown on top and very hot in the center when pierced with the tip of a paring knife, about 35 minutes on the convection setting, or 45 minutes if not using convection. Transfer the *timpano* still on the baking sheet to a rack and let rest for 15 to 30 minutes. The longer it rests, the sturdier it will be when you cut it. In the meantime, reheat the remaining tomato sauce and meatballs over medium heat.

16. Place the springform pan on a large, flat, round platter. With a pot holder, carefully unlock the sides of the pan, resisting any urge to run a knife between the crust and sides of the pan (this often ends up damaging the crust) unless absolutely necessary to release the crust from the sides. Cut the *timpano* into wedges and serve the pieces, upright, with some of the remaining tomato sauce and meatballs on the side.

SEAFOOD, POULTRY, AND MEAT MAIN DISHES

SEAFOOD, POULTRY, AND MEAT MAIN DISHES RECIPES

Seafood	Q	MA	V	Page
Grilled Skewered Shrimp with Romesco Sauce		•		136
California Crab Gumbo with Chicken and Sausage		•		138
Cracker-Crusted Nubble Point Scallops; Haddock, Cod, or Halibut Variation	•			142
Braised Calamari in Red Sauce	•	•		144
Sautéed Fillet of Sole with Tartar Sauce	•	•		145
Alaskan Halibut with Roasted Red Pepper Coulis	•	•		148
Steamed Salmon and Creamer Potatoes with Sauce Verte	•	•		150
Poached Salmon with Shortcut Hollandaise Sauce		•		152
Broiled Swordfish with Mango Salsa	•	•		155
Paella with Shellfish, Sausage, and Chicken		•		158

Poultry	Q	MA	V	Page
Chicken Salad Véronique with Whole Toasted Almonds		•		168
Thai-Style Minced Chicken with Basil and Chiles		•		170
Baked Portabello Mushrooms Stuffed with Turkey, Eggplant, and Fresh Bread Crumbs		•	•	172
Stir-Fried Velvet Chicken with Cashews	•			174
Garlicky Chicken Breasts	•	•		176
Turkey Piccata	•			177
Chicken Thighs Parmigiana		•		180
Grilled Stuffed Chicken Breasts with Prosciutto, Taleggio, and Pesto		•		183
Pesto	•	•	•	186
Classic Herb-Roasted Chicken		•		187

Q = Quick—prep to table in 45 minutes.
MA = Make ahead—part or all of the recipe can or must be made ahead.
V = Vegetarian—no meat, chicken, fish, or, with minor adjustments, such as substituting vegetable broth for chicken stock, can be prepared as a vegetarian recipe.

Poultry continued

	Q	MA	V	Page
Roasted Stuffed Turkey with Pan Gravy		•		188
Maple-Glazed Quail Stuffed with Wild Mushrooms, Sausage, and Sour Cherries		•		194
Herb-Crusted Chicken Potpies		•		198
Chicken Cacciatore		•		202
Turkey Mole		•		204

Meat

	Q	MA	V	Page
Grilled Pork Chops with Garlic and Fennel Rub	•	•		211
Vietnamese-Style Honey-Glazed Pork Skewers with Rice Vermicelli		•		212
Italian Sausage Contadina with Roasted Sweet Peppers, Potatoes, and Onions		•		215
Pork Loin Roast with Vanilla-Scented Applesauce; Crown Roast of Pork Variation		•		217
Honey-Mustard Glazed Ham with Grilled Pineapple Salsa		•		220
Grilled Leg of Lamb with Pomegranate Marinade and Muhammara; Venison Loin Variation		•		221
Rack of Lamb with Garlicky Bread Crumbs		•		224
Hamburgers, Italian Style	•	•		226
Rib-eye Steaks with Arugula, Blue Cheese, and Grilled Red Onions	•	•		228
Grilled Marinated Flank Steak au Jus	•	•		230
Slow-Roasted Beef Sirloin Tip with Pan Gravy or Creamy Horseradish Sauce		•		232
Osso Buco with Sweet Red Peppers and Gremolata		•		234
Braised Short Ribs with Frizzled Leeks		•		237
Pot Roast and Gravy with Peas and Carrots		•		241
Weeknight Chili	•	•		245

Q = Quick—prep to table in 45 minutes.

MA = Make ahead—part or all of the recipe can or must be made ahead.

V = Vegetarian—no meat, chicken, fish, or, with minor adjustments, such as substituting vegetable broth for chicken stock, can be prepared as a vegetarian recipe.

SECRETS FOR PREPARING FISH AND SHELLFISH SUCCESSFULLY

Each seafood recipe in this chapter features its own particular Secrets. In addition, here are general tips for preparing fish and shellfish.

STORAGE

- If possible, buy fish within 24 hours of when you plan to cook it, and no longer than 48 hours before cooking, and store in the coldest part of the refrigerator (or freeze for up to a month). If buying sooner, unwrap the fish so it doesn't sit in its juices, which can be a rich breeding ground for bacteria. Restaurants store large fish on ice in a perforated pan.

- Unless you know they're superfresh, purchase perishable clams and mussels no more than 36 hours before you plan to cook them. As soon as you get home, remove all the wrapping and place the shellfish in a clean, dry bowl. Dampen a paper towel and cover the mollusks, turning up a corner to give them a little air. Refrigerate until just before cleaning and cooking them. Squid, scallops, and shrimp are particularly perishable. Don't buy them sooner than the day before you plan to cook them. Keep in the coldest part of the refrigerator.

CLEANING CLAMS AND MUSSELS

- The fibrous tuft you see on some mussel shells is called a beard. It is what the mollusk creates for grabbing onto pilings or rocks. Pull off these beards, if present, from the edge of each mussel before scrubbing. (Farmed mussels usually don't have beards because of how they are raised.) A round, thin rubber disk used to open jars provides perfect tension for pulling off stubborn beards. Scrub the shells of clams and mussels with a stiff brush, ridding them of any sand.

DONENESS

- Chefs use a guideline of 8 to 9 minutes per inch of thickness if fish is at room temperature (68 degrees F) before cooking. Bringing fish to room temperature before cooking is critical for even cooking. If fish is just out of the refrigerator, estimate 10 minutes of cooking time per inch.

- Rather than using a thermometer to gauge doneness in fish, calculate 8 minutes of total cooking time per inch of thickness, then stick the tip of a paring knife into the densest part of the fish. If the knife doesn't penetrate with ease, cook the fish longer and continue checking at 1-minute intervals.

- Sushi-grade fish such as ahi tuna is sometimes seared, or cooked on the surface only, then served raw in the center.

- Many people prefer to eat impeccably fresh salmon on the rare side, about 115 degrees F internal temperature.

- Always consider the health and safety of the people you cook for and err on the side of caution, particularly when cooking for young children, people with compromised immune systems, and the elderly.

- The generally accepted (for healthy adults) range of internal doneness temperatures for fish is between 120 and 135 degrees F. Non-oily fish such as albacore tuna and halibut should be cooked to the lower end of this range to preserve succulence. Swordfish and other firm but oily fish can withstand temperatures at the higher end of this range.

FREQUENTLY ASKED QUESTIONS ABOUT
FISH AND SHELLFISH

How do I remove the pin bones from salmon and other fish?

Unless your fishmonger has already removed them, it's best to remove these before cooking. Fish tweezers or needle-nose pliers are the best tools for this job. Feel the flesh with your fingertips to find the line of bones, then, to prevent gaping holes, pull the bones out in the same direction they grew in.

Should I rinse fish and shellfish?

Consider the source and smell the fish first. Buy from a reputable fishmonger whenever possible. As a general rule, only rinse scallops, fish steaks, and fish fillets if they're not impeccably fresh. Fishmongers warn that otherwise you would rinse off the "ocean" flavor. Likewise, I typically do not rinse salad—or bay—shrimp, nor do I rinse rock shrimp. However, I do rinse shrimp just briefly after deveining them, and I always rinse thawed, peeled shrimp if I suspect that the fish market has not kept them in a perforated container that allows them to drain well. Mollusks such as clams and mussels must be washed—use a stiff brush—to rid them of any sand.

How can I prevent fish from drying out during broiling?

Slather fish fillets and steaks with a protective coating called a *glaçage* (pronounced glah-*sazh*). The simple version on page 157 is made with mayonnaise and mustard. Under the broiler, a *glaçage* creates flavorful caramelization on the surface of the fish and helps keep it moist. Beyond the evenly browned surface, it's almost impossible to detect the *glaçage* after the fish is cooked.

RECIPE SECRETS

To prevent bamboo skewers from splintering and help keep them from charring, soak in water for at least 30 minutes before threading them with the shrimp.

One of my students, Anna Fieler, showed me her mother's great trick for removing the shell and vein from shrimp in one easy step. With kitchen shears, starting at the head end, cut the shell along the outer curved side of the shrimp, removing the vein as you cut. (It may seem a little tricky, but the vein gets removed as you cut.) When you get to the tail, put the scissors down and pinch one of the tail shells as you twist out the tail.

Use 2 parallel skewers to thread each pair of shrimp. This way, when you grab a skewer on the grill, the shrimp will come with it, instead of the skewer spinning around in your tongs, which tends to happen with single skewers.

Almonds are a popular ingredient in Spanish cuisine. This recipe calls for 1 cup (about 4 ounces) of blanched (page 169) whole or slivered almonds, toasted. If you find a 3.5-ounce package, that would be sufficient here.

GRILLED SKEWERED SHRIMP
WITH ROMESCO SAUCE

This popular Spanish tapa is easy to prep ahead, then grill at the last minute on a George Foreman or stove-top grill, or even on a pancake griddle or in a cast-iron pan. You can also serve this full-flavored *romesco* sauce as they do in Spain, with roasted potatoes (page 271). Refrigerate or freeze any leftover sauce (it will keep for up to 5 days in the fridge and 1 month in the freezer; bring to room temperature and adjust the seasoning before serving) to have on hand as a last-minute dip for crudités or to spread on crostini. Have some crusty bread ready to dunk into any extra sauce—people just can't seem to get enough of it.

**Serves 6 to 8 as a first course
or 4 as a main course**

Shrimp

1 pound medium-sized shrimp, peeled and deveined (30 shrimp)

1 tablespoon bold-tasting extra-virgin olive oil

½ teaspoon kosher salt

¼ teaspoon granulated garlic powder

Romesco Sauce

1 tablespoon minced garlic, green germ removed if present

1 teaspoon kosher salt

3 ounces Italian or French bread (not sourdough), crusts removed

1 cup blanched whole or slivered almonds, toasted (page 89)

1 cup packed fresh basil leaves (about 1 small bunch)

1 jar (12 ounces) *piquillo* peppers or roasted red peppers, rinsed and drained

⅓ cup clam juice or water, or more if needed

2 to 3 tablespoons tomato paste

2 to 2 ½ tablespoons *pimentón dulce* or Hungarian sweet paprika

¼ to ½ teaspoon cayenne pepper

2 tablespoons brandy (optional)

2 to 3 tablespoons sherry vinegar or red wine vinegar

1 to 2 tablespoons freshly squeezed lemon juice

About ⅔ cup bold-tasting extra-virgin olive oil, preferably Spanish

1 or 2 pinches sugar, if needed

1. *Prepare the shrimp:* Soak 30 bamboo skewers, each 4 inches long, in water (a loaf pan works well) for at least 30 minutes. In a large bowl, toss together the shrimp, olive oil, salt, and garlic powder and marinate at room temperature for 20 minutes.

2. Hold 2 skewers parallel to each other, about 1 inch apart, and thread 2 shrimp onto them. Keep the shrimp close to the pointed ends of the skewers for easy eating (see illustration, page 138). Repeat with the remaining shrimp and skewers. Set aside. (This can be done up to 8 hours ahead; cover and refrigerate. Bring to room temperature before grilling.)

3. *Prepare the sauce:* In a mortar with a pestle or in a bowl with a fork, mash together the garlic and 1 teaspoon salt; set aside. Cut or tear the bread into ½-inch pieces; set aside.

4. Place the almonds in a food processor and process just until finely chopped. Add the basil and process until roughly chopped. Scrape down the sides of the work bowl. Add the bread and red peppers and process until the bread forms medium crumbs and the peppers are chopped. Scrape down the bowl. With the motor running, drizzle in ⅓ cup clam juice or water. Stop and scrape down the bowl again. Add the reserved garlic paste, 2 tablespoons tomato paste, *pimentón* or paprika, ¼ teaspoon cayenne, brandy (if using), 2 tablespoons vinegar, and 1 tablespoon lemon juice and process until smooth. Scrape down the bowl. With the motor running, drizzle in ⅔ cup olive oil through the feed tube. The oil should create an emulsion. If the oil begins to pool on top of the sauce, stop adding it. Scrape down the bowl. The mixture should be thin enough to drop from a spoon. Add more clam juice or water, if necessary. Taste and adjust the seasoning if necessary. It may be necessary to add more tomato paste, *pimentón,* cayenne, lemon juice, olive oil, and/or salt. If the sauce is too sharp, add the sugar. If it's bitter, add a little more salt. Let stand for 20 minutes to allow the flavors to bloom before serving, then taste and adjust the seasoning, if necessary. You should have about 2½ cups.

5. Drizzle a little of the sauce in a random pattern all over a large round platter. If available, use a plastic squeeze bottle to squirt it onto the platter. Place half of the remaining sauce in a small bowl in the center of the platter. Set aside.

/continued

RECILE SECRETS

RECIPE SECRETS

It's not typical, but I like one Spanish cook's trick of thinning *romesco* sauce with a little clam juice, which also adds a dimension of umami (page 38) to the sauce. I prefer St. Ours brand powdered natural clam broth, which is available at fine fish markets and upscale supermarkets; you can use bottled clam juice.

When preparing this sauce or any saucy mixture in a food processor, scrape the work bowl frequently to ensure that all the ingredients will be blended.

Depending on the heat of your *pimentón dulce* and cayenne, the acidity of your lemon juice and vinegar, and many other variables in the ingredients in this recipe, it's critical that you taste the *romesco* after blending it and adjust the seasoning so that the flavors will be in balance. When seasoning to taste, run down the list of ingredients and ask yourself if you can detect the contribution each is making to the sauce, then adjust accordingly. After the flavors have a chance to bloom, about 20 minutes after preparing it, taste the sauce again to see if everything is still in balance, and adjust accordingly.

6. *Grill the shrimp:* Preheat a stove-top grill over medium-high heat. To be sure the surface is hot, flick a few drops of water onto it. If they dance around and evaporate quickly, the grill is ready. Grill 8 to 10 skewers at a time (depending on the size of your grill), turning once, just until the shrimp turn pink, about 2 minutes per side. Transfer the skewers to the prepared platter, arranging them in a spoke pattern (pointed ends toward the center), and drizzle lightly with sauce. As you grill additional skewers, stack them on the platter and drizzle with more sauce.

7. Encourage people to spoon some sauce onto small plates for dipping their shrimp as they eat them off the skewers. Cover and refrigerate any leftover sauce for up to 5 days (bring to room temperature before serving) or freeze for up to 1 month.

2 shrimp skewered in opposite C-formation at the pointed end of two parallel bamboo skewers

CALIFORNIA CRAB GUMBO WITH CHICKEN AND SAUSAGE

If you're expecting a crowd for a holiday open house or weekend at the ski cabin, there's nothing like a big pot of gumbo on the stove to make it a special occasion. The smells will wow your guests as they enter the house, and if there's a party going on, they can help themselves to a bowl of crab-laced gumbo as it sits over the lowest heat on the back burner. Serve with steamed rice and a refreshing salad such as Shaved Celery with Medjool Dates, Feta, and Walnuts (page 88), or for a more formal dinner party, start with Butter Lettuce with Ruby Grapefruit, Avocado, and Glazed Walnuts (page 82). I'll tell you up front, making gumbo takes a fair amount of time and it's not an inexpensive proposition. It's a great project when you have visiting family members and friends who like to cook, and the rewards are memorable. To that end, I've divided this recipe into several steps you can either do ahead or divide up for a cooking party.

Serves 10 to 12

Chicken

1 whole chicken, 4 to 5 pounds

About 8 cups homemade chicken stock or broth (page 60 or 61) or purchased reduced-sodium broth

2 bay leaves, preferably imported

Velouté

½ cup (1 stick) unsalted butter

½ cup all-purpose flour

About 8 cups broth from steeping the chicken

Vegetables and Seasonings

¼ cup mild-tasting extra-virgin olive oil

2 large yellow onions, finely chopped

2 large red and/or green bell peppers, seeded, deribbed, and finely chopped

4 celery stalks with leaves, peeled if desired, then finely chopped

6 large fresh thyme sprigs

4 cloves garlic, green germ removed if present, minced

2 teaspoons Old Bay seasoning

1 teaspoon kosher salt

1 teaspoon *pimentón dulce* or Hungarian sweet paprika

¼ teaspoon cayenne pepper

1 can (28 ounces) diced tomatoes with juice

Crab

¼ cup kosher salt

2 live Dungeness crabs, about 2 pounds each

Sausage

4 flavorful smoked sausages such as turkey seasoned with sun-dried tomato

4 hot link sausages

½ cup water

For Serving

Steamed rice made with 3 cups white rice and 4¾ cups water

Kosher salt and freshly ground black pepper

RECIPE SECRETS

To keep the chicken moist, pour warm broth over it, just to cover, after removing the meat from bones.

The foundation, or sauce base, for gumbo is velouté (pronounced vel-oo-*tay*). In the classic French kitchen, velouté is made with chicken or fish stock and a blond roux. In this case, to add depth of flavor, color, and complexity to the gumbo, the roux is cooked slowly over medium-low heat to a darker mahogany color. Don't rush this step or you'll sacrifice big flavor. Having said that, one clever recipe tester, Michelle Winchester, shares her secret for microwaved mahogany roux in the accompanying box. She swears by it.

This calls for red and/or green bell peppers. Green bell peppers are simply unripe red bells. While green peppers are traditional in gumbo, some people find them too vegetal tasting and hard to digest. I prefer red bells, but the choice is yours.

/continued

RECIPE SECRETS

To remove the strong vegetal flavor that's sometime present in celery, peel the rounded outside part of the stalks with a swivel-blade vegetable peeler before chopping. If your bunch of celery doesn't have many leaves on the outside stalks, don't fret. You're sure to find some tender, sweet yellow leaves on the inner stalks.

To easily remove crabmeat from the shell, plunge the crabs into an ice-water bath immediately after cooking.

At the risk of committing culinary blasphemy, this gumbo doesn't call for okra. But feel free to slice and sauté a pound or so to add when you add the sausages. Or, add a 20-ounce package of frozen, sliced okra with the sausages. Okra adds body, or viscosity, to the gumbo, as well as distinctive flavor and texture. It's said to be effective in reducing cholesterol, too.

1. *Prepare the chicken:* Rinse the chicken and place in a 6-quart pot. Add enough stock or broth to cover. Place over high heat, bring to a boil, reduce the heat to low, and simmer for 10 minutes, skimming off the foam that rises to the surface. Turn off the heat, add the bay leaves, cover, and steep the chicken until the internal temperature of both thighs reaches 180 degrees, about 30 minutes. Remove the chicken from the broth and plunge it into a large bowl filled with ice water. When the chicken is cool enough to handle, remove it from the ice water. Tear and cut the meat into bite-sized chunks, discarding the skin and bones. Place the meat in a deep bowl, add enough of the warm broth just to cover the chicken, and refrigerate. Discard the bay leaves and reserve the remaining broth for the velouté. (This step can be done up to 24 hours in advance. Let the chicken and broth cool to room temperature, then refrigerate.)

2. *Prepare the velouté:* In a heavy 8-quart pot over medium heat, melt the butter. (This is the pot you'll use to prepare the gumbo and from which it will be served.) When foaming subsides, add the flour all at once. Reduce the heat to medium-low and whisk together the butter and flour until the roux turns mahogany brown, 20 to 35 minutes, depending on your stove. The more time you spend on this step, the more flavorful your gumbo will be. Add the broth to the roux, ¼ cup at a time at first, then ½ cup at a time, whisking constantly to break up lumps. (It helps to use a long-handled whisk or wear an oven mitt as you add the broth to the hot roux, as it will bubble up and create lots of steam. Have faith: It will become smooth eventually. Keep whisking and adding more broth as the previous addition is absorbed.) When the mixture becomes smooth, after adding about 2 cups of the broth, pour in the remaining broth all at once. Raise the heat to high and bring to a boil. Reduce the heat to low and simmer steadily for 5 minutes, stirring occasionally. The velouté should be perfectly smooth. If it is not, strain it through a medium-mesh strainer, pressing on the lumps with the back of a ladle, and return to the pot. (This step can be done up to 24 hours in advance. Let cool, cover, and refrigerate. Reheat over medium-low heat, stirring constantly with a wooden spoon.)

3. *Cook the vegetables:* Heat a 12-inch sauté pan over medium heat. Add the olive oil. When the oil is hot enough to sizzle a piece of onion, add the onions and sauté until soft and translucent, about 8 minutes. Add the bell peppers and celery and sauté until they soften, about 5 minutes. Add the thyme sprigs, garlic, Old Bay, salt, *pimentón,* and cayenne and sauté for 1 minute, stirring to prevent the garlic from browning. Add the tomatoes and their juices, stir, and bring to a simmer. Transfer the onion mixture to the pot with the velouté and stir to combine. Bring the mixture to a boil over high heat, reduce the heat to low, cover partially, and simmer until the flavors meld, about 20 minutes. Turn off the heat. (This step can be done up to 24 hours in advance. Let cool, cover, and refrigerate. Reheat over medium-low heat, stirring constantly with a wooden spoon.)

4. *Cook the crabs:* Bring a 12- to 16-quart pot of water to a boil (or use 2 smaller pots) over high heat. Add the salt and crabs. Cover and return to a boil. Starting when the water returns to a boil, cook the crabs for 18 minutes. Remove the crabs from the cooking liquid and plunge them into a bowl or sink filled with ice water. When cold to the touch, crack and clean the crabs and remove the meat, in large chunks, if possible, from the shells. Place the crabmeat in a bowl, cover, and refrigerate. (This step can be done up to 12 hours in advance.)

5. *Cook the sausage:* Place all the sausages and the water in a 12-inch sauté pan, cover, and bring to a boil over medium-high heat. Reduce the heat to medium-low, cover, and simmer for 5 minutes. Remove the lid and continue cooking over medium heat, turning the sausages as needed, until the water evaporates and the sausages are browned on all sides, about 12 minutes longer. Pour off any fat that renders while the sausages are cooking. Remove the pan from the heat. (This step can be done up to 24 hours in advance. Let cool, cover, and refrigerate the whole sausages.) When the sausages are cool to the touch, cut crosswise into ½-inch-thick slices and add to the gumbo.

6. *Serve the gumbo:* Prepare the rice about 30 minutes before serving the gumbo. Add the chicken (with broth) to the gumbo. To keep chicken moist and tender, bring the gumbo just to a simmer (do not boil), stirring occasionally. Reduce the heat to the lowest setting. Just before serving, add the crab, stir gently, and heat just until the crab is warmed through. Taste and adjust the seasoning with salt, pepper, *pimentón,* and/or cayenne. Serve the gumbo in bowls over rice.

MICHELLE'S MICROWAVED MAHOGANY ROUX

Expert recipe tester Michelle Winchester shares her method for preparing mahogany roux in the microwave oven. You may have to make slight adjustments to the timing, as microwave ovens behave differently. Each step here calls for microwaving on high. Use a 2-quart Pyrex liquid measure. Microwave the butter, uncovered, until bubbly and completely melted. Add the flour all at once and whisk until smooth. Cook, uncovered, for 3 minutes. Whisk and cook for 2 minutes longer. Repeat this last step 2 more times. As needed, continue cooking until the roux is a dark caramel color, stopping at 1-minute intervals to whisk. Let stand for 1 minute. The roux will continue to cook and develop a mahogany color. To make the velouté: Working carefully to prevent steam burns, add ½ cup of the broth and whisk. Continue adding broth ½ cup at a time, whisking after each addition, until you've added all the broth.

RECITE SECRETS

Bay scallops are the small, sweet scallops that measure about ½ inch in diameter and average about 100 pieces to the pound. Not to be confused with larger sea scallops, which are about three times the size, bay scallops are popular on the East Coast (see illustration on the facing page). In the fall, at the peak of their season, it's not unusual to find bay scallops in upscale fish markets all over the United States. They're worth seeking out for their incomparably sweet, tender meat.

If it's still attached, be sure to remove the tough membrane from the side of each scallop before cooking (see illustration on the facing page). This is what connects the scallop to its shell, and it's very tough to chew.

To preserve the flavor of the sea, many chefs don't rinse scallops before cooking them.

This simple and quick recipe calls for baking the scallops in a vermouth and butter mixture, and then broiling them to create a crisp cracker crust. Be sure to use a baking dish or pan that will withstand the direct heat of the broiler; porcelain or enamel-coated cast iron—such as Le Creuset—is a good choice. Or, divide the ingredients among three or four 6-inch porcelain ramekins and serve each person an individual portion.

CRACKER-CRUSTED NUBBLE POINT SCALLOPS

The seafood in California is nothing to complain about, but sometimes I yearn for the New England fish preparations I grew up with, such as these cracker-crusted bay scallops. After a visit to my friend Phyllis Fox's restaurant, located at breathtaking Nubble Point on the coast of Maine, I was inspired to re-create this typical New England seafood dish. The simplicity of this recipe belies its sophisticated flavor and delightful texture. Serve the scallops with Mashed Yukon Gold Potatoes (page 280) or Wild Rice Pilaf (page 276) to absorb the sauce, and "Roasted" Beets with Whole-Grain Mustard Sauce (page 268) or Romano Beans (page 258) to brighten the plate. Try this scrumptious cracker topping with fillets of haddock, cod, halibut, or other thick, flaky white fish, as directed in the variation that follows that recipe.

Serves 3 or 4

4 tablespoons unsalted butter, melted, divided	⅛ teaspoon fine, freshly ground white or black pepper
1 pound bay scallops, unrinsed, membranes removed if attached	15 Ritz crackers, classic or whole wheat
2 tablespoons dry white vermouth	1 tablespoon chopped fresh flat-leaf parsley
¾ teaspoon kosher salt	

---

1. Position one rack in the lower third of the oven and another rack 4 to 6 inches below the broiler element. Preheat the oven to 350 degrees F.

2. Lightly butter a 9- or 10-inch flameproof baking dish. Add the scallops in a single layer. Drizzle half of the melted butter over the scallops. Set aside the remaining melted butter. Sprinkle the scallops with the vermouth, salt, and white or black pepper. Bake on the lower rack for 15 minutes.

3. While the scallops bake, place the crackers in a plastic bag and crush with your fingers so the largest pieces are about ½ inch long. Transfer the crumbs to a small bowl. Drizzle the remaining melted butter (remelt, if necessary) over the crumbs and mix well. Stir in the parsley.

4. After the scallops have baked for 15 minutes, remove from the oven and turn on the broiler. Cover the scallops evenly with the cracker mixture. Place 4 to 6 inches under the broiler element (it's okay if it hasn't heated up fully) and broil just until the cracker topping starts to sizzle and to turn golden brown, about 1 minute. Remove from the broiler and let stand for 2 minutes before serving.

HADDOCK, COD, OR HALIBUT VARIATION
. . . .

Proceed as directed, substituting 1 pound fish fillet(s) for the scallops. Instead of baking for 15 minutes, bake until the tip of a paring knife penetrates the center of the fish easily, about 8 minutes per inch for halibut or 10 minutes per inch for haddock or cod. Top evenly with the crumbs and broil as directed.

Bay scallops and sea scallops with membrane attached

RECIPE SECRETS

When in season, buy fresh squid from a dependable fishmonger. Don't buy squid more than a day before you plan to cook them, and be sure to store airtight in the refrigerator.

If fresh squid aren't available, look for frozen blocks of squid—or calamari—in Asian markets and well-stocked grocery stores. Look for cleaned bodies, as opposed to bodies already cut into rings. You can thaw them in just minutes by running cold water over the block. One caveat: a box of frozen, cleaned squid marked 3 pounds is often closer to 1 pound after defrosting.

Slit the squid bodies so they'll curl up as they braise, trapping flavorful sauce inside each morsel. It's a matter of personal preference whether to leave the thin mottled skin on the squid. Usually, when you buy them cleaned, the skin has already been removed.

It's true what the experts say about squid: to keep them tender, you must cook them either very quickly or long enough for the chewiness to subside. This braise takes just 20 minutes, and the trick is to simmer the squid gently. A rolling boil would toughen them.

BRAISED CALAMARI in RED SAUCE

My grandmother served this simple, memorable squid stew as part of a family-style lunch with Linguine Aglio e Olio (page 109), fried sweet Italian peppers, and crusty homemade bread to sop up the piquant sauce. Even as a child I loved it. The everyday ingredients and quick cooking time belie the deep flavor of the finished dish. Substitute leftover 20-Minute Tomato Sauce (page 114) or marinara sauce for the diced tomatoes to enhance the complexity further. As with any braised dish, this is even better made a couple of hours ahead, left on a turned-off burner, and reheated gently at serving time. Instead of the linguine, you could serve this with buttered orzo and lightly dressed greens.

Serves 3 or 4

1½ pounds cleaned squid, whole bodies and tentacles (not rings)

4 tablespoons bold-tasting extra-virgin olive oil

1 small (about 5 ounces) yellow onion, chopped

3 cloves garlic, green germ removed if present, minced

½ teaspoon dried leaf oregano, crumbled between your fingers

⅛ to ¼ teaspoon red pepper flakes

¼ cup dry white wine or vermouth

½ cup seeded and diced canned Italian-seasoned tomatoes with juice or 20-Minute Tomato Sauce (page 114)

2 tablespoons chopped fresh flat-leaf parsley, divided

1 teaspoon kosher salt

¼ teaspoon freshly ground black pepper

---

1. Swish the squid bodies and tentacles in a bowl of cool water and drain. Trim off any hard cartilage from the tentacles and place them in a medium bowl. Separate the bodies into 2 piles: those 2½ inches and shorter, and the longer ones in the second pile. Lay the smaller squid flat on a cutting board and slit open on one side with a paring knife (see illustration). Open the squid flat and scrape away any slimy matter with the back of the paring knife. Transfer the slit squid to the bowl with the tentacles. Slit and open the longer squid similarly, and scrape as necessary. Cut these larger squid in half lengthwise and add to the bowl. Set aside. (This step can be done up to several hours ahead. Cover and refrigerate.)

2. Place a 10-inch sauté pan over medium heat. Add the oil. When the oil is hot enough to sizzle a piece of onion, add the onion and sauté until soft and translucent, about 8 minutes. Add the garlic, oregano, and red pepper flakes and sauté for 1 minute, stirring to prevent the garlic from browning. Add the wine all at once and cook until reduced by about one-half. Add the tomatoes and their juice (or the sauce) and simmer over low heat for 5 minutes to blend the flavors. Add the calamari, 1 tablespoon of the parsley, the salt, and the pepper. Bring to a boil (there won't be much liquid), then reduce the heat to low, cover, and simmer, stirring occasionally, until the squid are done, about 20 minutes. Add the remaining 1 tablespoon parsley, then taste and adjust the seasoning with salt and pepper.

Slitting squid along one side and opening flat

SAUTÉED FILLET OF SOLE WITH TARTAR SAUCE

Most of the sole available at American fish counters is from small flatfish, typically a species of flounder. These tender, boneless white fish fillets are mild flavored and perfect for sautéing. Larger fillets of petrale sole would also work well here. The simple tartar sauce is the perfect accompaniment. If time is short, just combine the mayonnaise and relish. Or, for a more refined version, mince cornichons to use in place of the relish and add a few sprigs of chopped fresh tarragon. If you prefer a zippier sauce, add a few shakes of Tabasco or some bottled horseradish. You may make the tartar sauce and bread the fish in advance; refrigerate until 30 minutes before cooking. The final step, sautéing in grapeseed oil, is quick and simple, so be sure to have your side dishes ready to serve when you start cooking. Consider serving the sole with Garlic Spinach with Currants, Pine Nuts, and Pecorino (page 265), "Roasted" Beets with Whole-Grain Mustard Sauce (page 268), or Romano Beans (page 258).

/continued

RECIPE SECRETS

Use the smaller amount of red pepper flakes to add complexity, the larger amount to add a spicier kick.

Use Tuscan-style extra-virgin olive oil. Don't be alarmed if the oil seems to float on the surface after you add the tomatoes. Once the squid release their juices, the oil will emulsify with the liquid, creating a rich, sauce.

ABOUT OREGANO

Oregano is one of the few herbs whose dried leaves have a more pungent flavor than the fresh. To release the volatile oils in dried leaf oregano—and other dried leaf herbs—crumble the leaves between your fingers as you add them to a recipe. Powdered dried oregano is not recommended.

RECIGE SECRETS

Breading serves two functions when sautéing: First, it prevents delicate fish fillets from falling apart. Second, it provides a protective coating, because fish this delicate and thin would dry out before browning to an appealing color. Breading fish *à l'anglaise,* or English style, as featured in this recipe, is a three-part process: First, in order to keep a moist egg wash on the fish, the fish is dredged—or lightly coated—with flour. Then, the floured fish is moistened with beaten egg. Finally, the fillets are coated in fine crumbs. If possible, use just one hand for each breading step, so you'll have a clean hand to lift the sides of the waxed paper to nudge flour or crumbs onto the fish.

Be sure to let excess egg wash drip off before dipping the fish in the crumbs. This prevents the breading from becoming too thick, which can cause it to separate from the fish during cooking.

You can use fine dried bread crumbs here, but I prefer the flavor and texture of cracker meal.

A by-product of wine making, grapeseed oil is inexpensive, relatively flavorless, and has a very high smoke point, which makes it ideal for sautéing. For health considerations, use expeller-pressed grapeseed oil (see page 87).

When making the tartar sauce, sprinkle the dry mustard all across the top of the mayonnaise, as it tends to clump if added in one glob.

Serves 3 or 4

Tartar Sauce	Fish
⅔ cup good-quality mayonnaise	2 large eggs
2 tablespoons grated yellow onion, grated on the large holes of a box grater	2 teaspoons canola oil
1 to 2 tablespoons sweet pickle relish with a little juice from the jar	2 teaspoons water
½ teaspoon dry mustard	1 teaspoon kosher salt, plus extra for sprinkling
½ teaspoon granulated garlic powder	Fine, freshly ground black pepper
A few drops of freshly squeezed lemon juice	1 pound sole fillets such as gray, English, or petrale
A few grinds of fine, freshly ground black pepper	½ cup all-purpose flour
	¾ to 1 cup cracker meal
	2 to 4 tablespoons grapeseed oil
	Lemon wedges, for serving (optional)

1. *Prepare the tartar sauce:* Combine all the ingredients in a small bowl and stir with a whisk to break up the dry mustard. Taste and adjust the seasoning as desired. Let stand for 10 minutes to allow the flavors to bloom. Cover and refrigerate if making more than 30 minutes ahead. You should have about ⅔ cup.

2. *Bread the fish:* In a shallow bowl (such as a glass pie plate) broad enough to accommodate the longest fish fillet, whisk together the eggs, canola oil, water, 1 teaspoon salt, and a few grinds of pepper; set aside.

3. Blot the fish dry with paper towels, arrange in a single layer, and season both sides lightly with salt and pepper. Place the flour on a 12-inch length of waxed paper. Place ¾ cup of the cracker meal on another 12-inch length of waxed paper. Line a baking sheet with waxed paper to hold the breaded fish.

4. Dredge both sides of a fish fillet in the flour to coat lightly and evenly. Tamp off the excess flour and dip the fish fillet into the egg mixture. Hold the fillet lengthwise over the egg mixture for a moment to allow the excess egg to drip off. Transfer to the cracker meal and lightly coat both sides, pressing to make the crumbs stick and lifting the sides of the waxed paper to coax the crumbs onto the fish as needed. Place the breaded fish on the prepared baking sheet. Repeat with the remaining fish, adding the remaining cracker meal to the waxed paper as needed. Cover the breaded fish with a clean sheet of waxed paper and pat lightly to make the crumbs adhere and to release any excess crumbs that would fall off and burn as the fish cooks. (The fish can be breaded up to 3 hours ahead. Cover and refrigerate, then bring to room temperature 30 minutes before cooking.)

5. *Sauté the fish:* Just before serving, heat a 12-inch nonstick skillet over medium-high heat. Add 2 tablespoons of the grapeseed oil. Tilt the pan gently, swirling to heat the oil. When the oil begins to ripple, drop in a few grains of cracker meal; if they sizzle immediately, the oil is ready. Slip the fish into the pan, working in batches if necessary to avoid crowding the pan.

6. Sauté just until the breading is light golden brown on the bottom, 2 to 4 minutes. To prevent the fish from breaking, use 2 wide, flat spatulas to turn the fish. Sauté on the second side until golden brown, 2 to 4 minutes. Transfer to a warmed platter or plates. Or, if cooking in batches, keep warm in the oven. Garnish each serving with lemon wedges, if using, and serve with a dollop of tartar sauce on the side.

ABOUT CRACKER MEAL

Cracker meal is made from finely ground cracker crumbs and is used to bread vegetables, cutlets of meat and poultry, and fish fillets before sautéing. Some cooks (this one included) feel cracker meal makes a lighter coating than fine dried bread crumbs. Look for boxed cracker meal in your supermarket where flour and baking products are displayed. To keep fresh after opening, freeze the entire box in a zip-top plastic bag. If unavailable, substitute fine dried bread crumbs.

BREADING FOOD BEFORE SAUTÉING

While it's certainly not necessary to bread food before sautéing it, breading is the secret to a crisp, delectable crust and to keeping delicate foods intact and moist. Select the style of breading based on how delicate your food is and how thick you like your crust:

• If you have perfectly fresh sand dabs, dust them with seasoned flour and sauté them in butter for the lightest breading. This style is known as *à la meunière.*

• My grandmother cooked vegetables like sliced eggplant and squash blossoms *à la parisienne,* or dipped in beaten egg and then fried.

• As has been pointed out, the sole fillets prepared in this recipe are breaded *à l'anglaise,* with flour, egg, and then cracker meal (or fine dried bread crumbs). The egg is beaten with a little oil to dissipate any foaminess and to ensure that the coating will stick.

• Chicken Thighs Parmigiana (page 180) are done *à la milanaise,* with finely grated Romano cheese mixed with bread crumbs, which stands in for the cracker meal.

• If your breading falls off with either of these last two styles, chances are your egg coating is too thick. Instead of dipping the food into the egg mixture, use a pastry brush to apply a lighter coating.

PROTECT YOUR PET BIRD

Be careful when preheating an empty nonstick pan. When certain types of nonstick pans are heated empty to an extremely high temperature, they give off fumes that can be fatally toxic to certain birds. The consumer relations department at a major American manufacturer of nonstick pots and pans assures consumers that this phenomenon, while certainly more than just an urban legend, does not pose a risk to humans. For safe sautéing in a nonstick pan, don't heat your empty cookware beyond warm.

RECIPE SECRETS

Coulis is a smooth, thick, sweet or savory sauce that is usually strained to eliminate seeds or skins. If you plan to strain the sauce, use a medium-mesh strainer and don't bother to peel the roasted peppers before puréeing them in the food processor.

Instead of broiling, you can grill the halibut over high heat for the same amount of time. Use these techniques and this recipe with any type of fish fillets or steaks. Keep in mind that just 1 minute extra of cooking time can render perfectly moist halibut dry and overcooked.

Removing the skin from a fish fillet

ALASKAN HALIBUT
with ROASTED RED PEPPER COULIS

I love the fresh, clean taste of halibut—almost as much as I love roasted peppers. In this quick preparation, they complement each other in both flavor and appearance: a bold, brilliant sauce drizzled over tender, delicate white fish. I prefer Alaskan halibut, available fresh in spring and summer, because it's oilier, and therefore moister, than other halibut, but you can substitute any firm white fish. The simple sauce is technically called a coulis (pronounced coo-*lee*). I have included a quick and easy variation using bottled peppers for when time is short. Drizzle coulis from a plastic squeeze bottle or spoon directly onto each piece of fish before serving. If you have leftover coulis, combine it with a little mayonnaise, sour cream, or crème fraîche (page 67) and use as a sandwich spread or vegetable dip. It keeps for several days in the refrigerator.

Serves 4

Coulis

2 red bell peppers, about 5 ounces each

1 clove garlic, green germ removed if present

Kosher salt and fine, freshly ground black pepper

2 to 3 tablespoons bold-tasting extra-virgin olive oil

Fish

4 skinless halibut fillets or steaks of uniform thickness, 6 ounces each, at room temperature

Garlic-flavored oil or extra-virgin olive oil and granulated garlic powder

Kosher salt and fine, freshly ground black pepper

Red pepper flakes (optional)

---

1. *Prepare the coulis:* Position the oven rack 4 inches below the broiler element and preheat the broiler. Cut off the top and bottom ends of each bell pepper and reserve for another use. Cut each pepper lengthwise into 4 pieces and remove the ribs and seeds. Line a baking sheet with aluminum foil and place the peppers, skin side up, on the pan. Broil with the oven door open a few inches if possible. Watch carefully, turning the pan to char the skins evenly. When the skins are blistered and charred, after about 3 minutes, transfer the peppers to a bowl, cover tightly with plastic wrap, and let them steam until cool enough to handle, 10 to 15 minutes. Leave the broiler on for the fish, but close the oven door. Peel off the pepper skins; if necessary use a paring knife to scrape off charred bits. Work over a bowl to catch any juices released from the peppers as you peel them.

2. Mince the garlic in a food processor. Scrape down the sides of the work bowl and mince again. Scrape the bowl again and add the roasted peppers and any pepper juices. Process until the peppers are puréed. Scrape the bowl and sprinkle the purée lightly with salt and pepper. With the motor running, drizzle in 2 tablespoons of the olive oil. Taste and add more salt and olive oil if necessary to achieve a rich-tasting, very smooth purée. Transfer to a bowl.

3. *Prepare the fish:* For easy cleanup, coat both parts of a broiler pan with vegetable oil spray. Place the fish pieces on the broiler pan with at least 1 inch between them to prevent steaming (steam impedes caramelization). Brush the tops of the fillets with garlic-flavored oil. Sprinkle lightly with salt, pepper, and with a few red pepper flakes, if using.

4. Place the fish under the broiler element and broil, with the oven door open a few inches if possible, for 4 minutes. Remove the pan from the broiler, turn the fish, and brush the tops with the garlic-flavored oil. Season with salt, pepper, and a few red pepper flakes. Broil for 4 minutes. Test the fish for doneness by inserting the tip of a paring knife into the center to see if the fish separates easily; if not, return to the oven and cook until done. Continue to test at 1-minute intervals.

5. Place a little coulis on the bottom of each plate, place a piece of fish on top, and drizzle the top of the fish with coulis in a random pattern. Serve any remaining coulis in a bowl on the side.

QUICK AND EASY ROASTED RED PEPPER SAUCE VARIATION

Substitute a 7-ounce jar of roasted red bell peppers for the roasted fresh bell peppers in the coulis. Strain the peppers, rinse well to remove any vinegar or brine flavor, and blot them dry with paper towels before adding to the food processor. Proceed as directed with the remaining ingredients.

RECIPE SECRETS

Smell your peeled garlic before adding it to the food processor for the coulis. If it seems particularly "hot" or sharp, poach it briefly to take away the sting: Place in a small saucepan, cover with about 1 inch water, and simmer for 5 minutes.

For simplicity and even cooking, buy skinless halibut fillets of the same thickness. If only halibut steaks are available, cook them with the skin on and peel it off after you transfer the steaks to the plates. To remove the skin from raw, skin-on fillets, place the fish skin side down on a cutting board. Grab a corner of the skin and tuck the center of the blade of a fillet or carving knife between the skin and flesh at the corner you're holding (see illustration on the facing page). Continue holding the corner of the skin with one hand as you slide the blade, parallel to the board, between the skin and flesh, separating the fish from the skin as you push the knife away from you. As you do so, press the blade down towards the skin, rather than upwards towards the flesh.

To imbue the fish with the sweet flavor of garlic without the risk of fresh garlic burning under the intense heat of the broiler, use garlic-flavored olive oil or extra-virgin olive oil and a sprinkle of granulated garlic powder. To prevent spoilage, store garlic-flavored oil in the refrigerator after opening. If the oil solidifies when chilled, remove it from the refrigerator about 15 minutes before using to restore it to pouring consistency.

RECIPE SECRETS

For homemade mayonnaise or delicate vinaigrettes such as *sauce verte*, be sure to use a mild-tasting extra-virgin olive oil, such as one from Provence or Liguria. A stronger, more peppery Tuscan-style oil would overpower the other flavors.

You'll need a large bamboo or aluminum stacking steamer with two racks for this recipe. To improvise a single-level steamer, place a 9-inch round wire cooling rack in a wok or Dutch oven and add water to within ½ inch of the rack. Place a dinner plate on the rack, cover the pot, and steam the salmon and potatoes on the plate.

In a two-level steamer, be sure to put the salmon on the lower level, so the fish juices don't drip onto other items.

Creamer potatoes are small new potatoes with a creamy, waxy texture that is enhanced by steaming. The most common varieties are red, white, and Yukon Gold. For a complete steamed meal, add carrot coins, broccoli florets, or asparagus spears to the steamer.

STEAMED SALMON AND CREAMER POTATOES WITH SAUCE VERTE

An adaptation of a French classic, this sprightly vinaigrette, known as *sauce verte* (pronounced vairt), or green sauce, is spectacular when paired with simple, rich steamed salmon. Make the sauce first (or up to 6 hours ahead) to allow enough time for the flavors to meld. For an interesting experiment, taste the sauce before and after you chill it. You'll be amazed at the difference in flavor. You'll have enough sauce here to drizzle on the salmon and the potatoes. Both the eye appeal and flavor of the potatoes are transformed when they soak up the vibrant herbs. You can refrigerate any leftover sauce for up to 5 days. It makes a great dip for crudités, or drizzle it over poached chicken or hot steamed vegetables.

Serves 4

Sauce Verte	Salmon and Potatoes
1 bunch (3 medium handfuls) watercress, large stems removed	1 pound smallest same-sized creamer potatoes, preferably Yukon Gold, scrubbed
1 handful fresh flat-leaf parsley leaves	4 salmon fillets or steaks, each about 6 ounces and 1 inch thick
3 cloves garlic, green germ removed if present	4 large outside romaine, butter, or other leafy lettuce leaves
1¼ teaspoons kosher salt	8 fresh chives, snipped into ¼-inch lengths
Fine, freshly ground black pepper	
1 teaspoon Dijon mustard, preferably imported	
¼ cup champagne vinegar or other white wine vinegar	
Leaves from 2 or 3 fresh basil sprigs	
¾ cup mild-tasting extra-virgin olive oil	

1. *Prepare the sauce:* Place the watercress, parsley, and garlic in a food processor or blender and process until smooth. Add the salt, a few grinds of pepper, the mustard, and the vinegar. Process, scrape down the sides of the work bowl, and process again. Scrape down sides and add the basil. With the motor running, slowly drizzle in the olive oil, processing until smooth. Taste and adjust the seasoning. Cover and chill for at least 20 minutes for the flavors to develop. You should have about 2 cups.

2. *Prepare the salmon and potatoes:* Select a Dutch oven, wok, or other pot and a stacking steamer. Fill the pot half-full with water and bring to a rolling boil.

3. If necessary, cut any large potatoes so that all the potatoes are about the same size. Place the potatoes in a single layer on the perforated rack of the stacking steamer, place the rack over—not touching—the boiling water, cover tightly, and steam for 20 minutes.

4. Place each piece of salmon on a leaf of lettuce and arrange in a single layer on another perforated steaming rack. Sprinkle with the chives. Place the rack with the fish directly over the boiling water, under the rack with the potatoes. Steam until salmon is cooked through to the desired degree of doneness, 7 minutes for rare and up to 10 minutes for well done. Remove the rack of fish as soon as the salmon is cooked. If necessary, continue to steam the potatoes until a paring knife enters and withdraws easily, indicating they are completely tender.

5. Transfer the salmon to warmed plates, leaving the lettuce leaves behind. Drizzle the fish with a little of the sauce. Cut the potatoes in halves or quarters, arrange on the plates, and drizzle with a little of the sauce. Serve the remaining sauce in a bowl on the side. Alternatively, if making ahead to serve chilled, arrange the salmon and potatoes on a platter, cover, and refrigerate.

WHAT'S THAT GREEN TINGE ON YOUR POTATOES?

The greenish tinge that sometimes develops on potatoes is solanine (*sole*-ah-neen). It develops when potatoes are stored improperly—in too much light. Although such green patches are often just skin-deep, solanine is toxic and bitter tasting, and should be peeled off before cooking the potatoes. The "eyes" on a potato contain solanine, and should be removed before cooking as well. To prevent the onset of solanine, store potatoes in a cool, dry, ventilated pantry or storage bin. When prepping potatoes, scrub them with a stiff brush and trim out any eyes. If you notice any solanine on the skin, peel off the affected area, continuing to peel more layers, as necessary, until there are no more signs of green.

RECIPE SECRETS

When making hollandaise sauce in the food processor or blender, be sure the clarified butter is warm enough to form an emulsion as you drizzle it into the egg yolk mixture. For the best flavor, use European-style or organic butter.

To keep the sauce warm and to prevent it from forming a skin, transfer it to a thermos. Prewarm the thermos by filling it with hot water, then pour out the water just before adding the hollandaise.

To make a smooth hollandaise, always add all the salt before you finish adding the clarified butter. Otherwise, the sauce will be grainy. Taste the sauce after you've added half the butter; if it doesn't taste a little too salty at that point, add a little more salt.

Since the egg yolks are not fully cooked in this recipe, if you're planning to serve this dish to young children, the elderly, or people with compromised immune systems, use pasteurized eggs.

If the salmon still has the skin on, see the illustration on page 148 for removing the skin.

It can be tricky to poach a whole (or a large side of) salmon and cook it evenly to perfect doneness throughout. The secret lies in having both the fish and the poaching liquid at the same temperature when you start.

POACHED SALMON
WITH SHORTCUT HOLLANDAISE SAUCE

While I was in cooking school, one of my favorite part-time jobs was Sunday brunch cook at the Sausalito Inn, just across the bay from San Francisco. Since I was the only cook, and we served seventy-five or more guests on an average Sunday, it was incumbent on me to come up with a hollandaise sauce that was quick, foolproof, and sturdy. My secret weapon was the food processor. To this day, when I teach hollandaise sauce in cooking classes, we always make it in the food processor. With this quantity, a blender works fine, too.

Serves 6 to 8

Court Bouillon

6 quarts water

6 carrots, thinly sliced

3 yellow onions, thinly sliced (not necessary to peel)

1 cup dry white wine or white vermouth

6 fresh thyme sprigs

6 fresh parsley stems

8 black peppercorns

1 bay leaf, preferably imported

Hollandaise Sauce

1 cup (2 sticks) unsalted butter

2 egg yolks, at room temperature

2 tablespoons warm water

¼ to ½ teaspoon fine sea salt

Pinch of cayenne pepper

2 to 3 teaspoons freshly squeezed lemon juice

Salmon

1 skinless whole salmon fillet, about 3 pounds, pin bones removed

About 2 tablespoons minced fresh chives, for garnish

---

1. *Prepare the court bouillon:* Combine all the ingredients in an 8-quart pot. Bring to a boil over high heat. Reduce the heat to low and simmer, uncovered, for 20 minutes. Strain through a chinois or fine-mesh strainer into a clean 6-quart pot; discard the solids. Place on a cooling rack and let cool to room temperature before using. (The court bouillon can be made up to 2 days ahead and refrigerated. Bring to room temperature before continuing.) You should have about 6 quarts.

2. *Prepare the hollandaise sauce:* First, clarify the butter (see page 155) and strain the clear liquid into a 1-quart saucepan. Keep the clarified butter warm over low heat. (This step can be done up to several days in advance. Reheat the clarified butter before continuing.)

3. Place the egg yolks, warm water, ¼ teaspoon of the salt, and the cayenne in a food processor or blender. Pulse to combine the ingredients, then scrape down the sides of the work bowl. With the motor running, slowly drizzle in about half of the warm clarified butter. (For pouring ease, you may want to transfer the warm butter to a liquid measuring cup.) When the sauce starts to thicken, add 2 teaspoons of the lemon juice. Process, scrape down the sides, and taste for seasoning; add additional salt and lemon juice, if necessary. (The sauce should taste a bit salty at this point, since you've only added half the butter. If you think it won't be salty enough when you add the remaining butter, add more salt now.) With the motor running, continue drizzling in the remaining butter. Taste and add more lemon juice, if necessary. Immediately transfer the sauce to a preheated widemouth thermos or clean stainless-steel bowl placed, uncovered, over a pot of warm (about 100 degrees F) water. (See page 138 for a tip on removing sauce from the food processor blade and bowl.) If the sauce thickens too much as it rests, whisk in a few drops of warm water. You should have about 1½ cups.

4. *Prepare the salmon:* Use a fish poacher with a rack, or improvise by placing a flat cooling rack in the bottom of a roasting pan. The poacher should be long enough to accommodate the fish in a single layer (except the tail end; see below) and deep enough for the entire piece of fish to be completely submerged in liquid, with a little headspace to spare. Place the salmon on the rack, "skin side" (flat side) down. To ensure even cooking, if the tail end is thinner than the rest of the fillet, fold it under so the entire piece of salmon is the same thickness. Place the rack with the fish in the poacher. Place the poacher on the stove. Depending on the size of your poacher, you may want to balance it over 2 burners. If you have a probe-type instant-read thermometer (see illustration), insert the temperature probe into the middle of the thickest part of the salmon and set the alert function to ring when the salmon reaches an internal temperature of 115 degrees F for rare, or 125 degrees F for medium. Gently pour the reserved room-temperature court bouillon into the poacher. To keep the salmon smooth and intact, don't pour the liquid directly onto the fish. You may not need all 6 quarts of court bouillon; use just enough to cover the fish.

/continued

Probe-type instant-read thermometer

> ## HOW TO FIX A "BROKEN" HOLLANDAISE
>
> If hollandaise sauce develops a curdled appearance while you're adding butter or when sitting above warm water waiting to be served, this is a sign that it has "broken," or fallen out of emulsion. To fix this broken emulsification, whisk 1 egg yolk and 1 tablespoon warm water in the top part of a double boiler (or in a stainless steel bowl placed over a pan of barely simmering water). Slowly drizzle in the broken sauce, whisking constantly until the sauce is completely incorporated and emulsified.

5. Slowly bring the bouillon to a gentle simmer over medium heat. This should take about 20 minutes. Don't rush this process—slow and steady cooks the fish most evenly. If necessary, gently ladle some warm bouillon over the fish to keep it submerged. When the bouillon is at a simmer, regulate the heat so the salmon continues to cook at a very gentle simmer until it reaches the desired internal temperature. If you don't have a probe-type thermometer, use a regular instant-read thermometer. Depending on the temperature of the court bouillon when you start poaching, it should take about 15 minutes for rare and a few minutes more for medium.

6. As soon as the fish is done, transfer the poaching pan with the fish in it to a safe spot beside the sink. Carefully transfer the rack with salmon on it into the empty sink and let drain for a minute. (This is where the handles on the rack of the fish poacher come in handy. If you're improvising with a cooling rack, slip the long prongs of 2 meat forks under the opposite ends of the cooling rack and lift the rack and fish out of the liquid. Or, put on a clean pair of rubber gloves and lift the rack out with your hands.) Use 2 large, flat offset spatulas to transfer the salmon from the rack onto a clean platter. Blot dry all over with a clean kitchen towel (not terrycloth).

7. If serving the hollandaise sauce on the side, sprinkle the salmon with the chives. If not, use a ladle to nap—or coat—the fish with the hollandaise and sprinkle with chives. Alternatively, if you prefer to serve the salmon chilled, allow it to cool to room temperature, then cover and refrigerate for up to 24 hours before serving. Discard the court bouillon or save and reuse for salmon only.

ABOUT CLARIFIED BUTTER

Clarified butter, similar to what Indian cooks call ghee (see page 240), is butter that has had its milk solids and other impurities removed. (In fact, ghee is clarified butter that is allowed to cook a bit longer, resulting in a deeper, richer flavor.) Clarified butter has a higher smoke point (see page 30) than regular butter, which means that you can sauté and brown foods in it at high temperatures. Thus, you get the great flavor of butter without the worry of it turning black and acrid before your food is browned. Also known as drawn butter, it is often served as a dipping sauce for lobster because it stays in a liquid state longer than regular melted butter. You can purchase clarified butter at upscale supermarkets or you can make your own.

To clarify butter, slowly melt a stick of good-quality unsalted butter in a small, heavy saucepan over medium heat. (Use European-style or organic butter for the best flavor.) Most of the water in the butter will evaporate and the milk solids will sink to the bottom. Skim off and discard any foam that rises to the surface. Pour the remaining clear yellow liquid through a fine-mesh strainer into a heat-proof jar with a tight-fitting lid, leaving the milk solids behind in the bottom of the pan. Cover and store clarified butter in the refrigerator for up to several weeks. Use a melon baller or heavy spoon to remove as much as you need, or let the jar of clarified butter stand at room temperature to soften before measuring.

BROILED SWORDFISH
WITH MANGO SALSA

While swordfish may still be available at restaurants and fish counters in the eastern United States, the fact remains that Atlantic swordfish—unlike its Pacific cousin—is an endangered species. While the greatest supply of fresh Pacific swordfish is available during the summer months, nonendangered frozen swordfish is available throughout the country year-round. Fresh albacore, also called tombo, belongs to the tuna family and is similar in texture and fat content to swordfish. It can be used here in place of the swordfish. For the freshest fish, look for steaks with a dark red, rather than brownish, bloodline running through the flesh. Despite its higher price tag and lower nutritional value, many people prefer swordfish or tuna over more widely available—and, some would argue, more flavorful—salmon because there's no chance you'll end up with fish bones in your mouth. The mayonnaise-mustard *glaçage*, or coating, featured in this recipe will do a fine job of preventing moisture loss to either fish under the high heat of the broiler. The tasty, protective coating caramelizes right onto the surface of the broiled fish. Serve with Orzo with Toybox Tomatoes and Fresh Mint (page 283) or Classic American Potato Salad (page 282). The mango salsa is also a good accompaniment to Garlicky Chicken Breasts (page 176).

/continued

KNOW YOUR BROILER

Some broilers allow you to choose a high or low broil setting. If yours does, use high to get the job done fast. The longer the fish is exposed to the intense, direct heat, the drier it becomes. Some ovens require you to close the oven door when broiling to prevent the electronic control panel from being exposed to too much heat. These ovens usually have a convection broil setting to dissipate the steam that builds up during broiling and can prevent caramelization. Be sure to use this setting if your oven has it.

RECIPE SECRETS

Unfortunately, the common practice of checking for doneness by seeing if the fish flakes isn't reliable. If the fish flakes, it's actually overcooked. Instead, for swordfish, apply the general rule of 10 minutes total cooking time per inch of thickness. For tuna, allow 8 minutes per inch. If the fish you have is thinner than 1 inch thick, decrease the time accordingly.

For the most flavorful salsa, use very ripe, juicy mangos. If unavailable, substitute a medium-sized ripe papaya or a large peach or nectarine. To select the most flavorful fruit, smell the stem end. If it's fragrant, you've got a winner. When ripe, fresh mangoes should feel heavy for their size. For this preparation, first peel the mango with a vegetable peeler. Hold the mango on a cutting board, stem up. (Use a paper towel to hold the slippery fruit in place; use a very sharp knife.) Make two lengthwise cuts down along both sides of the large, oval pit. Cut each half into ½-inch dice. Trim off and chop the remaining flesh from around the pit, too.

Use red wine vinegar when making mango salsa as an accompaniment for "meaty" proteins like swordfish or albacore. Substitute freshly squeezed lime juice for the vinegar when pairing the salsa with lighter foods such as shrimp, quesadillas, or tortilla chips.

Serves 4 to 6

Mango Salsa

1½ cups diced mango (½-inch dice from about 3 small or 1 large mango)

¼ cup minced red onion

½ cup quartered Sweet 100 or Sungold cherry tomatoes

¼ cup diced red bell pepper

1 jalapeño chile, seeded, deribbed, and minced

1 serrano chile, seeded, deribbed, and cut into fine ½-inch-long julienne

2 tablespoons chopped fresh cilantro

¼ teaspoon sugar, if needed

Kosher salt and fine, freshly ground black pepper

2 tablespoons red wine vinegar

2 tablespoons mild-tasting extra-virgin olive oil

Fish

2 pounds swordfish or albacore steaks, 1 inch thick

Kosher salt and fine, freshly ground black pepper

3 tablespoons good-quality mayonnaise (reduced fat is okay)

2 teaspoons Dijon mustard, preferably imported

1. *Prepare the salsa:* In a small bowl, gently mix together all ingredients in the order listed, adding the sugar only if the fruit is not sweet enough. Taste and adjust the seasoning with sugar, salt, pepper, and vinegar, if necessary. Let the salsa sit for 20 minutes before serving to allow the flavors to blend, or cover and refrigerate for up to 4 hours.

2. *Cook the fish:* Adjust a rack 6 inches below the broiler element and preheat the broiler. For easy cleanup, spray both the bottom of a broiler pan and its perforated rack with vegetable oil spray.

3. If the fish is bloody, rinse and blot dry with paper towels. Place the fish steaks on the prepared broiler pan with at least 1 inch between them to prevent steaming. Sprinkle both sides of the fish with salt and pepper. Combine the mayonnaise and mustard in a small bowl and spread half on top of the fish; set aside the remaining mayonnaise mixture. Center the fish under the broiler element and broil with the oven door ajar, if possible, for 5 minutes for swordfish, 4 minutes for albacore.

4. Remove the pan from the broiler, turn the fish, sprinkle lightly with salt and pepper, and spread with the remaining mayonnaise mixture. Broil for 4 more minutes for swordfish, 3 minutes for albacore. Test the fish for doneness by inserting the tip of a paring knife into it to see if it is done to your liking. If necessary, continue cooking to desired degree of doneness, testing at 1-minute intervals.

5. Transfer the fish to warmed plates and top each steak with a spoonful of salsa. Serve the remaining salsa in a bowl on the side.

RECIPE SECRETS

Two different chiles are used in the salsa. The milder jalapeño chile is diced, while the hotter serrano is sliced into delicate julienne, or slivers. (This makes it easier for less intrepid eaters to identify and remove the hottest chiles.) Be sure to wear latex gloves to protect your hands when working with chiles, and don't rub your eyes.

HOW TO SOOTHE STINGING HANDS AFTER WORKING WITH CHILES

It's always a good idea to wear latex gloves when working with fresh chiles, but once, while catering, I got cocky and didn't bother with the gloves. The next day I awoke with both hands ablaze. A friend reminded me that dairy neutralizes spicy heat, so I soaked my hands in a big bowl of yogurt. After about 20 minutes, the sting was gone.

DOES CILANTRO TASTE LIKE SOAP TO YOU?

Some people have an enzyme in their saliva that makes cilantro taste like soap. Fresh flat-leaf parsley is a suitable substitution.

PAELLA WITH SHELLFISH, SAUSAGE, AND CHICKEN

The name of this sensational Spanish rice dish is derived from the vessel it's prepared in, the *paellera* (pronounced pah-*eh*-air-ah). In Spain, especially during local festivals and celebrations, paella (pronounced pah-*eh*-yah) is cooked outside over a wood fire, often in huge quantities. While the ingredients for a Spanish paella vary from region to region (depending on local ingredients), in my California kitchen, I like to combine shellfish, chicken, and sausage in one robust dish. As long as your *paellera* will accommodate extra ingredients, add (or substitute) pork, rabbit, mussels, artichoke hearts, white beans, green beans, and so on as you like. Years ago, I learned a few key paella secrets, including the use of Italian Arborio rice, from renowned Spanish chef Julian Serrano in a class I took with him in San Francisco. Another secret, for marinating the chicken and shellfish a day ahead, comes from *Sunset* magazine. This is one of those magnificent stand-alone main dishes that really doesn't need a fancy first course. I either serve a shaved fennel salad as a side dish, or follow the paella with a refreshing salad such as Butter Lettuce with Ruby Grapefruit, Avocado, and Glazed Walnuts (page 82).

SEASONING YOUR *PAELLERA* OR WOK

Like spun-steel woks, *paelleras* are often coated in heavy oil before being transported across the ocean and sold in the United States. The oil prevents them from rusting, and it must be removed before you use the pan. First, wash the pan in hot, soapy water. Then, fill the pan with soapy water and bring to a boil. (Fill the pan half-full and carry it to the stove, then top it off as high as possible once it's secure on the burner.) Boil for 5 minutes. Use a ladle to remove half of the water, then pour the rest of the water out into the sink. Wash the pan again with hot, soapy water. Position a rack in the center of the oven and preheat to 250 degrees F. With paper towels or an old dish towel (not terrycloth), wipe the pan completely dry. With a wad of paper towels, rub 1 or 2 teaspoons of flavorless vegetable cooking oil, such as grapeseed oil, over the inside surface of the pan. Wipe the rim with the oil, too. The oil should be completely rubbed into the surface and any excess should be blotted up. Place the pan in the oven and let it remain there for 1 hour. Turn off the heat and let the pan remain in the oven until it's completely cool. Store the seasoned pan in a cool, dry place, and be sure to protect the surface with a paper towel if you stack anything on top of it.

Serves 6 to 8

Marinade for Chicken and Seafood
. . . .

1½ pounds bay or sea scallops, squid rings and tentacles, and/or peeled and deveined shrimp, in any combination

1 pound boneless, skinless chicken thighs, cut in half (1¾ pounds bone-in thighs, if you plan to bone them yourself)

½ cup bold-tasting extra-virgin olive oil

4 cloves garlic, gently crushed

Fresh basil leaves from 3 sprigs, torn in half

1 tablespoon dried leaf oregano, crumbled between your fingers

2 teaspoons kosher salt

¾ teaspoon fine, freshly ground black pepper

½ teaspoon red pepper flakes

4 fresh (not smoked) spicy Italian sausages or other flavorful sausages

Paella
. . . .

2 tablespoons extra-virgin olive oil

1 large yellow onion, chopped

1 red bell pepper, seeded, deribbed, and chopped into ¾-inch pieces

½ pound fresh button mushrooms, cut in half

1½ teaspoons kosher salt

½ teaspoon fine, freshly ground black pepper

3 cloves garlic, minced

1½ cups Arborio rice

3 cups homemade chicken stock or broth (page 60 or 61) or purchased reduced-sodium broth, heated

½ cup peeled, seeded, and diced Roma tomatoes with juices (fresh or canned)

Leaves of 5 fresh thyme sprigs

2 teaspoons saffron threads

1 can (15 ounces) garbanzo beans, drained and rinsed

½ cup fresh English peas or thawed frozen petite peas

½ cup small Spanish olives stuffed with pimientos, drained

¼ cup dry white wine

½ pound small clams or mussels, mussels debearded, if using, and well scrubbed

1 lemon, cut into wedges, for garnish (optional)

RECIPE SECRETS
. . . .

Here are a few flavor-enhancing secrets: If you have time, marinate the chicken and shellfish (not clams or mussels) a day ahead with the olive oil, garlic, spices, and herbs. Then sear the chicken and sausage quickly on a grill to imbue the paella with more complex flavors, but don't cook them all the way through on the grill. Rather, allow them to finish cooking in the paella, so they'll give their rich juices to the rice.
. . . .

Before you begin, be sure your paella pan fits in the oven and you can close the door. If not, start your paella on the stove top and finish it inside a kettle-style grill over a hot fire. Or, allow the paella to simmer, gently, on top of the stove over medium-low heat.
. . . .

For guaranteed perfect texture and separate grains of rice, use Italian Arborio rice.
. . . .

Shrimp are sold according to the number of pieces per pound. For paella, I like medium shrimp small enough to be eaten whole (41 to 50 shrimp per pound). But if you're feeling flush, don't hesitate to use larger, more expensive ones.

/continued

1. *Marinate the chicken and seafood:* If still attached, be sure to remove and discard the tough membrane from the side of each scallop (see illustration, page 143). To preserve the flavor of the sea, do not rinse the scallops. Do rinse and drain the squid and shrimp. Combine the scallops, squid, and/or shrimp, the chicken, and all the remaining marinade ingredients in a large, shallow bowl. Cover and marinate in the refrigerator for at least 3 hours or up to 24 hours. If possible, stir occasionally. (The olive oil will solidify, but that's okay.) Remove from the refrigerator 1 hour before proceeding with the recipe.

2. *Grill the chicken and sausage:* Preheat a gas grill to medium or a stove-top grill over medium heat, or position a rack 4 inches from the broiler element and preheat the broiler. Remove the chicken and shellfish from the marinade and drain off any excess oil or blot with paper towels. It's okay if the basil leaves stick to the chicken or shellfish. Discard the garlic and any excess marinade. Set the shellfish aside. Grill or broil the chicken and sausages just until seared on two sides, 3 to 4 minutes total. (Don't cook through; just brown the outside.) Transfer to a cutting board and let sit for 5 minutes. Cut each sausage on a sharp diagonal into 2 or 3 large chunks. Set aside.

3. *Prepare the paella:* Preheat the oven to 400 degrees F. Heat a 10-inch *paellera* (or a skillet with an ovenproof handle) over medium-high heat. Add the olive oil. When the oil is hot enough to sizzle a piece of onion, add the onion, bell pepper, and mushrooms, reduce the heat to medium, and sauté until the vegetables become limp, 6 to 8 minutes. Season with the salt and pepper, stir in the garlic and rice, and sauté for 1 minute. Add the stock, tomatoes, thyme, and saffron and raise the heat to medium-high. Add the grilled chicken and sausage pieces. With the back of a spoon, smooth the top of the mixture so that the rice and meat are completely immersed in the liquid. When the mixture comes to a good boil, immediately transfer the pan to the preheated oven and bake, uncovered, for 15 minutes. The liquid will no longer be visible on the surface, but the rice will still be hard.

4. Add the reserved marinated shellfish, garbanzo beans, peas, and olives. Smooth the top so that the rice, meat, and shellfish are completely immersed. Return the pan to the oven and bake just until the rice is tender and the shellfish are cooked through, 10 to 15 minutes.

5. Meanwhile, place the wine and the clams or mussels in a 2-quart saucepan, cover, and bring to a boil over high heat. As soon as each mollusk opens, after 1 or 2 minutes, use tongs to transfer them, one at a time, to a deep bowl. Discard any that do not open. Cover the clams or mussels. Strain the cooking liquid through a fine-mesh strainer and set aside.

6. When the rice is cooked and the paella is done, stir the clam or mussel cooking liquid into the paella. Taste and adjust the seasoning, if necessary, with salt and pepper. The rice should taste bright and flavorful. Fluff up the rice with a fork. Working quickly to prevent the paella from cooling, arrange the cooked clams or mussels around the outside edge of the pan, hinged side down. If you're not quite ready to serve, cover the paella with aluminum foil and let stand for 5 to 10 minutes. Garnish with lemon wedges, if using. Place the paella in the center of the table and serve directly from the pan.

SECRETS FOR SELECTING AND COOKING POULTRY SUCCESSFULLY

Each poultry recipe in this chapter features its own particular Secrets. In addition, here are some general tips, as well as responses to frequently asked questions about purchasing and preparing poultry.

INTERPRETING POULTRY PEDIGREES

Organic chickens and turkeys have not been treated with antibiotics and have been raised on crops grown in fields free of pesticides or chemical fertilizers for at least three years. **Free-range** chickens and turkeys are allowed to wander in enclosed outdoor pens, rather than being "cooped up" in closer indoor quarters that may encourage the spread of diseases. **Natural** chickens and turkeys are minimally processed and carry no preservatives or artificial ingredients, although antibiotics are allowed (their use is halted far enough in advance of slaughter to ensure their absence in the processed bird). The choice is yours.

To see how the various types of chickens actually taste, I invited some friends over and conducted a little experiment with four 4.3-pound chickens: three came from an upscale butcher shop and one came from a local branch of a nationwide chain supermarket.

The label on the supermarket variety simply read "young chicken," which means this chicken could have been fed antibiotics and/or animal by-products. Most likely, it was raised in a one-square-foot indoor pen. Because these chickens are produced in crowded, often sordid, quarters, their feed is augmented with antibiotics to minimize the spread of infectious diseases. However, such antibiotics do not prevent the spread of salmonellosis, which is said to be present on most raw poultry. At 99 cents per pound, this chicken cost $4.29.

The "natural" chicken was also likely raised in a small pen, but the butcher assured me that this particular brand of natural chicken had not been given antibiotics. While the USDA regulations for what constitutes a natural chicken are rather liberal, they currently do not allow the use of hormones or growth stimulants in poultry. The natural chicken cost $1.69 a pound for a total of $7.35.

The third chicken was "free-range and natural." I once imagined that free-range chickens languished about aimlessly in the great outdoors. But, as it turns out, most large producers tend their free-range chickens inside big coops with a single door that leads to a relatively small, enclosed outdoor pen. Apparently, when chickens are raised in large groups, they become aggressive if given too much freedom. Better to keep them close to home in tighter quarters. Contrary to what many consumers believe—or are led to believe—just because a chicken is free-range and natural, it's not necessarily organic. The free-range, natural chicken cost $2.59 a pound, or $11.16 total. Finally, the fourth chicken I tested was a "free-range, organic" chicken. The most expensive of the lot, it cost almost three times more than the supermarket variety, just under $12.

BLIND TASTING OF FOUR CHICKENS

Type	Taste	Texture	Overall Grade (A-to-F scale)
Supermarket variety	Most flavorful breast; rich-tasting thigh and leg	Tender, smooth on the tongue	A-
Natural	Bland breast; dark meat a little more flavorful	The driest of all	D
Natural, free range	Blandest-tasting chicken; unremarkable	Dry, mealy	D
Organic, free range	Breast and dark meat have good flavor	Not as tender as we'd like; thigh is tough	B

I prepared each chicken according to the recipe for Classic Herb-Roasted Chicken on page 187; all took the same amount of time for the densest part of the thigh to reach 180 degrees F. Eight people did a blind-tasting of the same parts of all four chickens side by side and compared their flavor and texture.

While many of the tasters had a slight preference for the flavor of the organic chicken, everyone was surprised to realize that we'd chosen the supermarket variety as our overall favorite. Our preferences, as reflected in the chart above, may reflect our proclivity to choose what is most familiar to us. The supermarket bird was tenderest, with a silky, smooth mouth-feel. Some tasters preferred the flavor of the supermarket chicken, too. I suggest you stage your own cook-off; I think you'd find it enlightening even if you compare only two chickens with different pedigrees.

SAFE HANDLING OF POULTRY

When working with any raw poultry, it's important to safeguard against cross contamination. Salmonellosis is said to be present on most raw poultry. It is killed by cooking poultry to a sufficient internal temperature and/or by washing everything that comes in contact with raw poultry—including your hands and the sink—with hot, soapy water. I wear disposable gloves and use plastic cutting boards when working with poultry; the boards can be washed and disinfected in the dishwasher.

The USDA issues recommended safe cooking temperatures for poultry. Typically, these are the temperatures printed on kitchen thermometers. In reality, chefs and fine cooks operate with another set of guidelines. Certainly, safety is of paramount importance, but texture and flavor are important, too. Both sets of guidelines are presented here. Use the one that *you* are comfortable with. Always consider the health and safety of the people you cook for and err on the side of caution, particularly when cooking for young children, people with compromised immune systems, and the elderly.

	Recommended Temperature (in degrees F):	
	USDA	Chefs
Chicken breast	170 to 180	145 to 150
Turkey breast, boneless	170	160
Chicken or turkey, leg or thigh	180 to 185	170 to 180
Chicken or turkey, ground	165	160
Stuffing (baked inside or outside of poultry)	180	160

FREQUENTLY ASKED QUESTIONS ABOUT COOKING POULTRY

Should I wash poultry before cooking it?

Since it's typically been sitting in its bloody juices, it's wise to rinse poultry in cool running water. Unless your next step will be poaching or brining, be sure to pat the poultry dry with paper towels.

How can I tell when poultry is done and safe to eat?

Consult the chart at left for particular types and cuts of poultry. Basically, **breast** meat is done when the internal temperature reaches 150 degrees F for chicken or 160 degrees F for turkey, while the preferred doneness for dark meat— legs and thighs—varies among cultures. Technically, **dark** meat is done and safe to eat at 170 degrees F, but some people find it more palatable at 180 degrees F. At the latter temperature there is no trace of pink at the joint. The best place to insert the thermometer to test white meat is in the densest part of the breast. To test doneness in dark meat, insert the thermometer into the densest part of the thigh, near the joint where the thigh attaches to the body. If you hit bone when you insert the thermometer, retract it a bit, as the temperature of bone is not an accurate indication of the temperature of the meat.

Another sign of doneness in poultry is when the juices run clear, rather than red or dark brown. First, pierce the meat with a long-tined meat fork. Immediately press the area where the prongs pierced through and look at the juices running freely from the hole. If the juices are clear or golden, the meat is done. If they are red or bloody, the bird needs more cooking time.

Why can't I just set a timer for a specific number of minutes to cook various chicken parts?

Doneness has more to do with internal temperature than with how long something is exposed to heat. Two 6-ounce chicken breasts cooked under the same broiler will be done at different times if one was placed under the broiler right out of the refrigerator and the other spent 20 minutes on the counter, coming to room temperature first. For accuracy, use a reliable, easy-to-read instant-read thermometer and consult the chart on the facing page.

How do I know how big a turkey to buy?

First, check the dimensions of your roasting pan and the internal dimensions of your oven to be sure you buy a bird that will fit. If you want to have enough turkey for leftovers, the guideline is to figure on about 1 pound raw, bone-in turkey per person.

Is white meat healthier than dark meat?

Breast, or white, meat has less internal fat than leg or thigh meat. To prevent leaner white meat from drying out during cooking, use quick cooking methods such as poaching, steaming, grilling, broiling, sautéing, and stir-frying. Also, marinades, brines, rubs, and velveting (a technique used for stir-fries) all help keep white meat moist and tender. Dark meat is better for braising because the fat helps keep the chicken moist during the long, slow simmer. Many people, including yours truly, prefer dark-meat poultry for its richer flavor. On the other hand, breast meat is a nice blank slate for all sorts of preparations.

Is boneless poultry less flavorful than bone-in?

Basically, yes. Any poultry, meat, or fish that's cooked on the bone and with the skin on is more flavorful than a boneless, skinless version, regardless of the cooking method used. Think about the difference in flavor between the first few bites of a pork or lamb chop and the meat right up against the bone.

If I don't want to eat the skin, does it matter when I remove it?

Chicken skin protects the meat from drying out during cooking, so if you prefer not to eat chicken skin, remove it after the chicken is cooked. When you braise chicken, the collagen in the skin melts, contributing unparalleled luster and body to the cooking liquids, resulting in a rich sauce.

What's the difference between "tenting" with foil and wrapping tightly with foil?

Plenty. When a roasted turkey just taken from the oven is covered tightly, the heat given off by the bird forms condensation on the underside of the foil. If the foil is tightly sealed, the turkey, in effect, sits in a steam chamber. Steam renders crispy skin flabby. Instead, fold and crease a sheet of aluminum foil and place it like a tent over the bird. The open ends of the tent provide an escape route for the steam, and the foil prevents the heat from dissipating while the turkey rests before carving.

What's wrong with just laying a sheet of foil flat on top of some grilled chicken breasts?

You might be tempted to do this to keep the breasts hot while you're waiting for a few more chicken pieces to be done on the grill. But as the cooked chicken gives off heat, it will be trapped as condensation on the underside of the foil. When you lift off the foil, a slick of water will slide right onto the expertly grilled chicken, and there goes your crispy skin. Tenting is the answer. In a pinch, however, if you're trying to keep heat in, use an inverted bowl with plenty of room between the top of the chicken and the underside of the bowl. The concave shape will trap the condensation, just like the sides of the foil tent. If possible, let a side of the bowl hang over the edge of the cutting board or platter to create an escape path for the steam.

What is trussing and why is it important?

Trussing keeps whole birds moist and encourages even cooking. By tying legs and wings close to the body, they're less exposed to the dry heat of the oven. Don't be intimidated by trussing a chicken. Your most important task is to secure the legs and wings close to the carcass. To truss a chicken, you'll need a length of kitchen string about one yard long. Follow these guidelines, or invent your own trussing technique: Be sure the bird is sitting breast side up. Trussing is easiest if you start by looping the midpoint of the string underneath the part of the bird that went over the fence last (1). Then, cross the string and bring it around the sides of the bird, over the legs and up to the wings (2). Turn the bird on its side and tie the two ends of string together on top of wings (3, 4). Tie a double knot and cut any excess string so that it doesn't get caught in the rack when you lift the bird after roasting.

What should I keep in mind when carving a chicken or turkey?

First of all, be warned: once your family and friends find out you have carving expertise, you will never be able to shun carving duty, unless there's someone else around who's equally adept. It can be downright painful to watch someone carve who doesn't know how. Carving is not that difficult, especially if you remember to remove the main parts from one side at a time in the following order (see illustrations on facing page): First, the leg and thigh. Next, the wing. Last, the breast. Use a sharp boning knife to separate and remove parts, and once the breasts are removed from the carcass, carve the breast meat into slices across the grain.

Chickens and turkeys have the same bone structure and musculature, so you can practice on a roasted chicken (page 187) before you move up to a turkey. (You can also practice on a raw chicken and use the cut-up—or carved—parts to make the Chicken Cacciatore on page 202.) The only difference in carving a chicken and a turkey is that you would serve a chicken thigh whole, but it's a good idea to cut the meat off the turkey thigh into serving-sized pieces before placing it on the platter.

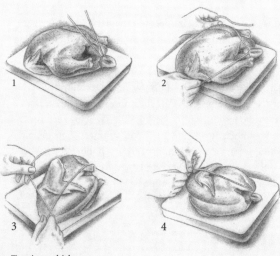

Trussing a chicken

CARVING A CHICKEN OR TURKEY INTO MAJOR MUSCLE GROUPS (LEG, THIGH, WING, BREAST)

Using a boning knife, first cut off the leg and thigh in one piece (1). Turn the cut piece skin side down and locate the white line that separates the leg and thigh (2). Cut through the line to separate the leg and thigh (3). For turkey, carve the meat off the thigh bone. Cut off the wing close to body (4). Cut off the breast in one piece (5), following the contour of the carcass with the boning knife and shaving (6), rather than slicing, along the body. Place the breast skin side up on a cutting board and use a carving knife to cut it into slices. Carve the second side of the bird the same way.

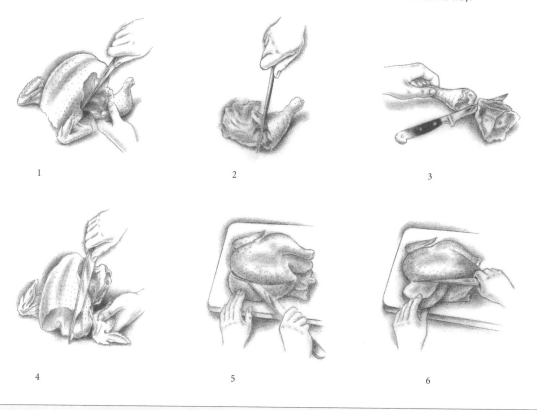

1

2

3

4

5

6

Finally, I never carve at the table, always at the kitchen counter. You need plenty of room to maneuver, and juices can squirt when and where you least expect. Besides, I like to hold a bone with one hand while holding the knife in my other—perhaps a bit déclassé at the dining room table. If you have any doubts about carving as you go along, just remove the parts that are protruding (leg, wing) from the body first, clearing the way to remove the breast meat in one large piece to be sliced crosswise (I don't recommend slicing breast meat with the grain "Norman Rockwell style"; it results in stringy meat). Be sure to smile while you're carving. You'll be rewarded by getting first dibs on the two "oysters" of dark meat nestled against the back of the bird. Yum!

RECITE SECRETS

If you cut the grapes in half (through the stem end), they're easier to eat and serve, and they are less likely to sink to the bottom of the serving bowl if you're serving this salad family style. Or for a more elegant look, leave them whole. Be sure to dry grapes well after washing to prevent them from watering down the dressing.

To ensure a delicate flavor and texture in this salad, use a vegetable peeler to remove the strings from the rounded outside of the celery stalks before mincing.

Use a good-quality commercial mayonnaise, such as Best Foods or Hellmann's, for the tastiest result.

CHICKEN SALAD VÉRONIQUE
WITH WHOLE TOASTED ALMONDS

There's nothing like a succulent, thyme-infused chicken salad made with tender chunks of moist poached chicken breast. The term Véronique (pronounced vair-on-*eek*) describes a dish prepared with seedless white grapes, the most famous of which is fillet of sole Véronique. Whole toasted almonds add a delightful crunch to this grape-studded, elegant but easy recipe. When fresh tomatoes are at their prime, serve the salad with thickly sliced heirloom tomatoes and crusty artisanal bread. In other seasons, start with a bowl of red bell pepper bisque (page 66). For a portable sandwich with sensational texture, line a pita bread half with leaf lettuce and stuff with the chicken salad. Use this chicken poaching technique to make chicken potpies (page 198), enchiladas, and any number of chicken-salad sandwich fillings. Be sure to strain the double-rich poaching liquid and save it. See page 59 for recipes in which you can put this broth into service.

Serves 4 to 6

6 cups homemade chicken stock or broth (page 60 or 61) or purchased reduced-sodium broth

2 bone-in whole chicken breasts or 4 bone-in half breasts, skin on

3 green onions, or 1 small yellow onion, quartered

5 fresh thyme sprigs, plus 2 teaspoons minced fresh thyme

1 bay leaf, preferably imported

½ pound flavorful seedless green grapes

2 large celery stalks, peeled and minced into ¼-inch pieces

¾ cup good-quality mayonnaise

Kosher salt and fine, freshly ground black pepper

1 cup blanched whole almonds, toasted (see page 89)

Red-leaf lettuce leaves, for serving

---

1. In a 4-quart saucepan over medium-high heat, bring the stock to a boil. Add the chicken breasts, onions, thyme sprigs, and bay leaf. Cook over medium-high heat until the stock returns to a steady boil, then cover and reduce the heat to the lowest setting. Simmer gently until the chicken reaches an internal temperature of 145 degrees F, or the juices run clear when the thickest part of a breast is pierced with a meat fork, 10 to 20 minutes; the timing depends on the size of the chicken breasts. When done, remove the chicken from the poaching liquid and set aside until cool enough to handle. Strain the poaching liquid for another use; let cool to room temperature before refrigerating. When the chicken is cool enough to handle, remove and discard the skin and bones, cut into roughly ¾-inch chunks, and transfer to a large bowl. (At this point, you can put the cut-up chicken in a deep bowl and add room-temperature broth just to cover. This will keep the chicken moist. Cover and refrigerate for up to 2 days. Be sure to drain the chicken well before using.)

2. Add the grapes, celery, and minced thyme to the chicken and toss to combine. Add the mayonnaise and stir gently. Season to taste with salt and pepper. (The recipe can be prepared to this point up to 8 hours in advance. Cover and refrigerate until ready to serve.)

3. Add the almonds and stir to combine. Line individual plates or a medium serving bowl with lettuce leaves and place the chicken salad on top. Serve at once.

ABOUT BLANCHED ALMONDS

Blanched almonds are whole almonds with the skins removed. Some fine cooks and chefs believe that the most flavorful almonds are those you blanch and toast yourself. If almonds have skins on, place them in a 4-quart pan of boiling water for 1 minute to blanch. Transfer to a sieve, drain, and peel off the skins. Then toast as directed on page 89.

RECIPE SECRETS

Black soy sauce, also known as sweet soy sauce, is soy sauce that has been augmented with molasses. It has a sweet, full-bodied flavor and is often used in braised dishes. Richer than regular soy sauce, black soy is also more viscous. If you are uncertain about what to buy, look for the sauce that leaves a dark coating inside the neck of the bottle after you shake it. Regular soy sauce is too thin to leave a heavy trace. If you can't find anything that resembles black soy sauce, stir a teaspoon of molasses into 1 tablespoon regular soy sauce.

According to *CookWise* author Shirley Corriher, the more you cut a chile, the more you release its spicy capsaicin. For a little bit of a spicy kick, cut 1 jalapeño crosswise into ¼-inch pieces, leaving seeds intact. For more of the same mild heat, use 2 jalapeños. For hotter heat, use 1 or 2 serranos.

Use the flat edge of your wok tool or a wooden spoon to break up chicken into clumps and sear in the wok or stir-fry pan. Wait until the underside is seared before stirring. Too much stirring as the chicken sears causes steam, which impedes caramelization. If you double this recipe, stir-fry the chicken in two batches, so that it caramelizes and doesn't steam.

THAI-STYLE MINCED CHICKEN
WITH BASIL AND CHILES

Inspired by a recipe from my favorite Thai cooking teacher, Kasma Loha-unchit, this quick stir-fry is a popular Sunday supper at my house. Known as *gai ka prow* in Thailand, many Thai restaurants in the United States prepare this dish with sliced chicken breast instead of the traditional hand-minced chicken thighs. When pressed for time, I ask the butcher for ground dark-meat chicken. This dish gets its characteristic taste from a harmonious combination of three flavors: sweet black soy sauce; salty, umami-rich fish sauce; and spicy chiles and white pepper. All are inexpensive and available in Asian markets or well-stocked supermarkets. To make this a complete meal and add a brilliant shot of color, add a large handful of blanched, 1-inch-cut green beans or elegant *haricots verts* with the basil. If you do, be sure to increase the sweet soy and Asian fish sauce.

Serves 2 or 3

1 pound boneless, skinless chicken thighs or ground dark-meat chicken

3 tablespoons peanut oil, divided

1 small yellow onion, ends removed, halved lengthwise, and sliced lengthwise into thin crescents

1 red bell pepper, seeded, deribbed, cut lengthwise into ½-inch-wide strips, and then cut on the diagonal into diamonds

1 tablespoon minced garlic, green germ removed if present

1 or 2 jalapeño or serrano chiles, cut crosswise into ¼-inch rings

1 tablespoon black soy sauce

1 tablespoon Thai or Vietnamese fish sauce

1 cup fresh basil leaves, preferably Thai basil

Fine, freshly ground white pepper

Al's Steamed White Rice, for serving (page 279)

---

1. If using chicken thighs, chop finely into ¼-inch pieces with a very sharp chef's knife. Alternatively, grind the chicken in a meat grinder, or cut into chunks and pulse 2 thighs at a time in a food processor.

2. Heat a wok or stir-fry pan over high heat. Add 1 tablespoon of the peanut oil. When the oil is hot enough to sizzle a piece of onion, add the onion and stir-fry for 1 minute. Add the bell pepper and stir-fry for 1 minute. Add the garlic and stir-fry 30 for seconds. Transfer the mixture to a bowl and set aside.

3. Return the pan to high heat. Add the remaining 2 tablespoons oil and swirl it up the sides to coat evenly. When the oil is hot enough to sizzle a piece of chicken, add the chicken. Use the edge of a wok spatula to break up the pieces of chicken and cover the bottom of the wok evenly. Do not stir the chicken yet. When the chicken is cooked on the bottom, after a minute or so, start to stir-fry it over high heat. If the chicken starts to give off lots of moisture, move it up the sides of the wok and let the liquid boil off in the bottom. Continue stir-frying just until the chicken is no longer pink inside, about 1 more minute.

4. Return the onion mixture to the pan. Add the chiles and stir-fry for 1 minute. Add the black soy sauce and stir-fry for 15 seconds. Add the fish sauce and the basil leaves and stir-fry just until the basil leaves are wilted, about 1 minute. Turn off the heat. Sprinkle lightly with white pepper. Taste and, if desired, adjust the sweetness with additional black soy, the saltiness with more fish sauce, and/or the spicy heat with more white pepper. Serve over rice.

WORKING WITH CHILES

Due to the popularity of stuffed chile "shooters," growers have bred much of the heat out of jalapeño chiles. For a hotter kick, use smaller serrano chiles (see illustration). The fiery part of the chile is concentrated in the seed-pod, which includes the ribs along the inside flesh and the seeds. Since it's impossible to determine a chile's heat until you taste it, to prevent the possibility of burning your fingers, always wear disposable gloves when working with chiles. If you fail to protect your hands and find that they are burning hours later, see my solution on page 157.

Jalapeño chile

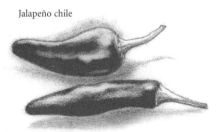

Serrano chile

RECIPE SECRETS

Besides providing a great use for day-old bread, fresh bread crumbs are simple to make and lend great texture to stuffings and casseroles. I love the way they soak up the flavorful juices of the other ingredients as they bake together. To make fresh bread crumbs, use a serrated knife to shave the crust off coarse-textured, day-old (or fresh) Italian bread. Tear the bread into 1-inch pieces and shred in a food processor or blender into crumbs no larger than ½ inch. Store extra fresh bread crumbs in the freezer and use in Baked Macaroni (page 110) or Rack of Lamb with Garlicky Bread Crumbs (page 224).

When sautéing ground meat or poultry, be sure the pan is hot enough to sear the meat, and don't add too much meat to the pan at one time, or it will steam instead of caramelize. It's better to sauté the meat in batches if your pan won't accommodate it in a single layer.

I prefer long, slender eggplants to the bulbous globe variety. The long ones are rarely bitter. But don't hesitate to use the globe variety if that's all that you can find. The secret to great-tasting eggplant in this dish is not cooking it too long. I don't peel either variety for this recipe.

To bring out the most flavor in dried herbs and spices, take a tip from Indian cooks and sauté the aromatics in the meat drippings or with the vegetables before adding liquids such as tomatoes. Frying releases the volatile oils in spices and herbs, contributing more vibrant flavor to the finished dish.

BAKED PORTABELLO MUSHROOMS STUFFED WITH TURKEY, EGGPLANT, AND FRESH BREAD CRUMBS

Sometimes you need a hardy but healthy, rib-sticking supper with flavor that's greater than the sum of its parts. For me, this is it. The turkey-eggplant-vegetable mixture freezes well, so I often make a double batch of filling and freeze it in individual freezer-to-microwave dishes that make a satisfying, effortless lunch. (See the Turkey-Eggplant Casserole with Fresh Bread Crumbs variation that follows.) For a vegetarian dish, simply omit the turkey. Like many tomato-based recipes, these behemoth stuffed mushrooms seem to get better as their flavors meld. Serve with Weeknight Green Salad (page 81) and Roasted Garlic Mashed Potatoes (page 281) or buttered orzo to balance the bold flavors.

Serves 6

6 fresh portabello mushrooms, each 3 to 3½ inches in diameter

2 tablespoons extra-virgin olive oil, divided, plus more for brushing on mushrooms

Kosher salt for sprinkling, plus 1½ teaspoons

Fine, freshly ground black pepper

10 ounces ground turkey or chicken meat (no skin)

1 yellow onion, chopped

1 red bell pepper, seeded, deribbed, and chopped into ½-inch pieces

3 cloves garlic, green germ removed if present, minced

½ teaspoon dried leaf oregano, crumbled between your fingers

¼ teaspoon fennel seeds

⅛ teaspoon crushed red pepper flakes

¾ pound long, slender eggplants, cut into roughly ¾-inch chunks

1 can (14½ ounces) diced tomatoes with juice

5 fresh basil leaves, each torn into 3 or 4 pieces, or ½ teaspoon dried leaf basil, crumbled between your fingers

¾ cup fresh bread crumbs from 2 or 3 slices Italian bread

6 ounces Monterey Jack cheese, shredded on the large holes of a box grater to yield 1½ cups

1 heaping tablespoon chopped fresh flat-leaf parsley

1. Preheat the oven to 350 degrees F. Select a deep baking dish or rimmed baking sheet large enough to accommodate the mushrooms in a single layer and spray it with vegetable oil spray (or brush lightly with olive oil).

2. Remove the stems from the mushrooms (leave the gills intact) and brush both sides of the caps generously with olive oil. Lightly sprinkle both sides with salt and pepper, then place gill side up in the prepared baking dish. Set aside.

3. Heat a heavy 6-quart Dutch oven over medium-high heat. Add 1 tablespoon of the olive oil. When the oil is hot enough to sizzle a small bit of turkey, add the turkey and, using a flat-bottomed wooden spatula, break up the meat into medium-sized clumps; they must not be too small. Do not stir the turkey yet. When the turkey is seared on the bottom, after about 5 minutes, start stirring. To keep the turkey moist and juicy, don't cook it completely at this stage; instead, cook it just until it is no longer pink. This should take about 10 minutes total. Transfer the seared turkey and any juices to a large bowl.

4. Add the remaining 1 tablespoon oil to the Dutch oven over medium-high heat. When the oil is hot enough to sizzle a piece of onion, add the onion and bell pepper and sauté until they begin to brown at the edges, about 10 minutes. Don't stir too much, and don't rush this step, as you want the vegetables to caramelize and develop deep flavor. Add the garlic, oregano, fennel seeds, and red pepper flakes and sauté for 1 minute. Add the eggplant and sauté for 2 minutes. Add the tomatoes and bring to a simmer. It's okay if the mixture seems dry. Stir in the basil, 1½ teaspoons salt, and a few grinds of pepper. Taste and add more salt and pepper, if desired. Transfer the mixture to the bowl with the turkey. Add the bread crumbs and stir to combine.

5. Spoon the mixture onto the mushrooms, dividing evenly. It's okay if some spills over onto the baking dish in between the mushrooms. Cover with aluminum foil and bake for 25 minutes. Remove the foil, divide the cheese evenly among the mushrooms, and return to the oven, uncovered. Continue baking until the cheese melts and the eggplant mixture is piping hot, about 10 minutes longer. Sprinkle evenly with the parsley and serve immediately.

TURKEY-EGGPLANT CASSEROLE WITH FRESH BREAD CRUMBS VARIATION

Omit the mushrooms. Prepare the remaining ingredients as directed. Rather than spooning the mixture onto the mushrooms, transfer it to a 9-inch square baking dish that has been coated with vegetable oil spray. Bake as directed. Serves 4.

SPRAYING BAKING DISHES WITH VEGETABLE OIL SPRAY

One of my pet peeves when using cooking spray is that the overspray often wafts all over the kitchen and lands in a sticky film on everything in its vicinity. To prevent this, when spraying a baking dish, open the dishwasher door (this trick is only good if the dishes inside are dirty), rest the baking dish on the inside of the door, and spray. Quickly remove the sprayed dish and shut the door, trapping the fumes and any overspray inside the dirty dishwasher. If this isn't convenient, place the baking dish in the sink and spray. With a little luck, the fumes will stay inside the sink. If all else fails, and you have easy access to the outdoors, step outside and spray the baking dish in the direction the wind is blowing.

RECIPE SECRETS

Late Chinese cooking authority Barbara Tropp turned me on to this simple velveting technique in which marinated chicken is blanched in hot water instead of the traditional hot oil. The result is incomparably tender and moist chicken breast chunks.

Cornstarch is used in both the marinade and sauce. To prevent cornstarch from becoming lumpy, always mix it with cold or room-temperature—never hot—liquids. Keep a spoon or chopstick handy to stir the mixture just before adding to the sauce, as the cornstarch tends to settle to the bottom.

Use the edge of a spoon to scrape off the peel before grating fresh ginger. To prevent it from becoming stringy, grate ginger crosswise on a Microplane grater or on the small holes of a box grater.

If you have only raw cashews, rather than roasted, fry them quickly in the hot peanut oil before you add the red pepper flakes. When they turn a deep golden brown, use a Chinese strainer or slotted spoon to transfer them to a heatproof bowl. Set aside and continue with the stir-fry.

STIR-FRIED VELVET CHICKEN WITH CASHEWS

Velveting is a traditional Chinese cooking technique most often used with chicken or shrimp. A simple procedure, it creates juicy, supersmooth morsels. For velveting, chicken is typically cut into bite-sized pieces, marinated in a seasoned egg white mixture, and then blanched in warm peanut oil, which binds the egg white to the chicken to produce a delectably soft exterior. This recipe demonstrates the effectiveness of using water instead of peanut oil for the blanching step. Serve this colorful stir-fry with steamed rice.

Serves 3 or 4

Marinade

1 tablespoon cornstarch

1 teaspoon kosher salt

1 tablespoon Shaoxing wine, white vermouth, or dry white wine

1 egg white

1 pound boneless, skinless chicken breasts (3 or 4 breast halves), cut into 1-inch pieces

Sauce

½ teaspoon cornstarch

¼ cup homemade chicken stock or broth (page 60 or 61) or purchased reduced-sodium broth

2 tablespoons soy sauce

1½ tablespoons Shaoxing wine, white vermouth, or dry white wine

1 teaspoon Asian toasted sesame oil

1 teaspoon sugar

Stir-Fry

2 tablespoons peanut oil

¼ to ½ teaspoon red pepper flakes

1 red bell pepper, seeded, deribbed, and cut into ½-inch strips, then cut on the diagonal into diamonds

½ pound pencil-thin asparagus, tough ends removed and cut on the diagonal into 1-inch pieces

3 green onions, green and white parts, cut on the diagonal into thin slices

1 teaspoon finely grated ginger

3 cloves garlic, green germ removed if present, cut into thin slices

⅓ cup unsalted roasted cashews

1. *Marinate the chicken:* In a medium bowl, combine the cornstarch and salt. Add the wine and egg white and whisk vigorously until the lumps disappear. Stir in the chicken chunks. Set aside to marinate for at least 10 minutes, or cover and refrigerate for up to 24 hours. (If refrigerated, bring the chicken to room temperature at least 30 minutes before continuing with the recipe.)

2. *Prepare the sauce:* In a small bowl, combine all the ingredients and stir until well blended. Set aside. (The mixture will need to be stirred again before adding to the pan.)

3. *To velvet the chicken:* In a 4-quart saucepan, heat 4 cups water almost to a simmer. Place a colander or strainer in the sink. Regulate the heat so the water is just steaming, not boiling or simmering. Using a Chinese strainer or large slotted spoon, transfer the marinated chicken to the steaming water. Stir with a chopstick to separate the pieces. The egg white will become stringy in the water. Cook just until the outside edges of the chicken pieces turn white, less than 1 minute (the chicken will not be cooked through). Transfer the chicken to the colander and leave to drain.

4. *Prepare the stir-fry:* Heat a wok or stir-fry pan over high heat. Add the peanut oil. When the oil is hot, add ¼ teaspoon red pepper flakes and stir-fry for 15 seconds. Add the bell pepper and asparagus and stir-fry for 2 minutes. Add the green onions and stir-fry for 30 seconds. Add the ginger and garlic and stir-fry for 30 seconds. Reduce the heat to low. Push the ingredients up onto the sides of the wok. Stir the sauce mixture, add it to the center of the wok, and stir constantly until it begins to bubble and thicken. Add the reserved velveted chicken and stir with the sauce. Slide the vegetables down to the bottom of the pan and cook, stirring often, until the chicken is hot in the center and just cooked through, about 1 minute. Turn off the heat and stir in the cashews.

ABOUT SHAOXING WINE

Also known as Shao Hsing wine, this amber-colored, mildly acidic Chinese cooking wine is made from fermented rice and can be aged between 10 and 100 years. Its age and quality are reflected in its price. If unavailable, substitute white vermouth, dry white wine, sake, or dry sherry. Store in a cool, dark place for up to several months.

RECITE SECRETS

For a tender, moist result, bring the chicken to room temperature before cooking and don't cook beyond an internal temperature of 150 degrees F.

The long strip of meat on the underside of a chicken breast is called the fillet strip or tenderloin. Sometimes these strips have been removed from the chicken breasts before they are sold. If they haven't been, I gently pull them off so the breasts will cook more evenly. The fillet strips are great in a stir-fry. To use them in this recipe, marinate and grill the strips separately.

Olive oil serves a trio of purposes here: it lubricates the chicken, preventing it from sticking to the grill; carries the flavors of the marinade; and contributes robust flavor of its own. Use a vibrant, bold oil (see page 80).

The high temperature of the grill or broiler would cause fresh garlic to burn, resulting in an acrid, off flavor. For the sweet taste of garlic without the risk of burning, use granulated garlic powder here instead of fresh garlic.

GARLICKY CHICKEN BREASTS

Grilled or broiled, these simple chicken breasts go together quickly for a week-night supper, yet make a flavorful addition to a mixed grill for company. Double the recipe to have a few extra on hand for lunchtime sandwiches and salads. It's your call whether to add green onions to the marinade. If you use them, leave them on when you cook the chicken. They'll char a bit, contributing fresh, bright flavor to the tender, juicy chicken breasts.

Serves 4

4 boneless, skinless chicken breast halves (about 1½ pounds), tenderloins removed if present

2 tablespoons bold-tasting extra-virgin olive oil

2 green onions, green and white parts, chopped (optional)

1 teaspoon kosher salt

½ teaspoon granulated garlic powder

¼ teaspoon fine, freshly ground black pepper

---

1. *Marinate the chicken:* Cut off any fat from the chicken. Combine the olive oil, green onions (if using), salt, garlic powder, and pepper in a 1-gallon zip-top plastic bag. Add the chicken and seal the bag, forcing out as much air as possible. Massage with your fingers to distribute the marinade. Leave to marinate, massaging occasionally, for at least 30 minutes or up to 24 hours. If marinating for 2 hours or more, refrigerate the bag; remove the bag from the refrigerator 1 hour before cooking the chicken.

2. *Cook the chicken:* Prepare a medium-hot fire in a charcoal grill, or preheat a gas or stove-top grill to medium-high. Alternatively, position a rack 4 inches from the broiler element and preheat the broiler. Remove the chicken from the marinade and discard the marinade. If grilling, place the chicken skin side (smooth side) down, with the pieces at least 1 inch apart to prevent steaming. If broiling, arrange the pieces skin side up on a perforated broiler pan and place in the broiler.

3. Cook the chicken on the first side for 5 minutes. If you're grilling and you want cross-hatching, rotate each piece a quarter turn after about 3 minutes. (An offset spatula is preferable to tongs for rotating the floppy pieces of chicken.) For moist meat, resist any temptation to press on the chicken as it cooks. Turn and cook the breasts on the other side for about 5 more minutes. The chicken is done when it reaches an internal temperature of 150 degrees F, or when the juices run clear when the chicken is pricked with a fork. To prevent cross-contamination, use a clean utensil to transfer the cooked chicken to dinner plates. If you plan to slice the chicken for sandwiches, let it rest for 5 minutes for the juices to retract before cutting.

TURKEY PICCATA

This quick Italian sauté traditionally features thin slices of veal or chicken breast, known as scaloppine. Here, turkey breast or breast tenderloins are cut, pounded, dredged in seasoned flour, and then quickly sautéed. Just before serving, they're enveloped in a zesty *à la minute* (at the last minute) pan sauce made from the flavorful pan drippings, enhanced with lemon juice and capers. Serve with Mashed Yukon Gold Potatoes (page 280) or Butternut Squash with Maple Syrup and Allspice (page 273) and Romano Beans (page 258) or Grilled Asparagus (page 250).

Serves 4

1 pound boneless, skinless turkey breast or turkey tenderloins

Kosher salt for sprinkling, plus 1 teaspoon

Fine, freshly ground black pepper for sprinkling, plus ¼ teaspoon

About ¼ cup all-purpose flour

1 tablespoon extra-virgin olive oil

4 tablespoons unsalted butter, divided

1 large lemon to yield about 1 teaspoon minced zest and ¼ cup juice, divided

2 cloves garlic, green germs removed if present, minced

2 tablespoons finely chopped fresh flat-leaf parsley

1 tablespoon capers, preferably salt-packed, rinsed and drained

ABOUT POUNDING MEAT AND POULTRY

Pounding serves two purposes: it tenderizes the meat or poultry and it creates cutlets of consistent thickness that brown evenly. Use the flat side of a meat pounder, not the end that looks like a medieval torture device (see illustration, page 181). If you don't have a meat pounder, use the bottom of a small, heavy saucepan. To keep the countertop clean when pounding meat, I place it on plastic wrap, then cover with waxed paper. (Two sheets of plastic wrap would stick together and not allow the meat to spread freely.)

/continued

RECIPE SECRETS

Both the type and size of your sauté pan make a difference when preparing *à la minute* sauces. In order to create the flavorful caramelized pan drippings that form the basis for the sauce, it's best to use a conventional, rather than nonstick, pan. If your pan is too big, the small amount of liquid in the sauce will evaporate before the caramelized bits stuck on the bottom are completely deglazed. If your pan is larger than 10 inches across the top, either use a smaller pan and cook in several batches, or double the sauce ingredients.

Because they're preserved in brine or salt, capers should always be rinsed and drained well. For the best flavor, look for salt-packed capers in upscale markets or Italian delicatessens. They have a more delicate taste than capers packed in vinegar or brine. If you love capers, double the amount called for in this recipe.

If both zest and juice are called for in a recipe, always remove the zest before you cut the lemon to squeeze out the juice.

This recipe utilizes either boneless turkey breast or the smaller fillet, or tenderloin, that runs along the underside of the breast. Sometimes the breast is sold with the fillet intact; if so, be sure to remove the tenderloin before you cut and pound the breast.

1. If you're using turkey breast with the tenderloin attached, gently pull off the tenderloin. If you're using turkey breast tenderloins, remove the white nerve from each: Cut the tenderloin in half lengthwise as close to the nerve as possible. Trim off and discard the nerve. If using turkey breast, remove any iridescent tissue—called silver skin—from the surface (see illustration on the facing page). If left on, the silver skin will shrink and curl up during cooking.

2. Cut turkey tenderloins crosswise into 1-inch pieces or cut the turkey breast crosswise into ½-inch-thick slices. Lay a sheet of plastic wrap on a flat surface. Place the pieces, cut side up and about 1 inch apart, on the wrap. Place a sheet of waxed paper directly on top to cover the turkey completely. With the flat side of a meat pounder, pound the turkey with a combination hitting-sliding motion, working from the center of each piece to the outside edge. Pound to a uniform thickness of about ¼ inch, being careful to avoid making holes. Lightly season the top side of the turkey pieces with salt and pepper.

3. Combine the flour, the 1 teaspoon salt, and the ¼ teaspoon pepper on a sheet of waxed paper; stir with a fork to blend. Dredge both sides of each piece of pounded turkey in the seasoned flour. Tamp off the excess flour and place the turkey slices on a clean sheet of waxed or parchment paper. (The turkey can be prepared to this point up to 3 hours in advance. Cover and refrigerate the turkey in a single layer; remove from the refrigerator 20 minutes before cooking.)

4. Preheat the oven to 180 degrees F. Place a large plate or small serving platter in the oven. Ten minutes before you're ready to serve the turkey, heat a 10-inch sauté pan or skillet over medium-high heat. Add the olive oil and 3 tablespoons of the butter. When the butter melts, swirl the pan to combine the butter and oil. Flick a few grains of flour into the fat. If they sizzle on contact, the pan is ready. If not, wait until the flour sizzles before adding the turkey.

5. Slide several scaloppine into the pan, keeping them in a single layer and leaving ½ inch of space around each piece. Don't crowd the pieces; you'll most likely have to cook the turkey in batches. To encourage caramelization, don't move the turkey except to turn it once with a meat fork or tongs. Sauté over medium-high heat just until golden brown, about 2 minutes on each side. Cooked scaloppine should be light golden brown on the outside and white inside. As the turkey cooks and shrinks in size, slip more scaloppine into the pan, always maintaining some separation among the pieces to prevent steaming. To prevent the butter from burning, don't create empty spots in the pan. As the turkey is done, shingle-stack the pieces on the warmed platter and place in the oven, uncovered, while you sauté the remaining pieces.

6. Keep the sautéed meat in the oven while you prepare the sauce: Holding the hot pan off the heat, add the remaining 1 tablespoon butter and the lemon juice. Return the pan to medium heat and, using a flat-bottomed wooden spatula, deglaze the pan by scraping up any caramelized bits stuck on the bottom. After 1 minute, reduce the heat to the lowest setting and add the lemon zest, garlic, parsley, and capers. After 30 seconds, stir and taste. Adjust the seasoning with salt and/or pepper, if necessary. Slip the scaloppine and any juices that have collected at the bottom of the platter back into the pan. Quickly turn the slices once to moisten them evenly with the caper mixure. Serve immediately with any remaining pan sauce and capers spooned over the scaloppine.

VARIATION

. . . .

Try this recipe with pork tenderloin, veal scaloppine, or boneless, skinless small chicken breasts instead of the turkey. Cut pork tenderloin as directed for turkey tenderloin. Pound pork or chicken breasts as directed. There is usually no need to pound veal scaloppine, but you may want to cut it into manageable pieces if it is too large.

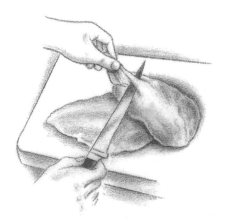

Removing silver skin

RECIPE SECRETS

If you prefer, substitute chicken breasts, but thighs are juicier, and many people find them more flavorful.

To prevent breading from becoming too thick and separating from the cutlets during cooking, let the excess egg wash drip off before dredging the chicken in the cracker meal. It's okay if all the parsley and grated cheese don't stick to the cutlets.

You can use fine dried bread crumbs here, but I prefer the flavor and texture of cracker meal (see page 147). It creates a lighter coating than bread crumbs.

For superquick sauces such as this one, I like imported Pomi brand chopped tomatoes, which are packed in 26½-ounce aseptic boxes with nothing added, not even salt. Whether using canned or fresh tomatoes in sauces or soups, use their flavorful packing juices, too.

For the best melting properties, use low-moisture mozzarella cheese, rather than fresh mozzarella packed in whey. Or, substitute sliced provolone.

CHICKEN THIGHS PARMIGIANA

Chicken parmigiana makes a great addition to an Italian family-style meal. The cutlets don't have to be absolutely piping hot when you eat them, and after the chicken is pounded and breaded, it creates an illusion of abundance. If you plan to serve a crowd—or for sensational leftovers—double the recipe. For a child-friendly version, cut the chicken into finger-sized strips before pounding. These breaded cutlets lend themselves to advance preparation: Marinate the chicken and make the sauce up to 24 hours ahead (or use leftover 20-Minute Tomato Sauce, page 114). Sauté the cutlets a couple of hours ahead, then, just before serving, top with the tomato sauce and pop them into the oven. Leftover chicken parmigiana makes fantastic hot sandwiches on crusty rolls: smear the inside of the roll with tomato sauce, top the chicken with a few Roasted Peppers (page 254), wrap in aluminum foil, and bake until hot.

Serves 4

Chicken	Tomato Sauce
2 large eggs	1 cup peeled, seeded, and diced tomatoes with juices (fresh or canned)
2 tablespoons freshly grated Romano or Parmesan cheese	1 tablespoon bold-tasting extra-virgin olive oil
3 tablespoons finely chopped fresh flat-leaf parsley, divided	1 clove garlic, smashed gently with the side of a chef's knife
½ teaspoon granulated garlic powder	1 teaspoon kosher salt
½ teaspoon kosher salt	⅛ teaspoon fine, freshly ground black pepper
¼ teaspoon fine, freshly ground black pepper	3 fresh basil leaves
1 pound boneless, skinless chicken thighs (about 4 thighs)	
¾ cup cracker meal	
3 to 5 tablespoons mild-tasting extra-virgin olive oil	
½ pound mozzarella cheese, preferably low moisture, cut into ¼-inch-thick slices	

1. *Marinate the chicken:* In a bowl, combine the eggs, cheese, 2 tablespoons of the parsley, the garlic powder, salt, and pepper. Mix well and set aside.

2. If necessary, trim off any fat or cartilage from the chicken. Lay a sheet of plastic wrap on a flat surface. Place the thighs, skin side (smooth side) up, on the wrap; be sure to leave a couple of inches around each piece for the chicken to spread. Place a sheet of waxed paper directly on top to cover the chicken completely. With the flat side of a meat pounder, pound the chicken with a combination hitting-sliding motion, working from the center of each piece to the outside edge. Pound to a uniform thickness of ¼ to ½ inch, being careful to avoid making holes. Transfer the pounded thighs to the egg mixture and stir to coat evenly. (This step can be done up to 24 hours in advance. Cover and refrigerate; stir occasionally. Bring to room temperature before breading the chicken.)

Meat pounder

Meat tenderizer

3. *Prepare the sauce:* Place the tomatoes in a nonreactive 2-quart saucepan. If using fresh tomatoes, bring them to a boil over medium-high heat, reduce the heat to low, and simmer until soft and reduced in volume, 5 to 8 minutes. If using canned tomatoes, there is no need to reduce the tomatoes; just bring them to a simmer over low heat. Slowly stir in the olive oil, then add the garlic, salt, and pepper. Cook, uncovered, over low heat until slightly thickened, 3 to 5 minutes. Tear the basil leaves into a few rough pieces and add to the sauce; stir to combine. Cover partially and remove from the heat. (The sauce can be prepared up to 8 hours in advance and left on a turned-off burner.)

4. *Cook the chicken:* Preheat the oven to 350 degrees F. Coat a rimmed baking sheet (large enough to hold chicken in a single layer) with vegetable oil spray or line with a silicone baking liner. Set aside.

5. Pour the cracker meal onto a 12-inch length of waxed paper. Using a meat fork, lift each chicken thigh out of the egg mixture, letting the excess egg wash drip off each piece, and dredge both sides in the meal, pressing lightly to coat all surfaces. Arrange the breaded chicken pieces in a single layer on a clean sheet of waxed paper. Cover with another sheet of waxed paper and gently press to adhere—and release excess—crumbs.

/continued

6. Place a 12- or 14-inch nonstick skillet over medium heat. When the pan is hot, add 3 tablespoons of the olive oil. When the oil is hot enough to sizzle a few crumbs of cracker meal, gently slide in the chicken. Don't crowd the pan; if necessary, sauté the chicken in batches. Cook the chicken, turning once, until golden brown on both sides, about 5 minutes on each. Drain on paper towels. If necessary, add more olive oil to the skillet and let it get hot before sautéing the remaining chicken. To prevent excess oil from being absorbed into the breading, regulate the heat as necessary to maintain a consistently high cooking temperature, and don't place the chicken in the pan until the oil is hot.

7. Arrange the browned chicken in a single layer on the prepared baking sheet. Remove and discard the garlic clove from the tomato sauce. Spread 1 to 2 table-spoons sauce on each piece of chicken. (You won't use all the sauce.) Bake the chicken until it is piping hot inside, 15 to 20 minutes. Test for doneness by inserting the tip of a paring knife into a piece of chicken. The knife tip should feel hot to the touch. Remove from the oven, top each piece with mozzarella, and return to the oven. Bake until the cheese melts, about 5 minutes.

8. Just before the chicken is ready, reheat the remaining tomato sauce. When the cheese has melted, remove the chicken from the oven and immediately sprinkle the remaining 1 tablespoon parsley over the melted cheese. Serve the chicken on warmed plates. Transfer the sauce to a warmed bowl to serve at the table.

GRILLED STUFFED CHICKEN BREASTS WITH PROSCIUTTO, TALEGGIO, AND PESTO

An adaptation of a dish I prepared on television in the PBS series *Cooking at the Academy,* these butterflied chicken breasts are elegant, yet simple to make. I often assemble a double batch the day before a dinner party, then grill or broil them at the last minute. I secretly hope for leftovers, as they're great the next day for a picnic, or sliced on the bias, slathered with pesto-laced mayonnaise, and tucked into a slab of crusty focaccia. Serve with Grilled Asparagus (page 250), Roasted Peppers (page 254), and Orzo with Toybox Tomatoes and Fresh Mint (page 283).

Serves 6

¼ pound Taleggio cheese	Kosher salt and fine, freshly ground black pepper
6 paper-thin slices (about 3 ounces) prosciutto	12 large fresh basil leaves
6 boneless, skinless chicken breast halves, at least 7 ounces each, butterflied	2 to 3 tablespoons extra-virgin olive oil
	1 cup Pesto (page 186)

1. Cut the Taleggio into 6 logs, each with a piece of rind on one edge, if possible. Wrap a slice of prosciutto around each log of cheese. Cover and set aside.

2. If the butterflied chicken breasts are too small to hold the cheese logs, pound the chicken a bit: Lay a sheet of plastic wrap on a flat surface. Open the butterflied breasts like a book, and place them skin side down on the wrap. Be sure to leave a couple of inches of room around each piece for the chicken to spread. Place a sheet of waxed paper on top of the chicken. With the flat side of a meat pounder, gently pound-stretch each piece of chicken until it becomes large enough to accommodate the log of cheese. Be careful not to tear the meat. Remove the waxed paper.

/continued

RECICE SECRETS

Taleggio is a rich, creamy Italian cow's milk cheese made in Lombardy. Among its distinguishing characteristics are its square shape and edible rind, perfect for stuffing into butterflied chicken breasts. Look for Taleggio in cheese shops and specialty markets where fine cheeses are sold. Or, substitute another semisoft cheese such as Brie, Camembert, or a good-quality Monterey Jack. Mozzarella and Fontina can become rubbery as they cool; Taleggio stays creamy. I use a cheese knife (see illustration below) to cut the Taleggio into evenly shaped logs.

You needn't use the finest-quality imported prosciutto in this recipe. Since the ham is wrapped around the cheese, then tucked inside the chicken breast, you might not appreciate the subtle nuances of flavor and texture that distinguish the best prosciutti. But, by all means, leave the fat on the prosciutto. As the chicken cooks, the fat melts and bastes the inside of the chicken with great flavor.

Wrapping the prosciutto around the cheese before tucking it into the butterflied chicken breast helps prevent the cheese from oozing out during cooking. (I'm pleased to say I learned this in class from a very astute student.)

For the best results, use large chicken breasts, about 7 ounces per half breast. Ask your butcher to butterfly them, or do it yourself (see illustrations on the facing page).

3. Lightly sprinkle the inside of each butterflied chicken breast with salt and pepper. Place 2 leaves of basil and a prosciutto-wrapped log of cheese on one side of each butterflied breast. Fold the other half over, covering the log, and secure the chicken with round toothpicks that have been dipped in olive oil (to make insertion easier). Use as few toothpicks as are necessary; the more you insert, the more you must remove from the hot chicken before serving. Brush both sides of the chicken with olive oil (it's okay to use the same oil you used for the toothpicks) and sprinkle lightly with salt and pepper. (The chicken can be prepared up to this point, placed on a plate or platter, covered, and refrigerated for up to 24 hours. Remove from the refrigerator 1 hour before grilling.)

4. Prepare a medium-hot fire in a charcoal grill, or preheat a gas or stove-top grill to medium-high. To grill, place the chicken skin side (smooth side) down, with the pieces at least 1 inch apart to prevent steaming. Cook, turning once, until the internal temperature of the densest part of the meat reaches 145 degrees F, about 5 minutes per side. Be sure to insert the thermometer into the meat, not the cheese; the latter can skew the reading. (As previously mentioned, white-meat chicken is done at 150 degrees. The residual heat from the melted cheese will elevate the internal temperature as the chicken rests.)

5. While the chicken is cooking, drizzle a little Pesto in a random pattern across the surface of a serving platter or onto individual plates.

6. With clean tongs (to prevent cross contamination), transfer the cooked chicken to a clean cutting board. Using needle-nose pliers, fish tweezers, or your fingers, twist and pull out every toothpick. Place the chicken on the prepared platter or plates, and drizzle a little more Pesto over the chicken. Pass the remaining Pesto in a bowl at the table.

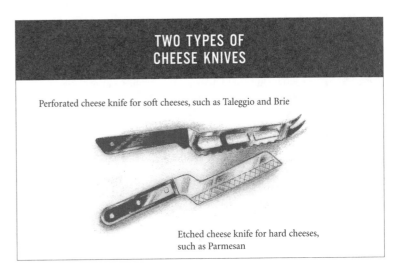

TWO TYPES OF CHEESE KNIVES

Perforated cheese knife for soft cheeses, such as Taleggio and Brie

Etched cheese knife for hard cheeses, such as Parmesan

It's easiest to butterfly chicken breasts when they are very cold. If necessary, remove the skin (1) and cut whole (double) breasts into 2 breast halves (2).

Gently cut or tear off the tenderloins or fillets, if present, and save for another use (3).

Trim off any cartilage or large pieces of fat (4).

Place a chicken breast skin side up on a clean cutting board. Using the sharp, rounded tip of a boning knife or a chef's knife, and keeping the knife blade parallel to the cutting board, make several small incisions down along the rounded side of the breast, eventually cutting the breast almost into two pieces (5). To keep yourself from inadvertently going off course and cutting a hole through the chicken, make several small slits, rather than a few large cuts. That way, if you do make a hole, it will be small enough to patch or cover with basil leaves. When you lift and open the top half (6)— as if you were turning a page in a book—the breast should be shaped like a butterfly, with the two halves connected down the center (7). This technique works well for small chicken breasts, when pounding is essential to expand the surface area in order to accommodate stuffing, such as a log of cheese. However, if your chicken breasts are larger, it is often not necessary to completely butterfly the breasts—all you need is a pocket large enough to accommodate the stuffing. (The advantage to creating a pocket, rather than butterflying, is that you won't have to insert—and remove—as many toothpicks.) To make a pocket, proceed as directed above, cutting an incision just long and wide enough to create a pocket that will accommodate your stuffing.

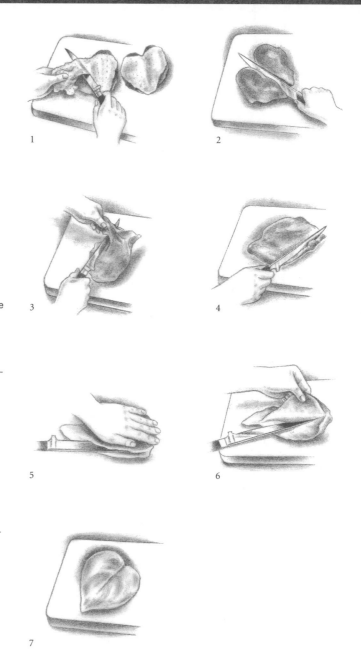

RECIPE SECRETS

Use mild-tasting extra-virgin olive oil, such as an oil from Liguria or Provence, for smooth-tasting pesto. Many upscale ethnic markets will let you taste their olive oils before buying. All you have to do is ask.

To help preserve the bright green in the fresh basil, chill the olive oil before adding it to the food processor. (The cold oil mitigates some of the heat from the processor.) Some cooks add a crushed vitamin C tablet or a little ascorbic acid to preserve the color. Others pour a thin layer of oil on top of the pesto before storing.

Choose sprigs of basil with the smallest leaves. They're the sweetest and most tender.

Pesto is traditionally made in a large mortar and pestle, and some Italians wouldn't think of toasting the pine nuts for pesto the way Americans do. This version uses a food processor or blender instead of a mortar and pestle, but be careful not to overprocess the pesto, or the leaves will bruise and turn from vibrant, bright green to mottled army green. By the way, if you love the flavor of toasted pine nuts, be my guest (see page 89 for how to toast pine nuts in a microwave).

PESTO

Being of Neapolitan descent, I had never even tasted pesto, a Ligurian specialty, until I was thirty years old. My first encounter with the unctuous green sauce was in a San Francisco restaurant. I must confess, it was a bit overwhelming. I loved the vibrant, fresh taste of summer it added to a plate of delicate cheese ravioli, but it was so rich that I could barely finish the plate of pasta. It took another five years before I started experimenting with pesto. Now I love it, but to this day, for me, a little goes a long way. Still, I wouldn't think of serving grilled chicken breasts stuffed with prosciutto and Taleggio (page 183) without a drizzle of fresh pesto to perk up both the flavor and presentation. Pesto is also terrific tossed with long *fusilli* pasta, either solo or as an accompaniment to grilled swordfish. And there's always cheese ravioli.

Makes about 1½ cups

⅔ cup mild-tasting extra-virgin olive oil

2 cups packed fresh basil leaves (from 1 large bunch)

3 cloves garlic, green germ removed if present

3 tablespoons pine nuts

1 teaspoon kosher salt

½ cup freshly grated *pecorino romano* or Reggiano-Parmigiano cheese, or a combination

---

1. Measure the olive oil into a liquid measuring cup and refrigerate it while you prep the remaining ingredients.

2. Swish the basil leaves around in a bowl of cool water. Lift them out with your fingers and spin dry in a salad spinner. (Or shake the leaves dry in a sieve, then roll them gently in kitchen towels to rid them of excess water.) Spread the leaves on a clean, dry kitchen towel to continue drying. Set aside.

3. Smell the garlic. If it seems particularly "hot" or sharp, place it in a small saucepan, add water to cover by 1 inch, and simmer for 5 minutes. Drain the garlic and transfer to a food processor or blender.

4. Process the garlic until finely minced. Scrape down the sides of the work bowl and process again. Add the pine nuts, basil, and salt. Process just until the leaves are chopped; scrape down the bowl. With the motor running, drizzle in about two-thirds of the cold olive oil. Scrape down the bowl and add the cheese. Process to combine the ingredients; scrape down the bowl. With the motor running, drizzle in the remaining olive oil. The mixture should have a flowing consistency, but not be overly runny. (If it is too runny, add more basil and/or cheese.) Scrape down the bowl and taste. Add more salt, if necessary, to make the mixture taste bright.

5. If you're not using the pesto immediately, or to store leftover pesto, transfer it to a covered container with minimal headroom. Refrigerate for up to a few days. Bring to room temperature before serving.

CLASSIC HERB-ROASTED CHICKEN

Nothing makes my mouth water more than the smell of chicken roasting in the oven. This foolproof recipe requires little fuss, and is my first choice when I want to serve a comforting home-cooked meal. If you're in a hurry, don't bother tucking the thyme sprigs under the skin or stuffing chunks of onion into the cavity. But do take a minute or two to season the chicken inside and out with the savory rub of oregano, granulated garlic powder, salt, and pepper. It smells and tastes great.

Serves 4 to 6

1 teaspoon dried leaf oregano, crumbled between your fingers	¼ teaspoon fine, freshly ground black pepper
1 teaspoon granulated garlic powder	1 chicken, 3 to 4 pounds
1 teaspoon kosher salt	Several fresh thyme sprigs
	1 small yellow onion, cut into 4 pieces

---

1. Position a rack in the lower third position of the oven and preheat to 425 degrees F. Spray a roasting pan and rack generously with vegetable oil spray and set aside.

/continued

RECIPE SECRETS

Fresh thyme tucked between the skin and breast meat flavors the chicken with a lovely perfume. As the fat in the skin melts, it bastes the breast meat with thyme-flavored juices.

I start the chicken at a high temperature and then reduce the heat. This ensures crisp, golden brown skin. If you want to shave off a little roasting time, it's okay to roast the chicken at the higher temperature for the entire time, as restaurant chefs do, but I find this causes excessive splattering, making a mess in the oven.

Trussing keeps the chicken moist by preventing exposed parts from drying out while surrounded by the dry heat of the oven. Don't be intimidated by trussing a chicken; see page 166 for easy-to-follow steps. Or, invent your own trussing technique.

2. In a small bowl, mix together the oregano, granulated garlic powder, salt, and pepper; set aside.

3. Remove the packaged giblets from the chicken cavity, if included, and reserve for another use or discard. Rinse the chicken inside and out and blot dry inside and out with paper towels. Place the chicken, breast side up, on a clean cutting board. Carefully insert an index finger between the skin and breast meat to make a pocket. Tuck a few thyme sprigs into the pocket, spreading them with your fingers over the breast meat. Sprinkle the neck and body cavities with the oregano mixture, reserving some for the outside of the bird. Place the onion pieces and a few sprigs of thyme in each cavity. Pat the remaining seasoning mix all over the outside of the chicken.

4. If desired, truss the chicken (page 166) and place, breast side up, on the rack in the prepared roasting pan. Roast for 20 minutes. Reduce the heat to 350 degrees F and continue roasting until the internal temperature tested near the hip joints of each thigh (but not touching bone) reaches 170 to 180 degrees F, 50 to 60 minutes. Remove from the oven, tent with aluminum foil, and let stand for 10 minutes for the juices to retract before carving. See page 167 for carving tips.

ROASTED STUFFED TURKEY with PAN GRAVY

For the past several years, each fall I've taught a class called Your First Turkey. It's one of my favorite classes because the students are always full of enthusiasm. Many come from cultures that don't have an annual turkey-eating tradition, but they've had a taste of American Thanksgiving and want to create a special holiday feast of their own. At first, I expected only young or novice cooks at these classes, but I'm always pleased to see more experienced cooks, eager to learn how to brine a bird or how to perfect the gravy that's plagued them for years. (Because brining, stuffing, roasting, and carving a turkey require certain equipment that new cooks might not have on hand, you'll find a checklist of equipment at the beginning of this recipe.) While I haven't strayed much from my mother's satisfying classic bread stuffing, it's fair to say that my approach to preparing the traditional Thanksgiving bird has changed since I began teaching Your First Turkey classes. Now I wouldn't think of roasting a turkey I hadn't brined first. Today, consumers are bombarded with more and more information about the pedigree of turkeys. To my taste, a fresh natural bird is more tender and flavorful than a free-range turkey, and less expensive, too. For more information on selecting a turkey, see page 162.

Serves 10 to 12 with leftovers

Special Equipment

. . . .

Large stockpot or clean, food-safe plastic bucket (a 16-quart stockpot accommodates a 14-pound turkey)

Roasting pan with rack

4 or 5 metal poultry skewers, each about 3 inches long

Cheesecloth

Fine-mesh skimmer

Fat-separator measuring cup

Flat whisk

Cutting board large enough for the turkey

To Brine the Turkey

. . . .

1¾ cups kosher salt

8 cups hot water

About 2 gallons cold water, divided

1 tablespoon black peppercorns

1 tablespoon granulated garlic powder

1 bunch fresh thyme or 1 table-spoon dry leaf thyme, crumbled between your fingers

1 fresh turkey, 10 to 12 pounds, with giblets

Broth for Gravy and Stuffing

. . . .

Giblets from turkey

8 cups water

1 large yellow onion, unpeeled, washed, and cut in half

2 carrots, unpeeled, cut into 2-inch pieces

1 celery stalk, cut into 2-inch pieces

5 fresh thyme sprigs

4 fresh flat-leaf parsley sprigs

2 cloves garlic, peeled but left whole

8 black peppercorns

2 whole cloves

1 bay leaf, preferably imported

/continued

RECIPE SECRETS

For a tender, juicy, and flavorful bird, brine the turkey in a salt-water solution for 24 to 48 hours before roasting. This step is especially important for free-range turkeys, as it also seems to tenderize their tougher muscles.

To determine cooking time, figure on about 15 minutes per pound for an unstuffed turkey. Then, add 30 minutes to the total cooking time if the turkey is stuffed. To be safe, test the internal temperature of the thigh about 30 minutes before you figure it should be done. When done, the internal temperature of the thickest part of the thigh (without touching the thermometer to the bone) should be 180 degrees F, so you can remove the turkey from the oven when it reaches 175 degrees. The residual heat in the bird will cause the temperature to climb as it rests outside the oven.

Let the roasted turkey rest for 30 minutes (tented loosely with aluminum foil to keep it warm) before carving. This allows the juices to be absorbed back into the meat, and it gives you time to make the pan gravy.

Stuffing

¾ cup (1½ sticks) unsalted butter

¾ cup minced yellow onion

¾ cup minced celery

3 tablespoons minced fresh flat-leaf parsley

2½ teaspoons kosher salt

1 teaspoon fine, freshly ground black pepper

1 tablespoon plus ½ teaspoon Bell's Seasoning or other poultry seasoning

2¼ teaspoons dry mustard

4½ quarts ½-inch bread cubes (from about 1½ pounds day-old white bread with crusts removed)

2 large eggs, lightly beaten

½ cup raisins, rehydrated in hot water and drained (optional)

About 2¼ cups broth (recipe on pages 189, 191)

To Roast Turkey

About 1½ teaspoons fine, freshly ground black pepper

½ cup (1 stick) unsalted butter

Gravy

Up to 3 tablespoons unsalted butter, if needed to supplement fat from turkey drippings

Up to 2 cups broth (recipe on pages 189, 191) to supplement pan juices from roasting

¼ cup all-purpose flour

Kosher salt and fine, freshly ground black pepper

1. *Brine the turkey:* Plan on starting the brining 24 to 48 hours before roasting. In a large stockpot or plastic bucket, combine the salt and hot water. Stir until the salt dissolves completely. Add 1 gallon of the cold water, the peppercorns, garlic powder, and thyme. Stir to combine.

2. Remove the giblet package from the turkey cavity and refrigerate the giblets for the turkey broth. Rinse the turkey inside and out with cool running water. Remove any plastic inserts, including a pop-up thermometer and plastic or metal "harness" if present. Peel off and discard any large pads of fat (but leave the skin flaps intact) around the openings of the cavity. Place the turkey in the brine. Continue to add cold water until the turkey is completely submerged. Stir, cover, and refrigerate for 24 to 48 hours.

3. *Prepare the broth:* You can make the broth up to 48 hours before roasting. Open the reserved package of giblets. Discard the liver (or save for another use), and rinse the giblets in cool water. Place the giblets in a 4-quart saucepan and add the water. Bring to a boil over high heat, reduce the heat to a simmer, and, using a fine-mesh skimmer or a ladle, skim off any impurities that rise to the surface. Simmer for 10 minutes, skimming as needed. Add the onion, carrots, celery, thyme sprigs, parsley sprigs, garlic, peppercorns, cloves, and bay leaf. If necessary, add more water just to cover the giblets. Simmer for 1 hour, uncovered, skimming any scum that rises to the surface. Strain the broth through a fine-mesh sieve into a 2-quart liquid measure or bowl. Measure out 2¼ cups for preparing the stuffing, and let cool to room temperature. Set aside the remaining broth for preparing the gravy. If the broth is done more than 4 hours before using, let cool to room temperature, cover, and refrigerate. Let any leftover broth cool, then cover and refrigerate or freeze (page 58) and use in place of chicken stock in soups, risottos, and the like.

4. *Prepare the stuffing:* Up to 2 hours before roasting the turkey, heat a 12-inch sauté pan or skillet over medium-high heat. Add the butter. When the butter is hot enough to sizzle a piece of onion, add the onion and celery and sauté until the onion is soft and translucent, 6 to 8 minutes. Add the parsley, salt, and pepper and sauté for another minute. Add the poultry seasoning and dry mustard, remove from the heat, and stir until all the ingredients are combined evenly.

5. Place the bread cubes in a large bowl. Add the onion mixture and toss to mix. Stir in the eggs and the raisins, if using. While stirring with a large spoon, pour 1½ cups of the reserved hot broth all over the mixture. You may not need more broth if the bread is soft and fresh. If the bread is on the dry side, add enough broth, up to another ¾ cup, to moisten the bread fully without completely soaking it. You should be able to distinguish individual cubes of bread in the moist stuffing.

/continued

RECIPE SECRETS

Use a sturdy roasting pan or rimmed baking sheet (with a rack) large enough to accommodate the bird with space around it on all sides. If you are buying a roasting pan, measure your oven to make sure your purchase will fit. If you don't want to invest in a roasting pan, buy 2 disposable pans and stack them for extra support.

While it's roasting, cover the turkey with a piece of cheesecloth saturated in melted butter—you'll never have to baste the bird.

Don't be surprised if you detect a very slight pink tinge in the breast meat of a brined turkey. As with hams, the color is a by-product of brining.

Store any leftover gravy, covered, in the refrigerator, and use any remaining turkey broth, carving juices, or water to thin the gravy when you reheat it.

6. *Roast the turkey:* One hour before roasting the turkey, remove the turkey from the brine and rinse under cool running water. Blot dry inside and out with paper towels. Discard the brine. To ensure that the turkey will cook evenly, let it rest at room temperature for about 1 hour before roasting.

7. Position a rack in the oven at the lowest level necessary to accommodate the turkey and preheat to 425 degrees F. Generously coat a roasting pan and rack with vegetable oil spray.

8. Lightly sprinkle the turkey inside and out with the pepper. Lightly pack the stuffing into the neck and body cavities of the bird, leaving enough loose skin at both cavities to arrange over the openings. Secure the openings by weaving the skin together with metal poultry skewers. (To prevent the possible growth of bacteria, do not refrigerate a stuffed turkey either before or after roasting.)

9. Place the turkey, breast side up, on the rack in the roasting pan. In a 2-quart saucepan, melt the butter over low heat. Cut a piece of cheesecloth as long as the turkey, unfold the cheesecloth completely, and fold in half. Dip the folded cheesecloth into the melted butter to absorb all the butter completely and saturate the cheesecloth. Arrange the soaked double layer of cheesecloth over the surface of the turkey, covering as much of the bird as possible. Drizzle any remaining melted butter onto the cheesecloth. If using, insert an ovenproof thermometer into the densest part of a thigh, where the thigh meets the carcass, not touching the bone.

10. Roast the turkey for 30 minutes. After 30 minutes, reduce the oven temperature to 325 degrees F. Calculate the remaining cooking time: Figure on 15 minutes per pound and add 30 minutes for the stuffing. Then subtract 1 hour for the time already in the oven and to build in a fudge factor. Set a timer. Every half hour or so, peek to be sure the cheesecloth isn't getting too dark. When the cheesecloth becomes very dark brown, remove the turkey from the oven and gently peel off the cheesecloth. Return the turkey to the oven and continue roasting. Depending on the size of both the turkey and your oven, you may not have to remove the cheesecloth until the turkey is done.

11. When the timer rings, remove the turkey from the oven and check the temperature in the densest part of each thigh (but without touching the bone). The thermometer should register 175 degrees when it's time to remove the turkey from the oven. If the breast is getting too brown, cover only the breast with a loose tent of aluminum foil. When the turkey is done, transfer the rack and turkey to a heavy, rimmed baking sheet. Carefully remove and discard the cheesecloth if you haven't already done so. Tent the turkey loosely with aluminum foil and let rest in a warm place for 30 minutes while you make the pan gravy. In the turned-off oven, warm a serving platter, a large bowl for stuffing, and a gravyboat or bowl.

12. *Prepare the gravy:* Pour off all of the pan juices from the roasting pan into a fat-separator measuring cup or into a 4-cup heatproof liquid measure. Spoon off 3 tablespoons of the fat that rises to the top and add it back to the pan. If there is insufficient turkey fat, make up the difference with butter. If you are not making additional gravy, discard the remaining fat from the surface of the pan juices. Add enough of the reserved homemade turkey broth to the pan juices to total 2 cups liquid. Set aside.

13. Place the roasting pan with the fat on the stove top over medium-high heat. Use a flat whisk to scrape up the browned bits from the pan bottom. Depending on the size of your roasting pan, you may want to balance it over 2 burners, or rotate it around 1 burner. Reduce the heat to medium and make a roux: Sprinkle the flour into the pan all at once and cook, whisking constantly, until the mixture is smooth and golden brown, 3 to 5 minutes. Slowly pour in the 2 cups broth, a few tablespoons at a time at first, whisking constantly. After you've added about ½ cup broth, it's okay to add the rest all at once. Have faith; as you stir constantly and the mixture comes to a boil, the lumps will dissipate. Simmer until the gravy reaches the thickness you like, usually 5 to 10 minutes. Season with salt and pepper to taste. Because the turkey has been brined, the gravy may require less salt than you might expect. If desired, strain the gravy through a medium-mesh strainer into a small saucepan (or directly into a warmed gravyboat, if using right away). Cover and keep the gravy in a warm place while carving the turkey.

14. At serving time, carve the turkey (page 167) and shingle-stack, or slightly overlap, the slices on the warmed platter. Remove the metal skewers and spoon the stuffing out into the warmed bowl. Reheat the gravy over low heat, if necessary, and transfer to the warmed gravyboat or bowl. Serve at once.

RECIPE SECRETS

If available, use partially boned fresh quail. When the breastbone has been removed, it's easier to eat the quail, but you'll need a few more toothpicks to secure the stuffed cavity closed. When fresh or semiboneless quail aren't available, I buy frozen, bone-in quail at a reasonable price in Chinese markets or in grocery stores that specialize in Asian ingredients. They require a bit more effort when eating, but hold their shape better for stuffing. Or, use this stuffing for game hens, poussins, or other game. If the quail have necks attached (they may if you buy directly from the farm), cut the necks off at the base.

To infuse the birds with plenty of flavor, marinate them overnight. Don't chop sage for the marinade too finely, and let some sage and thyme flecks remain on the birds as they roast.

Walnut oil has a voluptuous smell and flavor. It's used to great benefit in the marinade, and is also a bridge ingredient in the dressing, linking the flavors of the greens to the quail. For the best flavor, look for cold-pressed toasted walnut oil in specialty markets, but any walnut oil will work here. Store in the refrigerator after opening.

MAPLE-GLAZED QUAIL STUFFED WITH WILD MUSHROOMS, SAUSAGE, AND SOUR CHERRIES

This flavorful marinade is adapted from a recipe by game cookery expert Gloria Ciccarone-Nehls, chef at San Francisco's The Big Four restaurant. The stuffing, which got particularly high marks from my recipe testers, was inspired by a dish created by chef Rosemary Campiformio, which appears in *Savoring the Wine Country,* a cookbook that features her St. Orres restaurant in Mendocino County, California. I put the two recipes together for a class I taught at Barbara Dawson and Matt Katzer's In Good Taste cooking school in Portland, Oregon—imagine a California girl teaching quail in the game capital of the West. When the cooking was finished, we all gathered around the table, gnawing on quail bones and listening to quail tales of the Pacific Northwest.

Begin marinating the quail and infusing the cherries the day before serving. You can even make the stuffing—but don't stuff the quail—the day before you roast these little game birds. This dish is versatile when it comes to serving: As a first course, serve 1 quail per person on a bed of watercress or mixed baby salad greens lightly dressed with walnut oil and balsamic vinegar. For a luncheon, augment the salad greens with julienned apple or pear, toasted pecans, and shaved red onion and use as a bed for 1 or 2 quail per person. For a family-style dinner, figure on 2 quail per person, arranged on the greens on a large, colorful platter. Serve with "Roasted" Beets With Whole-Grain Mustard Sauce (page 268), Savory Corn Pudding (page 256), Butternut Squash with Maple Syrup and Allspice (page 273), or Wild Rice Pilaf (page 276).

**Serves 8 as a main course,
or 16 as a first course**

Marinade

. . . .

¼ cup balsamic vinegar

¼ cup walnut oil

¼ cup mild-tasting extra-virgin
olive oil

1 tablespoon fresh thyme leaves

1 tablespoon chopped fresh
sage leaves

1 tablespoon pure maple syrup

½ teaspoon granulated garlic
powder

½ teaspoon fine, freshly ground
black pepper

¼ teaspoon fine sea salt

½ teaspoon pure vanilla extract

⅛ teaspoon red pepper flakes

1 bay leaf, preferably imported

. . . .

16 quail, about ¼ pound each,
preferably with breastbones
removed

½ cup dried pitted sour cherries
or dried cranberries

⅓ cup white vermouth or dry
white wine

3 cloves garlic, green germ
removed if present, minced

3 tablespoons chopped fresh flat-
leaf parsley

2 tablespoons minced fresh sage

1 tablespoon minced fresh thyme

4 tablespoons unsalted butter

½ pound fresh (not smoked)
pork or turkey sausage, casings
removed

1 leek, white part only, chopped

1 small yellow onion, chopped

1 cup chopped fresh wild mushrooms and/or cultivated shiitake
and cremini mushrooms

1 teaspoon kosher salt, plus more
for sprinkling

½ teaspoon fine, freshly ground
black pepper, plus more for
sprinkling

1¼ teaspoons dry mustard,
preferably Colman's

3 tablespoons pure maple syrup,
divided

3 cups fresh bread crumbs made
from ¾ pound Italian or French
bread (weighed with crust)

About 1 cup homemade chicken
stock or broth (page 60 or 61) or
purchased reduced-sodium broth

About 2 tablespoons mild-tasting
extra-virgin olive oil

8 cups watercress, large stems
removed, or mixed baby salad
greens, rinsed and spun dry

2 tablespoons walnut oil

2 teaspoons balsamic vinegar

RECIPE SECRETS

. . . .

Wild mushrooms add a big dose of
delectable umami (page 38) to this
stuffing. If you prefer to use dried
mushrooms instead of fresh, substitute
½ ounce dried assorted wild mushrooms for 3 ounces fresh mushrooms.
Rehydrate dried mushrooms in warm
water for about 20 minutes, then strain
the soaking liquid and use in place of
some of the chicken stock.

. . . .

To prepare fresh bread crumbs, start
with a 1-pound loaf of Italian or
French bread (not sourdough). Using
a serrated knife, remove and discard
the crusts from the bread and tear the
bread into roughly 1-inch pieces.
Place in a food processor or blender
and grind into crumbs no larger than
¼ inch. For best results, you may have
to do this in batches. This makes about
4 cups fresh bread crumbs. You'll need
3 cups to make this stuffing. Store any
leftover crumbs in a zip-top plastic bag
in the freezer and use to prepare stuffed
portabello mushrooms (page 172) or
baked macaroni and cheese (page 110).

/continued

1. *Marinate the quail:* Begin marinating the quail 8 hours before roasting. In a bowl, whisk together all the marinade ingredients. Place the quail in a heavy-duty, 1-gallon zip-top plastic bag, add the marinade, and seal the bag, forcing out as much air as possible. If the bag feels flimsy, place the bag of quail inside another zip-top bag and seal it. With fingers, gently massage the marinade into the birds. Place on a plate and refrigerate for 8 hours, turning every so often to redistribute the marinade.

2. *Soak the cherries:* At the time you begin marinating the quail, combine the cherries or cranberries and wine in a small bowl, stir, cover, and set aside at room temperature for 8 hours.

3. Place the garlic, parsley, sage, and thyme in a small bowl (you don't have to mix them) and set aside. Place a 12-inch sauté pan or skillet over medium heat. Add the butter. When the butter is hot enough to sizzle a piece of the onion, add the sausages and break them up into ½-inch pieces with a flat-bottomed wooden spatula. Sauté until no longer pink, 3 to 4 minutes. Raise the heat to medium-high, add the leek and onion, and sauté until the onion is soft and translucent, but not brown, 6 to 8 minutes. Add the mushrooms, 1 teaspoon salt, and ½ teaspoon pepper and sauté for 5 minutes. Add the reserved garlic and herbs and sauté for 1 minute. Add the cherries or cranberries and their soaking liquid and cook for 1 minute.

4. Remove the pan from the heat and sprinkle the sausage mixture with the mustard, crumbling it with your fingers to break up any lumps. Stir to combine. Drizzle in 1 tablespoon of the maple syrup and stir to combine. Transfer to a large bowl. Add the bread crumbs and stir to combine. Add ¾ cup of the stock and stir to mix thoroughly. The stuffing should be very moist and hold together. If it's too dry, add more stock, 1 tablespoon at a time. Taste and adjust the seasoning, adding maple syrup, salt, and pepper until flavors are bright and in harmony. Set aside to cool. (The stuffing can be made 24 hours ahead, cooled to room temperature, covered, and refrigerated separately. For safety reasons, do not stuff the quail until just before roasting them.)

5. *Roast the quail:* Position a rack in the upper third of the oven and preheat to 425 degrees F (or 400 degrees F on the convection setting). Place a rack or racks inside a rimmed baking sheet large enough to accommodate the quail with a bit of space around each bird. Coat the rack(s) and pan liberally with vegetable oil spray and set aside.

6. Remove the quail from the marinade and discard the marinade. Stand the quail on end in a colander placed in a bowl to allow excess marinade to drain off. Place 32 round toothpicks in a small bowl with the olive oil.

7. Stuff each quail with about 3 tablespoons of the cooled stuffing mixture. Use an iced-tea spoon or shape stuffing into a cylinder with your fingers, then insert into the quail. Close the cavity of each quail with 2 toothpicks crossed in an X to keep the stuffing in place. Set aside the toothpicks bowl with any remaining olive oil. Place the quail, breast side up and as upright as possible, on the prepared rack(s) in the pan. Don't worry if they fall to one side. Sprinkle the tops with salt and pepper. Roast for 20 minutes and remove from the oven.

8. Reduce the oven temperature to 350 degrees F (or 325 degrees F on the convection setting). If any quail have leaned to one side, turn them to lean on other side and sprinkle the other side with salt and pepper. If the quail are dry on the surface, brush with some of the reserved toothpick oil. Lightly brush all the quail with some of the remaining maple syrup, but don't use it all. Roast the quail for another 20 minutes. Remove from the oven and insert a thermometer into the meaty part of a thigh (not touching bone); it should register 160 degrees F when the quail are done. Alternatively, the quail are done if a leg has some give when you grab it, or the juices run clear when the meat is pierced with a meat fork. If not done, brush any light-colored surfaces with olive oil and maple syrup and continue roasting until done.

9. Near the end of the roasting time, in a large bowl, toss the watercress with the walnut oil, balsamic vinegar, and salt and pepper to taste. When the quail are done, transfer the salad to a serving platter or individual plates and top with the quail.

RECIPE SECRETS

Use fine sea salt—instead of kosher salt—in the dough. This way you won't taste crunchy unmelted grains of salt in the tender crust.

To bring out the flavor of root vegetables and cook them without browning, chefs and fine cooks sweat, or stew, vegetables in their own juices in a covered pan over low heat. A little butter adds exponential flavor when sweating vegetables.

Thicken saucy mixtures such as this one with flour and butter mixed together into a *beurre manié* (pronounced *burr* mahn-*yay*), literally "handled butter." Freeze any extra in a plastic bag. Use for thickening pan gravies and cooking juices from stews and other braised dishes. It's quicker than cooking a roux.

After peeling, keep white root vegetables, such as potatoes and parsnips, in cold water to prevent them from turning brown. Occasionally, parsnips have a tough, fibrous core. Cut them lengthwise into quarters and trim away the core, if present, before dicing.

Unlike black pepper, white pepper has a tendency to become bitter if cooked too long. With light-colored foods and sauces where ground black pepper would look unappealing—or when you want the distinctive, subtler flavor of white pepper—season with white pepper when cooking is done.

HERB-CRUSTED CHICKEN POTPIES

For most of my cooking life, I've had fear of crust. There, I've said it. Fortunately, a fondness for *timpano* (page 126) and potpies has given me reason to overcome my trepidation. After much trial and error, I'm now a proponent of the foolproof method of rolling out pastry dough between two sheets of waxed paper. These butter-rich potpies are based on a recipe by my colleague, and former California Culinary Academy student, chef Nicholas Petti, owner of the highly acclaimed Mendo Bistro in Fort Bragg, California. In Nicholas's version of the classic comfort food recipe, herb-flecked pastry circles top individual ramekins filled to the brim with tender chunks of chicken and perfectly cooked root vegetables, all suspended in a savory sauce. You'll need 6 ramekins, each 4 inches in diameter and 1½ inches deep. If you don't have them, look for E-Z Foil disposable baking pans in well-stocked supermarkets. This is a terrific use for some of the homemade broth, along with the succulent steeped chicken, from Shortcut Chicken Broth with a Dividend (page 61). This may seem like a complicated recipe, but you can make the broth and chicken in the morning or a day ahead, or substitute purchased broth and leftover roasted chicken or turkey. While the chicken steeps, prepare the dough and cut out the crusts, chopping together the herbs for the filling and crust at the same time. Once you prep the vegetables, the filling comes together simply and rather quickly. Drizzle some fresh greens with good olive oil and vinegar to round out this homey meal in a bowl.

Serves 6

Pastry

1½ cups all-purpose flour

2½ teaspoons baking powder

¼ teaspoon fine sea salt

2 tablespoons cold unsalted butter, cut into 8 pieces

¾ cup heavy (whipping) cream

2 teaspoons minced fresh chives

1 teaspoon finely chopped fresh flat-leaf parsley

1 teaspoon chopped fresh sage leaves

Filling

. . . .

½ cup (1 stick) unsalted butter, at room temperature, divided

6 tablespoons all-purpose flour

1 small yellow onion, finely chopped

3 carrots, peeled and cut into ½-inch dice

2 large celery stalks, peeled and cut into ¼-inch dice

6 ounces fresh button mushrooms, cut into ¼-inch-thick slices

2 Yukon Gold or other potatoes, about 7 ounces total, peeled and cut into ½-inch dice

1 parsnip, about 7 ounces, peeled, cut into quarters lengthwise, and cut into ½-inch dice

2 tablespoons finely chopped fresh flat-leaf parsley

1 tablespoon fresh thyme leaves

1 teaspoon chopped fresh sage leaves

1 bay leaf, preferably imported

About 4 cups homemade chicken broth (page 61) or purchased reduced-sodium broth, divided

3 to 4 cups 1-inch cooked chicken chunks from making broth (page 61) or poached chicken (page 168)

⅔ cup fresh English peas or frozen petite peas

2 teaspoons kosher salt

1 tablespoon minced fresh chives

½ teaspoon finely ground white pepper, preferably freshly ground

1. *Prepare the pastry:* Sift together the flour, baking powder, and salt into a bowl. With your fingers, work the butter into the flour until the butter is the size of small peas. Add the cream, chives, parsley, and sage and mix with a fork, then by hand, just to combine. On a lightly floured surface, shape the dough into an oval disk, wrap in plastic wrap, and refrigerate until firm enough to roll, about 45 minutes.

2. Line a rimmed baking sheet with parchment paper or a silicone baking liner. Place six 1-cup ramekins, each 4 inches in diameter and 1½ inches deep, on the prepared sheet; set aside. Line a second baking sheet or cutting board with waxed paper to hold the pastry circles and set aside.

/continued

3. Place the dough disk between two 24-inch-long sheets of waxed paper (not parchment paper). Using a rolling pin, roll out the dough. After every few rolls, turn over the package of dough and roll on the other side. If any waxed paper becomes imbedded in the dough, peel off the paper, smooth it, and replace. Continue rolling until you have an oval measuring about 12 by 15 inches and ¼ inch thick, or large enough to cut out five 4-inch circles. (You'll make a sixth circle from the dough scraps.) If it's hot in the kitchen, chill the dough for about 20 minutes before cutting out the circles.

4. Carefully peel off the top sheet of waxed paper and set aside, sticky side up. Press an inverted ramekin into the dough to create 5 circles. With a pastry wheel, pizza wheel, or butter knife, cut out the pastry circles. Use a bench scraper or offset spatula to loosen and transfer the circles to the reserved baking sheet. If they become a little misshapen in the transfer, gently reshape them into 4-inch rounds.

5. Gather up the dough scraps into a ball, press into a disk on the waxed paper, and cover with the reserved sticky waxed paper. Roll out ¼ inch thick and large enough to press out another dough circle. Similarly, cut out this last circle and transfer it to the pan with the other circles. Refrigerate for up to 24 hours, covering the circles with waxed paper if refrigerating for longer than 2 hours. Discard the remaining dough scraps or reserve for another use.

6. *Prepare the filling:* To make the *beurre manié,* combine 6 tablespoons of the butter with the flour in a small bowl. Mash with a fork until the mixture is completely combined. Set aside, uncovered, in the refrigerator.

7. Heat a 4-quart saucier or saucepan over medium heat. Add the remaining 2 tablespoons butter. When the butter is hot enough to sizzle a piece of onion, add the onion, carrots, celery, and mushrooms. Heat until the mixture sizzles, stirring to coat with the butter, then cover, reduce the heat to low, and let the vegetables soften and sweat until the onion becomes translucent, about 10 minutes. Add the potatoes, parsnip, parsley, thyme, sage, and bay leaf. Add enough broth just to cover the vegetables, about 2 cups. Bring to a boil, reduce the heat to medium-low, cover, and cook until the potatoes and parsnips are just tender, about 10 minutes.

8. Position a rack in the upper two-thirds of the oven and preheat to 450 degrees F.

My colleague Charlene Vojtilla makes beautiful pastry. Here are some of her secrets to success.

- Temperature is the key to success when rolling pastry dough: If the dough cracks around the edges when you begin to roll, it is too cold; let it sit at room temperature for a few minutes. If the dough becomes sticky and hard to work with, it is too warm; slide it onto a baking sheet or other flat surface and refrigerate for about 10 minutes.

- Let the rolling pin do the work; in other words, don't press down excessively when rolling, or you'll sacrifice the flakiness which defines good pastry.

- If you'll be working with pastry dough a lot, you may want to invest in a fairly large, heavy rolling pin (they're relatively inexpensive). It will do most of the work, and do it more quickly than a smaller, lighter one.

- For the most even thickness, always roll from the center toward the edge. Also, lift up slightly on the rolling pin as you near the edge. This will help prevent thin edges.

- As you roll, rotate the dough frequently, a quarter turn at a time. If maintaining a round shape is important, as when making pie crust, rotate an eighth turn.

- If you aren't rolling between sheets of waxed paper, lightly sprinkle the work surface, rolling pin, and the top of the dough with flour (a metal shaker with a fine-mesh top is ideal for this). Professional pastry chefs keep a dry pastry brush (used exclusively for pastry, never used for oil or butter) at hand to brush excess flour from the dough (too much flour will make your dough tough).

9. Add the chicken, peas, salt, and enough of the remaining broth just to cover the top of the chicken, about 2 cups. Raise the heat to medium-high, bring to a boil, then reduce the heat to low. Add about two-thirds of the reserved *beurre manié* in clumps and stir to combine. The sauce will thicken and develop a sheen. If necessary, add more *beurre manié* until the sauce reaches napé, or is thick enough to coat the back of a wooden spoon. Run your finger down the back of the spoon. If the track of your finger remains distinct, the sauce is done. If not, or if you prefer a thicker sauce, add more *beurre manié*, a little at a time, and simmer gently until the sauce reaches the desired consistency.

10. Stir in the chives and white pepper. Taste and adjust the seasoning by adding enough salt and white pepper to bring the flavors into balance and to make the sauce taste bright. Remove and discard the bay leaf. (The filling mixture can be prepared to this point up to 24 hours ahead. Let cool to room temperature, cover, and refrigerate. Remove from the refrigerator 1 hour before using and reheat over low heat, stirring constantly.)

11. Divide the filling mixture equally among the reserved ramekins. Place a pastry circle on top of each ramekin. (No vents are necessary.) Bake until the tops are medium to dark brown, 15 to 20 minutes. Serve at once.

RECIPE SECRETS

As is typical with braising, the first step here is to toss the chicken pieces in seasoned flour and brown them in hot oil. Use long-handled tongs to turn the chicken while you brown it. A fork would pierce the skin and cause juices to run out and burn.

. . . .

If you prefer not to eat the chicken skin, remove it after the chicken is cooked, as it serves a dual purpose in braising: First, the skin protects the meat from becoming tough or dried out at the edges. Also, the collagen in the skin contributes unparalleled luster and body to the sauce as it cooks.

. . . .

Like nearly all braised dishes, this one improves with age. It tastes best when prepared a day in advance and reheated in a 325 degree F oven until piping hot. This gives you a chance to skim off any fat solidified on the surface before reheating it.

CHICKEN CACCIATORE

In Italian, *cacciatore* (pronounced cotch-yah-*tor*-eh) describes a dish prepared "hunter style," that is, braised with tomatoes, vegetables, herbs, and wine. To me, cacciatore is Italian soul food. This is a variation of the dish my mother often prepared for supper on cold winter weeknights. I'll never forget the smell of it wafting out from the kitchen exhaust fan as we made angels in the snow in our backyard after school. She added big chunks of russet potatoes, but I omit them and instead serve Creamy, Soft Polenta (page 274) on the side. This is the perfect dish to take to a potluck or to a friend just home from the hospital. When I make it for a crowd, as I do in braising classes, I use 8 to 10 bone-in, skin-on chicken thighs instead of a whole cut-up chicken.

Serves 4 to 6

1 chicken, 3 to 4 pounds, cut into 6 to 8 pieces, or 8 to 10 bone-in thighs, skin on

½ cup all-purpose flour

3 teaspoons kosher salt, divided

1 teaspoon fine, freshly ground black pepper, divided

3 tablespoons mild-tasting extra-virgin olive oil

1 yellow onion, cut in half lengthwise, then thinly cut crosswise into half-moons

1 teaspoon dried leaf oregano, crumbled between your fingers

3 cloves garlic, smashed gently with the side of a chef's knife

½ cup dry white or red wine

3 large carrots, peeled and cut into 2-inch sticks

1 red bell pepper, seeded, deribbed, and cut into ¾-inch squares

1 can (28 ounces) diced tomatoes with juice

½ pound green beans, preferably Romano beans, stem ends trimmed and cut into 2-inch lengths or left whole

3 tablespoons chopped fresh flat-leaf parsley, divided

1 bay leaf, preferably imported

½ cup water

½ cup fresh English peas or frozen petite peas

2 tablespoons chopped fresh basil

---

1. Preheat the oven to 325 degrees F. Trim off any excess fat from the chicken and set aside.

2. Put the flour, 1½ teaspoons of the salt, and ½ teaspoon of the pepper in a 1-gallon zip-top plastic bag and seal the bag, forcing out as much air as possible. Shake to combine ingredients. Set aside.

3. Heat a 6-quart Dutch oven or roasting pan over medium heat. Add the olive oil. While the oil is heating, place the chicken pieces in the bag with the seasoned flour and seal the bag, forcing out as much air as possible. Shake to coat the chicken evenly with the flour. When the oil is hot enough to sizzle a few flecks of flour, tamp off the excess flour from the chicken (so it doesn't burn before chicken browns) and slip the pieces, skin side down, into the oil. Raise the heat to medium-high and add only as many pieces of chicken as you can fit into the Dutch oven without crowding; you may have to brown the chicken in batches. Cook, turning once, until golden brown, about 5 minutes on each side. The chicken will still be raw inside. Transfer to a platter.

4. With the Dutch oven still over medium-high heat, add the onion and sauté, stirring with a flat-bottomed wooden or heatproof rubber spatula to release the caramelized bits from the bottom. When the onion softens, after 6 to 8 minutes, add the oregano and garlic. Sauté 1 minute, stirring constantly. Add the wine and reduce by half. Add the carrots, bell pepper, and dark meat, including wings, back, legs, and thighs. Pour the tomatoes with their juices over the chicken and stir in the green beans, 2 tablespoons of the parsley, the bay leaf, and the remaining 1½ teaspoons salt and ½ teaspoon pepper. Rinse the tomato can with the water and add to the Dutch oven. Bring the entire contents to a steady boil, cover, and place in the oven to braise for 40 minutes. (You can instead braise on the stove top. Omit preheating the oven. Once the mixture is at a steady boil, reduce the heat to low, cover, and cook for 40 minutes.)

5. Remove the pot from the oven (or remove the cover if braising on the stove top) and add the chicken breasts, peas, and basil. Stir, cover, and continue braising for another 20 to 25 minutes. To test for doneness, insert a thermometer into the largest chicken breast or thigh (not touching bone); when done, the breast should register 150 degrees F and the thigh 180 degrees F. Taste and adjust the seasoning with salt and pepper as needed to bring the flavors into balance. Remove and discard the bay leaf and garlic. If you're not planning to serve the chicken right away, it's okay to leave it, covered, on top of the stove on a turned-off burner for up to 1 hour. The residual heat will keep the dish warm enough for serving without sacrificing the tenderness of the chicken. If any oily puddles rise to the surface, use a ladle or large spoon to remove and discard the oil. Stir well before serving.

6. Place the chicken pieces in the center of a warmed serving platter, arrange the vegetables around the chicken, and pour a little sauce over all. Sprinkle with the remaining 1 tablespoon parsley. Pour the remaining sauce into a warmed gravyboat and serve.

RECIPE SECRETS

There are as many versions of mole as there are Mexican cooks. After making many batches of this unctuous, dark, complex sauce, this recipe represents my favorite combination of chiles, tomato, spices, and chocolate. It calls for ancho chiles, "the workhorse of the Mexican kitchen," as Mexican cooking authority Rick Bayless has dubbed this mild-tasting dried chile. If you prefer your mole with a bit of a kick, add the optional guajillo chiles, which are also dried. Look for dried chiles in well-stocked upscale markets or in the produce or Mexican section of your grocery store. They should be pliable and leathery, but not brittle. Store dried chiles in a cool, dark place for several months, or freeze them in a zip-top plastic bag.

The plantain adds both viscosity and sweetness to the sauce. Use one that is so ripe its skin is black. If plantains are unripe or unavailable, substitute a ripe (not black) banana, the plantain's more pedestrian cousin.

Mexican cooks prefer the clean, pure flavor of white onions over the yellow onions more widely available in the United States. For mole, I agree.

To ensure flavorful, tender, moist braised turkey, use turkey on the bone and keep the temperature at a simmer.

TURKEY MOLE

The summer before I officially opened my cooking school, I decided to get some practice by offering classes for young cooks. The kitchen remodel was almost complete, it was summertime, and I figured kids wouldn't be too critical of unfinished details like a missing backsplash. As with many new businesses, the first week was slow, but I had vowed to hold class even if only one student signed up. I also pledged not to dumb down the recipes and techniques just because the students were ten to fourteen years old. The third Young Cooks class featured a Mexican menu with a mole (pronounced *mow*-lay) recipe complex enough to keep many little hands busy all morning long. The only problem was that on that day there was only one pair of hands in the kitchen in addition to mine. Fortified with a pitcher of *agua de jamaica,* twelve-year-old Elliot and I chopped, charred, roasted, blended, braised, and stirred together for almost four hours, creating a riot of smells and sensations as I initiated him into the savory world of mole.

Finally, it was time to sit down together and taste our complex, chocolate-enriched sauce. We filled our plates with chunks of braised turkey thigh, handmade corn tortillas fresh from the griddle, and copious amounts of thick, rich mole sauce. As we tucked napkins under our collars, I said a silent prayer that Elliot would like this meal. With due reverence, he tore off a piece of tortilla, picked up some turkey with it, swished it around in the heady sauce, and closed his eyes, chewing ever so slowly. As he gradually opened his eyes, he stared straight ahead, his face expressionless for what seemed like an entire minute. I began to wonder if he'd be comfortable telling me he'd prefer a peanut butter sandwich, or whether I should just offer him one. Finally, I asked if he was okay. "Yes," he explained, "I'm just sitting here trying to figure out how I can convince my father to hire you to cater my bar mitzvah." As *my* father would have said, "Only in America."

Serves 8 to 10

Braised Turkey

. . . .

3½ to 4 pounds bone-in turkey thigh(s)

2 white onions, quartered

1 head garlic, unpeeled, cut ¼ inch deep around its equator

2 teaspoons kosher salt

6 black peppercorns

2 fresh mint leaves

1 bay leaf, preferably imported

Mole

. . . .

⅓ cup sesame seeds

4 teaspoons cumin seeds

2 teaspoons coriander seeds

1 teaspoon aniseed

2 tablespoons dried Mexican oregano

4 to 6 ancho chiles

2 or 3 guajillo chiles (optional)

1 tomato

1 slice white onion, ½ inch thick

4 cloves garlic, unpeeled

5 whole allspice

3 whole cloves

About 2½ cups broth from braising the turkey thigh(s)

1 ripe plantain, peeled and cut into ¼-inch-thick slices

1 piece Mexican cinnamon, about 5 inches long, broken into a few pieces

1 to 2 tablespoons kosher salt

2 to 3 teaspoons sugar

1½ tablespoons mild-tasting olive oil

1 ounce Mexican chocolate

. . . .

About 1 cup crème fraîche, homemade (page 67) or purchased, or sour cream, for garnish

8 to 10 lime wedges, for serving

12 corn tortillas, warmed, for serving

/continued

RECIPE SECRETS

. . . .

In Mexican cooking, a variety of cinnamon called *canela* is used in both savory and sweet recipes. The cinnamon most commonly available in the United States is cassia. *Canela* is more delicate, almost paperlike, and breaks up easily if crumbled between your fingers. Look for it in stores with extensive selections of dried spices in bulk. If you can't find it, substitute the more ubiquitous cassia.

. . . .

Imported Mexican chocolate adds a dark complexity to mole without making it sweet. Ibarra brand—in a distinctive yellow and red hexagonal box—is augmented with sugar and cinnamon, as are many Mexican chocolates, and has a gritty texture. If you can't find Mexican chocolate, substitute the same amount of unsweetened baking chocolate.

. . . .

For the best texture and flavor, warm the tortillas before serving. Wrap a few in a kitchen towel and microwave on high for 25 to 30 seconds.

. . . .

There's nothing wrong with eating this mole the moment it's cooked. But it's even better when made the day before serving. If preparing the mole a day ahead, let it cool to room temperature, cover, and refrigerate until ready to serve, then reheat slowly over medium heat, with the lid ajar, until the mole and turkey are piping hot throughout.

1. *Cook the turkey:* Place the turkey in a 6-quart Dutch oven or stockpot and add water to cover by 1 inch. Bring to a boil, uncovered, over high heat. Reduce the heat to a simmer. Using a fine-mesh skimmer or a ladle, skim off the foam that rises to the top. Continue simmering and skimming for 10 minutes, or until no more foam rises to the surface. Add the onions, garlic, salt, peppercorns, mint, and bay leaf. Cover and continue to simmer over low heat until the turkey registers an internal temperature of 180 degrees F, 20 to 45 minutes; the timing will depend on the size of the thigh(s). Remove from the heat and uncover. Let the turkey cool in the broth until the meat is cool enough to handle. Transfer the turkey to a cutting board, remove and discard the skin, and shred the meat by hand into 2- to 3-inch chunks and strips. Strain the turkey broth through a fine-mesh strainer into a bowl and discard the solids. Set the broth aside.

2. *Prepare the mole:* In a small, dry skillet, toast the sesame seeds over medium heat, stirring often, until they brown lightly and begin to give off their fragrance, 2 to 3 minutes. Transfer the seeds to the bowl of a medium-sized mortar. (If you don't have a mortar and pestle, use a spice grinder.) Using the same skillet, toast the cumin seeds in the same way and transfer to the bowl with the sesame seeds. Repeat, toasting the coriander seeds and aniseed separately, adding each to the bowl of toasted seeds. Toast the oregano similarly and transfer it to a separate small bowl. Set aside.

3. Preheat a stove-top grill or a 9-inch cast-iron or other heavy skillet over low heat or preheat a gas grill on low. Wipe the chiles with a damp paper towel to remove any dust. Remove the stems, split the chiles open, and tear each chile into 3 or 4 pieces. Remove and discard the seeds and ribs, or veins. Raise the heat to medium and place the chile pieces on the grill or skillet. Using an offset metal spatula to flatten them, toast the chile pieces quickly on both sides just until they give off an aroma and the inside turns reddish brown, about 20 seconds total. If you toast them too long, they'll develop a bitter flavor. You may want to do this in batches. Place the chiles in a bowl and cover with very hot water. Place a small plate over the chiles to keep them submerged, and let soak for 20 minutes. Drain, reserving 3 tablespoons of the soaking liquid.

4. While the chiles are soaking, place the whole tomato on the grill or skillet and lightly roast on all sides over medium heat until the skin becomes blistered and loose, about 4 minutes total. Transfer the tomato to a bowl to capture the juices. Using a paring knife, cut out the core. Roast the onion slice and garlic cloves on the grill or skillet (place the garlic on a small piece of aluminum foil, if necessary, to prevent the cloves from falling through the grill grate), until lightly charred on both sides, about 5 minutes total. Set the onion and garlic aside. When the garlic is cool enough to handle, peel it. Set all the roasted vegetables aside.

5. Using a pestle, grind the cooled, toasted sesame, cumin, coriander, and aniseeds in the mortar (or grind in the spice grinder). Add the oregano, allspice, and cloves and grind to the consistency of coarse salt. Set aside.

6. In a blender, combine the chiles, the 3 tablespoons reserved soaking water, and 1 cup of the reserved turkey broth and process to a thick purée. Add the tomato, onion, garlic, ground spice mixture, plantain, cinnamon, 1 tablespoon salt, 2 teaspoons sugar, and 1½ cups additional broth. (If necessary, purée the ingredients in batches.) Process until smooth. Taste and add more salt and sugar if necessary. If the mixture tastes bitter, add salt. (Salt mitigates bitterness better than sugar, which can add an undesirable sweet flavor. Sugar balances acid.)

7. Heat a medium-sized Dutch oven or other wide, heavy pot over medium-high heat. Add the olive oil. When the oil is hot enough to sizzle a drop of mole mixture on contact, add the mole mixture, pouring away from you. Be cautious, as the mixture will sputter and steam. Stir constantly to develop the flavors, about 5 minutes.

8. Set a medium-mesh strainer (see illustration, page 67) over a clean 6-quart Dutch oven or pot. Pour the mole through the strainer, using the back of a spoon or ladle to coax all the sauce through. Discard the solids. (The straining step is optional; if you like a pulpy sauce, don't strain the mole.) Reheat the mole over medium heat. If desired, add more reserved turkey broth to thin the mole; it should be thick enough to coat the back of a wooden spoon. Add the chocolate and stir until melted, 2 to 3 minutes. Taste and add more salt and sugar, if necessary to balance the flavors. Add the reserved turkey and simmer gently over low heat, stirring often, until the turkey is heated through and the mole is piping hot, 10 to 15 minutes.

9. Ladle the turkey and mole into warmed soup plates and drizzle with the crème fraîche or sour cream. Serve with lime wedges and tortillas. Let any remaining mole cool to room temperature, then cover and store in the refrigerator. It will keep for up to 3 days.

SECRETS FOR PREPARING MEATS SUCCESSFULLY

Each pork, lamb, and beef recipe in this chapter features its own particular Secrets. In addition, here are some general tips, as well as responses to frequently asked questions about preparing different cuts of meat.

SEASONING AND MARINATING

- For the best flavor and texture, season meats with salt and pepper before cooking. Seasoning after cooking results in less flavorful meat, with discernible flecks of salt and pepper that are less satisfying to the palate. Season steaks, short ribs, roasts, and chops, and refrigerate, uncovered, for up to 36 hours before cooking (page 44). Let large cuts sit at room temperature for 1 hour and smaller chops and steaks for 20 minutes before cooking.

- Marinate tough, lean cuts of meat such as flank steak to break down fibers and boost flavor. Raw garlic becomes acrid when burned, so remove it from marinades before cooking in the direct, dry heat of a grill, broiler, or sauté pan. As an alternative, I use granulated garlic powder (page 82) in marinades in which I want the garlic flavor to permeate the meat. Typically, it's not wise to include acids such as vinegar or lemon juice in an overnight marinade, as the acid breaks down the protein fibers and makes the meat mushy over time. Also, overmarinated meat takes on a liver-y flavor. Tougher muscles such as flank steak and tri-tip can withstand the acid's tenderizing effect longer than smaller, tenderer cuts.

- Before cooking, blot up excess marinade so meat will sear, rather than steam. Searing, or caramelization of the meat's natural sugars, is what promotes great flavor in cooked meats.

COOKING

- If your oven has a convection setting, use it for roasting meats. The circulating dry heat helps caramelize the surface. Set the temperature 25 degrees F lower than the directed conventional temperature and reduce the roasting time by 10 percent.

- Lean cuts of beef and lamb are juiciest and most tender when cooked to rare or medium-rare. For the best eating, cut these meats across the grain, on the diagonal, into thin slices.

- The little pieces of meat and fat that turn brown and stick to the bottom of the roasting pan are the *fond,* or pan drippings, and they are the perfect foundation for pan gravy. To prevent pan drippings from burning during roasting, choose a roasting pan only slightly larger than the meat. If the *fond* begins to burn before the roast is done, add about ½ cup cold water to the pan. (Don't pour the water directly over the meat.)

INTERNAL DONENESS TEMPERATURES FOR MEAT

As with internal doneness temperatures for poultry (page 164), there are two sets of guidelines for cooking meats. The same cautions apply here.

	Recommended Temperature (in degrees F):	
	USDA	Chefs
Beef, lamb, veal—rare	140	125 to 130
Beef, lamb, veal—medium	160	135 to 140
Beef, lamb, veal—well done	170	not recommended
Beef, lamb, ground	160	personal preference
Ham, cooked (to reheat)	130	130
Ham, smoked	160	140
Pork chops	160 to 170	140 to 145
Pork roast—medium (pale pink, juicy)*	not recommended	145 to 150
Pork roast—well done	160 to 170	not recommended
Pork, ground; sausage	160	155

*Trichinae, if present, are killed at 137 degrees F.

PRESSURE-TESTING TO DETERMINE DONENESS

If you've ever sat at the counter in a busy restaurant watching line cooks work the grill, you've probably seen them poking the steaks and chops with an index finger. The pace is far too hectic to check every steak with a thermometer, so they rely on this time-honored pressure test to determine doneness: Bend one hand into a weak fist, exerting no pressure at all. With the index finger of your other hand, poke at the flabby piece of skin between your index finger and thumb. That's how rare meat feels. Now exert a little more pressure in making the fist, but don't squeeze your fist as tight as possible. That's how meat cooked to medium doneness feels. Next, squeeze hard and make a fist. See how that piece of skin has firmed up? That's what well-done meat feels like.

ABOUT CARAMELIZING

One way to enhance a food's flavor and appearance is by caramelizing the surface. Caramelization occurs when the natural—or added—sugars in foods are cooked in a dry-heat cooking method, such as in stir-frying, sautéing, deep-frying, grilling, broiling, and roasting. Also, before most foods are braised, they are quickly browned first to caramelize their outer surfaces; the actual cooking takes place later during braising. When caramelized, meats and other foods generally appear dark brown on the surface; however, some caramelized vegetables such as onions, are more distinguishable by their soft, limp texture and sweet flavor, rather than a dark brown appearance.

FREQUENTLY ASKED QUESTIONS ABOUT MEATS

What's that iridescent membrane I sometimes see on the surface of pork tenderloin, turkey breast, and some cuts of beef?

Occasionally (when the butcher hasn't removed it first), you'll find a layer of silver skin, a shiny whitish membrane that separates muscle groups, running along the surface of certain muscles of meat. Silver skin is tough to chew and it shrinks and curls up when it cooks, so it's critical that you remove it before marinating or cooking. Use a boning knife to trim off the silver skin by slicing along the grain, parallel to the meat (see illustration, page 179).

Why is it important to let meat rest before carving?

Small cuts such as chops, burgers, and small steaks can be served right away. But it's important to let larger cuts such as roasts and large steaks sit a bit before carving. When meat is cooking, its juices flow toward the source of the heat. If you cut into a roast right out of the oven, you'll see all sorts of juice squirting out, and you might think you have a juicy roast. But, in fact, what you have is a juicy cutting board. If you want the meat to be juicy, you need to allow time for the juices to settle back into the meat. Because the air in the kitchen is cooler than the center of the meat, the juices will now flow back inward, becoming reabsorbed as the meat sits. During the resting period, the internal temperature of a large roast with a fair amount of residual heat will rise between 5 and 10 degrees F. Take this into consideration when judging when to remove a roast from the oven.

Why does my roast sometimes come out with a solid red core and gray edges?

The roast with the red core was too cold when it went into the oven. For even cooking, be sure that meats are at room temperature before cooking. This helps to achieve restaurant-quality roasts with a caramelized exterior and an interior that's evenly pink—or medium-rare—throughout.

How do restaurants manage to serve hot, yet rare, prime rib?

This is a wonderful trick I learned when I worked in a restaurant that served prime rib. The whole roast would come out of the oven just before dinner. Then, as dinner service progressed, the chef would carve off pieces to order. To reheat, he'd put a slab of meat on an aluminum pie plate, cover it with a large outer leaf of romaine lettuce, and pop it under the broiler. In this example, the pan gets hot and transfers heat to the meat, and the lettuce keeps the meat both red and moist under the direct heat of the broiler. By the time the lettuce starts to shrivel, the meat is hot.

GRILLED PORK CHOPS
WITH GARLIC AND FENNEL RUB

These chops are quick enough for a weeknight supper and special enough for company. If time is short, just pat the spice mix into the chops and grill them right away. But, for the best flavor, marinate the chops in the rub for up to 24 hours before cooking. In the summertime, I serve these pork chops with Savory Corn Pudding (page 256) and heirloom tomato salad. In the winter, they're great with Vanilla-Scented Applesauce (page 217) and Mashed Yukon Gold Potatoes (page 280). If you don't care for fennel seeds, simply omit them.

Serves 4

4 rib-end pork chops, about 1½ pounds total weight and each ¾ inch thick

1½ teaspoons kosher salt

½ teaspoon fennel seeds

½ teaspoon dried leaf oregano, crumbled between your fingers

Scant ½ teaspoon freshly ground black pepper

¼ teaspoon granulated garlic powder

---

1. Using a paring knife, scrape both sides of the chops to remove any bone chips or bloody residue. Trim off any excess fat from the edges. Arrange the chops in a single layer on a flat platter or cutting board.

2. In a small bowl, combine the salt, fennel seeds, oregano, pepper, and garlic powder. Sprinkle the top of each chop with a heaping ¼ teaspoon of the spice mixture, being sure to distribute the fennel seeds equally. With the heel of your hand, pat the spices into each chop. Turn over the chops and sprinkle with the remaining spices, dividing them evenly. Refrigerate the chops for up to 24 hours (no need to cover them).

3. If the chops have been refrigerated for more than 2 hours, bring to room temperature about 30 minutes before cooking. Prepare a hot fire in a charcoal grill, or preheat a gas grill or stove-top grill to high. Alternatively, position a rack 2 to 3 inches below the broiler element and preheat the broiler.

4. Grill or broil the chops for 6 minutes on the first side, leaving some space around each chop so any steam can escape and the surface of the chops can caramelize. (If broiling, leave the oven door ajar—if your oven allows—for the steam to escape.) If you'd like to mark the grilled chops with cross-hatching, rotate each chop about 45 degrees after 4 minutes. Otherwise, don't disturb the chops as they sear and caramelize. Turn over the chops and cook until the internal temperature reaches 140 degrees F, about 4 more minutes. Serve on warmed plates.

RECIPE SECRETS

The most flavorful pork chops come from the rib end of the loin, which is closer to the shoulder and a bit fattier than the popular center cut. Look for chops with a curved bone, with the meat on one side of the bone. (Center-cut chops often have a T-shaped bone with meat on both sides of the bone.)

The longer you leave the rub on the meat, the more flavorful your chops will be. For the best results, sprinkle the chops with the seasoning rub the night before—or morning of—the day you plan to cook them.

Because today's pork is leaner—it has about one-third fewer calories—and higher in protein than what was produced in the United States as recently as in the mid-1990s, it has less flavor and loses moisture when overcooked even a little. There's no need to cook pork to 180 degrees F, as directed on old-fashioned meat thermometers, since trichinae (which cause trichinosis) are killed at 137 degrees. For ¾-inch-thick pork chops, remove them from the grill or broiler when the internal temperature reaches 140 degrees F.

Turn the chops with tongs or a metal spatula. If you stick thin chops or steaks with a fork, you'll lose some of the flavorful juices.

RECIPE SECRETS

To prevent bamboo skewers from splintering, soak them in water for at least 30 minutes before threading the meat onto them. You'll need sixteen 6-inch bamboo skewers for this recipe.

To turn the skewered meat on the grill easily, use 2 skewers to thread each serving of meat. This way, when you grab a skewer, the meat will come with it, instead of the skewer spinning around in your tongs and the meat sticking to the grill, which tends to happen with single skewers.

To cut pork, chicken, or beef as thinly as possible before marinating, place it in the freezer for 1 hour to freeze partially before cutting. Use the sharpest, thinnest blade in your knife block, and cut across the grain. Alternatively, ask your butcher for a pound of thinly sliced pork for sukiyaki. Traditionally, a marbled cut of pork, such as pork shoulder or country-style ribs, is preferred, but pork loin or tenderloin is a suitable—and leaner—alternative, although not as flavorful.

VIETNAMESE-STYLE HONEY-GLAZED PORK SKEWERS WITH RICE VERMICELLI

I've been known to drive across town in the middle of a hot summer day for a big bowl of this cool, refreshing salad at my favorite Vietnamese restaurant (Le Cheval in Oakland, California). Any time of year, *bun cha* (pronounced *boon chaw* in Vietnamese) makes a substantial lunch or simple one-dish supper. If you prefer, substitute shrimp, beef, or boneless, skinless chicken breasts or thighs for the pork. Look for Asian fish sauce and rice noodles in the Asian section of well-stocked supermarkets. Serve this colorful dish in your deepest, largest pasta bowls, or layer the ingredients on dinner plates, so there's enough room to toss the ingredients together as you eat.

Serves 4

Pork

¼ cup packed light or dark brown sugar

¼ cup soy sauce

1 teaspoon granulated garlic powder

1 pound thinly sliced pork from country-style ribs or tenderloin

¼ cup honey

Vegetable oil for grill

Dressing

⅓ cup Asian fish sauce

½ cup freshly squeezed lime juice (from 3 to 6 limes, depending on size)

½ cup granulated sugar

1 cup hot water

Salad

10 ounces dried rice vermicelli (also called rice sticks)

2 teaspoons kosher salt

1 small head romaine lettuce

1 small English cucumber

1½ cups (4 ounces) bean sprouts, picked over

½ cup packed fresh mint leaves

2 carrots, peeled and shredded on the medium or large holes of a box grater

4 green onions, tender green parts only, shredded (see page 214)

½ cup salted, roasted peanuts, chopped into ¼-inch pieces

---

1. *Marinate the pork:* Soak 16 bamboo skewers, each 6 inches long (if you can find only 10-inch skewers, they'll be fine), in water (a loaf pan works well) for at least 30 minutes. In a shallow bowl or baking dish large enough to marinate the meat, combine the brown sugar, soy sauce, and garlic powder. Add the pork, stir to coat the meat, and marinate at room temperature for 30 minutes.

2. *Prepare the dressing:* In a bowl, whisk together all the ingredients until the sugar dissolves completely. Taste and adjust the seasoning, if necessary. Set aside at room temperature for the flavors to blend. (The dressing can be made up to 24 hours ahead, covered, and refrigerated; bring to room temperature before using.)

3. *Prepare the salad:* Bring a 4-quart pot of water to a rolling boil. When the water boils, add the vermicelli and salt. Cook until just tender, 4 to 5 minutes. The vermicelli should be resilient, chewy, and not chalky inside. Drain in a colander and immediately rinse with cold water until cool to the touch. With kitchen shears, cut into roughly 6-inch lengths. Set aside.

4. Cut out the core from the romaine lettuce, then cut the leaves crosswise into ½-inch-wide ribbons; set aside. Cut the cucumber crosswise into thin slices. Stack a few slices on top of one another and cut into julienne (matchstick-sized pieces); set aside.

5. Equally divide and layer the salad ingredients among 4 large, shallow pasta bowls in the following order: romaine, cucumber, bean sprouts, mint leaves, noodles, and carrots. Set the bowls aside. (This step can be done up to 2 hours in advance. If doing ahead, cover and set aside in a cool place, but do not refrigerate, as the texture of the noodles would suffer.)

6. Prepare a hot fire in a charcoal grill, or preheat a gas or stove-top grill to high. Meanwhile, hold 2 skewers parallel to each other, about 1 inch apart, and thread one-eighth of the pork slices onto them, gathering up the pork into ruffles as you weave the slices. The pork should be bunched up, not flat, so it stays moist while grilling. Repeat with the remaining pork and skewers. There won't be much of the skewers showing by the time you thread on all the pork. As each pair of skewers is loaded, place on a rimmed baking sheet. Place the honey in a small, shallow bowl. When the grill is hot, carefully oil the grill grate with some wadded-up paper towels dipped in vegetable oil (use tongs to hold the wad of paper towels). Using a pastry brush, coat both sides of the pork with about two-thirds of the honey. Grill the pork, basting with the remaining honey as it cooks, just until cooked through and charred on all sides, 6 to 8 minutes total. Turn the skewers frequently to prevent the meat from drying out while cooking.

ABOUT MARBLED MEAT

Marbling is the term used to describe the lines of internal fat you see running through the flesh of some meats, such as country-style pork ribs and rib-eye steaks. During cooking, this fat melts, naturally basting the meat from within. For the best flavor and texture, choose meats that are well marbled.

/continued

7. Lay 2 skewers of grilled pork on top of each salad in a crisscross pattern. (Or, remove the pork from the skewers and divide among the salads.) Scatter the green onions and peanuts on top of the salads. Stir the dressing and drizzle 3 tablespoons over each salad. Pass the remaining dressing in a bowl at the table.

HOW TO SHRED GREEN ONIONS

Cut off the root tip and the stem ends from green onions. If using green parts only, cut off the white parts and reserve for another use.

Cut onions into roughly 2-inch lengths.

Gather the pieces together side by side across your cutting board.

Holding your chef's knife parallel to the onions, cut the onions lengthwise into shreds, working your way across the collection of onions, back and forth, with the blade parallel to the onions at all times.

Shredded onions will look rougher and more uneven than perfectly trimmed, julienned onions.

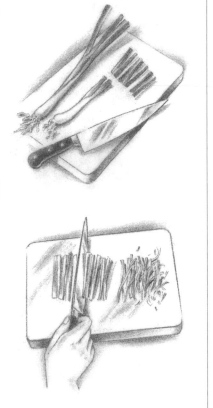

ITALIAN SAUSAGE CONTADINA WITH ROASTED SWEET PEPPERS, POTATOES, AND ONIONS

In Italian cooking, *contadina,* or "country style," is often used to describe what might be called peasant food. This robust dish of plump sausages roasted with peppers, onions, and potatoes is satisfying, yet simple to prepare. It travels well to potluck suppers and is sturdy enough not to suffer from being reheated. I like to use a combination of hot and mild sausages, but whichever you choose, be sure to buy the finest-quality fresh—not smoked—sausage. Serve with a salad and crusty bread for spreading the meltingly soft roasted garlic.

Serves 4 to 6

2 small yellow onions, about ½ pound total	⅛ teaspoon freshly ground black pepper
12 cloves garlic, unpeeled	4 red, yellow, or green bell peppers or a combination
1 pound Yukon Gold or new potatoes (about 5 medium)	1½ pounds fresh (not smoked) hot or mild Italian sausages, or a combination
2 tablespoons plus 1 teaspoon extra-virgin olive oil, divided	Crusty Italian bread, for serving
1 teaspoon kosher salt, divided	

---

1. Preheat the oven to 425 degrees F (or 400 degrees F on the convection setting). Coat a 17-by-12-inch rimmed baking sheet generously with vegetable oil spray. Set aside.

2. Trim off the hairy parts of the roots close to the base of each onion (see illustration, page 216), cut off the stem ends, peel down the skins to the root ends, and cut off the peels as close to the base as possible without cutting off the root. (This will keep the onion wedges intact during roasting.) Cut lengthwise into quarters and place the onions in a large bowl. Set aside.

3. Remove all but the last papery layer of peel from the garlic cloves. Trim off any long, scraggly ends so they don't burn. Add the garlic to the bowl with the onions.

/continued

RECIPE SECRETS

Roast the sausages, peppers, potatoes, and garlic on a rimmed baking sheet to allow the oven heat to caramelize the food on all sides. The high sides of a roasting pan would not be as effective here.

Rinse and dry the potatoes and peppers well before tossing with olive oil to prevent them from steaming and to encourage optimal caramelization in the oven.

Check the potatoes carefully for solanine (page 151), and peel away any green spots and "eyes."

Green bell peppers are unripe red peppers, and have a distinctive herbaceous taste that is often mitigated by roasting. Feel free to use them in this recipe in place of—or along with—red and yellow peppers.

For the sweetest flavor, be sure to use sprout-free garlic for roasting in this recipe (page 110).

If you have a convection setting on your oven, this is the perfect recipe for it.

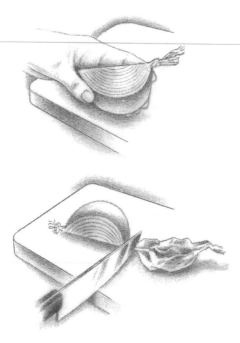

Peeling and trimming an onion so the wedges stay intact during roasting

4. Cut the potatoes into quarters and place in the bowl with the onions and garlic. Toss with 1 tablespoon of the olive oil, ½ teaspoon of the salt, and the pepper. Transfer to the prepared baking sheet and reserve the bowl. As necessary, turn the pieces of potatoes and onions cut side down. Roast for 15 minutes.

5. While the potatoes are roasting, seed and derib the bell peppers, then cut lengthwise into strips about ¾ inch wide. Place in the reserved bowl and toss with 1 tablespoon of the olive oil and the remaining ½ teaspoon kosher salt. After the potatoes and onions have roasted for 15 minutes, scatter the pepper strips evenly over the baking sheet without moving the other items on the sheet. (It's okay if the peppers are on top of the potatoes and onions.) Roast for 10 minutes. Remove from the oven and use a thin pancake turner or icing spatula to turn the potatoes cut side up.

6. While the peppers are roasting, heat a 10-inch sauté pan over medium heat. Add the remaining 1 teaspoon olive oil and swirl to film the bottom of the pan lightly. With the tip of a paring knife, prick the sausages a few times on each side to allow the fat to drain off as they brown. Add the sausages to the pan and sauté, turning them as they brown, until they are brown on all sides, but not cooked through, about 8 minutes. Use a splatter screen, if desired. Transfer the sausages to a cutting board and let sit for 5 minutes to allow the juices to retract. Cut each sausage into 4 chunks.

7. Remove the baking sheet from the oven and arrange the sausage chunks on top of the peppers. Roast until the potatoes are creamy soft inside and crisp on the outside, 10 to 20 minutes longer. Transfer the sausages and vegetables to a warmed bowl and serve family style, encouraging guests to squeeze the roasted garlic onto the bread.

PORK LOIN ROAST
WITH VANILLA-SCENTED APPLESAUCE

Ever since I was a kid, roast pork has been one of my favorite Sunday dinners. This herb rub, inspired by a recipe in an old issue of the terrific *Cook's Illustrated* magazine, elevates the roast of my childhood memories to new levels. For special occasions and holidays, I prepare the Crown Roast of Pork variation at the end, filling the center cavity with root vegetables tossed with peas for color, which makes for a memorable meal. Serve either roast any time of year with warm applesauce, roasted potatoes (page 271), and Garlic Spinach with Currants, Pine Nuts, and Pecorino (page 265). If you use the optional kale or broccoli rabe (pronounced *rob*) to garnish your platter, save the greens for braising (page 266) or add them to a pot of soup the next day. Imbued with the flavorful pork juices, they'll add incomparable depth of flavor to your cooking.

Serves 4 to 6

Pork

1 bone-in rib-end pork loin roast, 3 to 4 pounds (5 or 6 chops), frenched and tip of the chine bone removed

1 tablespoon kosher salt

1 teaspoon granulated garlic powder

1 tablespoon chopped fresh thyme, sage, and/or rosemary or 1 teaspoon dried mixed herbs, crumbled between your fingers

1 teaspoon freshly ground black pepper

½ teaspoon fennel seeds

1 tablespoon extra-virgin olive oil

Applesauce

2 pounds Golden Delicious, Cortland, or other favorite local apples

1 pound Jonathan, Rome Beauty, or other favorite local red-skinned apples

½ small lemon

½ cup water

About 1 tablespoon sugar

1 cinnamon stick

1 teaspoon pure vanilla extract, preferably Tahitian

Orange wedges and kale or broccoli rabe, for garnish (optional)

/continued

RECIPE SECRETS

The rib end of the pork loin is closer to the shoulder and thus a bit fattier—and more flavorful—than the ubiquitous center-cut roast. For the best flavor, order a bone-in pork roast. Ask the butcher to remove the tip of the chine bone, or backbone, to make carving easier.

For an elegant presentation, have the butcher french the bones for you, that is, trim out the meat and fat between the bones. (If you make your own sausage, be sure to ask the butcher to save the trim, too—you're paying for it, after all.) I must confess, however, that since this meat between the bones is so rich and flavorful, I often specifically ask the butcher *not* to french the bones when I order a rib-end pork roast. If you don't have the bones frenched, ignore the step below about covering the bones with aluminum foil before placing the roast in the oven.

Adding lemon to the apples as they cook leaches some of the color from red apple skins, giving homemade applesauce a lovely pink hue.

If you use a food mill to purée apples for applesauce, you don't have to peel them. Otherwise, peel apples, cook, and stir vigorously with a wooden spoon to achieve a saucy consistency. If you've peeled the apples and want pink applesauce, add some of the red skins to the pot when you cook the applesauce; remove them before stirring.

1. *Prepare the pork:* About 4 hours before serving time, remove the meat from the refrigerator and bring to room temperature.

2. About 3 hours before serving time, position a rack in the lower-middle of the oven and preheat to 250 degrees F. Choose a roasting pan and rack about the same size as the pork roast, and coat the pan and rack generously with vegetable oil spray.

3. In a small bowl, combine the salt, garlic powder, herb(s), pepper, and fennel seeds. Set aside.

4. Blot the roast dry with paper towels and rub with the olive oil. Pat the salt mixture onto all the surfaces, distributing the fennel seeds evenly. Place the roast, meat side up, on the rack. Cover the frenched bones (bones only) with aluminum foil. Roast until the internal temperature registers between 120 and 130 degrees F, about 1½ hours.

5. *Prepare the applesauce:* If you plan to use a food mill, simply cut the apples into quarters. If you don't plan to use a food mill, peel and core the apples and add some of the red peels to the pan to give the finished sauce a pink tinge. Place the apples in a heavy 4-quart saucepan. Squeeze juice from the lemon into the pan and add the spent rind, then add the water, sugar, and cinnamon stick. Bring to a boil over medium-high heat, cover, and reduce the heat to low. Cook until the apples are soft and collapsed, 10 to 25 minutes, depending on their size and type.

6. Remove and discard the cinnamon stick (or rinse and reuse), lemon rind, and apple peel, if using. In batches, pass the apple mixture through a food mill fitted with a medium disk held over a bowl. Scrape the underside of the food mill to capture all the sauce. Alternatively, leave the apples in the pan and beat into a sauce with a wooden spoon. Stir in the vanilla extract. Taste for sweetness and add more sugar, if desired. Keep warm. (The applesauce can be made up to 24 hours in advance. Let cool, cover, and refrigerate. Reheat gently before serving.)

7. *Finish roasting the pork:* When the internal temperature of the pork reaches 120 to 130 degrees F, raise the oven temperature to 425 degrees F and remove the foil from the bones. If you notice that the pan drippings are starting to smoke, add 1 cup water to the pan (don't pour it over the roast). Roast until the internal temperature registers 145 degrees F, about another 20 minutes.

8. Remove the roast from the oven, tent with foil, and let rest for 15 minutes. Transfer the pork to a warmed serving platter. Cut between the bones with a sturdy boning knife to separate the part of the loin. If desired, garnish the platter with orange wedges and kale or broccoli rabe. Serve the applesauce alongside.

CROWN ROAST OF PORK VARIATION

Ask the butcher to tie together 2 rib-end pork roasts into a crown. Be sure to specify the rib end, as crowns are typically made with the less marbled center-cut part of the loin. Based on my experience, a 16-chop crown roast weighs about 10 pounds and serves 8 to 10 people. (I like to offer guests a "double chop.") For the best flavor, specify that you *don't* want the bones frenched, but if you are planning an elegant presentation, do have them frenched. Remove the crown roast from the refrigerator a good 2 hours before cooking to guarantee it's at room temperature when you put it into the oven; this ensures it will cook evenly. Rub all the surfaces with olive oil, triple the amount of seasonings in the pork loin roast recipe, and pat the seasonings all over the outside and inside of the crown. Position the crown upside down (meat up, bones down) on the rack to keep it juicy during roasting. Roast on a rimmed baking sheet in an oven preheated to 350 degrees F for the first 20 minutes, then reduce the heat to 325 degrees F for the duration. Test for doneness 1 hour after putting the roast in the oven by inserting a thermometer into the densest section of the meat. For tender, pink meat, remove the roast from the oven when the thermometer registers 140 degrees (which will rise to about 145 degrees F as the meat rests). For meat that is firmer and less pink, but still juicy, remove the roast when the internal temperature registers 145 degrees F (which will rise to about 150 degrees F). If you cook pork any longer, you risk serving dry, tough meat. (You can always return a few chops to the oven for people who might prefer meat well done.) Tent the roast with aluminum foil and let rest for 15 minutes. Place the crown, bones up, on a platter or cutting board and remove any visible string used to sew or tie the crown together. If presenting the entire crown, fill the center cavity with Roasted Root Vegetables (page 269) mixed with 1 cup seasoned, cooked English peas. Alternatively, on a cutting board, cut the crown into chops and arrange, overlapping, on a warmed platter. Garnish the platter as directed for the loin roast.

ORDERING A CROWN ROAST OF PORK

Call several butchers for cost estimates a week or so before ordering a crown roast. You're likely to find the best price in Chinatown meat markets. For organic pork that's also juicy, tender, and full of flavor, order from Niman Ranch (see Sources). As I learned in my catering days, everything that's considered a specialty item, such as this roast, costs more around the holidays. If the cost of a crown is prohibitive, consider roasting two rib-end pork roasts separately. Present them standing on a platter, propped up against each other with the bones of each roast intertwined.

RECIPE SECRETS

These days, all hams, boneless and bone-in, are precooked, so all you have to do is reheat them. For the best results, take the ham out of the refrigerator and bring it to room temperature before baking. If you buy a ham that's labeled "cook before eating," cook it to an internal temperature of 160 degrees F. Otherwise, 140 degrees F is sufficient.

In this recipe, testers preferred Annie's Naturals Organic Honey Mustard and Jack Daniel's Honey Dijon. Maille Honey Mustard gave the baked ham a bitter flavor.

Be sure to wear latex gloves when working with the jalapeño, and don't rub your eyes. For an antidote to chile burns, see page 157.

In a "The Doctor Is In" seminar with food science authority Shirley Corriher, I learned that some people have an enzyme in their saliva that makes cilantro taste like soap. If you don't like cilantro, feel free to substitute finely chopped flat-leaf parsley or minced chives here.

Use a Granton edge carving or slicing knife (page 232) to slice very thin slices of ham or other meats.

HONEY-MUSTARD GLAZED HAM
WITH GRILLED PINEAPPLE SALSA

While I was working on the business plan for my cooking school, I was offered a job demonstrating equipment at the brand new Berkeley and San Francisco, California, Sur La Table cookware stores. It was springtime and a crowd was expected for the demonstration on stove-top grills. I had to decide what would smell good enough to draw people over to the kitchen *and* demonstrate the versatility of the grill, yet not break the bank or tie me down to the stove for two hours. The answer came to me as I wandered through the produce market one day and the fragrance of fresh pineapple drew me in. Pineapple always reminds me of ham, so I challenged myself to come up with a new way to pair the ubiquitous combination. After a few trials, a new recipe was born. Whether you use a stove-top, gas, or charcoal grill, the high heat caramelizes the pineapple, giving it a complementary smokiness that works well with the ham. Here's a great dish for a crowd—at home or away at a potluck dinner. Ham has the added benefit of tasting great whether it's served piping hot or at room temperature.

Serves 6 to 8

Ham

1 boneless ham, 3 to 4 pounds	About 2 teaspoons sugar or honey
Prepared honey mustard to brush on ham	⅓ cup minced red onion
	¼ cup diced red bell pepper

Salsa

4 slices fresh pineapple, each ¼ to ½ inch thick, cores removed	½ to 1 green jalapeño chile, seeded, deribbed, and cut into slivers
¼ cup mild-tasting extra-virgin olive oil	2 tablespoons chopped fresh cilantro
2 tablespoons rice vinegar (seasoned or unseasoned)	Kosher salt and fine, freshly ground black pepper

---

1. *Prepare the ham:* Preheat the oven to 325 degrees F. Coat a roasting pan and rack with vegetable oil spray. Place the ham on the rack and lightly brush the top and sides with the honey mustard. Bake until the internal temperature registers 140 degrees F, 30 to 60 minutes, depending on size.

2. *Prepare the salsa:* While the ham is in the oven, prepare a hot fire in a charcoal grill, or preheat a gas or stove-top grill to high. Lightly brush both sides of the pineapple slices with a little of the olive oil. Pour the remaining oil into a medium bowl and set aside.

3. Grill the pineapple, turning the slices as needed, until seared on both sides, 8 to 10 minutes total. When done, the pineapple should be caramelized with visible grill marks. Transfer the grilled pineapple to a cutting board. When cool enough to handle, chop into ¼-inch pieces and set aside.

4. Whisk the rice vinegar and sugar or honey into the reserved oil. Add the onion, bell pepper, jalapeño, and cilantro and stir to combine. Season to taste with salt and pepper. Let the salsa sit for at least 20 minutes for the flavors to meld. You should have about 1½ cups.

5. Slice the ham and serve with the salsa on the side. Cover and refrigerate (separately) any leftover ham or salsa for up to a few days.

GRILLED LEG OF LAMB
WITH POMEGRANATE MARINADE
AND MUHAMMARA

Pomegranate molasses, a thick, syrupy, sweet-tart reduction of pomegranate juice that adds incomparable flavor to marinades, is a natural with grilled lamb. This marinade works well with lamb chops and venison, too (see variation). I love to serve grilled—or broiled—leg of lamb with muhammara (pronounced moo-*hahm*-mer-ah), an addictive Middle Eastern spread or condiment made with roasted red peppers, walnuts, and pomegranate molasses. For side dishes, serve roasted potatoes (page 271) or Kalijira Rice Pilaw (page 277) and a tangle of Romano Beans (page 258). Cold, sliced leftover leg of lamb is a great foundation for composed summer salads with roasted peppers and goat cheese, or stuffed into a pocket-bread sandwich with feta, cucumber, and shaved red onion. When fresh pomegranates are in season in the fall, use a handful of fresh pomegranate seeds to garnish a side dish you're serving with the lamb, such as salad or rice. The vibrant pomegranate seeds will serve as a flavor bridge between the marinated lamb and the other dish.

Boneless, butterflied leg of lamb, cut into main muscle groups

/continued

RECILE SECRETS

. . . .

If you can't find a boneless, butterflied leg of lamb, buy a bone-in leg and ask your butcher to bone it and butterfly it.

. . . .

I love grilled leg of lamb cooked rare or medium-rare. Once it's cooked beyond bright pink, however, lamb starts to taste gamy to me. Grilling a butterflied leg of lamb to even doneness throughout can be tricky because the three main muscles in the leg are of different thickness and density. To solve this problem, cut the butterflied leg into three pieces along the natural separations. This way, it's easy to cook each piece to the desired doneness, or to cook one piece longer for someone who prefers well-done lamb.

. . . .

For a crusty, charred exterior, blot up all excess marinade before grilling. Otherwise, the meat will steam instead of sear, making it difficult for a flavorful crust to form. Also, when you grill more than one piece of meat, be sure to leave some space around each piece for steam to escape.

. . . .

While it's important to salt meat generously before grilling, do not add salt to the marinade. Salt the meat before cooking so it will cook into—and flavor—the crust of the meat.

. . . .

Muhammara gets its hauntingly addictive flavor from both pomegranate molasses and Aleppo pepper, a coarsely ground, sun-dried pepper from Syria with a warm, mild heat. Look for Aleppo pepper in Middle Eastern markets (see Sources) or substitute Hungarian paprika, if unavailable.

Serves 4 to 6; makes about 1 cup muhammara

Lamb	Muhammara
1 boneless leg of lamb, 3 pounds, butterflied	1 cup walnuts, toasted (page 89)
½ cup extra-virgin olive oil	1 slice Italian bread, torn into pieces
2 tablespoons pomegranate molasses	1 cup roasted red pepper strips, fresh (page 254) or jarred
1 tablespoon balsamic vinegar	2 tablespoons extra-virgin olive oil
1 tablespoon dry rosé, white wine, or white vermouth	2 tablespoons pomegranate molasses
1 teaspoon whole allspice or ¼ teaspoon ground allspice	1 tablespoon tomato paste
6 black peppercorns	1 teaspoon kosher salt
2 bay leaves, preferably imported	1 teaspoon ground cumin
Leaves from 1 fresh rosemary sprig (6 inches long) or ½ teaspoon dried rosemary leaves	½ to 1 teaspoon coarsely ground Aleppo pepper or Hungarian paprika
½ teaspoon granulated garlic powder	½ teaspoon sugar (optional)
½ teaspoon dry leaf oregano, crumbled between your fingers	
⅛ teaspoon crushed red pepper flakes	
About 2 teaspoons kosher salt	

1. *Marinate the lamb:* If the lamb is tied into a roast, remove and discard the butcher's string or mesh bag holding it together. Open up the leg of lamb onto a cutting board. If the meat is bloody, rinse and blot dry with paper towels. Cut the lamb at its natural separations into 1 large and 2 smaller pieces (see illustration, page 221) and trim off all exterior fat. Set aside.

2. Combine the olive oil, pomegranate molasses, vinegar, wine, allspice, peppercorns, bay leaves, rosemary, garlic powder, oregano, and red pepper flakes in a 1-gallon zip-top plastic bag. Add the lamb, press out the air from the bag, seal closed, and massage marinade into meat. Lay the bag flat and marinate the lamb in a cool place in the kitchen for 3 hours, turning the bag and massaging the meat periodically. (If the kitchen is warmer than 70 degrees F, refrigerate the bag with lamb and marinade for 2 hours, then bring to room temperature for the remaining 1 hour.)

3. *Prepare the muhammara:* Place all the ingredients in a blender or food processor and purée into a smooth paste, stopping occasionally to scrape down the sides of the jar or bowl. Taste and bring the flavors into balance with more salt, Aleppo pepper, pomegranate molasses, and/or sugar, as necessary. Transfer to a bowl, cover, and refrigerate. Bring to room temperature and adjust the seasoning, if needed, before serving.

4. *Cook the lamb:* Prepare a medium-hot fire in a charcoal grill, or preheat a gas grill to medium-high heat. Alternatively, position a rack about 6 inches from the broiler element and preheat the broiler.

5. Remove the lamb from the marinade and blot off the excess marinade with paper towels (it's okay to leave any herb flecks in place). Discard the marinade. Sprinkle the lamb generously with the salt. Place the lamb on the grill (or on a broiler pan fitted with a perforated top pan or rack), being sure to allow at least 1 inch of space around each piece. Cook the lamb, turning to brown all sides, until the internal temperature of each piece reaches 130 degrees F for medium-rare meat, about 10 minutes on each side for the thickest piece, less for the thinner pieces. If you want all of the lamb to be cooked to the same degree of doneness, transfer the smaller pieces to a cutting board as soon as they come to temperature and tent with aluminum foil while the larger piece continues to cook. Let the lamb rest, tented with foil, for 5 minutes for the smaller pieces, 10 minutes for the larger piece. Carve the meat across the grain. If some lamb is less done inside than desired, return individual slices to the grill (or broiler) until they are done to your liking. Serve with the muhammara on the side.

VENISON LOIN VARIATION

Add 1 teaspoon juniper berries to the marinade. Because venison is very lean, don't cook it beyond 125 degrees F internal temperature, or it will be dry and gamy.

ABOUT POMEGRANATE MOLASSES

Pomegranate molasses might remind you of the grenadine used in kids' Shirley Temple and Roy Rogers "mocktails." In fact, grenadine is a sweet, light syrup made from pomegranates, but it would not be a suitable substitute for pomegranate molasses.

Pomegranate molasses is a Middle Eastern condiment—also called pomegranate paste or pomegranate concentrated juice—with a distinct flavor profile that tastes both sweet and tart. It reminds me of tamarind in the way that it adds a complex, subtly limy, distinctively bright flavor to marinades, dressings, and spreads. Unfortunately, pomegranate molasses varies in quality from one producer to the next. Sometimes, when the pomegranate juice is reduced too much or some of it has scorched in processing, the molasses can have a burned aroma or aftertaste. To be sure I have a good bottle, I open it—after paying for it—and taste it before leaving the store. Look for pomegranate molasses in upscale supermarkets or in Middle Eastern markets (see Sources). I have had good luck with Sadaf brand.

RECIPE SECRETS

Have the butcher remove the chine bone (backbone) to make carving easier (see illustration on the facing page). You or the butcher can either trim the racks down to the silver skin (the iridescent membrane that separates the two muscle groups) or trim the fat down to the top flap of meat and leave the next thin layer of fat intact. The latter method is less wasteful and allows the meat to self-baste during roasting. It's the method I use.

For a classic presentation and easier carving, you or the butcher can french—or scrape clean—the bones and remove the meat from between them (see illustration on the facing page). If you prefer not to french the bones, just roast the rack and gnaw on the bones for a delicious treat. If you do french the bones, discard the fat, but save the lamb scraps for stew, or grind it for lamb burgers.

Depending on how a rack of lamb is butchered, it may have 7 or 8 ribs, or chops. Plan on serving 3 or 4 chops per person. To prevent too many crumbs from falling off while carving, and to keep the meat hot, I like to serve 2 double chops per person, instead of 4 single chops. People with smaller appetites may be satisfied with 1 double chop, depending on the side dishes.

RACK OF LAMB
WITH GARLICKY BREAD CRUMBS

Special enough for company or holiday dinners, this roast of tender, little lamb chops is coated with garlicky fresh bread crumbs that give off a seductive fragrance as they mingle with the lamb juices in the oven. In this recipe, garlic and parsley are combined with buttered fresh bread crumbs and "glued" onto the lamb with Dijon mustard. This is a rather simple recipe, and you can do much of it a day ahead. Serve with roasted potatoes (page 271) or Roasted Garlic Mashed Potatoes (page 281) and Garlic Spinach with Currants, Pine Nuts, and Pecorino (page 265).

Serves 4

2 racks of lamb, about 3 pounds total, trimmed of visible fat and frenched, if desired

1 tablespoon extra-virgin olive oil

Kosher salt for sprinkling, plus ½ teaspoon

Freshly ground black pepper for sprinkling, plus ⅛ teaspoon

6 ounces day-old dense Italian or French bread

4 tablespoons unsalted butter

2 tablespoons minced fresh flat-leaf parsley

2 small cloves garlic, green germ removed if present, minced

About 1 tablespoon Dijon mustard, preferably imported

---

1. Preheat the oven to 400 degrees F (or 375 degrees F on the convection setting). Coat an 17-by-12-inch rimmed baking sheet with vegetable oil spray. Completely cover the bottom and ends of the pan with aluminum foil, wrapping foil around both ends. Place the racks, meat side up, on the foil. Brush the tops and sides of the racks (including the bones) with the olive oil and sprinkle lightly with salt and pepper. Roast until the internal temperature registers 120 degrees F, 15 to 20 minutes. Remove from the oven.

2. In the meantime, prepare the crumbs: Using a serrated knife, remove and discard the crusts from the bread (page 106). Tear the bread into roughly 1-inch pieces. Process in a food processor or blender, grinding into crumbs no larger than ½ inch. Melt the butter in a 10-inch nonstick skillet over medium-high heat. When the butter is hot enough to sizzle a bread crumb on contact, add the bread crumbs and stir constantly until they turn very pale golden brown, 5 to 7 minutes. Transfer to a bowl and toss together with the parsley, garlic, ½ teaspoon salt, and ⅛ teaspoon pepper.

3. If you're not using the convection setting, once the lamb reaches 120 degrees F, position a rack 6 inches below the broiler element and preheat the broiler. Otherwise, raise the heat to 500 degrees F on the convection setting.

4. If there is a fair amount of grease on the foil after roasting the lamb, transfer the racks to a cutting board, carefully fold up and discard the foil, and return the racks to the pan.

5. Brush all surfaces of the meat with the mustard. With your hand, firmly pat all of the bread crumb mixture onto the mustard. Place the lamb back in the convection oven or under the broiler. Watch very carefully and turn the pan as needed to prevent the crumbs from burning. If you like your lamb rare, remove the lamb from the oven when the crumbs are golden brown. If you prefer medium-rare lamb, brown the crumbs a little darker, another 3 minutes or so. Tent the lamb loosely with foil and let stand for 10 minutes. Don't turn off the heat in the oven or broiler yet.

6. Transfer the lamb to a cutting board and cut between the bones into double chops (2 bones per slice). If the meat is too rare for you, place the chops on their sides on a clean baking sheet, and return to the oven or broiler. Check every 30 to 60 seconds until the chops are done to your liking. Serve 2 double chops per person.

Rack of lamb, not frenched, with chine bone

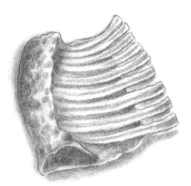

Rack of lamb, frenched, chine bone removed

RECIPE SECRETS

....

If you have a convection setting on your oven, this is the time to use it. The circulating dry heat does a great job of caramelizing the meat, then toasting the bread crumbs.

....

To prepare most of this recipe up to a day ahead, roast the meat to an internal temperature of 120 degrees F as directed, then coat it with the mustard and crumbs. Allow the meat to cool to room temperature, cover, and refrigerate for up to 12 hours. Bring the meat to room temperature before continuing.

RACK OF LAMB FOR NONINTERVENTIONIST COOKS

Browning the racks in the oven before you add the crumbs caramelizes the meat and adds flavor, but it adds a step, too. For simplicity, here's how recipe tester Susan Galindo-Schnellbacher does it: Season the raw racks with the salt and pepper (omit the olive oil), brush with the mustard, and pack the racks with the "raw" garlic-parsley crumbs (Susan doesn't sauté the crumbs). Roast the lamb in an oven preheated to 325 degrees F until the internal temperature reaches 130 degrees F, about 35 minutes, for medium-rare meat, or until the meat is done to your liking.

RECIPE SECRETS

For tender, flavorful hamburgers, don't use the leanest ground beef, such as sirloin. I prefer ground chuck.

Combine the meat mixture with your hands just enough to blend all the ingredients. Overmixing compacts the mixture and can make hamburgers tough and dry.

Resist any urge to press on the hamburgers while they cook. It just presses out the juices and results in dry burgers.

HAMBURGERS, ITALIAN STYLE

One of my first taste memories as a kid was going to my godmother's house when her mother was frying meatballs. As soon as I opened the front door, that unforgettable smell grabbed me and I became instantly hungry. Godmother par excellence Patty DeFeo broke off a piece of "bare" meatball (it was a huge treat to get one before it hit the tomato sauce), blew on it, and fed it to me with her fingers. I can still taste the hot, tender meat brightened with fresh Italian parsley, salty grated cheese, and sweet sautéed onions. Over the years, my mother would shape and bake this same mixture into a meat loaf, or when time was short, thick patties (or flat meatballs, depending on your perspective) and sauté them. We always ate these "Italian hamburgers" with ketchup, but never on a bun—that these have bread *in* them was part of the rationale, I suspect. Serve with Savory Corn Pudding (page 256) or Classic American Potato Salad (page 282) and Romano Beans (page 258) or braised summer squash (page 262).

Serves 4

3 slices day-old Italian or French bread (not sourdough), ½ inch thick, crusts removed

3 to 4 tablespoons milk (nonfat or low fat is okay)

4 tablespoons mild-tasting extra-virgin olive oil, divided

½ cup finely chopped yellow onion

1¼ teaspoons kosher salt, divided

1 large egg

¼ cup freshly grated Romano cheese

About 1 tablespoon finely chopped fresh flat-leaf parsley

¼ teaspoon granulated garlic powder

⅛ teaspoon fine, freshly ground black pepper

1 pound ground beef chuck

---

1. Tear the bread into roughly 1-inch pieces and place in a medium bowl. Pour 3 tablespoons milk over the bread and let stand until the bread is moistened, about 10 minutes. Squeeze the bread with your fingers; if it feels dry, add the remaining 1 tablespoon milk. Shred the bread into roughly ½-inch pieces and set aside in the bowl.

2. Heat a 12-inch skillet or sauté pan over medium heat. Add 1 tablespoon of the olive oil. When the oil is hot enough to sizzle a piece of onion, add the onion and sauté, stirring occasionally, for 5 minutes. Reduce the heat to low, sprinkle the onion with about ¼ teaspoon of the salt, and continue cooking until the onion begins to get sticky, about 5 more minutes. Remove the pan from the heat and set aside.

3. In a small bowl, mix the egg lightly with a fork. Add the cheese, parsley, the remaining 1 teaspoon salt, the garlic powder, and pepper and stir with the fork to combine. Transfer to the bowl holding the bread and stir to combine. Add the ground beef and sautéed onion and mix with a fork or your hands until all the ingredients are evenly incorporated.

4. Shape a little of the mixture into a small patty and fry (or microwave) to test for seasoning. Taste and add more cheese, salt, pepper, and/or garlic powder, if necessary, to bring the flavors into balance.

5. Divide into 4 equal portions and shape into roughly ½-inch-thick patties. Rinse your hands with cold water to prevent the mixture from sticking as you gently compress the patties. (The patties can be shaped up to 24 hours ahead. Cover tightly with plastic wrap and refrigerate. Bring to room temperature before cooking.)

6. Return the pan used for cooking the onions to medium-high heat. Add the remaining 3 tablespoons oil. When the oil is hot enough to sizzle a tiny bit of beef, add the patties and sauté, turning once, until browned nicely on both sides and just barely pink inside, 5 to 6 minutes on each side. Serve hot, warm, or at room temperature.

RECIPE SECRETS

When I moved to California, I could never find the tender, flavorful, boneless Delmonico steaks I grew to love on the East Coast. When I took a butchery class in cooking school, I learned that butchers in different locations have different names for the same cut of meat. In the Northeast, Delmonico steaks, cut from the rib roast, were given the name of the New York restaurant that made them famous. In California, the same cut is sold as rib-eye steaks.

For the best flavor and texture, season the steaks 36 hours before grilling.

I love *Fine Cooking* magazine, especially for their great tips and secrets, such as how to grill thickly sliced onions. To ensure they'll cook all the way through before the outside edges burn on a hot grill, give them a head start in the microwave or in a steamer. To prevent the onion slices from coming apart on the grill, skewer them with toothpicks. If available, use round toothpicks, and twist them in, leaving no exposed ends to burn. Otherwise, soak toothpicks in water first.

RIB-EYE STEAKS WITH ARUGULA, BLUE CHEESE, AND GRILLED RED ONIONS

Early in life, I discovered an affinity for blue cheese when my father took the family to his favorite lunch spot near his office in Brookline, Massachusetts. Jack and Marion's has long since been shuttered, but I'll never forget their superthick grilled hamburger, piled precariously high with a dome of soft, creamy—and yes, strong—blue cheese and a hefty slab of red onion. Here, that classic flavor combination is augmented with a sprightly arugula salad in a family-style meal that's fit for a special occasion. Add a big platter of corn on the cob and a crusty loaf of bread, and the feast is complete.

Serves 3 or 4

Steaks	Onion Slices
3 boneless rib-eye steaks, about 2 pounds total and ¾ inch thick	1 large red onion, cut into 3 or 4 slices, each ½ inch thick
1½ teaspoons kosher salt	About 3 tablespoons bold-tasting extra-virgin olive oil, divided
¾ teaspoon freshly ground black pepper	Kosher salt and fine, freshly ground black pepper
¾ teaspoon granulated garlic powder	2 bunches arugula, about 6 ounces total, tough stems removed, rinsed, and spun dry
1 tablespoon minced fresh thyme	Large handful of flavorful cherry tomatoes, cut in half through the stem end
¼ pound Maytag blue, Stilton, or other firm but crumbly blue cheese	1 tablespoon balsamic vinegar

1. *Prepare the steaks:* Trim away all the external fat from the steaks and place in a single layer on a large plate or platter. Season the steaks on both sides with salt, pepper, and garlic powder. Press the seasoning into the steaks with the heel of your hand. Sprinkle each side of each steak with ½ teaspoon thyme; press in. Refrigerate the steaks, uncovered, for up to 36 hours.

2. Remove the steaks from the refrigerator 1 hour before cooking. Prepare a hot fire in a charcoal grill, or preheat a gas grill to high.

3. *Grill the onions:* Skewer each slice of onion with 2 toothpicks twisted in crosswise from opposite sides to hold the layers together while grilling. Push the toothpicks in as far as possible to prevent any exposed ends from burning. Place the onions on a microwave-safe plate and microwave on high for 3 minutes to cook partially. (Or steam on a steamer rack above boiling water for 5 minutes.) Brush both sides of the onions with 1 tablespoon of the olive oil and sprinkle lightly with salt and pepper. Grill the onions, turning as necessary, until soft and golden brown on both sides, about 10 minutes total. Transfer to the bowl you'll use for the salad and set aside until cool enough to handle.

4. *Cook the steaks:* While the onions cool, grill the steaks on both sides to desired doneness, 5 to 7 minutes total for rare (125 degrees F), 7 to 10 minutes total for medium (135 degrees F), or until done to your liking.

5. Twist the toothpicks out of the onion slices, separate into rings, and leave the onion rings in the salad bowl. Add the arugula, tomatoes, the remaining 2 tablespoons olive oil, and the balsamic vinegar. Toss well. Season to taste with salt and pepper. Transfer the arugula salad to one side of a serving platter large enough to also accommodate the sliced steaks.

6. When the steaks are done, transfer to a cutting board, tent with aluminum foil, and let rest for 5 minutes. Slice the steaks across the grain into strips about ½ inch wide. With a large spatula, and in one motion, transfer the slices onto the platter. Drizzle the steak with any remaining carving juices and crumble the blue cheese over the meat. Serve at once.

RECIPE SECRETS

Occasionally, you'll find a layer of silver skin running along the surface of the flank steak. Be sure to remove it before marinating (see page 179).

I wouldn't even consider cooking a flank steak that hasn't been marinated to break down some of its fibers and boost its flavor. While it's not typical to include an acid, such as lemon juice, in an overnight marinade, the tough protein fibers of flank steak benefit from the acid's tenderizing effect without the steak becoming mushy. You could also use this marinade for chicken legs and thighs, pork tenderloin, or lamb chops. For the best results with flank steak, marinate overnight, cook rare, and cut across the grain on the diagonal into ¼-inch-thick slices.

You'll notice that beyond the sodium in the soy and Worcestershire sauces, no additional salt is added to this marinade. By all means, do season with salt—and pepper—before grilling to create an integrated, flavorful crust. Seasoning *after* grilling would result in less flavorful meat, with discernible flecks of salt and pepper that are not as pleasing to the palate.

GRILLED MARINATED FLANK STEAK AU JUS

Flank steak is a tasty cut of beef that proves the point "the tougher the meat, the better the flavor." A lean, long muscle from the underside of the steer toward the back end of the animal, this satisfying steak has a distinctive and pronounced grain that runs the full length of the cut. Au jus (pronounced oh-*zhoo*), a French term usually applied to beef, describes meat that's served with its natural juices, instead of with a separate sauce. A cutting board with a built-in well, or trough, is the best way to capture these juices that are released when carving. Serve flank steak with Orzo with Toybox Tomatoes and Fresh Mint (page 283), Roasted Peppers (page 254), Romano Beans (page 258), and/or Sautéed Mushrooms with Sherry and Garlic (page 271). Refrigerate any leftover flank steak and slice for sandwiches or salads. Or, for an unbeatable quesadilla, layer a flour tortilla with chopped leftover flank steak, sliced green onions, and shredded Cheddar cheese. Top with another tortilla and cook on a hot griddle until the cheese melts.

Serves 6 to 8

1 flank steak, about 1½ pounds

2 cloves garlic, crushed

2 tablespoons Dijon mustard, preferably imported

2 tablespoons soy sauce

2 tablespoons Worcestershire sauce

2 tablespoons freshly squeezed lemon juice

1 tablespoon chopped fresh thyme or 1 teaspoon dried leaf thyme, crumbled between your fingers

½ teaspoon freshly ground black pepper, plus more for sprinkling

½ cup boldly flavored extra-virgin olive oil

Kosher salt

---

1. Trim off any fat and silver skin from the flank steak, and pierce both sides all over with a meat fork to tenderize the meat and open its pores. Rub both sides of the steak with the crushed garlic. Place the steak and garlic in a 1-gallon zip-top plastic bag.

2. In a small bowl, whisk together the mustard, soy sauce, Worcestershire sauce, lemon juice, thyme, and the ½ teaspoon pepper. Slowly drizzle the olive oil into the mixture as you whisk steadily to form an emulsion. Pour the marinade into the bag with the steak and seal the bag, pressing out as much air as possible. With your fingers, massage the marinade into the steak. Lay the bag flat in the refrigerator and marinate for 2 to 24 hours, turning the bag and massaging the meat periodically.

3. About 1 hour before serving, remove the bag from the refrigerator and allow the steak and marinade to come to room temperature. Prepare a hot fire in a charcoal grill, or preheat a gas or stove-top grill to high. Remove the steak from the marinade and blot off excess marinade with paper towels, removing any pieces of raw garlic. Season the top side lightly with salt and pepper. Discard the marinade.

4. When the grill is very hot (you can hold your hand over it for only 2 seconds), place the steak on it, seasoned side down. Don't try to adjust the position of the steak at this point, as the meat won't release from the grill until it's sufficiently seared. Cook the steak on the first side for 3 minutes for rare, or for 4 minutes for medium-rare. If you want to create cross-hatching, rotate the steak a quarter turn after 2 minutes, then cook for 1 or 2 more minutes.

5. Lightly sprinkle the top of the steak with salt and pepper, and turn to sear the second side. If desired, rotate the steak a quarter turn after 2 minutes to achieve cross-hatching. After 3 minutes total cooking on the second side, test the internal temperature of the steak. Because flank steak is very lean, it's advisable not to cook it beyond rare (125 degrees F) or medium-rare (130 degrees F). Insert the thermometer on a slant into the center of the steak to test. If the steak is not done, continue grilling and test again after 1 minute. (If your thermometer has a plastic—not glass—housing covering the dial, don't leave it in the meat while it's on the grill, or the plastic will melt.)

6. When the steak is done, transfer it to a cutting board, preferably one with a trough or well to capture the juices when carving. Tent it with aluminum foil, or cover completely with an inverted bowl, and let stand for 5 minutes to allow the juices to retract into the meat. Using a carving knife, and holding it at a 45-degree angle, cut the steak across the grain into thin slices. If the steak is more rare than you prefer, place individual slices back on the grill. The residual heat will continue to cook them until they reach your desired doneness. Arrange the slices, shingle-style (see page 179) to retain heat, on a warmed platter. Use a spoon or metal bench scraper to scoop up juices and drizzle them over the sliced steak.

RECIPE SECRETS

See the headnote on page 110 for tips on making a roux. This gravy recipe yields about 1½ cups. For more gravy, double the amount of each ingredient.

For juicy sliced roast beef for sandwiches, let the meat cool to room temperature before slicing. A Granton edge knife (see illustration below) makes cutting thin, even slices easy.

Granton edge slicer

SLOW-ROASTED BEEF SIRLOIN TIP WITH **PAN GRAVY** OR **CREAMY HORSERADISH SAUCE**

Boneless beef sirloin tip is a relatively lean yet flavorful, moderately priced cut that's my favorite for Sunday roast beef dinners. Depending on the butcher and what part of the country you're in, this cut is also called a face round roast, crescent roast, or knuckle roast. It feeds at least six people, with enough left over for delicious sandwiches during the week. When I had a catering business, this was the recipe we used for party sandwiches, which were served on small dinner rolls with arugula and mayonnaise laced with horseradish. Making gravy with the flavorful pan drippings is simple and straightforward, and this version comes out so smooth you don't even have to strain it. In the summertime, instead of hot gravy, I prefer to serve the roast beef with the cool, creamy horseradish sauce made with crème fraîche. This roast is short on preparation time and long on flavor. Serve it with either sauce, accompanied by Roasted Garlic Mashed Potatoes (page 281), roasted potatoes (page 271), or roasted acorn squash with butter and brown sugar.

Serves 8 to 10

Roast Beef

1 boneless beef sirloin tip or round tip roast, 3 to 4 pounds

About 1 tablespoon extra-virgin olive oil

About 2 teaspoons kosher salt

About ½ teaspoon granulated garlic powder

About ½ teaspoon coarse, freshly ground black pepper

Horseradish Sauce

1 cup crème fraîche, homemade (page 67) or purchased, or sour cream

3 to 4 tablespoons bottled cream-style horseradish

Gravy

Up to 4 tablespoons unsalted butter if needed to supplement fat from roasting pan

About 2 cups homemade chicken stock or broth (page 60 or 61), homemade beef stock, or purchased reduced-sodium chicken or beef broth

3 tablespoons all-purpose flour

Fine, freshly ground black pepper and kosher salt

1. *Prepare the roast:* Remove the beef from the refrigerator 3 to 4 hours before you plan to serve the roast. Blot the roast dry with paper towels, rub with the olive oil, and sprinkle all sides generously with the salt, garlic powder, and pepper. Let stand at room temperature for at least 30 minutes or up to 2 hours.

2. Preheat the oven to 425 degrees F (or 400 degrees F on the convection setting). Choose a shallow roasting pan and rack about the same size as the beef roast and coat the pan and rack generously with vegetable oil spray. Place the roast, fat side up (don't worry if there's no external fat), on the rack. Roast for 15 minutes. Reduce the heat to 325 degrees F (or 300 degrees F on the convection setting) and roast until the internal temperature registers 125 degrees F for rare or 130 degrees F for medium-rare, 1 to 1½ hours, depending on the thickness of the roast and the desired doneness. Transfer the roast to a cutting board with a trough or well to collect the juices when carving. Tent the roast with aluminum foil and let stand for 15 to 20 minutes.

3. *Prepare the gravy:* Pour off all of the fat and any pan juices from the roasting pan into a fat separator measuring cup or heatproof bowl. Spoon ¼ cup of the fat that rises to the top back into the pan. If there is insufficient fat, make up the difference with butter. If you are not making additional gravy, discard the remaining fat. If there are any dark-colored pan drippings, add them back to the pan.

4. Place the pan with the fat on the stove top over medium-high heat. Use a flat whisk to scrape up the browned bits from the pan bottom. Depending on the size of your roasting pan, you may want to balance it over two burners, or rotate it around on one burner. Reduce the heat to medium and make a roux: Sprinkle the flour into the pan all at once and cook, whisking constantly, until the mixture is smooth and golden brown, 3 to 5 minutes. Slowly pour in the 2 cups broth, a few tablespoons at a time at first, whisking constantly. Have faith; as you stir constantly and the mixture comes to a boil, the lumps will dissipate. Simmer until the gravy reaches the thickness you like, usually 5 to 10 minutes. Season with salt and pepper to taste. You may not have to add any salt, depending on whether you use canned or homemade broth, and how much salt you used to season the beef. If you object to any chunky bits of pan drippings in the gravy, strain it through a medium-mesh sieve. Keep the gravy warm over very low heat until ready to serve. (If you make the gravy well ahead of serving time, transfer it to a small saucepan, cover with a concave lid—to prevent condensation from dripping into the gravy when you remove the lid— and place it on a turned-off burner.)

/continued

WOOD IS GOOD

When stirring a pan gravy or delicate sauce or custard with a metal spoon, you run the risk of dislodging any stuck-on or burned bits of food on the bottom of the pan. A wooden spoon glides right over the surface, keeping the sauce smooth. When making a pan gravy, use a metal whisk to dislodge pan drippings before you make the roux, then switch to a wooden spoon to stir as the gravy simmers and thickens.

HOW TO SEASON GRAVY

If you're unsure of how much salt to add when making gravy, transfer a couple of tablespoons of gravy to a small bowl and add salt a little at a time, tasting after each addition. The gravy should taste bright and compelling, not flat or dull. When it tastes perfect, do a little experiment and add a bit more salt. If the gravy tastes better now, use this as a flavor benchmark to refer to when seasoning the rest of the gravy. If it tastes too salty, just pour the salty gravy back into the pan and season to taste.

5. Before carving the roast, remove any butcher's string, if present. Carve into thin slices across the grain and shingle-stack the slices (see page 179) on a warmed serving platter. Spoon any juices that collect on the carving board over the meat or add to the gravy, if desired. Pour the gravy into a warmed gravy-boat or bowl and serve at once.

6. *Prepare the horseradish sauce:* While the roast is resting, in a small bowl, combine the crème fraîche or sour cream and 3 tablespoons of the horseradish. Taste and add more horseradish if you prefer a spicier kick. Refrigerate for at least 10 minutes for the flavors to meld; serve chilled.

OSSO BUCO WITH SWEET RED PEPPERS AND GREMOLATA

Like most long-simmered dishes, these braised veal shanks taste even better when reheated the next day. For the choicest part of the shank, call ahead and ask the butcher for center-cut pieces to order. This dish was inspired by a recipe in *Northern Italian Cooking* by Biba Caggiano. For a classic Italian combination, garnish the braised veal shanks with zesty *gremolata* and serve with the classic Italian osso buco side dish, Risotto Milanese (page 98). Instead, Creamy, Soft Polenta (page 274) or Mashed Yukon Gold Potatoes (page 280) would be another perfect accompaniment. If desired, give each person a marrow spoon (or crab or lobster pick) to extract the rich, gelatinous marrow from the narrow hole in the center of the bone and spread the marrow on crusty Italian bread. Be sure to have plenty of bread available for sopping up the luscious sauce, too.

Serves 6

Veal

. . . .

⅓ cup all-purpose flour

3 teaspoons kosher salt, divided, plus more for sprinkling

½ teaspoon fine, freshly ground black pepper, plus more for sprinkling

6 center-cut slices veal shank, 1¼ inches thick

¼ cup plus 2 tablespoons clarified butter or ghee (page 155) or coconut oil (see page 236), divided

3 large red bell peppers, seeded, deribbed, and cut lengthwise into strips about ½ inch wide

2 large yellow onions, cut in half through the stem end, then thinly sliced crosswise into half-moons

5 cloves garlic, green germ removed if present, minced

1 cup dry white or red wine

1 cup homemade chicken stock or broth (page 60 or 61) or purchased reduced-sodium broth, as needed

1 cup peeled, seeded, and diced tomatoes with juice (fresh or canned)

2 tablespoons tomato paste

5 fresh thyme sprigs

Gremolata

. . . .

3 tablespoons chopped fresh flat-leaf parsley

1½ teaspoons minced lemon zest

1 clove garlic, green germ removed if present, minced

1. *Prepare the veal:* Preheat the oven to 325 degrees F. Place the flour on a sheet of waxed paper. Add 1 teaspoon of the salt and ¼ teaspoon of the pepper to the flour and stir with a fork to distribute evenly. Set aside.

2. Using kitchen string, tie each shank around its equator. Don't leave more than ½ inch of string dangling. Sprinkle both sides of each shank with salt and pepper.

RECIPE SECRETS

. . . .

Brown the shanks before braising to both caramelize the meat and develop a flavorful *fond* on the bottom of the pan. For the quickest, most even browning, and the best flavor, use either clarified butter, ghee, or coconut oil.

. . . .

To prevent the meat from falling off the bone while cooking, tie each piece with kitchen string around its "equator."

. . . .

After the shanks are braised, make the rich, thick sauce by puréeing, then straining, half the vegetables with the braising liquid. If you use a blender to purée the sauce, fill no more than half full, and be sure to hold the lid down as you slowly increase the speed. Or, purée the sauce right in the roasting pan with an immersion blender. A food processor will do the job, but the purée won't be as smooth, and you must be careful not to fill the work bowl more than one-third full to prevent leaking. After puréeing, strain the purée through a medium-mesh strainer. Don't use a finer mesh, or you'll trap too much of the pulp and end up with a watery sauce.

3. Place a 6- to 8-quart Dutch oven, 12 inches in diameter, or a heavy 12-inch sauté pan over medium-high heat. (The taller the sides of the pan, the less the shanks will splatter onto your stove.) When the pan is hot, add the ¼ cup clarified butter or coconut oil. When the butter is hot enough to sizzle a pepper strip, add the peppers and sauté until slightly softened, about 5 minutes. Add the onions and cook until limp, about 5 minutes. Using a slotted spoon, transfer the vegetables to a bowl, season with 1 teaspoon of the salt and the remaining ¼ teaspoon pepper, stir well, and set aside. Add the remaining 2 tablespoons clarified butter or coconut oil to the pan and reduce the heat to low.

4. Dredge the veal shanks in the seasoned flour to coat the tops and bottoms evenly. Raise the heat to medium-high. When the butter is hot enough to sizzle a few flecks of flour, tamp off any excess flour (which would burn before the meat is browned) from the veal and place the shanks in the pan in a single layer. To encourage browning, don't crowd the veal; you may have to brown the pieces in batches. Sauté, turning once, until the veal is brown on both the top and bottom, 10 to 15 minutes total. If the veal is still cold, you may want to raise the heat right after you add the shanks so the butter temperature stays constant and shanks don't absorb the fat. Transfer the browned veal to a roasting pan large enough to accommodate all the shanks in a single layer with a little extra wiggle room.

5. After all the shanks have been removed from the Dutch oven, raise the heat to high, add the garlic, and sauté for 30 seconds. Add the wine all at once and deglaze the pan, using a flat-bottomed wooden spatula to scrape up caramelized bits from the bottom of the pan. When the wine has reduced by about half, after about 5 minutes, add the stock, tomatoes, tomato paste, and thyme. Add the remaining 1 teaspoon salt and a few grinds of pepper. Stir, bring to a boil, and pour the mixture over the shanks. The liquid should almost reach the top of the shanks. If not, add stock or water as needed. Bring the liquid to a steady boil as you scatter the reserved bell peppers and onions evenly on top of the shanks. Cover, place in the oven, and braise for 1 hour, checking occasionally to be sure the liquid maintains a steady simmer throughout, and adjust the oven temperature if necessary. After the veal has braised for 1 hour, cut off a small piece and taste for tenderness. When done, a paring knife should penetrate the meat easily, and the meat should easily pull away from the bone and taste tender, not chewy. If necessary, continue simmering until tender.

6. *Prepare the gremolata:* While the veal shanks are braising, combine the parsley, lemon zest, and garlic in a small bowl. Cover and set aside.

7. *Prepare the sauce:* With tongs and a slotted spoon, transfer all the veal and about half of the peppers and onions to a warmed large, shallow bowl or deep platter, cover tightly with aluminum foil, and keep warm. Remove and discard the thyme sprigs from the braising liquid. Using an immersion blender, purée the remaining contents of the roasting pan, then strain through a medium-mesh sieve. Alternatively, pass the pepper mixture and braising liquid through a food mill fitted with a disk with the smallest holes.

8. Return the strained sauce to the roasting pan. Carefully return the veal and vegetables to the pan. Place on the stove top over medium heat and bring to a gentle simmer. Cook just long enough for all the ingredients to be heated through completely. Taste the sauce and adjust the seasoning with salt and pepper, if necessary.

9. To serve, remove the shanks from the pan and place on a cutting board. Cut off the string and transfer each shank to a warmed dinner plate (use a pancake spatula to transfer the veal if it's falling off the bone). Spoon some sauce and vegetables around the sides and on top of each shank. Top each shank with a spoonful of *gremolata* and serve at once.

BRAISED SHORT RIBS WITH FRIZZLED LEEKS

I've yet to meet a beef eater who doesn't love short ribs. These braised ribs derive exceptional flavor from a generous advance seasoning—called a rub—of fresh thyme, salt, and pepper. For the rub to have full impact, allow the seasoned ribs to sit for up to 24 hours before cooking. Or, if you're short on time, rub the ribs with seasonings and set them aside as you prep the other ingredients. Short ribs taste even better the next day, which makes them a perfect make-ahead dish for company. To gussy up the ribs, serve them on a bed of Horseradish Mashed Potatoes (page 281) or White Cheddar Polenta (page 275), and top with a flavorful tangle of frizzled leeks. The leeks look pretty piled up on the monochromatic ribs and sauce, and taste like delicate onion rings. They provide a crunchy contrast to the sticky-tender meat. Serve with Brussels sprouts or green beans and some crusty bread to sop up the rich sauce. This recipe makes plenty of sauce; if you have some left over, thin it with stock or broth and use as a base for beef barley soup. Or, freeze the sauce until you need some "instant" homemade gravy for beef sirloin tip roast (page 232).

/continued

RECIMENT SECRETS

For a generous estimate, I figure on 1 pound bone-in short ribs per person (more if I'm hoping for copious leftovers—these are terrific the next day). In the supermarket, short ribs are usually sold in 2- to 3-inch roughly square chunks, with a small, flat bone per chunk. If your meat market carries longer, uncut 1-pound slabs, ask the butcher to cut each slab into 2 or 3 chunks; depending on the cut, there may be 1 long or 3 smaller bones. The bone(s) will determine the number of chunks per slab.

For the best flavor and tenderness, choose short ribs that have some visible interior fat, or marbling. Look for chunks of even thickness; avoid those that taper off with less meat at the ends.

To prevent the meat from falling off the bones as the ribs braise, tie each chunk with kitchen string before cooking. Use a tight square knot, rather than a bow, which can get caught and pulled off by your meat fork. Remove the strings in the kitchen just before serving, after transferring the ribs to serving plates.

For the fastest, most even caramelization—not to mention great flavor—brown the seasoned ribs in ghee (see pages 155, 240) or clarified butter (page 155). Or, use mild-tasting extra-virgin olive oil or coconut oil (page 236).

Serves 3 or 4

Short Ribs

3 pounds bone-in beef short ribs

4 teaspoons kosher salt

1 teaspoon fine, freshly ground black pepper

1 tablespoon chopped fresh thyme, plus 3 sprigs

½ ounce dried porcini or other dried wild mushrooms

2 cups lukewarm water

3 tablespoons ghee (see pages 155, 240), clarified butter (page 155), or coconut oil

1 large yellow onion, cut in half through stem end and sliced into half moons

1 large carrot, peeled and chopped

1 large celery stalk, chopped

1 cup dry red wine

1 cup peeled, seeded, and diced tomatoes with juice (fresh or canned)

6 cloves garlic, smashed gently with the side of a chef's knife

1 bay leaf, preferably imported

2 tablespoons chopped fresh flat-leaf parsley, divided

Frizzled Leeks (optional)

1 leek

About ½ cup all-purpose flour

1 teaspoon kosher salt

¼ teaspoon fine, freshly ground black pepper

About 3 cups expeller-pressed canola or peanut oil (see page 87), for deep-frying

1. *Season the ribs:* Up to 24 hours in advance, rinse the ribs with cool water if they are bloody and blot dry with paper towels. Trim off and discard any external fat. If you have slabs of ribs with 3 separate bones attached, cut into 3 chunks with 1 bone each. Place the ribs in a rectangular nonreactive baking dish. Sprinkle the salt and pepper evenly over all surfaces of the ribs, patting the seasoning into the meat with your fingers. Sprinkle all surfaces with the chopped thyme, and press it into the meat. If time allows, refrigerate, uncovered, for up to 24 hours, or let the ribs stand at room temperature while you prep the remaining ingredients.

2. *Prepare the porcini:* Place the porcini or other mushrooms in a medium bowl, add the water, and set aside until the mushrooms soften, about 20 minutes. Using your fingers, transfer the mushrooms to a strainer, reserving the soaking liquid. To rid the mushrooms of any remaining sediment, toss them in the strainer as you spray or rinse them with warm water. Squeeze dry and chop roughly. Carefully strain almost all the soaking liquid through a fine-mesh strainer into a small clean bowl, leaving the sediment behind in the original bowl. Set aside the mushrooms and strained soaking liquid separately.

3. *Cook the ribs:* Preheat the oven to 325 degrees F. To keep the bones attached during braising, tie each rib around the middle with a piece of kitchen string. Choose a 5-quart Dutch oven, sauteuse (sauté pan without the long handle), or roasting pan large enough to hold the ribs snugly in a single layer during braising, and place over medium-high heat. Add the ghee or clarified butter. When the ghee is hot enough to sizzle a piece of onion, add the ribs (leave the seasonings on the meat) and sear on all sides until the surfaces are dark brown and caramelized, about 3 minutes on each side. For the best caramelization, don't crowd the ribs in the pan; if necessary, brown them in batches. Transfer to a plate and set aside.

4. With the pan still over medium-high heat, add the onion, carrot, and celery. Sauté until the onion is soft and translucent, 6 to 8 minutes. Add the wine all at once, and deglaze the pan, using a flat-bottomed wooden spatula to scrape up any caramelized bits from the bottom of the pan. Simmer until the wine is reduced by about half, 5 to 10 minutes. Stir in the tomatoes, garlic, bay leaf, and the reserved porcini and their soaking liquid. Add the ribs and any juices that may have collected on the plate. If the tops of the ribs protrude above the liquid, add enough water just to reach the top of the meat. Bring the liquid to a steady boil, cover, and place in the oven.

5. Braise at a steady simmer until the meat is tender, 2 to 2½ hours, checking periodically and regulating the heat as necessary to maintain a simmer. When the ribs are very tender (a meat fork penetrates and comes out with little resistance), use a slotted spoon to transfer them to a bowl (it's okay if some onions are attached). Cover tightly with aluminum foil and keep warm. Remove and discard the bay leaf. With a ladle, skim off any grease from the surface of the braising liquid; there may be as much as ⅔ cup, depending on how fatty the ribs were. Discard the grease. It's your call whether to discard all or some of the garlic, or purée it with the braising liquid. (I leave it in.)

/continued

ABOUT DRIED PORCINI

Dried porcini (pronounced poor-*chee*-nee) mushrooms, with their rich glutamate content, contribute a complex dimension of flavor to the sauce for the short ribs as well as to other sauces. This is a good example of how adding ingredients rich in umami (see page 38) can make a good sauce great. Look for dried porcini in upscale supermarkets or see Sources. You may find them labeled cèpes (pronounced *sep*), the French equivalent. If unavailable, substitute other thinly sliced dried wild mushrooms or 2 mashed anchovy fillets.

6. Using an immersion blender, or using a stand blender and working in batches, purée the braising liquid until very smooth. In the case of the stand blender, fill it no more than half full each time, and hold the lid down firmly as you gradually increase and decrease the speed.

7. If desired, strain the sauce through a medium-mesh sieve into a clean 4-quart saucepan. (This is a rustic dish, so I don't bother straining the sauce.) Add all but about 2 teaspoons of the parsley. Strip the leaves from the 3 thyme sprigs and add the leaves to the sauce. If the purée is not thick enough for your taste, bring it to a boil, uncovered, over high heat and allow it to reduce, stirring occasionally, until it reaches the desired consistency. Taste and adjust the seasoning with salt and pepper, if necessary. Return the ribs to the sauce.

8. *To prepare the recipe to this point up to 24 hours ahead:* Let the ribs and sauce cool to room temperature. Place a piece of waxed paper directly on the ribs to prevent them from drying out, cover the pot, and refrigerate. Bring to room temperature 2 hours before serving, removing the waxed paper and any fat that may have solidified on top. Proceed with the reheating instructions below.

9. *Prepare the frizzled leeks, if using:* Cut off the root end and green leaves from the leek. If the remaining white part is longer than 3 inches, cut it in half crosswise. Cut the piece(s) in half lengthwise, then cut each half lengthwise into julienne strips ⅛ to ¼ inch wide. Swish the julienned leeks in a bowl of warm water and lift into a medium-mesh strainer with your fingers. If the leeks feel gritty, repeat the washing. Shake well and spread the leeks in a single layer on a clean, dry kitchen towel. Cover with another kitchen towel and roll together to dry the leeks. Unroll, remove the top towel, and fluff the leeks with your fingers. Set aside to air-dry completely.

10. Place the flour in a bowl, add the salt and pepper, and stir to combine. Toss a handful of the leeks in the seasoned flour and transfer to a dry wide-mesh strainer or colander. Shake the strainer over a bowl to let the excess flour fall away. Dump the floured leeks onto a clean, dry rimmed baking sheet. Repeat with the remaining leeks.

11. Line a rimmed baking sheet with paper towels and set aside. Pour the oil to a depth of about 2 inches into a 2-quart saucepan and heat over medium heat to 365 degrees F on a deep-frying thermometer, or until hot enough to sizzle a piece of leek on contact. Add a handful of leeks to the hot oil and deep-fry until golden brown and crisp, about 1 minute. Stir the leeks occasionally with a wooden chopstick (or the handle of a wooden spoon) to separate them as they cook. With a slotted spoon or Chinese strainer, transfer the leeks to the prepared baking sheet. Repeat with the remaining leeks, frying them a handful at a time. Set aside until ready to serve. (The leeks can be fried up to 8 hours in advance, set aside, and reheated in an oven preheated to 400 degrees F until they are hot, 3 to 5 minutes.)

12. *To serve the ribs:* Reheat the short ribs and sauce over medium heat, stirring occasionally, until the sauce comes to a boil and the ribs are piping hot. Reduce the heat to low and keep warm as you serve. If serving with potatoes or polenta (see introduction), make a bed of either in the center of warmed plates. Place 2 ribs on each bed. Cut off the strings, and spoon some of the sauce over the ribs. Top with a handful of frizzled leeks, if using. Sprinkle with the remaining 2 teaspoons parsley, and pass the remaining sauce in a warmed bowl at the table.

POT ROAST AND GRAVY WITH PEAS AND CARROTS

This recipe was inspired by the Sunday Supper Beef Chuck Roast prepared by chef Kimball Jones when he was affiliated with Wente Vineyards. The occasion was one of many eightieth-birthday celebrations for Chuck Williams, founder of Williams-Sonoma. As we savored this exceptionally tender chuck roast, several colleagues took delight in the play on words and "roasted" Chuck, recounting memories of the legendary cookware-store pioneer. I often include this recipe when I teach classes on braising. Much to my delight, a retired butcher and his wife attended one of these classes. After watching another student try to cut the tender pot roast into thin, even slices, the butcher shared an elegant carving secret—included here—with the class. I'll never forget how he broke into a big, beautiful smile when the entire class—teacher included—oohed and aahed at his revelation. Serve this pot roast with mashed potatoes with roasted garlic (page 281) or White Cheddar Polenta (page 275) and plenty of crusty bread to sop up the rich gravy.

/continued

RECIPE SECRETS

This braised chuck roast derives exceptional flavor from a generous advance seasoning—or rub—of fresh thyme, salt, and pepper. For the rub to have full impact, allow the seasoned roast to sit for 5 to 24 hours before cooking. However, if you're short on time, even 30 minutes under the rub makes a noticeable difference.

. . . .

The size of your braising pan really matters here. It should be just large enough to accommodate the roast, which will shrink during cooking. If you need to add more than 2 to 3 cups water for the liquid to reach the top of the meat, chances are your pan is too big. Better to transfer everything to a smaller pot, so the gravy will have the proper consistency and rich flavor. It's okay when you start braising if the carrot sticks aren't submerged.

. . . .

Here's the butcher's carving secret: Don't wait until the roast is completely cooked before you cut it into slices. Partway through the braising period, cut the roast—but not all the way through—and tie some kitchen string around the whole thing to keep it intact as it finishes cooking. After you transfer the roast to your serving platter, cut off the string, give the meat a little nudge, and your pot roast will fan out into neat, even slices. It will be piping hot when you serve it, too.

Serves 6

1 boneless beef chuck roast, 3 to 4 pounds

4 teaspoons kosher salt

1 teaspoon freshly ground black pepper

1 tablespoon chopped fresh thyme leaves

½ ounce dried porcini mushrooms

2 cups lukewarm water

6 large, thick carrots, peeled

2 leeks

3 tablespoons ghee (pages 155, 240), clarified butter (page 155), or coconut oil

1 yellow onion, chopped

1 large celery stalk, chopped

1 cup dry red wine

1 cup tomato purée or homemade tomato sauce

6 cloves garlic, smashed gently with the side of a chef's knife

1 bay leaf, preferably imported

1 cup fresh English peas or frozen petite peas

2 tablespoons chopped fresh flat-leaf parsley or minced fresh chives, for garnish

---

1. *Season the roast:* Up to 24 hours in advance, rinse the roast with cool water if it is bloody, and blot dry with paper towels. Trim off and discard any external fat. Place the roast in a nonreactive baking dish. Sprinkle the salt and pepper evenly over all surfaces of the roast, patting them into the meat with your fingers. Sprinkle all surfaces with the thyme, pressing it into the meat. Refrigerate the roast, uncovered, for at least 5 hours or up to 24 hours.

2. *Prepare the vegetables:* Place the porcini in a bowl, add the water, and set aside until the mushrooms soften, about 20 minutes. Using your fingers, transfer the porcini to a strainer, reserving the soaking liquid. To rid the mushrooms of any remaining sediment, toss them in the strainer as you spray or rinse them with warm water. Squeeze dry and chop roughly. Carefully strain almost all the soaking liquid through a fine-mesh strainer into a small, clean bowl, leaving the sediment behind in the original bowl. Set aside the mushrooms and strained soaking liquid separately.

3. Trim off and discard both ends of the carrots. Cut the thicker, top half (or so) of each carrot into roughly 3-inch lengths. Chop the smaller, bottom halves into roughly ½-inch pieces (they will be puréed with the sauce) and set aside. Cut the 3-inch pieces lengthwise into sticks about ¼ inch thick (they will be served with the pot roast) and set aside.

4. Cut off and discard the root ends and dark green parts of the leeks. Make 2 perpendicular cuts in the top third of the remaining leek and rinse well under warm water. Cut the leeks into ¼-inch pieces; you'll end up with some chopped pieces and some whole rounds. Swish the leeks in a bowl of warm water until any remaining dirt falls to the bottom. With your fingers, transfer the leeks to a strainer. Rinse well and set aside.

5. *Cook the meat:* Preheat the oven to 325 degrees F. Choose a 6-quart Dutch oven, sauteuse (sauté pan without the long handle), or roasting pan just large enough to hold the roast, and place over medium-high heat. Add the ghee or clarified butter. When the ghee is hot enough to sizzle a piece of onion, add the roast (leave the seasonings on the meat) and sear on all sides until the surfaces are dark brown and caramelized, 3 to 4 minutes on each side. Transfer the roast to a plate and set aside.

6. With the pan still over medium-high heat, add the onion, celery, leeks, and chopped carrots (reserve the carrot sticks) and sauté until the onion becomes soft and translucent, 6 to 8 minutes. Add the wine all at once and deglaze the pan, using a flat-bottomed wooden spatula to scrape up any caramelized bits from the bottom of the pan. Simmer until the wine is reduced by about half, about 5 minutes. Stir in the tomato purée or sauce and the reserved porcini and their soaking liquid. Push the vegetables to the sides of the pan and place the meat in the center of the pan. Add the garlic, bay leaf, and enough water just to reach the top of the meat, about 2 cups. Stir to combine. Add the carrot sticks, arranging them on the sides and over the top of the meat. Bring the liquid to a steady boil, cover, and place in the oven. Braise at a steady simmer for 1 hour.

7. Remove the pan from the oven and transfer the roast to a cutting board, preferably one with a trough or well to collect the juices when carving. Test the doneness of the carrot sticks with the tip of a paring knife. If tender, transfer to a plate, cover tightly, and keep in a warm place. Cut the roast across the grain (widthwise) into ¼-inch-thick slices, stopping ⅛ to ¼ inch from the bottom, so that you don't actually cut off the slices completely. Tie the roast around its equator with kitchen string. Using tongs and a large offset spatula, return the roast, cut side up, to the pan, along with any liquid from the cutting board. Spoon some of the braising liquid over the meat, immersing it as much as possible. Bring to a boil on the stove top over medium-high heat. As soon as the liquid comes to a steady boil, cover and return the roast to the oven.

8. Braise until the meat is tender, another 1½ to 3 hours, depending on the thickness of the roast and the amount of connective tissue there is to break down. Check periodically to be sure the braising liquid is simmering. Remove and reserve the carrot sticks when tender, keeping them covered and warm, if you haven't already done so.

/continued

9. When the meat is very tender (you can insert a dinner fork into the center and the tines penetrate with no resistance), transfer the roast, cut side up, to a warmed oval platter, preferably one that's deep enough to hold some sauce, too. Cover tightly with aluminum foil and keep warm. Remove and discard the bay leaf. With a ladle, skim off any grease from the surface of the braising liquid and discard. It's your call whether to discard all or some of the garlic, or purée it with the braising liquid. (I leave it in.)

10. Using an immersion blender, or a stand blender and working in batches, purée the braising liquid and chopped vegetables until very smooth. In the case of the stand blender, fill it no more than half full each time, and hold the lid down firmly each time you gradually increase and decrease the speed. If desired, strain the gravy through a medium-mesh strainer into a clean saucepan. (This is a rustic dish, so I don't bother to strain the gravy.) If the gravy is not thick enough for your taste, bring it to a boil, uncovered, over high heat and allow it to reduce, stirring occasionally, until it reaches the desired consistency.

11. *To serve the pot roast:* Add the peas and the reserved carrot sticks to the gravy and simmer until the carrots are piping hot and the peas are cooked, about 5 minutes for fresh peas or 2 minutes for frozen. Taste the gravy and adjust the seasoning with salt and pepper, if necessary.

12. Cut the string and remove it from the meat. Push the roast with a long, flat spatula, tipping it just enough to allow the slices to fan out a bit. Ladle some gravy over the sliced pot roast and carrots and sprinkle with the chopped parsley or chives. Fill a warmed gravyboat or bowl with extra gravy and serve on the side.

WEEKNIGHT CHILI

My Italian American mother made tomato sauce, meatballs, and macaroni or spaghetti once a week for supper, and there was always a little tomato sauce left over. With that sauce she transformed English muffins into mini-pizzas, or a pound of ground beef and a can of kidney beans into this hardy chili, made in a pressure cooker, creating one of our family's favorite wintertime suppers. Some of us liked the chili soupy, ladled over some torn-up, day-old Italian bread; this is still my favorite way to eat it. The bread soaks up the rich juices and gives the chili a delightful texture. All you need to round out this meal is a simple green salad (page 81). I find I can whip up this recipe quickly enough in a heavy pot, without using a pressure cooker as my mother did. If you have chili left over, let cool to room temperature, cover, and refrigerate for up to 4 days or freeze for up to 1 month.

Serves 4 to 6

2 tablespoons mild-tasting extra-virgin olive oil

1 yellow onion, chopped

1 large carrot, peeled and cut into ¼-inch dice

1 large celery stalk, peeled and cut into ¼-inch dice

3 to 4 teaspoons mild chili powder

1 teaspoon kosher salt

½ teaspoon dried leaf oregano, crumbled between your fingers

¼ to ½ teaspoon cayenne pepper

2 cloves garlic, green germ removed if present, minced

1¼ pounds ground beef

1 cup tomato sauce (homemade or canned)

1 can (15 ounces) red kidney beans

1 cup water

1 bay leaf, preferably imported

4 to 6 slices day-old crusty Italian or French bread, for serving (optional)

/continued

RECIPE SECRETS

Peel the outer, rounded part of the celery stalk with a vegetable peeler to remove any strings that can get caught in your teeth. The flavor of peeled celery is more delicate, too.

. . . .

Sauté the spices and dried oregano with the vegetables before adding the liquids. Cooking them first in the olive oil releases their volatile oils and brightens their flavors differently than if you were to add them directly to the hot liquid. Crumbling the oregano between your fingers as you add it helps to awaken its flavors even more.

. . . .

To keep the meat tender and juicy, cook the chili at a steady simmer, not a rolling boil. If necessary, place a Flame-Tamer™ between the burner and the pot to prevent the chili from cooking too briskly on the lowest setting.

1. Heat a 6-quart Dutch oven or other heavy pot over medium heat. Add the olive oil. When the oil is hot enough to sizzle a piece of onion, add the onion, carrot, and celery and sauté, stirring occasionally, until the onion is soft and translucent, 6 to 8 minutes. Resist any urge to stir frequently, so the vegetables will caramelize rather than steam. Add 3 teaspoons of the chili powder, the salt, oregano, ¼ teaspoon of the cayenne, and the garlic and sauté for 1 minute until fragrant.

2. Push the vegetables to the sides of the pan, raise the heat to medium-high, and place the ground beef in the center. Use the edge of a wooden spatula or spoon to break up the meat into roughly ¾-inch pieces. Let the beef sear over medium-high heat until it begins to brown on the bottom. Don't stir until the beef sears and you see steam begin to rise. Cook, stirring occasionally, until the beef is no longer pink, about 5 minutes.

3. Add the tomato sauce and kidney beans, including the liquid in the can. Rinse the tomato sauce can (or the container from the homemade sauce) with the water and add to the pot. Add the bay leaf. Bring to a rolling boil, then quickly reduce the heat to low. Taste and add more cayenne if you'd like the chili to be spicier, and more chili powder if you'd like the chili to have a deeper flavor. Cover and cook at a steady, gentle simmer, stirring occasionally, until the largest pieces of carrot are tender, 20 to 30 minutes. Remove and discard the bay leaf. Taste and adjust the seasoning, if necessary.

4. If serving over bread, tear a slice of bread into roughly ¾-inch pieces and place in the bottom of each wide, shallow soup plate or bowl. Ladle the chili into the bowls and serve at once.

ON THE
SIDE

Recipe	Q	MA	V	RT	Page
Grilled Asparagus	●	●	●	●	250
Fresh Fava Beans with Pecorino and Meyer Lemon Olive Oil		●	●	●	252
Roasted Peppers	●	●	●	●	254
Savory Corn Pudding	●	●	●		256
Romano Beans	●	●	●	●	258
Eggplant Parmigiana		●	●		259
Braised Summer Squash with Sweet Peppers, Tomatoes, and Basil		●	●		262
Escarole with Garlic and Red Pepper Flakes	●	●	●		263
Garlic Spinach with Currants, Pine Nuts, and Pecorino	●		●		265
Braised Greens with Sausage and Onions		●	●		266
"Roasted" Beets with Whole-Grain Mustard Sauce		●	●	●	268
Roasted Root Vegetables; Roasted New Potatoes Variation		●	●		269
Sautéed Mushrooms with Sherry and Garlic	●		●		271
Butternut Squash with Maple Syrup and Allspice	●	●	●		273
Creamy, Soft Polenta; White Cheddar Polenta Variation	●		●		274
Wild Rice Pilaf		●	●		276
Kalijira Rice Pilaw	●		●		277
Al's Steamed White Rice	●		●		279
Mashed Yukon Gold Potatoes; Horseradish Mashed Potatoes Variation, Roasted Garlic Mashed Potatoes with Chives Variation		●	●	●	280
Classic American Potato Salad	●	●	●	●	282
Orzo with Toybox Tomatoes and Fresh Mint	●	●	●	●	283

Q = Quick—prep to table in 45 minutes.
MA = Make ahead—part or all of the recipe can or must be made ahead.
V = Vegetarian—no meat, chicken, fish, or, with minor adjustments, such as substituting vegetable broth for chicken stock, can be prepared as a vegetarian recipe.
RT = Okay to serve at room temperature.

SECRETS FOR PAIRING SIDE DISHES WITH MAIN DISHES

How do you know which vegetables to serve with which meats? Do certain starches go better with seafood? Does it even matter? These questions come up invariably in cooking classes. After all, we aren't born into this world knowing the answers. So how do you decide? In many cases, classic combinations provide good guidelines. Think of pot roast with mashed potatoes, carrots, and peas or roast pork with applesauce and roasted root vegetables. These alliances have withstood the test of time for good reason: they taste great together.

Another approach is to consider what's in season. You'll be rewarded with the best nutrients, price, flavor, and availability when you choose seasonal produce. Then, think about how the flavor, texture, and appearance of certain side dishes will complement the texture of your chosen protein.

When it comes to flavor, pair something bold and vibrant, such as braised summer squash with peppers, tomatoes, and onions (page 262) with a simply grilled piece of meat, chicken, or fish. Likewise, the complexity of a Thai-flavored stir-fry with chicken, basil, and chiles (page 170) needs nothing more than simple steamed rice as an accompaniment.

Complementary textures on the same plate keep things interesting, too. Sticky, gooey braised short ribs topped with crispy frizzled leeks (page 237) are a natural for a side of creamy polenta (page 274) or horseradish mashed potatoes (page 281). Crisp-skinned roasted and grilled meats are also well paired with soft, comforting accompaniments. Keep in mind that starchy vegetables such as corn and butternut squash are often suitable substitutes for potatoes, rice, or pasta.

It can't be disputed that our eyes send a message to our brain before food even touches our tongue. To that end, don't rule out the importance of varied colors on the plate. If the meat is brown, look to green and red vegetables to perk things up. Leave the red skins on roasted potatoes, and roast three different colors of peppers to keep the plate interesting.

Above all, as I see it, the most important consideration is that the foods be nutritiously dense and good for our bodies. Try to weave in such nutritional powerhouses as cruciferous vegetables, cooked tomatoes, legumes, and dark, leafy greens as you plan your menus. And rather than thinking of these foods as accompaniments, try planning the rest of the plate around such vegetables (as you see in many healthful cuisines other than the typical Western diet).

Finally, be realistic. If time is short when you're having a crowd for dinner, consider side dishes that can be prepared in advance and served at room temperature (see the chart on page 248). You don't have to do it all yourself, either. While few pastimes give me greater pleasure than cooking, I'm the first one to save time by buying prewashed spinach (and other greens) and boneless, skinless chicken breasts. If I don't have time to prepare roasted chicken, broccoli, and mashed potatoes for supper, I'm just as happy with a fresh spinach salad topped with a perfectly grilled chicken breast. If cherry tomatoes are in season, I'll add some to this salad for flavor and color. Instead, if citrus is at its prime, I'll substitute orange or grapefruit segments. Use the pairings suggested in the seasonal menus on page 319 to jump-start your meal planning. Remember to be flexible and have fun.

RECIPE SECRETS

When buying asparagus, look at the cut ends. If they are brown or shriveled, the spears aren't very fresh. White ends indicate asparagus that have been recently been cut (albeit sometimes by a shrewd produce clerk). When you get home, cut off about ½ inch from the cut ends and place the spears, cut end down, in a tall container filled about one-third full with water. Refrigerated this way, asparagus will keep for several days. When ready to cook, grab both ends of a spear and flex the asparagus until it breaks. Save the tender, upper part and discard the bottoms, which are stringy and fibrous.

. . . .

If asparagus are of medium thickness or the thinner "pencil" size, it's not necessary to peel them, as their skin isn't too fibrous. It's your choice whether to peel larger asparagus. For a rustic preparation such as this, it's not necessary. But if the skins seem tough, use a swivel-blade vegetable peeler, lay the asparagus on a cutting board, and remove the thinnest layer of skin from the bottom one-third to two-thirds of each spear (after breaking off the bottom part).

GRILLED ASPARAGUS

When shipped in boxes with wet packing material at the bottom, asparagus will continue to draw up water and grow even after they're harvested. On a visit to a Monterey County, California asparagus farm, I learned that the spears are given a little headroom in the packing crates, but sometimes it's not enough, so occasionally you'll find asparagus with curved tips, the result of their continued growth in transit. While at the farm, I was struck by how randomly the asparagus just seem to pop out of the ground in tall, slender spears with no leafy ground cover or orderly rows. In this recipe, the spears are blanched, marinated, and grilled, which can all be done in advance, and then served at room temperature as a side dish. They're perfect with salmon (page 150 or 152) just as they are. Or, you can gussy up grilled asparagus in a variety of ways: After grilling, drizzle with mayonnaise spiked with lemon and anchovy, or sprinkle with crumbled, sautéed pancetta and toasted pine nuts for an elegant appetizer. For a simple, colorful hors d'oeuvre, roll grilled asparagus in sliced prosciutto. Refrigerate any leftover grilled asparagus, then cut into 1-inch pieces and toss into a risotto, omelet, or pasta dish for a smoky-tasting, colorful addition.

Serves 4 to 6

1 tablespoon plus 1 teaspoon kosher salt, divided, plus more for cooking

About 2 tablespoons garlic-flavored olive oil

1½ pounds medium-thick asparagus, tough ends removed and ends cut on the diagonal

1. Bring a 6-quart pot of water to a boil. In the meantime, prepare an ice-water bath in a large bowl and stir in 1 tablespoon of the salt; set aside.

2. Pour the garlic oil onto a large rimmed baking sheet and tip the pan so the entire surface is covered with oil. Sprinkle 1 teaspoon of the salt evenly over the entire surface of the oil; set aside.

3. When the water boils, add enough salt to make the water taste like the ocean. Drop a handful of the asparagus into the rapidly boiling water and blanch for 1 minute. Use a Chinese strainer, tongs, or a slotted spoon to transfer the asparagus immediately to the reserved ice-water bath. Leave the asparagus in the ice water just until they are cool to the touch, then drain and transfer to the baking sheet with the seasoned oil. Roll the asparagus in the oil to coat evenly. Repeat with the remaining asparagus. Let the asparagus marinate at room temperature for at least 10 minutes or up to 8 hours.

4. Prepare a medium-hot fire in a charcoal grill, or preheat a gas or stove-top grill to medium-high. Grill the asparagus in batches, turning frequently with tongs, until grill marks appear on all sides, about 8 minutes total. Transfer to a serving platter.

RECIPE SECRETS

As is the case with many green vegetables, the secret to keeping asparagus green after cooking is to blanch them first, then shock the spears in an ice-water bath to stop the cooking and set the color. Salt both the blanching water and the ice-water bath to ensure that your asparagus will be well seasoned.

If garlic-flavored olive oil is unavailable, marinate blanched asparagus in extra-virgin olive oil mixed with about ½ teaspoon granulated garlic powder.

For the best caramelization, don't crowd the asparagus on the grill. If necessary, cook them in batches.

RECISE SECRETS

. . . .

Buy fava bean pods that are shiny and relatively free of blemishes. Store in a plastic bag in the refrigerator for just a day or two, or better still, cook them the day you purchase them. To get to the beans, you have to tear open the leathery pods, which have a protective Styrofoam-like lining. Very young favas, about the size of a small fingernail, can be eaten as is. But before eating the larger beans, they must be blanched to remove their thick skins. To prevent favas from tasting flat, salt both the blanching water and their subsequent ice-water bath.

. . . .

Generally, 1 pound favas in the pod yields about ½ cup beans, which makes them labor intensive—perfect for keeping kids or guests occupied as you make other preparations in the kitchen. If fresh fava beans are unavailable, substitute half the weight of shelled *edamame* (pronounced ed-a-mahmay), or soybeans. The color and texture are similar, but once removed from their pods, *edamame* have no thick skin to reckon with.

FRESH FAVA BEANS WITH PECORINO AND MEYER LEMON OLIVE OIL

. . . .

Available in farmers' markets and produce markets in California from early spring through summer, neon green fava beans have been debuting across the country in recent years. Traditionally prized by gardeners because of their ability to add nitrogen back to the soil, fava plants produce long seedpods that dangle from incredibly tall bushes. I wouldn't be surprised if the fava bush is what inspired the story *Jack and the Beanstalk.* If you've never tasted fresh mint in a savory side dish, you might be pleasantly surprised at the refreshing role it plays here. Serve these with Grilled Stuffed Chicken Breasts with Prosciutto, Taleggio, and Pesto (page 183) or Turkey Piccata (page 177). For a gorgeous springtime pasta course, cook ½ pound *farfalle* or *gemelli* pasta and toss the warm pasta with this finished fava side dish. Toss with enough additional lemon oil to coat the pasta, and pass extra grated cheese at the table.

Serves 4 to 6

3 pounds fresh fava beans

1 tablespoon kosher salt, plus more for cooking and seasoning

2 to 4 tablespoons Meyer lemon extra-virgin olive oil

1 tablespoon chopped fresh mint and/or oregano leaves

2 ounces *pecorino romano* cheese, chopped into pellet-sized pieces

Coarse, freshly ground black pepper

---

1. Remove the fava beans from their pods. If, as you're doing so, it appears that you have some large (about ¾ inch long) and some small (½ inch or shorter) beans, divide them into 2 piles, according to size.

2. Bring a 4-quart saucepan of water to a boil. In the meantime, prepare an ice-water bath in a large bowl and stir in 1 tablespoon salt.

3. When the water boils, add enough salt to make the water taste like the ocean. If the beans are divided by size, add the larger beans to the boiling water, blanch for 2 minutes, and, using a Chinese strainer or slotted spoon, transfer the favas immediately to the ice-water bath. Repeat with the small favas, blanching them for only 1 minute, then drain and transfer them to the ice-water bath.

4. To remove the tough, transparent skins from the beans, locate the part of each bean that connected it to the pod. Pinch open the opposite end and slip the bean out. You should have about 1½ cups peeled beans.

5. Place the beans in a bowl and toss with the lemon oil and herbs. Add the cheese and toss. Season to taste with salt and pepper.

CAUTIONARY NOTE ABOUT EATING FAVA BEANS

People who take MAO-inhibitor antidepressants are advised not to eat fava beans. Also, favas have been known to cause severe anemia in people who suffer from an inherited deficiency known as glucose-6-phosphate dehydrogenase. Elizabeth Schneider writes in her encyclopedic *Vegetables from Amaranth to Zucchini*, "One hopes they know who they are before they sit down to your table."

RECIPE SECRETS

Look for delicately flavored Meyer lemon oil in the oils section in well-stocked supermarkets or gourmet stores. "O" is a popular and delicious California brand. Lemon oil makes a great dipping sauce for fresh fennel or celery. Or, toss hot pasta, smoked salmon, and fresh dill with the oil. Many recipe testers for this book reported great success when making their own lemon-flavored oil. Here's how: add the zest of an organic lemon to ¼ cup mild-tasting extra-virgin olive oil and let stand until the oil is fragrant and lemony, about 10 minutes.

For an interesting texture, rather than grating the cheese, chop it into pellets: cut into ½ -inch chunks and pulse in a food processor or blender until you have pea-sized or smaller pellets.

Serve this side dish warm or at room temperature. Many side dishes dressed with oil are more pleasing to the palate—and more vibrant to the taste buds—when served warm or at room temperature, rather than hot or cold. If preparing ahead, cover and refrigerate the beans, then bring them to room temperature before serving. Legumes soak up flavors as they sit, so be sure to taste and reseason the favas just before serving.

RECISE SECRETS

Green bell peppers are simply unripe red bell peppers. If you tend to avoid green bell peppers because they "repeat" on you, or they taste too vegetal or grassy, you may find these qualities delightfully absent from ripe, sweet red or yellow bell peppers. Don't be tempted by the Technicolor peppers in orange, purple, brown, and the like, that you sometimes see in markets. While they make a vibrant addition to a crudité platter, when cooked, their bright hues—and flavor—revert to green.

Choose peppers that are evenly shaped and dimple free. The smoother the surface, the easier it is to remove the skins after roasting.

Be sure to dry peppers well after rinsing. Otherwise, the moisture on the surface will create steam, which impedes the blistering process.

For ease in removing blistered skins from peppers after roasting, let them sit, covered, until cool enough to handle. The steam they generate will make the skins separate from the flesh. Then, lift off the skins in large pieces.

ROASTED PEPPERS

Simple as it is, this is one of my mother's most popular recipes. Every Fourth of July our kitchen was filled with the smell of peppers "roasting" in a tin pie plate on top of the stove. I wonder if the family friends who hosted our annual holiday picnic would have made us turn the car around if we showed up without Flo's famous peppers. Every year they elicited groans of delight as the grown-ups grabbed toothpicks and stabbed garlicky roasted pepper strips during the cocktail hour. My mother always roasts green bell peppers, but I prefer the less-grassy-tasting red and yellow bells. As you'll see here, there's more than one way to roast a pepper. Although only one of these methods technically qualifies as roasting, any way you cook these will give you satisfactory results. Serve roasted peppers as part of an antipasto platter, or as a side dish with grilled meats or fish. Tuck leftover roasted peppers into an Italian sandwich or hot oven grinder, and be sure to brush the bread with the flavorful pepper juices.

Serves 4 to 6

4 large red bell peppers, or a mixture of red, yellow, and green

1 large clove garlic, cut in half crosswise

2 tablespoons bold-tasting extra-virgin olive oil

1 teaspoon kosher salt

---

1. Rinse the peppers and dry thoroughly, then roast according to one of the following methods.

Broiler method: Position a rack 4 inches below the broiler element and preheat the broiler. Cut off both ends from the peppers and reserve for another use (such as Stir-Fried Velvet Chicken, page 174). Remove the ribs and seeds and cut each pepper lengthwise into 4 pieces. Line a rimmed baking sheet with aluminum foil. Place the peppers, skin side up, on the prepared baking sheet. If necessary, use the heel of your hand to flatten them. Place the pan under the broiler element and leave oven door ajar, if possible. (This allows the steam to escape.) Watch carefully, turning the pan often, and broil until the pepper skins are evenly charred, 5 to 10 minutes.

Grill method: Prepare a hot fire in a charcoal grill, or preheat a gas or stove-top grill on high. When the fire is ready, place the whole peppers on the grate and grill, turning with tongs (don't puncture the skins) as necessary, until the skins are charred and blistered evenly on all sides, about 10 minutes total.

Oven method: Position an oven rack in the center and a second rack in the lower third of the oven and preheat to 425 degrees F (or 400 degrees F on the convection setting). Line a rimmed baking sheet with aluminum foil and place the pan in the oven on the bottom rack. Place the whole peppers directly on the top rack, over the pan, so the pan will catch any juices that drip during roasting. Roast, turning with tongs (don't puncture the skins) as necessary, just until the skins are charred and blistered evenly on all sides, about 10 minutes total.

2. *After the peppers are roasted:* When the skins are blistered and charred evenly, transfer the peppers to a deep bowl and cover with plastic wrap. Alternatively, place the peppers in a brown paper bag, close the top, and place the bag in a bowl (to prevent the bottom of the bag from giving out). Allow the peppers to steam until cool enough to handle, about 10 minutes.

3. Rub the cut surface of the garlic all over the sides and bottom of a shallow serving bowl. Cut each clove half into 2 or 3 pieces and place in the bowl.

4. Peel off the pepper skins with your fingers or a paring knife. If the peppers are whole, start from the non-stem end and tear the peppers along their seams, then remove the seedpods and trim off the ribs. Discard all the loose seeds, but allow any juices from inside the peppers to drip into the bowl with the garlic.

5. Cut the peeled peppers lengthwise into strips ½ inch wide, and place in the bowl with the garlic. Add the olive oil and salt and stir to combine. Taste and add more olive oil and salt, if necessary. Let stand for 20 minutes for the flavors to meld. Just before serving, toss, taste, and adjust the seasoning, if necessary. If you have any leftover peppers, remove and discard the garlic, cover the peppers, and refrigerate them for up to 3 days.

SAVORY CORN PUDDING

It's worth waiting for the sweetest corn of summer to make this delicate, creamy soufflé-like side dish that's a perfect accompaniment to grilled or roasted meats. In cooking classes, this is a big hit when served with Broiled Swordfish with Mango Salsa (page 155). When fresh corn is out of season, or when time is short, substitute 2 pounds (6 cups) thawed, frozen petite white corn kernels. The pudding can be assembled completely up to a day ahead, refrigerated, and baked just before serving. For a special presentation, bake individual corn puddings for 15 to 20 minutes, invert onto a plate, and drizzle with red pepper coulis (page 148).

Serves 6 to 8

7 ears sweet corn

1½ cups whole milk, divided

2 teaspoons unsalted butter, for baking dish

5 large eggs

1 tablespoon plus 1 teaspoon all-purpose flour

¼ pound Monterey Jack cheese, coarsely shredded on the large holes of a box grater to yield 1 cup

2 tablespoons minced fresh chives, divided

1 teaspoon kosher salt

¼ teaspoon Tabasco sauce

1. Cut off the kernels from the ears of corn (page 69) and reserve 1 cup. Place the remaining corn and 1 cup of the milk in a blender. Hold the blender lid in place as you gradually increase and decrease the speed. Process at the highest speed for a full 3 minutes. If necessary, interrupt blending to scrape down the sides. You should have a thick, smooth purée.

2. In the meantime, position a rack in the center of the oven and preheat to 325 degrees F. Prepare a bain-marie (hot-water bath): Choose a roasting pan large enough to hold a 9-inch round or square baking dish with 2-inch sides. Line the bottom of the roasting pan with a paper towel (to prevent the pudding from sliding around) and set aside. Butter the bottom and sides of the baking dish and set aside. Bring a kettle of water to a boil. Set aside.

3. In a bowl, whisk the eggs lightly. Add the blended corn mixture and whisk to combine. Sprinkle with the flour and whisk to blend thoroughly. Add the remaining ½ cup milk, the cheese, all but about 1 teaspoon of the chives, the salt, the Tabasco, and the reserved corn kernels and stir to combine. Pour into the prepared baking dish and sprinkle with the remaining 1 teaspoon chives. (The pudding can be prepared up to this point up to 24 hours in advance, covered, and refrigerated. Bring to room temperature before baking.)

4. Pull out the oven rack halfway. Place the baking dish on the paper towel in the bain-marie and place in the center of the oven rack. Carefully pour the hot water from the kettle into the bain-marie to reach halfway up the sides of the baking dish. Gently slide the oven rack into place. Bake the pudding until the blade of a paring knife inserted in the center comes out almost clean, 45 to 60 minutes, depending on the depth of the baking dish. The top of the pudding should be firm and pale and the edges should begin to pull away from the sides of the baking dish.

5. Remove the bain-marie from the oven. With oven mitts and/or a long, wide offset spatula, carefully transfer the baking dish from the bain-marie to a cooling rack. Let cool for 5 minutes for pudding to set up a bit before serving.

RECIPE SECRETS

To make an even richer pudding, substitute half-and-half or heavy (whipping) cream for the milk. Likewise, to cut back on some of the fat, substitute a 12-ounce can evaporated low-fat milk for the whole milk. Evaporated milk gives baked custards a very creamy texture.

The Tabasco sauce here is just enough to add a bit of complexity, without overpowering the sweet corn flavor. If you prefer, substitute ¼ teaspoon cayenne pepper.

RECIPE SECRETS

Season the cooking water with plenty of salt, so the beans will absorb some of the flavored water as they cook.

As soon as you drain the beans, toss them with the olive oil, garlic, and salt. They absorb the flavors right away when they are hot.

A few drops of vinegar, added just before serving, adds a welcome bit of acid to brighten the flavor of any green beans. But if you add the vinegar too soon, the beans—or any green vegetables—will turn an unappetizing shade of gray-green.

Romano beans with stem and blossom end

ROMANO BEANS

Starting in July, and continuing throughout the summer, look for flat, wide Romano beans—also called Italian green beans or Roman beans—at your local farmers' market. If you can't find Romanos, substitute Kentucky Wonder or Blue Lake green beans and cook them for a shorter time. Choose beans that have no blemishes and look supple, not shriveled. With their substantial, almost meaty texture, Romano beans taste best when cooked completely through (well beyond the crisp stage) in plenty of boiling, salted water, rather than in a steamer. Serve the beans hot or at room temperature.

Serves 4

1 pound Romano beans	1 clove garlic, green germ removed if present, cut into
Kosher salt	4 slivers
1 to 2 tablespoons bold-tasting extra-virgin olive oil	1 teaspoon wine vinegar, preferably white

---

1. Bring a 6-quart pot of water to a boil.

2. Clean the beans in a bowl of tepid water, rubbing them with your fingers, if necessary, to remove any dirt. Trim off the stem end of each bean, cutting on the bias (for aesthetics); leave the blossom end—with its edible tail—intact.

3. When the water boils, add enough salt to make the water taste like the ocean. Add the whole beans to the boiling water and adjust the heat, as necessary, to maintain a steady boil. Cover partially and cook until the beans are tender enough for your teeth to bite through them easily, with no crispness remaining, 7 to 14 minutes, depending on their size. The beans should flop over a bit when you lift a couple out of the water with a fork, but they shouldn't be mushy. Test often once they lose their crispness, to be sure not to overcook them.

4. Drain the beans in a colander and return the empty pot to the stove. Add 1 tablespoon of the olive oil, the garlic, and a little salt. Swirl to coat the bottom of the pan. Return the drained beans to the pot and toss with the olive oil mixture. Taste and add more olive oil and salt, if necessary. If serving immediately, drizzle with the vinegar and toss to combine. Otherwise, wait until just before serving to toss with the vinegar. Remove the garlic before serving.

EGGPLANT PARMIGIANA

It seems as if there are as many variations of this eggplant dish as there are Italian cooks. Over the years, I've perfected my version based on tips I've picked up from my mother and grandmother, a class I took in Sicily (where eggplant is king), and from eating this beloved dish in restaurants from coast to coast. For Friday suppers during Lent, when we couldn't eat meat, my mother served thinly sliced eggplant layered with tomato sauce and mozzarella in a hearty casserole. Here, the eggplant is sliced thicker and each piece is topped with tomato sauce and mozzarella. This recipe makes 8 large slices, which you could serve as a first course, main course, or substantial side dish with simple broiled fish or grilled chicken breasts and a salad. For a special treat the next day, make hot oven grinders with the leftovers tucked into crusty rolls, wrapped in foil, and baked until the cheese melts.

Serves 8 as a first course or side dish, or 4 as a main course

Eggplant

1 globe eggplant, 1½ pounds

1½ teaspoons kosher salt, divided

2 large eggs

2 tablespoons freshly grated Romano or Parmesan cheese

½ teaspoon granulated garlic powder

⅛ teaspoon fine, freshly ground black pepper

1 cup mild-tasting extra-virgin olive oil

½ pound mozzarella cheese, preferably low moisture, cut into 8 slices

3 fresh basil leaves

Tomato Sauce

2 cups peeled, seeded, and diced tomatoes with juice (fresh or canned)

2 tablespoons bold-tasting extra-virgin olive oil

1 clove garlic, smashed gently with the side of a chef's knife

2 teaspoons kosher salt (less if using canned tomatoes with added salt)

¼ teaspoon fine, freshly ground black pepper

5 fresh basil leaves

/continued

RECIPE SECRETS

The more seeds in an eggplant, the more bitter it will taste. Salt the eggplant slices before cooking to leach out any bitterness. I've compared the results from putting a weight on the eggplant after salting it, as many cooks do, and just letting it rest in a colander. Using a weight doesn't seem to make a difference in the bitterness, and the weight sometimes compresses the eggplant too much for my taste. Be sure to rinse and dry each piece well before sautéing.

. . . .

In order to prevent eggplant fibers from absorbing too much oil during frying, cut the eggplant lengthwise into long slices, rather than crosswise into circles. For even less oil absorption, you can brush the sliced eggplant with olive oil and broil it (don't dip it in egg). For the best results in this recipe, choose a shiny eggplant that's short and round, as opposed to long and narrow or bulbous at the bottom.

. . . .

When frying, don't use a fork to turn eggplant, or the oil will seep in. Instead, use tongs or a spatula. This may seem like a lot of oil for shallow-frying the eggplant, but don't worry. It won't all be absorbed during cooking.

. . . .

The tomato sauce recipe is lightning-fast to prepare, but don't hesitate to substitute 1 cup (leftover) 20-Minute Tomato Sauce (page 114) instead.

. . . .

Use low-moisture mozzarella, as opposed to the fresh cheese in this recipe, as it melts better. Or, substitute sliced provolone.

1. *Prepare the eggplant:* Cut off the stem and blossom ends of the eggplant and cut lengthwise into 8 slices, each a scant ½ inch thick. Layer the slices in a bowl, sprinkling them on both sides with a total of 1 teaspoon of the salt as you stack them. Let stand for 30 minutes.

2. *Prepare the sauce:* While the eggplant is standing, place the tomatoes in a nonreactive 2-quart saucepan. If using fresh tomatoes, bring to a boil over medium-high heat, then reduce the heat to low and simmer, uncovered, until soft and reduced in volume, 5 to 8 minutes. If using canned tomatoes, crush into smaller pieces with a fork and heat just to a simmer over low heat; there's no need to boil or reduce them. Slowly stir the olive oil into the simmering tomatoes. Add the garlic, salt, and pepper and cook, uncovered, over low heat until thick, 3 to 5 minutes. Tear each basil leaf into a few pieces and stir into the sauce. Taste and adjust the seasoning, if necessary. Remove from the heat and partially cover the pan. (The sauce can be prepared up to 8 hours ahead, covered, and left on a turned-off burner.)

3. Preheat the oven to 350 degrees F. Line a baking sheet with several layers of paper towels and set aside. In a shallow bowl, mix together the eggs, grated cheese, garlic powder, the remaining ½ teaspoon salt, and the pepper; set aside.

4. Rinse the eggplant under running water to remove the salt. Drain the eggplant and blot completely dry with paper towels.

5. *Sauté the eggplant:* In a 12-inch skillet (the sloping sides make it easier to turn the eggplant), heat the olive oil over medium-high heat to 325 degrees F on a deep-frying thermometer. (Or place the end of a wooden chopstick into the oil; when it sizzles on contact, the oil is ready.) Working in batches, and being careful not to crowd the pan, dip the eggplant slices in the reserved egg mixture, allowing the excess egg to drip off, then slip them into the hot oil. Fry until lightly browned on the bottom, 3 to 5 minutes. Turn, without puncturing the eggplant, and fry until the second sides are browned, 2 to 4 minutes longer. Using tongs or a spatula, transfer the eggplant to the prepared baking sheet, allowing any excess oil to drain back into the pan. As necessary, regulate the heat to keep the oil at 325 degrees F. Use a slotted spoon to remove any pieces of cooked egg that float to the surface of the oil. Fry the remaining eggplant in the same way. Gently blot up any excess oil from the fried eggplant with paper towels. Discard the oil.

6. Coat a large, rimmed baking sheet with vegetable oil spray or line with a silicone baking liner. Arrange the fried eggplant in a single layer on the prepared baking sheet. Remove and discard the garlic clove from sauce. Spread each eggplant slice with a heaping tablespoon of tomato sauce. (The recipe can be prepared to this point up to 24 hours ahead, covered, and refrigerated. Bring to room temperature before baking.)

7. Bake until the tip of a paring knife inserted into the eggplant comes out piping hot, about 10 minutes. Top the eggplant with the mozzarella and bake until the cheese melts, about 5 minutes. Tear the basil leaves into small pieces and scatter them over the eggplant the moment it comes out of the oven. Heat any remaining sauce and serve in a bowl on the side.

HOW TO PEEL, SEED, AND DICE A TOMATO FOR FRESH TOMATO SAUCE OR TOMATO CONCASSÉ

To yield about 3 cups peeled, seeded, and diced tomatoes, use 3 pounds firm, ripe tomatoes. Bring a 6-quart pot of water to a boil. At the same time, create an ice-water bath by filling a large bowl three-fourths full with water and ice. Using a paring knife, cut out the core from each tomato. Then, cut a skin-deep X in the blossom end of each tomato. Immerse the tomatoes, a few at a time, in the boiling water and blanch until the skins start to curl at the X on each tomato, 10 to 60 seconds, depending on ripeness and the thickness of the skins. With a slotted spoon or Chinese strainer, immediately transfer the tomatoes to the ice-water bath. This "shocks" the tomatoes and stops the cooking. Blanch and shock the remaining tomatoes. When the tomatoes are cool to the touch, remove them from the ice-water bath and cut in half widthwise (through their equators). Place a fine-mesh sieve over a bowl and squeeze the tomatoes gently to remove the seeds. If necessary, use your finger to dislodge any stubborn seeds. Discard the seeds and transfer the tomato liquid to a 4-cup liquid measure. Cut the tomatoes into 1-inch chunks and add to the tomato liquid. Use a bench scraper to transfer the juices from the cutting board to the tomatoes.

Uniformly chopped tomatoes used for a garnish are called tomato *concassé* (pronounced kon-kah-*say*). Ideally, they should be as dry as possible after chopping. Discard the liquid that comes out when you remove the seeds, as well as any excess liquid remaining on the cutting board when you chop tomatoes (or save for another use). Be more precise in chopping the tomato halves into ½-inch dice: cut the halves into ½-inch-thick slices, stack the slices, and make perpendicular ½-inch cuts to create uniform ½-inch dice.

RECISE SECRETS

RECIPE SECRETS

Make no mistake; this isn't one of those California-crisp vegetable dishes. To develop deep flavor when braising, first brown the vegetables in olive oil. Then, cover the pan and let the vegetables cook in their own juices until tender. When done, you should be able to easily slip the tip of a paring knife—with no resistance—into the cooked vegetables.

This qualifies as one of those Mediterranean recipes in which olive oil is not only a sautéing medium, but also a significant ingredient. If you're watching your fat grams, use less oil, but use it wisely: Heat the pan before adding the oil, and don't add the vegetables until the oil is hot enough for them to sizzle on contact. That way, you'll use the least amount of oil when sautéing, and prevent the vegetables from absorbing oil as they cook.

To prevent fresh basil from discoloring in this rustic dish, tear the leaves, rather than cutting them with a knife.

BRAISED SUMMER SQUASH WITH SWEET PEPPERS, TOMATOES, AND BASIL

Nothing says summer to me the way this dish does. About once a week, when squash and tomatoes were ready to be harvested from the garden, my grandma Guglietta would slowly simmer a colorful batch of yellow crookneck squash, green zucchini, and sweet red peppers. I never asked her to translate the name for this dish, which, in her Neapolitan dialect, sounded something like *"cucuzza,"* but whenever she said it, I made sure I was around for the next meal. You can't go wrong with this combination. It's tasty when eaten freshly cooked, but is just as terrific a few hours later when the flavors have had a chance to meld. Serve it with Grilled Pork Chops (page 211), Italian Sausage Contadina (page 215), or Creamy, Soft Polenta (page 274). This recipe makes enough for a side dish for six people, plus some terrific leftovers. My favorite time to enjoy the leftovers is at breakfast, stirred into softly scrambled eggs with ricotta, and then spooned onto toasted and buttered Italian bread. *Buon appetito!*

Serves 8

3 tablespoons bold-tasting extra-virgin olive oil, divided, plus more for drizzling (optional)

1 large yellow or red onion, cut lengthwise into ½-inch-wide crescents

2 red bell peppers (or 1 red and 1 yellow), seeded, deribbed, and cut lengthwise into ½-inch-wide strips

2 small green zucchini, cut into ½-inch-thick rounds

2 medium yellow crookneck squash, cut into ½-inch-thick rounds, large pieces cut in half crosswise

2 or 3 cloves garlic, minced

2 teaspoons kosher salt

Freshly ground black pepper

2 large, juicy ripe tomatoes, cut into 1-inch chunks, juices reserved

3 tablespoons chopped fresh flat-leaf parsley

10 fresh basil leaves, torn in half

---

1. Heat a 12-inch skillet, stir-fry pan, or wok (choose a pan with a lid) over medium-high heat. Add 2 tablespoons of the olive oil. When the oil is hot enough to sizzle a piece of onion, add the onion and bell peppers. Sauté until the onions are soft and translucent, about 8 minutes.

2. Add the zucchini and crookneck squash and sauté, stirring often, until the squashes are crisp-tender, about 8 minutes. Push the vegetables to one side, tilt the pan, and add the remaining 1 tablespoon olive oil to the empty part of the pan. When the oil is hot enough to sizzle a small piece of garlic, stir in the garlic, salt, and a few grinds of black pepper. Stir well, cover, reduce the heat to medium-low, and braise the vegetables in their own juices until the bell peppers are soft, about 10 minutes.

3. Add the tomatoes and their juices and most of the parsley and basil, reserving some of the herbs for garnish. Bring to a simmer, cover, and continue braising until the tomatoes collapse and give up their juices and all the vegetables are cooked through, 10 to 15 minutes. Taste and adjust the seasoning with salt and pepper, if necessary.

4. Transfer to a serving bowl. If desired, drizzle with a little olive oil. Garnish with the reserved parsley and basil. Serve hot or at room temperature.

ESCAROLE WITH GARLIC AND RED PEPPER FLAKES

This is one of those leafy greens I grew up with that made me realize I was different from the other kids in my small Massachusetts town. My Italian grandmother and mother called escarole something that sounded like "'schkadoll," with the first letter pronounced more as a gasp for breath than an actual syllable. I never saw schkadoll in the school cafeteria, and my all-American friends' mothers never served it when I ate supper at their houses. Consequently, I never made the connection between the big bowl of braised greens, redolent of garlic and olive oil, that my family served and the gorgeous heads of abundantly leafy escarole (pronounced es-kah-roll) that I saw in the produce market. Finally, in my twenties, it occurred to me to ask my mother how to spell the vegetable we were eating. All I had to hear were the first three letters, and the lights came on. Lately, given all the health benefits of eating leafy greens, I make escarole at least once a week when it's in season, often for lunch when I'm working at home; it's not beyond me to devour a whole pot of 'scarole over the course of the day. Fortunately, it's available almost year-round in California where I live now—another good reason to call it home.

/continued

RECIPE SECRETS

Look for leafy heads of escarole in winter and spring near the lettuces and other greens in well-stocked grocery stores and produce markets. The best heads have a moist stem end and not more than a few brown tips at the ends of the leaves.

Since the outer leaves can have a bitter flavor, it's important to cook escarole in plenty of boiling, salted water to leach out some of the bitterness.

Some cooks save the pale inner leaves of escarole for salads. They add a distinctive crunch and flavor. Try an escarole salad with fresh mandarin segments and shaved red onion, tossed with some toasted walnuts and a splash of robust olive oil and white balsamic vinegar.

**Serves 2 to 4,
depending on size of escarole**

1 head escarole, 1 to 1½ pounds, or 2 smaller heads	⅛ to ¼ teaspoon red pepper flakes
3 teaspoons kosher salt, divided	1 clove garlic, green germ removed, if present, cut lengthwise into 4 slivers, or ½ teaspoon granulated garlic powder
About 2 tablespoons bold-tasting extra-virgin olive oil	

1. Fill a 6-quart pot half-full with water and bring to a boil.

2. Trim off about 1 inch from the white base of the escarole, as well as any bruised or discolored parts from the leaves. Separate the outer leaves, stopping when you get to the small, pale green cluster of leaves inside. Cut the outer leaves crosswise into 2- to 3-inch-wide ribbons and place in a large bowl of cool water. (Or, fill a clean sink with water to give the greens plenty of room to float and release any dirt.) Tear off the inner leaves individually, and add them to the water. If the inner leaves are more than about 3 inches long, cut them in half crosswise. Swish the greens around in the water, allowing any dirt or sediment to fall to the bottom. Lift the escarole with your fingers into a colander. Pour out the water and repeat with another 1 or 2 rinsings until there is no trace of grittiness or dirt.

3. Add the escarole and 2 teaspoons of the salt to the boiling water. You may have to wait until the first leaves wilt a bit before adding the rest. Let the water return to a boil, reduce the heat to low, cover partially, and simmer until the escarole is tender, about 10 minutes. It's traditional for Italian braised greens such as these to be on the soft, tender side, but if you prefer crunchier greens, simmer for just 5 minutes.

4. Drain the escarole in a colander and shake a few times, but don't press out every last drop of water. Return the empty pot to the burner. Add the 2 tablespoons olive oil, the red pepper flakes, garlic, and the remaining 1 teaspoon salt to the hot pot. Over low heat, swirl the pot for a minute or so just to warm the garlic and release the flavor of the red pepper flakes. (If using garlic powder, just let the mixture warm from the residual heat in the warm pot.)

5. Add the drained escarole and toss with tongs to coat it evenly with the olive oil. If necessary, drizzle in more oil so the greens are loose and evenly coated. Taste and add more salt or garlic, if necessary. Serve immediately while the greens are hot, or cover and serve later at room temperature. If using fresh garlic, remove it before serving.

GARLIC SPINACH WITH CURRANTS, PINE NUTS, AND PECORINO

We've been making this gussied-up spinach side dish in cooking classes and team-building cooking parties for years. The food department of the *San Jose Mercury News* so loved this dish that they featured it on the front page of their Thanksgiving issue one year. My clever sister taught me the secret of grating a little sharp *pecorino romano* cheese into the hot spinach. It melts right in, adding incomparable flavor—a perfect example of umami (page 38) at work. The pine nuts and currants, a Spanish touch, make this suitable for special occasions. But don't overlook this—with or without the pine nuts and currants—as a weeknight side dish with Classic Herb-Roasted Chicken (page 187) or Grilled Pork Chops with Garlic and Fennel Rub (page 211). This dish works well for a big crowd, too. Just triple—or quadruple—the ingredients and use the same-sized pot, but add the spinach in batches, allowing it to wilt before adding more.

Serves 3 or 4

2 tablespoons dried currants

2 packages (10 ounces each) leaf spinach, preferably prewashed baby spinach

2 tablespoons bold-tasting extra-virgin olive oil

½ teaspoon kosher salt

⅛ teaspoon granulated garlic powder

2 tablespoons freshly grated *pecorino romano* cheese

1 tablespoon pine nuts, toasted (page 89)

Fine, freshly ground black pepper

---

1. In a small bowl, combine the currants with hot water to cover. Let stand for about 15 minutes to plump up. Drain and set aside.

2. Rinse the spinach in a large bowl of cool water. (Or, fill a clean sink with water to give the greens plenty of room to float and release any dirt.) If the spinach is not prewashed, repeat with another 1 or 2 rinsings until there is no trace of grittiness or dirt. Transfer the spinach—with the rinsing water clinging to the leaves—to a dry 6-quart pot. It's okay to pack it in quite tightly. Place the pot over medium-high heat, cover, and steam the spinach, stirring occasionally and scraping down the sides of the pot, just until the leaves are evenly wilted, about 5 minutes.

/continued

RECIPE SECRETS

I prefer baby spinach for this recipe. The stems are so tender that it's not necessary to remove them.

If you prefer, substitute raisins or sultanas (golden raisins) for the currants.

Parmesan or Asiago cheese is a good substitute for the *pecorino romano*.

A long-handled meat fork works well to stir spinach. The leaves don't stick to it as much as they stick to tongs.

3. Drain the spinach in a colander and return the hot pot to the stove. Don't press every last teaspoon of water out of the spinach, just shake the colander a few times to remove the excess liquid.

4. Add the olive oil, salt, and garlic powder to the hot pot and warm over low heat, swirling to combine. Add the drained spinach and toss to combine. The spinach should glisten with olive oil; if necessary, drizzle in a bit more. Remove from the heat.

5. Stir in the cheese and toss well, allowing the cheese to melt. Add the currants and pine nuts and toss well. Sprinkle lightly with pepper. Taste and add more salt, pepper, and/or garlic powder, if necessary. Serve immediately, or cover and set aside for up to 20 minutes before serving.

BRAISED GREENS
WITH SAUSAGE AND ONIONS
. . . .

The flavorful liquid produced when you cook braising greens is called pot liquor, and this recipe produces some sensational pot liquor, thanks to the low and slow caramelizing of the onions in the beginning. I've been known to eat a big bowl of this for lunch, then saunter back to the pot with my spoon throughout the afternoon until suppertime. When time is short, use a 1-pound bag of prewashed, precut mixed braising greens. In fact, a recipe on a bag of Trader Joe's greens inspired this dish. One night I was trying to figure out what to do with not-quite-enough leftovers from the previous night's Italian Sausage Contadina with Roasted Sweet Peppers, Potatoes, and Onions (page 215). I combined the leftovers with the bag of greens and some chicken broth and a new dish was born. For another complete meal in a bowl, add a can of drained and rinsed garbanzo or cannellini beans as you're cooking the greens and serve over steamed brown rice. Any combination of sturdy greens, such as mustard, turnip, collard, chard, or kale, works well here. The greens are great ladled over Creamy, Soft Polenta (page 274), or served as a side dish in individual bowls with the pot liquor drizzled on top. For a vegetarian option, omit the sausage.

Serves 3 or 4

1 pound mixed sturdy braising greens

2 tablespoons bold-tasting extra-virgin olive oil

1 yellow onion, chopped

½ pound fresh (not smoked) sweet Italian pork or chicken sausages, casings removed

1 clove garlic, minced

¼ teaspoon red pepper flakes

2 cups homemade chicken stock or broth (page 60 or 61) or purchased reduced-sodium broth

Kosher salt and fine, freshly ground black pepper

RECIPE SECRETS

Don't rush the cooking time when caramelizing onions. If you cook them slowly, the onions will imbue the greens with deep, complex flavor and you'll be rewarded for your patience.

To remove the casing from fresh sausage, slit the casing lengthwise with a paring knife. Remove the casing in one piece as if you're taking a jacket off a baby.

1. Trim off the ends and any discolored spots from the greens. Chop the greens crosswise into roughly 2-inch pieces (it's okay to leave the stems intact). Swish the greens around in a bowl of warm water. Lift the greens with your fingers into a colander. If the greens feel gritty or if the water is particularly dirty, wash the greens again. Set aside.

2. Heat a heavy, 6-quart Dutch oven or similar pot over medium-high heat. Add the olive oil. When the oil is hot enough to sizzle a piece of onion, add the onion, stir once, and reduce the heat to medium-low. Slowly cook the onions, stirring only occasionally, until very soft and lightly browned, 10 to 15 minutes.

3. Raise the heat to medium-high and add the sausages. Using a flat-bottomed wooden spatula, break them into bite-sized pieces. Cook the sausages and onions, stirring occasionally, until the sausage is no longer pink and begins to brown, about 5 minutes. Add the garlic and red pepper flakes and sauté, stirring constantly, for 1 minute. Add the stock and greens. If the pot is too small to add them all at once, wait until a handful of greens wilts before adding more. Bring to a boil, reduce the heat to a steady simmer, cover, and cook until the greens are very soft and tender, about 35 minutes. For the best flavor, don't skimp on the cooking time.

4. A fair amount of pot liquor is desirable (especially if you're serving this over polenta), but if you feel you have too much once the greens are cooked, turn the heat up to high and reduce the liquid to a desirable amount. Taste and season with salt and pepper. If the greens taste bitter, add salt to balance the bitterness. Serve in individual bowls, with some of the pot liquor ladled over each serving.

RECIPE SECRETS

When it comes to sweetness and tenderness, small or medium-sized beets (no larger than an average-sized lemon) are best. For even cooking, select bunches whose beets are all about the same size. The freshest beets are sold with their edible, nutritionally dense, leafy greens still attached. If the greens are attached, cut off and discard (or reserve for another use) all but 1 inch, and leave any long root ends intact. This helps prevent beets from bleeding as they cook and keeps them as neat as possible for peeling.

When cooking variously sized beets, steam similar sizes together in the same package so you can remove the individual packages from the oven as they are done. Use a marker pen to note the size of the beets on each foil package. When testing for doneness, test the package with the smallest beets first; if they're not done yet, there's no need to test the others. Recipe tester Kay Austin suggests using a toothpick to test for doneness, sticking it right through the foil.

In her encyclopedic masterpiece, *Vegetables from Amaranth to Zucchini*, author Elizabeth Schneider suggests roasting each beet in a separate square of foil, then gently rubbing each cooked beet through the foil to loosen the skin, sliding the beet away from its skin as you open and peel down the foil.

"ROASTED" BEETS
WITH **WHOLE-GRAIN MUSTARD SAUCE**

Although these beets are cooked in the oven, technically they are steamed, rather than roasted. They are enclosed in aluminum-foil packets that trap the steam, which keeps the beets moist, helps them cook evenly, and makes it easier to remove the skins. Oven cooking sure beats boiling, which leaches out their color and many nutrients and can be rather messy. For this room-temperature side dish, use red, orange, golden, or concentrically striped, eye-catching Chiogga (pronounced key-*oh*-gah) beets, or a combination of colors. You may prepare this entire dish up to 24 hours ahead. Cover and refrigerate the beets, then bring them to room temperature before serving.

Serves 6 to 8

3 bunches medium beets, about 3 pounds total (about 12 beets)

1 tablespoon whole-grain mustard, preferably imported

1 teaspoon Dijon mustard, preferably imported

1 tablespoon honey

1 teaspoon champagne vinegar or other white wine vinegar

¼ teaspoon kosher salt

Fine, freshly ground black pepper

1 tablespoon toasted walnut oil or extra-virgin olive oil

⅛ to ¼ teaspoon ground cloves

ABOUT DIJON MUSTARD

With its characteristic yellow-gray color, Dijon mustard is made from dark mustard seeds, white wine, and unfermented grape juice. Mustard is a natural emulsifier and is used frequently in vinaigrettes to bind oil and vinegar and add complexity. For a smooth, clean flavor, use imported Dijon mustard from France.

1. Preheat the oven to 375 degrees F. Scrub the beets gently, being careful not to pierce the skins, and place 3 or 4 beets of similar size in the center of a square of aluminum foil. Gather the 4 corners together at the top and seal the foil. Wrap the remaining beets similarly, and place the beet packages on a rimmed baking sheet. If the beets are of varying sizes, mark the packages that contain the smallest beets so you can test them for doneness first. Place the pan in the oven and cook until the beets are tender, for 30 to 60 minutes, depending on size.

2. While the beets are "roasting," prepare the mustard sauce: In a bowl, whisk together the whole-grain mustard, Dijon mustard, honey, vinegar, salt, and a few grinds of pepper. Drizzle in the walnut oil while whisking. Stir in the cloves. Taste and adjust the seasoning, if necessary. Set aside.

3. The beets are ready when a toothpick or paring knife can be inserted in the center and withdrawn with little resistance. (It's not necessary to open the packets if using a toothpick.) While the beets are still warm, but cool enough to handle, cut off the stem and root ends of beets and peel away the skins. If working with red beets, you may want to put on gloves to prevent them from staining your hands. Cut each beet into 6 or 8 wedges, depending on size, and add to the mustard sauce. Stir to combine, taste, and adjust the seasoning, if necessary. Serve immediately while the beets are still warm, or let stand and serve at room temperature. If making ahead, be sure to taste and adjust the seasoning just before serving.

RECIPE SECRETS

If preparing a combination of different-colored beets, prevent red beets from "bleeding" and staining lighter-colored beets by dividing the mustard sauce into separate bowls and tossing each color separately. Combine in a single serving bowl just before serving.

For the best flavor, use good-quality imported mustards. Maille (pronounced *my*) brand is widely available, and comes in both whole-grain and Dijon styles.

ROASTED ROOT VEGETABLES

Rather than filling the center of a crown roast of pork (page 219) with a tradi-tional bread stuffing, which can get greasy, I add a cup of green peas to these colorful, caramelized vegetables and heap them into the cavity of the roast. Also, this is a great combination to serve alongside roasted chicken or lamb, and the recipe makes enough for leftovers to reheat and serve throughout the week. Add your favorite vegetables, such as peeled golden beets (red beets would stain everything), rutabagas, or unpeeled whole garlic cloves. Likewise, omit your least favorite root vegetables from the list below. Just don't leave out the shallots—everyone seems to love them. See the variation that follows for "solo" roasted new potatoes.

/continued

RECIPE SECRETS

To give dense root vegetables a chance to cook through before burning on the outside, cover and steam with a little water for the first 20 minutes. The steam softens them before their exposure to the hot, dry oven heat for the final roasting.

To ensure that vegetables develop a caramelized exterior, roast at a high temperature and place the vegetables directly on the surface of a spacious, unlined shallow pan, such as a large, rimmed baking sheet, not a deep roasting pan or lined baking sheet. And don't crowd them. For ease in clean-up, spray the pan first with vegetable oil spray.

The secret to great roasted root vegetables is to roast them to the point that they are creamy and soft inside, with crisp, wrinkled skins on the outside.

To preserve the sweet garlic flavor during high-heat roasting, I use granulated garlic powder, rather than fresh garlic. If you prefer, omit the granulated garlic powder and use garlic-flavored olive oil instead of the extra-virgin olive oil. (Garlic oil is perishable; refrigerate it after opening.)

For an attractive presentation and to create the broadest surface area for caramelization during roasting, cut long, dense root vegetables such as carrots and parsnips into paysanne, or roll-cut, pieces (see page 21).

Serves 6 to 8

4 small new potatoes, about 1½ inches in diameter, peeled or unpeeled, cut in half crosswise

4 carrots, peeled and cut into 2-inch paysanne cut

2 sweet potatoes, peeled or unpeeled, cut crosswise into 2-inch chunks

½ pound parsnips, peeled and cut into 2-inch paysanne cut

½ pound turnips, peeled and quartered (or cut into sixths if very large)

8 shallots, any "twins" separated

About 3 tablespoons extra-virgin olive oil

1 teaspoon kosher salt

½ teaspoon fine, freshly ground black pepper

½ teaspoon granulated garlic powder

½ teaspoon ground allspice

10 fresh thyme sprigs

2 bay leaves, preferably imported

¼ cup water

---

1. Preheat the oven to 425 degrees F (or 400 degrees F on the convection setting). Generously coat the sides and bottom of a large, rimmed baking sheet or very shallow roasting pan with vegetable oil spray.

2. In a large bowl, combine the potatoes, carrots, sweet potatoes, parsnips, turnips, and shallots. Drizzle with the 3 tablespoons olive oil, tossing to coat every surface of the vegetables.

3. In a small bowl, combine the salt, pepper, garlic powder, and allspice. Sprinkle the mixture evenly over the vegetables and toss well. Toss in the thyme sprigs and bay leaves. Transfer the mixture to the prepared pan, arranging the vegetables in a single layer. It's okay if they're rather crowded at this point. Drizzle with the water. Cover tightly with aluminum foil (or another rimmed baking sheet, inverted).

4. Bake the vegetables for 20 minutes. Uncover the vegetables and stir. If necessary, transfer some to a second (sprayed) pan to accommodate all the vegetables in a single, uncrowded layer. To caramelize the flat surfaces, arrange the vegetables cut side down. Roast, uncovered, until the vegetables are very tender and the flat surfaces are browned, another 15 to 25 minutes. For the best flavor, it's better to err on the side of overroasting.

5. Remove and discard the thyme sprigs and bay leaves. Taste and adjust the seasoning with salt and pepper, if necessary. Transfer to a warmed bowl, or arrange on a serving platter around a roasted chicken or other main dish.

ROASTED NEW POTATOES VARIATION

Preheat the oven to 425 degrees F (or 400 degrees F on the convection setting). Cut in half 2½ pounds of small or medium-sized unpeeled new potatoes and place in a large bowl. Add 2 tablespoons extra-virgin olive oil, 1 teaspoon kosher salt, and ¼ teaspoon freshly ground black pepper and toss to coat evenly. If desired, toss in several unpeeled whole garlic cloves and leaves stripped from a few sprigs of fresh thyme and rosemary. Arrange the potatoes in a single layer, cut sides down, on a rimmed baking sheet coated with vegetable oil spray. Roast, uncovered, until the bottoms are brown and crispy, about 20 minutes. Turn the potatoes with a thin metal spatula. Continue roasting until creamy soft inside and crispy at the edges, 10 to 20 minutes longer. It's better to overroast a bit if you're unsure about doneness. Serves 4.

ABOUT NEW POTATOES

New potatoes, which come in many varieties, are immature potatoes that are harvested in the spring. With characteristically thin skins yielding to an exceptionally tender and creamy flesh, new potatoes are prized for both their texture and flavor. My favorite new potatoes are Yukon Gold and Yellow Fingerlings, both of which make terrific roasted potatoes.

SAUTÉED MUSHROOMS WITH **SHERRY** AND **GARLIC**

One of my indelible memories of La Boqueria, the huge central marketplace in Barcelona, is the vast array of mushrooms displayed there in the fall. I enjoyed them with all sorts of fish preparations, or simply sautéed like this and served as a tapa or side dish. When I teach Tapas Party classes, this "sleeper" recipe is the one that surprises people the most. It's relatively simple to prepare, and the sherry adds a delightful complexity to the flavor of the finished dish. One student told me, "I never thought I could create flavors like this. I thought I had to go to a restaurant to taste mushrooms this good."

RECIPE SECRETS

When you sauté mushrooms, be sure to give them plenty of room in the pan. A good guideline is to sauté no more than ½ pound at a time in a 10- to 12-inch pan. If you want to cook more—as in this recipe—they'll caramelize better, and steam less, when cooked in batches or in a larger pan.

To prevent mushrooms from absorbing oil, be sure the pan is hot before adding the olive oil, then heat the olive oil. When the oil is hot enough to sizzle a mushroom, add the rest.

Serves 4 to 6

1 pound same-sized fresh button mushrooms, divided

2 tablespoons bold-tasting extra-virgin olive oil, divided

1 tablespoon minced fresh thyme, divided

1 teaspoon kosher salt

Fine, freshly ground black pepper

3 cloves garlic, green sprout removed if present, minced

¼ cup medium-dry sherry or dry white vermouth

1 tablespoon minced fresh flat-leaf parsley

1 teaspoon unsalted butter

/continued

RECIPE SECRETS

Monter au beurre (page 39) is the French technique of swirling a lump of butter into a sauce at the end of cooking. It adds a distinctive glossy sheen to the finished dish, then coats your tongue with butterfat with each taste, enhancing your enjoyment of the mushrooms. One teaspoon is enough butter to do the trick here. Try a little experiment: Taste the mushrooms before and after you add the butter. Pay attention to the flavors you detect and how the mouth-feel differs before and after.

. . . .

When it comes to selecting mushrooms, some fine cooks insist that the bottoms should be tightly closed and attached to the stem, conveying freshness. Others favor mushrooms whose caps have started to pull away from the stem, citing this sign of maturity as an indicator of flavor. Personally, I can't say I've been able to notice a difference. What I do look for, however, are supple but dry mushrooms with no trace of sliminess. Avoid those whose stems are shriveled or brown at the bottom. For information on cleaning mushrooms, see page 119.

. . . .

Use a nutty, medium-dry, medium-bodied sherry such as Amontillado (pronounced ah-mohn-tee-*yah*-doe) in this recipe. If serving these mushrooms as a tapa or hors d'oeuvre, serve with the same sherry you use for cooking.

1. If the mushrooms are larger than 1 inch in diameter, cut into quarters. If not, leave whole.

2. Heat a 10- or 12-inch skillet (preferably nonstick) over medium heat. Add 1 tablespoon of the olive oil. When the oil is hot enough to sizzle a piece of mushroom, add half of the mushrooms and half of the thyme. Raise the heat to medium-high and sauté, stirring only occasionally, until the mushrooms are golden brown, 8 to 10 minutes. (If you stir too often, the mushrooms won't caramelize; let them brown on the bottom before stirring.) Season with ¼ teaspoon of the salt and a few grinds of pepper. Transfer the sautéed mushrooms to a bowl. Repeat with the remaining olive oil, mushrooms, thyme, salt, and a few grinds of pepper. Add the garlic and sauté for 1 minute, stirring constantly. Return the reserved sautéed mushrooms (with any juices that have accumulated in the bottom of the bowl) back to the sauté pan. Add the wine and parsley and boil until the liquid is reduced to a thick consistency, another minute or so.

3. Add the butter and gently swirl the pan as the butter melts and emulsifies with the sauce. Taste and adjust the seasoning with salt and pepper. Serve at once or at room temperature.

BUTTERNUT SQUASH
WITH MAPLE SYRUP AND ALLSPICE

. . . .

Every Thanksgiving I look forward to this side dish as if it's an old friend coming to visit. I'm so fond of "butternut" that I include it in Your First Turkey classes each fall, always amazed that such a simple recipe consistently elicits oohs and aahs from the students. This can be multiplied easily for a big crowd, and is fine when prepared completely a day ahead (let cool, cover, and refrigerate). Add a little cream, if necessary, to thin it down as you slowly reheat it. The sweetness and smooth texture of butternut squash make it a good foil for a variety of meats, including chicken, flank steak, or pork tenderloin, that have been marinated in a bold, jerk-type mixture made with vinegar and chiles.

Serves 4 to 6

2 pounds butternut or Hubbard squash	¼ teaspoon ground allspice
	¼ teaspoon ground cinnamon
2 teaspoons kosher salt, plus more for seasoning	⅛ teaspoon ground cloves
1 cinnamon stick	⅛ teaspoon ground ginger
3 whole cloves	A few grates of whole nutmeg
1 tablespoon unsalted butter	Pinch of fine, freshly ground black pepper
2 tablespoons maple syrup or brown sugar	

1. Peel the squash with a vegetable peeler. Cut in half lengthwise and use a grapefruit spoon or melon baller to remove the seeds and strings. Cut the flesh into uniform, roughly 2-inch chunks. Place in a 4-quart saucepan and add cold water just to cover. Add the salt, the cinnamon stick, and the whole cloves. Cover and bring to a boil over high heat. Reduce the heat to low and simmer, covered, until the squash is tender, 20 to 30 minutes, depending on the density of the chunks. When a fork penetrates the biggest pieces with no resistance, the squash is done.

/continued

RECIPE SECRETS

. . . .

Figure on ½ pound of winter squash per person. To remove the skin efficiently and safely, use a swivel-blade vegetable peeler instead of a knife. Continue peeling until you no longer see green lines or other traces of skin.

. . . .

The safest way to cut up a dense winter squash is to let gravity and a heavy cleaver or chef's knife do the work for you. Impale the middle-to-back end of the blade into the squash about 1 inch deep so it's firmly imbedded. Lift the blade—attached to the squash—and bang both together, firmly, but gently, onto a heavy-duty cutting board. Repeat as the blade slowly penetrates, eventually severing the squash.

. . . .

For even cooking, and to prevent dense vegetables such as winter squash and root vegetables from becoming waterlogged during boiling, start them in cold water.

. . . .

For the freshest nutmeg flavor, buy a whole nutmeg and grate it over the smallest holes of a box grater, or use a Microplane or a special nutmeg mill, similar to a pepper mill.

. . . .

When seasoning with ground cloves, a little goes a long way. If you double this recipe, don't multiply the whole or ground cloves. Instead, when seasoning, start with ⅛ teaspoon, and add more to taste. Also, it's not necessary to double the cinnamon sticks.

. . . .

You can reuse cinnamon sticks. Just rinse well and air-dry completely before storing.

2. Drain the squash well in a colander, and keep the pan nearby. Remove and discard the cinnamon stick (or reserve for another use) and cloves. Return the squash to the pan and add the butter and maple syrup or sugar. Mash to a smooth purée with a potato masher. Season with the allspice, ground cinnamon, ground cloves, ginger, nutmeg, and pepper. Stir well, taste, and add more maple syrup, salt, and/or spices, if necessary. If the squash tastes flat, first add more salt to bring out the other flavors. Transfer to a warmed serving bowl, or cover the pan and keep the squash warm, reheating when ready to serve.

RECIPE SECRETS

. . . .

Polenta is dried corn that is milled to produce a coarse grain. The word *polenta* refers to both the uncooked grain and the cooked dish. For the best flavor and texture, look for stone-ground polenta in specialty-food markets and health-food stores.

. . . .

Traditionally, Italians stir a steady stream of dry polenta into simmering water a little at a time to prevent lumps from forming. Never having been instilled with such a tradition, I find it far less cumbersome to whisk together the polenta and stock, then cook over low heat, covered, until the polenta absorbs the liquid. I prefer to use a sloping-sided saucier with no "corners" where the polenta might stick, but a saucepan works fine. Alternatively, you can bake polenta in a covered baking dish in a moderate oven (about 325 degrees F), which is particularly convenient if you already have a roast in the oven.

CREAMY, SOFT POLENTA

. . . .

My late father was amazed when I told him I teach people how to make polenta. "They actually pay you for that?" He was incredulous that anyone would choose to prepare—or eat—the "cornmeal mush" that sustained him and his family—and countless other Italian Americans—in hard times. Fortunately, from his perspective, but sadly, from mine, we never had polenta when I was growing up. I don't think my father would have even allowed it in the house. We never made polenta when I was in French-focused cooking school, either. You could say I'm self-taught in this subject. I became a quick study the first time I tasted the incomparable creamy, soft polenta smothered with turkey Bolognese at my favorite local specialty-food store, The Pasta Shop in Oakland and Berkeley, California. (See the variation below for my version of this favorite.) Serve polenta as a side dish to complement Chicken Cacciatore (page 202), Grilled Pork Chops with Garlic and Fennel Rub (page 211), or Pot Roast and Gravy with Peas and Carrots (page 241). Or, substitute white Cheddar for the Fontina and Parmesan here and serve alongside braised short ribs (page 237); see the variation below.

Serves 6 to 8

1½ cups polenta	1 teaspoon kosher salt
5 to 6 cups homemade chicken stock or broth (page 60 or 61) or purchased reduced-sodium broth, divided	2 ounces Italian Fontina, diced or shredded
	½ cup freshly grated Parmesan cheese

---

1. In a 3-quart saucier or saucepan, whisk together the polenta, 5 cups of the stock, and the salt. Bring to a boil over medium-high heat. Stir, cover, reduce the heat to the lowest setting, and cook for 8 minutes. Stir with a heatproof rubber spatula and taste. When done, the polenta grains should be tender, but firm, and not mushy. If not done, add about ¼ cup of the remaining stock, stir, and continue cooking over low heat until the liquid is absorbed. Continue to cook, taste, and add stock, a little at a time, until the polenta is done. You won't necessarily use all the stock, but add enough so the polenta is sufficiently loose to spread when you spoon some onto a plate, but not so loose that liquid seeps out at the edges. The cheese will tighten it up some, so it's better to err on the side of it being too loose here.

2. Remove the pan from the heat and stir in the Fontina. When the Fontina has melted, stir in the Parmesan. Taste and add salt, if needed. If not serving immediately, cover and keep off the heat in a warm place. If the polenta thickens too much as it stands, thin with any remaining stock or a little milk.

WHITE CHEDDAR POLENTA VARIATION

Prepare the polenta as directed, substituting ¼ pound white Cheddar cheese, shredded on the large holes of a box grater, for the Fontina and Parmesan cheeses. Serves 6.

POLENTA WITH "BOLOGNESE SAUCE" VARIATION

Prepare the "Bolognese" Sauce (page 124) up to 24 hours before serving. Prepare the polenta with the Fontina and Parmesan cheeses as directed and divide among 6 warmed, shallow soup plates. Ladle about ½ cup piping-hot sauce over each portion. Sprinkle with additional grated Parmesan cheese and serve immediately. Serves 6.

RECIPE SECRETS

For enhanced flavor and added protein, use chicken stock instead of the traditional water to cook polenta.

When adding the cheese, remove the pan from the heat to prevent the cheese from becoming rubbery.

Fontina from Italy, called Fontina Val d'Aosta, has a buttery, almost nutty flavor. If unavailable, substitute Danish or another Fontina, sliced provolone, or Monterey Jack. All are great melting cheeses.

Any number of dairy products—cream, cheese, or milk—will keep polenta soft and flowing. Otherwise, as it cools, it firms up considerably.

RECIPE SECRETS

Most wild rice packages lead you to believe that the contents will be cooked to perfection in 20 to 30 minutes. Not so! Depending on the age of the rice, it can take as long as an hour for the grains to soften and begin to burst, which is how you know when wild rice is cooked. To my taste, it's better to err on the side of overcooking wild rice, rather than serving hard shards that can impale your gums.

Ideally, the grains of wild rice should be whole when you buy them, rather than broken with the center white core showing. For this reason, I recommend that you buy only tightly sealed packages, instead of rice scooped out of a bin.

To clean wild rice, agitate it in a bowl of cold water. Let the rice settle for a few minutes, allowing any debris to float to the surface. Skim off the debris and lift the wild rice out with your fingers, inspecting grains for pebbles or dirt. Place wild rice in a strainer or sieve and rinse with cool water.

For best flavor, sauté the onions in European-style or organic butter or ghee (pages 155, 240). Cook slowly, allowing the onions to develop flavor.

WILD RICE PILAF

Despite its name, wild rice isn't a rice at all. It's actually a marsh grass indigenous to North America. Its distinctive dark brown color, chewy texture, and nutty flavor make it a complementary side dish to serve with fish or fowl. If you're planning to use wild rice as an ingredient in a stuffing or mixed grain salad, simply cook it in salted water until tender. For a side dish, prepare it pilaf style by sautéing it first in butter with onions, then adding chicken stock. Use this basic pilaf formula as a jumping-off point for all sorts of variations. For a delightful texture and color combination, try substituting brown rice for half the wild rice in this recipe. Add chopped, rehydrated dried mushrooms when you sauté the grains, and use the strained mushroom soaking liquid in place of part of the stock. Stir in a handful of chopped, toasted nuts and some dried cherries or cranberries just before serving. For a main-dish salad, toss wild rice with bite-sized chunks of smoked or roasted chicken or turkey, toasted pecans, nectarines, walnut oil, and rice vinegar.

Serves 4 to 6

2 tablespoons unsalted butter or extra-virgin olive oil	½ teaspoon kosher salt
1 small yellow onion, minced	¼ teaspoon freshly ground black pepper
1 cup wild rice, well rinsed	¼ cup chopped toasted pecans, walnuts, pine nuts, or sliced almonds (optional)
3 fresh thyme sprigs	
2 cups homemade chicken stock or broth (page 60 or 61) or purchased reduced-sodium broth	¼ cup dried currants, sultanas (golden raisins), or other chopped dried fruit (optional)
1 bay leaf, preferably imported	

---

1. Heat a 4-quart saucepan over medium-high heat. Add the butter. When the butter is hot enough to sizzle a piece of onion, add the onion and sauté, stirring occasionally, until soft and translucent, 6 to 8 minutes. Reduce the heat to low and continue cooking the onion, allowing it to caramelize and become sticky without browning, about 10 more minutes. Add the wild rice and thyme and stir to combine. When the grains glisten, after about 1 minute, add the stock, bay leaf, salt, and pepper. Raise the heat to high and bring to a boil. Reduce the heat to low, cover, and simmer steadily until the grains are tender and some have burst open, 40 to 60 minutes. Taste after 30 minutes and then every 5 to 10 minutes thereafter to judge doneness.

2. If there's a substantial amount of liquid remaining in the bottom of the pot, transfer the contents to a colander placed inside a bowl. Let the liquid cool and save it to use in a soup recipe. Alternatively, if the pilaf seems dry enough to serve as is, leave it in the pot without straining.

3. Remove and discard the thyme sprigs and bay leaf. Stir in the nuts and dried fruits, if using. Fluff the pilaf with a fork. Taste and adjust the seasoning with salt and pepper, if necessary. Transfer the pilaf to a warmed serving bowl, or keep warm until ready to serve.

KALIJIRA RICE PILAW

This recipe comes from my friends Ken Lee and Caryl Levine, who import an impressive array of distinctive rices from around the world and package them under their Lotus Foods label. Among my favorites is the quick-cooking baby basmati rice from Bangladesh called Kalijira (pronounced kal-ih-*jee*-rah). This recipe for traditional rice pilaf—or *pilaw* (pronounced *plow*), as it's called in Bangladesh and India—was reportedly a favorite of the Moguls who built the Taj Mahal. Serve it with Grilled Leg of Lamb with Pomegranate Marinade (page 221), Garlicky Chicken Breasts (page 176), or Broiled Swordfish with Mango Salsa (page 155). For special occasions, *pilaw* is garnished with a generous sprinkling of currants and sautéed almonds.

Serves 6	
2 cups Kalijira rice	1 cinnamon stick
1 tablespoon plus 2 teaspoons ghee (pages 155, 240) or unsalted butter, divided	1½ teaspoons kosher salt
	1 bay leaf, preferably imported
½ cup minced yellow onion	3 cups water
¼ teaspoon ground turmeric	⅓ cup dried currants or raisins
3 whole cloves	½ cup slivered almonds
3 cardamom pods	

/continued

WHEN IS IT APPROPRIATE TO SERVE RICE?

Traditionally, rice is served with fish or shellfish, but not exclusively so. Consider the classic combination of *risotto milanese* with osso buco or shish kebab with saffron rice.

If a seafood preparation is saucy, rice is a nice vehicle for the sauce, as it is with saucy stir-fried dishes. Rice is never verboten, but I wouldn't serve it—or any other starch, for that matter—after a first course of risotto or pasta. Nor would I serve plain, steamed rice with roasted meats. Rice pilafs, on the other hand, can add texture and interest to roasted and grilled poultry and game. What it boils down to is this: What do *you* like to eat with rice?

RECIPE SECRETS

Kalijira rice, also known as baby basmati or *gobindavog* rice, has a fragrant, delicate flavor and, due to its tiny size, cooks in no time flat. It's ideal for rice puddings and quick pilafs, such as this one. Look for it in specialty-food stores or in Middle Eastern or Indian markets (see Sources). Look for the spices used here at the same market. It's okay to substitute regular long-grain basmati rice in this recipe; just increase the cooking time by 5 minutes.

Whether making a *pilaw* or a curry, Indian cooks sauté their spices in ghee before adding any liquid. This step awakens—or volatilizes—the flavors of the spices, making them more fragrant and lively than if they were simply added with the water.

For the best texture, it's important not to disturb the rice when you cook a *pilaf* by the absorption method, as in this recipe. If you uncover rice as it cooks, you'll release the steam that's necessary for the grains to become tender. If you stir the rice as it cooks, the grains will release starch, resulting in a heavier pilaf with sticky rice, rather than a lighter pilaf with fluffy, separate grains.

1. *Prepare the rice:* Place the rice in a fine-mesh strainer, rinse with cool water, and drain well. Set aside.

2. Heat a 4-quart saucepan over medium heat. Add the 1 tablespoon ghee or butter. When the ghee is hot enough to sizzle a piece of onion, add the onion and sauté until soft and translucent, but not brown, 6 to 8 minutes. Add the turmeric, cloves, cardamom pods, cinnamon stick, salt, and bay leaf and stir to toast the spices for 1 minute. Add the drained rice and stir until the grains become shiny, about 1 minute. Add the water and bring to a boil. Cover, reduce heat to the lowest setting, and cook, undisturbed, for 15 minutes (or 20 minutes if using regular basmati rice). Remove from the heat and let stand, covered and undisturbed, for 5 minutes.

3. *Prepare the currants and almonds:* While the rice is cooking, place the currants or raisins in a small bowl with hot water to cover and let stand just long enough to plump, about 10 minutes for currants or a bit longer for raisins. Drain well and set aside. Heat a 6- to 8-inch skillet over medium-high heat. Add the 2 teaspoons ghee. When the ghee is hot enough to sizzle an almond, add the almonds and sauté until they are fragrant and golden brown, about 5 minutes. Transfer the toasted almonds to a large plate and let cool completely in a single layer until they become crunchy.

4. When the rice is done and has rested for 5 minutes, stir gently with a fork to fluff the grains and distribute the spices. (It's customary to serve *pilaw* studded with the whole spices, but you may remove them before fluffing, if desired.) Taste and adjust the seasoning, if necessary. Transfer to a warmed shallow serving bowl and garnish with the almonds and currants. Serve at once.

AL'S STEAMED WHITE RICE

I never learned to steam rice—at home or in cooking school. My mother never served it, and in school we either used a rice cooker, made pilaf, or boiled converted rice in monumental amounts of water. My husband makes the rice at our house, and he never worries about "boil-overs" with this microwave method. I recommend steaming jasmine rice from Thailand or Indian basmati. Both have long grains with a lovely fragrance and texture—perfect for this simple recipe. Serve with Thai-Style Minced Chicken with Basil and Chiles (page 170), Stir-Fried Velvet Chicken with Cashews (page 174), or a saucy stir-fry.

Serves 4

1 cup jasmine or basmati rice

1½ to 1¾ cups water

1 teaspoon kosher salt (optional)

---

1. Place the rice in a strainer and rinse with cold water until the water runs clear. Transfer the rice to a deep, 3-quart microwave-safe dish with a tight-fitting lid. Alternatively, use an 8-cup Pyrex liquid measure and cover tightly with plastic wrap.

2. Stir in the water, using the lesser amount if you have new-crop rice, and the salt, if using. Cover tightly. Place in the microwave and cook on high for 4 minutes, then on medium for 10 minutes. When the microwave stops, check to see if the rice is done to your liking (times vary with different microwave ovens). If not, return the rice to the microwave and cook on high for 2 to 3 more minutes. If the rice seems very dry, add 1 tablespoon water.

3. Let the rice stand, uncovered, for 5 minutes. Fluff with a fork or rice paddle and place a paper towel between the rice and the lid to absorb condensation. Let stand for 3 to 5 minutes before serving.

RECIPE SECRETS

Read the label to see if you have "new crop" rice. If so, use the lesser amount of water. If the label doesn't specify, assume it's not new crop rice, and use the greater amount of water: Older rice absorbs more liquid.

You can use the same method for cooking long-grain brown rice, but cook on high for 5 minutes and medium for 30 minutes.

To give the rice an Asian accent, add a slice of fresh ginger with the salt.

RECILE SECRETS

It's your choice whether to peel potatoes for mashing. The skins contain
valuable nutrients and fiber, and they
add a rustic look to mashed potatoes.
If you plan to whip potatoes with an
electric mixer, the peels tend to get
gummed up in the beaters, so I'd advise
peeling them. You may find that peeled
potatoes cook a bit faster. Regardless,
cut potatoes into uniform pieces so
they'll cook evenly. To prevent peeled
potatoes from oxidizing, or turning
brown, immerse them in cold water
immediately after peeling.

Potatoes—and other root vegetables—
cook evenly if you start with cold
water. Plunging them into boiling water
cooks the outsides before the centers
are done.

To make fluffy mashed potatoes and
prevent them from becoming gummy,
heavy, or waterlogged, drain the cooked
potatoes and return them to the hot,
dry pan. Toss them over low heat until
a starchy film forms on the bottom of
the pan.

Heat the milk to prevent it from
pulling the heat out of the potatoes.

MASHED YUKON GOLD POTATOES

Here's a foolproof technique for fluffy hand-mashed potatoes, the perfect complement to Rack of Lamb with Garlicky Bread Crumbs (page 224), Grilled Pork
Chops with Garlic and Fennel Rub (page 211), Roasted Stuffed Turkey with
Pan Gravy (page 188), or a slow-roasted beef sirloin tip (page 232). If you like
your potatoes lighter and airier, whip them (instead of mashing by hand) with
an electric mixer, adding the milk slowly as you whip. Make these as rich or
light as you like, using as much butter as your heart desires and either half-and-
half or heavy (whipping) cream, or nonfat, low-fat, or full-fat milk. When you
use flavorful, buttery potatoes, such as Yukon Golds, you may be surprised at
how good they taste prepared with nonfat milk and just a teaspoon of butter.
Just be sure to add enough salt and pepper to bring out the potato flavor.
Don't miss the variations at the end with horseradish and with roasted garlic
and chives.

Serves 4

1½ pounds Yukon Gold potatoes
(about equal in size)

2 teaspoons kosher salt, plus
more for seasoning

1 tablespoon butter, or more if
desired

½ cup milk or cream, heated

Fine, freshly ground pepper,
preferably white

---

1. Place the unpeeled, whole potatoes in a 4-quart saucepan and add cold
water to cover. If some potatoes are much bigger than others, cut them so they
are all about the same size. Add 2 teaspoons of the kosher salt, cover, and bring
to a boil over high heat. Reduce the heat to low and simmer until tender, 15 to
20 minutes. To test for doneness, transfer one of the larger potatoes to a plate,
cut it in half, and taste a piece from the center to see if it's tender. Return the
test potato to the pan and continue to cook, if necessary.

2. Drain the potatoes well in a colander or strainer. Return the potatoes to the
same pan and place over low heat. "Dry out" the potatoes by tossing them in
the pan until no liquid remains and a starchy film begins to coat the bottom of
the pan, 1 to 2 minutes. Turn off the heat.

3. Add the butter and mash the potatoes with a potato masher. Add the hot milk or cream a little at a time, stirring with the masher as you add it. Season to taste with salt and white pepper. Serve immediately, or cover and place over the lowest setting. When the potatoes are piping hot, after about 5 minutes, turn off the heat and let stand, covered, for up to 15 minutes.

HORSERADISH MASHED POTATOES VARIATION

Proceed as directed above, reducing the amount of milk or cream to ¼ cup. Add ¼ cup room-temperature crème fraîche, homemade (page 67) or purchased, 1 heaping tablespoon prepared cream-style horseradish, and 2 tablespoons minced fresh chives. Serve with roast beef and gravy (page 232) or saucy dishes such as pot roast (page 241) or Braised Short Ribs with Frizzled Leeks (page 237).

ROASTED GARLIC MASHED POTATOES
WITH CHIVES VARIATION

At least 45 minutes or up to 2 days before cooking the potatoes, preheat the oven to 425 degrees F. Cut off about ½ inch from the top of a head of garlic. Peel until only a thin layer of papery skin covers the bulb. Brush the cut surface with about ⅛ teaspoon olive oil. Wrap in aluminum foil and roast, oiled side up, until the cloves are soft enough to squish, 45 to 60 minutes. Set aside (or refrigerate if preparing more than 4 hours ahead). Cook the potatoes as directed above. After drying out the cooked potatoes, squeeze the garlic pulp from its papery sheath into the pan. Mash the garlic and potatoes together. If desired, add 2 tablespoons finely minced fresh chives. Serve with Cracker-Crusted Nubble Point Scallops (page 142), Sautéed Fillet of Sole with Tartar Sauce (page 145), Grilled Marinated Flank Steak au Jus (page 230), or Grilled Leg of Lamb with Pomegranate Marinade (page 221).

RECIPE SECRETS

Rather than chopping hard-cooked eggs, I find it quicker and neater to shred them on the large holes of a box grater.

. . . .

To remove the strings and eliminate the strong vegetal flavor sometimes present in celery, before dicing, peel the rounded outside part of the stalks with a swivel-blade vegetable peeler.

. . . .

For the best flavor, toss starchy foods such as potatoes and pasta while they're hot with flavorful dressings. They soak up the flavors better when hot.

CLASSIC AMERICAN POTATO SALAD

There must be as many variations of potato salad as there are cooks. This is an eggy version, adapted from my mother's recipe. For the best texture, use waxy new potatoes, which are young potatoes whose sugar hasn't completely converted to starch. Their skins are tender, so I leave them on for color and their nutritional benefits. My favorite new potatoes are red creamers and Yukon Golds, but more pedestrian round red and white potatoes would be fine. For the best flavor, serve the salad while the potatoes are still warm.

Serves 6 to 8

2 pounds waxy new potatoes

3 teaspoons kosher salt, divided

1 teaspoon dry mustard

¼ teaspoon granulated garlic powder

¼ teaspoon fine, freshly ground black pepper

½ to ⅔ cup best-quality mayonnaise

3 hard-cooked eggs (page 129)

2 tablespoons cider vinegar or champagne vinegar

¼ cup minced red onion

2 to 4 celery stalks, peeled and diced

---

1. Place the unpeeled, whole potatoes in a 4-quart saucepan and add cold water to cover. If some potatoes are much bigger than others, cut them so they are all about the same size. Add 2 teaspoons of the kosher salt, cover, and bring to a boil over high heat. Reduce the heat to low and simmer until tender, 15 to 20 minutes. To test for doneness, transfer one of the larger potatoes to a plate, cut it in half, and taste a piece from the center to see if it's tender. Return the test potato to the pan and continue to cook, if necessary.

2. While the potatoes are cooking, in a small bowl, whisk together the remaining 1 teaspoon kosher salt, the dry mustard, garlic powder, and pepper. Add ½ cup mayonnaise and whisk to combine. Taste and adjust the seasoning. Set aside.

3. Peel the hard-cooked eggs and shred on the large holes of a box grater onto a piece of waxed paper; set aside.

4. When the potatoes are done, drain well in a colander and transfer to a large bowl. Carefully cut the hot potatoes into quarters. Sprinkle with the vinegar and toss well. Add the eggs, onion, and celery and toss to combine. Add the reserved mayonnaise dressing and toss to combine. If the mixture seems dry, add more mayonnaise. Taste and adjust the seasoning, if necessary. Serve immediately, or cover and refrigerate for up to 3 days.

ORZO WITH TOYBOX TOMATOES AND FRESH MINT

Orzo is small, dried pasta in a distinctive, elongated oval shape. Don't be fooled by its tiny size; it can take as long to cook as larger macaroni. This side dish is a good accompaniment to Grilled Stuffed Chicken Breasts with Prosciutto, Taleggio, and Pesto (page 183), or is a nice addition to a summertime picnic or buffet. The recipe yields a lot, and you can prepare it several hours ahead. If you do make it in advance, don't refrigerate it, or the texture will suffer and the pasta won't soak up as much of the flavorful tomato juices. (Do refrigerate leftovers, however.) I sometimes toss this orzo—or leftovers—with a handful of julienned prosciutto and diced mozzarella or crumbled feta. In the middle of summer, when tomatoes are at their peak and the home team's in town, it's my favorite picnic food to take to the ballpark.

/continued

RECIPE SECRETS

What makes this pasta so tasty is tossing it with the tomato–olive oil mixture while it's hot. Whether you actually serve this hot or at room temperature, it's filled with flavor.

You might be surprised to find fresh mint in this savory recipe. A cousin of basil, mint is a delightful foil for tomatoes, and in the right amount, it contributes a distinctive, refreshing flavor. If you prefer, substitute fresh basil, but tear—don't chop—the basil leaves to prevent them from discoloring.

Toybox tomatoes (see illustration, page 284) are a gorgeous combination of various sizes, shapes, and colors of cherry tomatoes. Look for them at summertime farmers' markets or in produce stores. Substitute a combination of flavorful cherry tomatoes in season, or use good-quality sun-dried tomatoes out of season.

Store tomatoes on the counter-top, rather than in the refrigerator, as cold has a negative effect on their texture.

Serves 8 to 10

Kosher salt for cooking pasta, plus 1 teaspoon

¾ pound orzo, *riso,* or *semi di melone* pasta

1 basket (about 2 cups) Toybox tomatoes or a combination of flavorful cherry tomatoes

2 tablespoons chopped fresh mint

¼ cup bold-tasting extra-virgin olive oil

½ teaspoon granulated garlic powder

1. Bring a 4-quart pot of water to a boil. Add enough salt to the boiling water to make it taste like the ocean. Cook the pasta according to package directions, stirring occasionally, until al dente.

2. While the orzo is cooking, cut the tomatoes in half through the stem end and place in a bowl. Add the mint, olive oil, garlic powder, and 1 teaspoon salt and toss to mix.

3. When the orzo is done, drain well and toss immediately with the tomato mixture. Taste and adjust the seasoning with more olive oil, garlic powder, and/or kosher salt, if necessary. Serve hot, or cover loosely and set aside, stirring occasionally. If preparing this dish more than 30 minutes ahead, be sure to taste and adjust the seasoning again just before serving.

Toybox tomatoes with a sprig of mint

SWEET
ENDINGS

SWEET ENDINGS
RECIPES

Recipe	Q	MA	Page
Grilled Peach Ice Cream Sundaes with Shortcut Caramel Sauce	●	●	289
Apple Crisp with Brandy and Sp'Ice Cream		●	291
Bittersweet Chocolate Bread Pudding with Kahlúa Sauce		●	293
White Chocolate Cheesecake with Oreo Crust and Raspberry Coulis		●	295
Devil's Food Cake with Dark Chocolate Ganache or Chocolate Fudge Frosting		●	298
Lemon Marzipan Cake		●	301
Zucchini–Olive Oil Snack Cake with Lemon Icing		●	303
Zabaglione with Fresh Berries and Peaches	●		305
Rich Chocoholic Pudding	●	●	307
Strawberry Granita Parfaits		●	309
Orange-Mint Sorbet in Orange Shells		●	311
Dark Chocolate–Pistachio Wafers	●	●	313

Q = Quick—prep to table in 45 minutes.
MA = Make ahead—part or all of the recipe can or must be made ahead.

SECRETS FOR CHOOSING AN APPROPRIATE DESSERT

Every special dinner deserves a distinctive dessert, and I've included twelve of my favorites in this book. But how do you know which dessert to serve when?

It's important to consider the context of the entire meal when planning dessert. But before I tell you about how to select an appropriate dessert, let me tell you how to plan a menu when a particular dessert is a foregone conclusion. That's my challenge every year on my husband's birthday, when he makes his annual bid for white chocolate cheesecake. Since the dessert is sacrosanct, I work backwards when planning the rest of the menu.

When I use the so-called "seesaw" approach to planning his birthday menu, to prevent fatigue, I alternate between light and heavy courses. Here's an example:

Chicken Soup with Glass Noodles (page 70)
....

Broiled Swordfish with Mango Salsa (page 155)
....

Savory Corn Pudding (page 256)
....

Romano Beans (page 258)
....

Weeknight Green Salad (page 81)
....

White Chocolate Cheesecake with Oreo Crust and Raspberry Coulis (page 295)

In this seesaw menu, a light and brothy soup is followed by a rich fish dish and a substantial corn pudding. Then we're back to lightness with a simple salad, followed by the heavy, rich cheesecake crescendo for dessert.

There are two other sound menu-planning approaches you can follow: starting with a light first course and progressively moving to a heavy dessert, or starting with a rich, heavy first course, such as Fettuccine Alfredo with Baby Shrimp and Peas (page 113), and ending up with a light Orange-Mint Sorbet in Orange Shells (page 311).

If you consider dessert in the context of everything else, you'll likely create a satisfying menu. Try to imagine what you'll feel like eating after a bold and flavorful meal like Turkey Mole (page 204) or paella (page 158). As you scan the list of desserts on the previous page, ask yourself how each would taste after the mole or paella. Chances are good you'll welcome the refreshment of Strawberry Granita Parfaits (page 309) or the orange-mint sorbet, maybe with a plate of Dark Chocolate–Pistachio Wafers (page 313) on the side. But if the Rich Chocoholic Pudding (page 307) seems more fitting, give it a try.

One last word: the seasonal dessert recipes and menus on pages 316–18 and 319–25, respectively, provide guidelines for when to prepare certain seasonal fruit-based desserts. As with every other course, when you prepare these recipes with ingredients in season, the enjoyment will stretch beyond your palate, rewarding you with nutritional—and cost-saving—dividends as well.

SECRETS FOR PREPARING SUCCESSFUL DESSERTS

Each recipe in this chapter features its own particular Secrets. In addition, here are some general tips, as well as some information on the three most common ingredients called for in these recipes.

INGREDIENTS

- **Butter** is a fat made from churned cream, which, by law, must contain at least 80 percent butterfat—the rest can be water and milk solids. **Salted** butter can contain up to 7 percent salt, which is added to lengthen shelf life and "enhance" flavor. Typically, **unsalted** butter is made from the freshest cream, and is prized by fine cooks for its purer flavor. **European-style** butter has a higher percentage of butterfat, and can derive its characteristic deep, rich, satisfying flavor from cream that has been allowed to mature before churning. The cream used to make **organic** butter comes from antibiotic- and hormone-free cows that eat an organic diet. **Cultured organic** butter has a distinctive tang. Store well-wrapped unsalted butter for up to 2 weeks in the refrigerator and salted butter for up to 2 months. Freeze any butter for up to 6 months. For the best flavor, I prefer to use European-style or organic unsalted butter. To soften cold butter, cut into several pieces, arrange in a single layer on a microwave-safe plate, and microwave on defrost for 20 seconds at a time until soft.

- **Cream** is the fat-rich layer that forms at the top when fresh, unhomogenized milk is left to stand. Almost all commercial cream has been pasteurized, but much of the cream sold in large chain grocery stores today is ultrapasteurized and contains a list of additives. These can change cream's behavior in baking and whipping, as well as its flavor. For example, while pasteurized heavy (whipping) cream can be whipped hours in advance without separating, whipped ultrapasteurized cream loses its loft relatively quickly. For best results, look for pasteurized heavy (whipping) cream with no additives.

- **Vanilla extract** is the fragrant, smooth, pure-tasting extraction of vanilla beans aged in alcohol. Widely available, imitation vanilla, which can have a harsh flavor and high chemical content, is a poor substitute. To taste and compare vanilla extracts, do what the pros do and dissolve a little in some milk. Vanilla is most often used to enhance the flavor of baked goods and desserts, especially those made with chocolate. Because of its high alcohol content, when using vanilla extract in cooked recipes, wait until the sauce or custard is off the heat, lest it dissipate. Look for deep-flavored Madagascar Bourbon or Tahitian vanilla extract (a bit more expensive). The latter, with a light, floral scent, particularly complements fruit-based desserts. Mexican vanilla is also available, but there are presently no government standards regulating the vanilla extract sold in Mexico. So if you purchase Mexican vanilla, be sure it is from a reputable source. Store vanilla extract, tightly sealed, in a cool, dark place.

TIPS AND TECHNIQUES

- To enhance the **chocolate** flavor in a dessert, add coffee, vanilla extract, and/or salt.

- In baked goods, I prefer to use **finely ground sea salt** (not kosher salt), to be sure the grains melt completely. This is especially important when baking at low temperatures, such as for Lemon Marzipan Cake (page 301), which is baked at 300 degrees F.

- Instead of chopping chocolate, I shave it into large shards with a sturdy serrated knife. I find that it melts more quickly and evenly than chopped chocolate.

- For quick and efficient sifting, use a medium-mesh strainer, rather than a special sifter.

GRILLED PEACH ICE CREAM SUNDAES WITH SHORTCUT CARAMEL SAUCE

When you fire up the grill for dinner, take advantage of hot coals and make these juicy grilled peaches. You can cook the peaches up to 2 hours ahead, transfer them to a baking pan, then just before serving, reheat them in a flash in a preheated 500 degree F oven. Top with your favorite vanilla ice cream and some crumbled crunchy amaretti cookies, then drizzle with this incredibly simple shortcut caramel sauce—no more standing over a pot of molten sugar with a candy thermometer.

Serves 4

Sauce	Sundaes
6 tablespoons unsalted butter	⅓ cup granulated sugar
½ cup heavy (whipping) cream	1 tablespoon ground cinnamon
½ cup granulated sugar	2 large, ripe freestone peaches
½ cup packed light brown sugar	Almond oil, canola oil, or other flavorless cooking oil, for brushing on peaches
Pinch of kosher salt	
¾ teaspoon pure vanilla extract, preferably Tahitian	1 pint vanilla ice cream
1 tablespoon dark rum (optional)	8 crunchy-style amaretti cookies, crumbled

/continued

RECIPE SECRETS

Caramel sauce is typically made with melted, or caramelized, sugar to which you add heavy (whipping) cream. It can be tricky to make, and can seize up and solidify if you're not careful. This method makes a butterscotchy sauce that thickens beautifully as it cools. Make the sauce first—or earlier in the day—so it has a chance to thicken a bit as it cools. Cool any extra sauce to room temperature, cover, and refrigerate for up to a week.

Freestone peaches come apart easily from the pit when you cut them around the seam and twist the halves in opposite directions. True to their name, the flesh of *cling* peaches clings to the pit, making it harder to separate them into halves. Here's how to choose the sweetest peaches in the produce market: Smell the stem end of the peach. If it smells sweet, chances are it's a good one. When ripe, peaches should feel heavy for their size.

Coating the peach halves in cinnamon sugar before grilling adds another level of caramel flavor to this dessert.

These peaches tend to leave a fair amount of sticky residue on the grill grate. So, in class, when we cook them a couple of hours ahead on a gas grill, we use only half of the grill for peaches, leaving some of the grate clean for grilling our steaks or chicken later.

ABOUT AMARETTI COOKIES

Not to be confused with amaretto liqueur, amaretti are imported, crunchy Italian cookies made from ground apricot kernels. Their texture is light and airy, and their flavor unparalleled. Amaretti di Saronno brand cookies are packed in pairs, wrapped in tissue paper, and sold in distinctive red tins. I use this brand in any recipe in which a dry, crunchy cookie is preferred, such as these ice cream sundaes. Look for Amaretti di Saronno in the cookie section of upscale markets or in Italian delicatessens where packaged ladyfingers are sold. If unavailable, use another packaged amaretti cookie and, if necessary, dry out the crumbs in the oven until they're crunchy instead of chewy.

1. *Prepare the sauce:* Heat the butter in a heavy 2-quart saucepan over medium heat just until almost completely melted. Stir in the cream, then add the granulated sugar, brown sugar, and salt. Bring to a boil, reduce the heat to low, and simmer steadily for 5 minutes, stirring occasionally. Remove from the heat and stir in the vanilla and the rum, if using. Set aside to cool and thicken. If the sauce begins to separate as it cools, stir with a whisk to re-emulsify.

2. *Grill the peaches:* Prepare a hot fire in a charcoal grill, or preheat a gas or stove-top grill to high. In a small, shallow bowl, combine the sugar and cinnamon and set aside.

3. Cut the peaches in half along the seam (through the stem end), twist to separate the halves, and lift out and remove the pits. Do not peel, as the skin holds the peach together on the grill. Cut a thin slice off the round side of each peach half so it will sit flat, pitted side up, on a plate.

4. Brush the 2 cut sides of each peach half lightly with oil. Dip the oiled surfaces into the cinnamon sugar. Place the halves, cut side down, on the grill and grill until hot and the sugar caramelizes, 3 to 5 minutes. The peaches should retain their shape. Turn and grill the second sides until caramelized.

5. *Assemble the sundaes:* Place each hot peach half, pitted side up, on a dessert plate or soup plate. Top each with a scoop of ice cream, drizzle with caramel sauce, and sprinkle with crumbled amaretti. Serve immediately with the remaining caramel sauce on the side.

APPLE CRISP WITH BRANDY AND SP'ICE CREAM

If you like apple crisp that has a cinnamony topping with lots of texture from rolled oats, this crisp is for you. It is one of the only desserts I love equally warm right out of the oven or cold right out of the refrigerator. Truth be told, I usually prefer the former for dessert, and the latter for breakfast the next morning. You can make both the crisp and the ice cream early in the day. To reheat the apple crisp, place it in a preheated 325 degree F oven until a paring knife inserted in the center comes out warm, 10 to 15 minutes. For the best texture, make the "homemade" ice cream at least 4 hours ahead. One of the secrets I learned in cooking school is how to "cheat" with style, in this case using top-quality store-bought ice cream as a base. This trick for doctoring up ice cream with brandy and spices came from former Sonoma chef Charles Saunders. Don't be surprised to discover that the ice cream decreases in volume as it softens. It will be denser than the store-bought version you started with, but it'll still be creamy, like gelato. If you prefer, serve the apple crisp with a dollop of crème fraîche, homemade (page 67) or purchased, in place of the ice cream.

Serves 8

Brandy and Sp'Ice Cream

1 quart top-quality vanilla ice cream, preferably vanilla bean, softened, but not completely melted

¼ cup brandy

½ teaspoon ground cinnamon

¼ teaspoon nutmeg, preferably freshly grated

⅛ teaspoon fine, freshly ground black pepper

⅛ teaspoon ground allspice

Apple Crisp

1 cup all-purpose flour

1 cup packed light brown sugar

¾ cup rolled oats (old-fashioned or quick cooking)

2 tablespoons wheat germ (optional)

1 teaspoon ground cinnamon

¼ teaspoon fine sea salt

½ cup (1 stick) unsalted butter, at room temperature, cut into 8 pieces

2 tablespoons freshly squeezed lemon juice

3 pounds Golden Delicious apples (about 9 medium)

/continued

RECIPE SECRETS

Golden Delicious apples are often used in baked apple recipes because they keep their shape when cooked. They're also easy to find. Select ripe apples with a golden, rather than greenish, hue.

If desired, add a little wheat germ to the topping mixture for additional nutrients and a nutty flavor.

While it's important for the butter to be soft enough to blend with the oats mixture, if the topping mixture is too warm, it will melt into the apples as the crisp cooks. If it's a warm day, chill the topping while you cut up the apples.

Don't pour the topping mixture over the apples. Instead, grab clumps of it in your fist and distribute them over the apples—make some clumps large, others smaller. They'll bake into delicious, crunchy sections, creating a nice contrast to the soft apples.

If you like your apple crisp really crunchy on top, sprinkle it with only half of the topping, in clumps, and bake for 15 minutes. Then add clumps of the remaining topping and bake for another 25 minutes.

Don't use your best brandy in this recipe. The cold temperature of the ice cream won't let you appreciate its nuances. Be sure not to add more than the specified amount of brandy, or the ice cream will not freeze solid (alcohol inhibits freezing).

1. *Prepare the ice cream:* Scoop the soft ice cream into a bowl and return the empty carton and lid to the freezer. Add the brandy and stir just enough to combine.

2. In a small bowl, combine the cinnamon, nutmeg, pepper, and allspice. Sprinkle the mixture over the ice cream and stir just enough to combine, breaking up any spice clumps with the spoon. Spoon the ice cream back into the carton and refreeze until solid, about 4 hours.

3. *Prepare the apple crisp:* In a bowl, stir together the flour, brown sugar, rolled oats, wheat germ (if using), cinnamon, and salt. Cut the butter into the flour mixture with a pastry blender, potato masher, or table knife. The mixture should be crumbly. If it's fairly warm in the kitchen, refrigerate the topping.

4. Preheat the oven to 375 degrees F (or 350 degrees F on the convection setting). Coat a 9-by-13-inch baking dish with vegetable oil spray. Set aside.

5. Pour the lemon juice into a large bowl. Peel and core each apple and cut into eighths. Add the apples immediately to the lemon juice and turn to coat them on all sides. As you cut the apples, stop every now and then to stir the apples already in the bowl to prevent browning. When all the apples are cut, pour the apples and lemon juice into the prepared baking dish.

6. Arrange the topping mixture in large and small clumps evenly over the apples. Bake until the apples are tender when pierced with a paring knife, 30 to 40 minutes.

7. Transfer to a cooling rack and let stand for 10 minutes to set a bit before cutting. For a more formal presentation, cut the crisp into squares and serve on dessert plates. Alternatively, spoon the crisp into small bowls. Top each serving with a scoop of the ice cream. Serve at once.

BITTERSWEET CHOCOLATE BREAD PUDDING WITH **KAHLÚA SAUCE**

One winter several years ago, I flew to Colorado to cook for a family during their ski week in Vail. At the end of the week, the mom lamented all the leftover bagels and asked if I could do something with them. (You might be surprised at how frequently people confuse chefs with magicians.) Anxious to face the challenge, I shaved off all the sesame and poppy seeds, cut up the bagels, and decided to make bread pudding. Just as I was pouring the custard into the baking pan, I noticed a big bar of imported dark chocolate on the counter. I melted some chocolate and stirred it into the bread pudding before popping it into the oven. While the experiment baked, I scattered the remaining onion and garlic bagels in the snowy yard for the birds, then returned to the kitchen and whipped up a Kahlúa sauce to gild the lily. Not surprisingly, the chocolate bagel bread pudding was a big hit. Now I don't even bother to wait for bagels to get stale—this recipe, made with day-old, dense Italian bread, is just as good. The Kahlúa sauce is a cinch; you can make it in no time while the pudding bakes. It's rather sweet to play off the bittersweet chocolate in the bread pudding. Feel free to substitute whiskey or another liqueur, such as Frangelico or Baileys Irish Cream, for the coffee-flavored Kahlúa. Cover and refrigerate any leftover bread pudding and sauce. Reheat the sauce over low heat, stirring constantly. Cold bread pudding tastes great with reheated sauce.

RECIPE SECRETS

For the best texture, use day-old, dense, chewy artisanal Italian bread, such as Pugliese or *ciabatta*. This works well with day-old bagels or French bread, or a standard Italian loaf from the bakery. Just don't use sourdough bread.

To remove the crusts easily without taking off too much of the bread, cut the loaf in half crosswise. Place each half on the cutting board, cut side down. With a serrated knife, shave off the crust in thin pieces, starting from the top.

Give the bread chunks a good, long soak in the chocolate milk so there's time for the liquid to permeate every square inch.

Serves 6

Bread Pudding	Kahlúa Sauce
2 cups whole milk	6 tablespoons unsalted butter
4 ounces bittersweet or other dark chocolate, chopped	¾ cup confectioners' sugar, sifted
¼ cup granulated sugar	¼ cup Kahlúa
1 loaf day-old dense Italian or other plain bread, crusts removed and cut into ¾-inch cubes to yield 3½ cups	2 large egg yolks
	½ cup heavy (whipping) cream or low-fat evaporated milk
2 large eggs	1 cup whipped cream, for serving (optional)
1 teaspoon pure vanilla extract	6 strawberries or 18 chocolate-covered espresso beans, for garnish (optional)

/continued

When making this chocolate bread pudding in one of our corporate team-building cooking classes, my friend Kara Nielsen, a former pastry chef, created a lovely presentation for this dessert, transforming the pudding into something nice enough to serve company. Here's how you can do the same: Ladle some Kahlúa sauce into the center of a light-colored dinner plate, leaving a wide band of empty plate showing around the perimeter to create a frame. Place a rectangle of bread pudding in the center of the plate. Ladle a little sauce over the top, just to moisten the pudding and make it glisten. Top the bread pudding with a dollop of softly whipped cream, or if you really want to be fancy, pipe whipped cream out of a pastry bag fitted with a star tip. Place a few strawberries on a cutting board and make several parallel cuts in the bottom, but don't cut all the way through the hull. Press the cut parts gently with your finger, fanning out the strawberry. Place the strawberry fan on top of the whipped cream. If you wish, prop up another pair of strawberry fans against one side of the bread pudding. Voilà!

1. *Prepare the bread pudding:* Preheat the oven to 325 degrees F. Butter the sides and bottom of a 2½-quart shallow baking dish.

2. In a Dutch oven or broad saucepan, combine the milk, chocolate, and sugar and heat over medium heat, stirring occasionally, just until the chocolate melts. Remove from the heat, stir in the bread cubes, and set aside for 15 minutes. While the bread is soaking, gently push the cubes into the chocolate milk with a slotted flat spatula or potato masher. (Don't mash the bread, just submerge it completely.)

3. In a small bowl, whisk together the eggs and vanilla extract. Stir the egg mixture into the bread mixture and mix well with a rubber spatula. Transfer to the prepared baking dish. Bake until a knife inserted in the center comes out with just a little chocolate residue on it, 20 to 30 minutes. The pudding should be firm and dry on top. Transfer to a cooling rack and let cool for 10 minutes.

4. *Prepare the sauce:* While the bread pudding is baking, in a 3-quart saucier or saucepan, melt the butter over medium heat. When the butter is almost completely melted, gradually whisk in the confectioners' sugar. Add the Kahlúa and stir well.

5. Remove the pan from the heat and add the egg yolks one at a time, whisking constantly. Add the cream and stir to combine. Return the pan to medium heat and cook, stirring constantly with a slotted wooden spoon, until the sauce thickens slightly, about 5 minutes. Don't raise the temperature, or the eggs will scramble. To test if the sauce is ready, drag your finger along the back of the spoon; the track should remain for a few moments before it fills in. This stage of doneness in a sauce is called *napé* (page 112).

6. Place the pan of sauce on a rack and stir occasionally until it cools a bit, from hot to warm. It will thicken as it cools. To hasten thickening, place the pan in a bowl filled with ice water to reach about two-thirds up the sides of the pan. Stir constantly until the desired temperature and consistency are reached. Serve the sauce warm.

7. To serve, ladle a little sauce onto each plate and top with a piece of bread pudding. Ladle more sauce on top, and garnish with a dollop of whipped cream and a strawberry or a few chocolate-covered espresso beans, if using. Alternatively, for a fancier presentation, see the suggestion at right. Transfer any remaining sauce to a bowl and serve on the side.

WHITE CHOCOLATE CHEESECAKE WITH OREO CRUST AND RASPBERRY COULIS

My husband, Allen, is a white chocolate fanatic. Don't get me wrong, he loves the dark stuff, too. And yes, he does realize the only thing chocolate about white chocolate is its name. I concocted this recipe one year for his birthday, and it's been a family favorite ever since. Even people who don't like white chocolate have to admit it's one of the creamiest cheesecakes they've ever had. I like to serve it with raspberry coulis (pronounced coo-*lee*), but he finds that blasphemous—nothing should come between this man and his white chocolate.

Serves 12 to 16

Crust
. . . .

20 Oreo cookies (use cookies and filling)

5 tablespoons unsalted butter, melted and cooled to room temperature

Cheesecake
. . . .

1 pound white chocolate, chopped or shaved

2 pounds cream cheese, at room temperature

1 cup granulated sugar

4 large eggs

1 large egg yolk

1 tablespoon pure vanilla extract

Raspberry Coulis
. . . .

3 to 5 teaspoons superfine sugar

1 bag (10 to 12 ounces) frozen raspberries with their juices, thawed

. . . .

10 to 12 Oreo cookies, for decoration (optional)

/continued

RECIPE SECRETS

Pastry chef, cookbook author, and friend Nick Malgieri has taught me a thing or two about cheesecakes. For years I used crumbly "natural" cream cheese that's packaged in a tube and sold by the slice. Instead, for the best texture, Nick prefers the more widely available packaged cream cheese that has gum arabic added. A natural emulsifier used in ice creams and other sweet treats, gum arabic comes from the bark of certain acacia trees. Now I wouldn't use anything but the ubiquitous—and less costly—silver package of Philadelphia brand cream cheese from the local supermarket. It definitely makes a creamier cheesecake.

. . . .

To prevent the cake from rising and falling, which can cause the top of the cake to crack, Nick advises not to beat the mixture too much, especially after adding the eggs. The less volume you create, the less the cake will rise.

. . . .

My own personal cheesecake-crack prevention program has consistently proven the importance of one little step. As soon as the cheesecake comes out of the oven, run a knife around the edge, releasing the seal between the cake and the pan. As the cake cools, it will drop uniformly, without cracking.

RECIPE SECRETS

For the best flavor and texture, use top-quality white chocolate, not the white baking chips commonly available in supermarkets. I prefer Callebaut brand, a Belgian import available in specialty-food shops and where fine baking ingredients are sold (see Sources).

To ensure even baking, bake the cheesecake in a shallow bain-marie (page 27). Line the bottom of the bain-marie with a paper towel to prevent the cheesecake from sliding around. To prevent water from seeping into the cheesecake, wrap the bottom and sides of the springform pan with aluminum foil, with the shiny side out to prevent overbrowning.

For serving ease, before you grease the springform pan, invert the bottom piece so the lip faces downward. It might be a bit trickier to lock the springform in place, but later on it's much easier to slide a cake server onto the pan bottom as you remove each wedge.

1. *Before making the cheesecake:* Position an oven rack in the lower third of the oven and preheat to 350 degrees F. For serving ease, if possible, invert the bottom of a 9½-inch springform pan, so the lip around the edge faces downward, and lock in place. Wrap the bottom and sides of the pan with heavy-duty aluminum foil, shiny side out. Coat the inside of the pan with vegetable oil spray. Select a roasting pan large enough to accommodate the springform pan and place a paper towel in it. Bring a kettle of water to a boil. Set aside.

2. *Prepare the crust:* Place the cookies in a 1-gallon zip-top plastic bag, and seal the bag, pressing out as much air as possible. With a rolling pin, crush the cookies into crumbs no larger than peas. Add the butter, reseal the bag, pressing out the air, and massage the butter into the crumbs. Dump the crumbs into the prepared pan and press evenly into the bottom and about ½ inch up the sides. Don't pack down too tightly or the crust will be difficult to cut. Bake in the bottom third of the oven for 10 minutes. Reduce the oven temperature to 300 degrees F.

3. *Prepare the cheesecake:* Place the white chocolate in a microwave-safe bowl and melt in the microwave on medium power for 4 minutes, stopping at 1-minute intervals to stir. Stop microwaving when the chocolate is melted and smooth. Set aside.

4. In a stand mixer with the paddle attachment, if available (or in a bowl with a handheld mixer), beat together the cream cheese and sugar on low speed just until incorporated and smooth. On low speed, beat in the eggs and egg yolk one at a time. Don't overmix. Add the melted white chocolate and vanilla and mix on low speed just to combine. Pour into the baked crust and place in the prepared bain-marie pan.

5. Pull out the oven rack halfway. Center the pan on the rack. Pour the hot water from the kettle into the bain-marie to reach halfway up the sides of the springform pan. Bake until the top is golden brown, but the cheesecake is still loose in the center, 1 hour and 10 minutes to 1 hour and 20 minutes. Remove the bain-marie from the oven. With oven mitts, carefully transfer the cheesecake to a cooling rack and remove the foil. Immediately run a knife around inside edge to loosen the cake from the pan. Let stand for 30 minutes, then refrigerate the cheesecake on the rack until the center is very cold, at least 6 hours, or up to 24 hours.

6. *Prepare the raspberry coulis:* In a food processor or blender, combine 3 teaspoons of the sugar and the raspberries and process until puréed. Stop, scrape down the sides, taste, and add more sugar, if necessary. Strain the coulis through a fine-mesh strainer or chinois into a bowl. Use the back of a small ladle to push the coulis through. Be sure to scrape any purée from the underside of the strainer, adding it to the bowl. Discard the seeds. Transfer the coulis to a pitcher or bowl, cover, and chill before serving or for up to a few days.

7. Remove the springform sides and place the cheesecake on a flat platter. To cut the cake, dip a sharp knife with a thin blade into a glass filled with hot water. Shake off the water (away from the cake) and promptly make the first cut. Wipe the blade clean on a paper towel, dip it into hot water, shake, and make the second cut. Continue wiping and dipping the knife as you make each cut. If using Oreo cookies to decorate the cake, push one capriciously into each wedge at an angle near the wider end. Serve with a little raspberry coulis beside each slice of cheesecake. If there is additional coulis, pass it at the table.

RECIPE SECRETS

To my taste, the best raspberry sauce is made with frozen raspberries. *Cooks Illustrated* magazine once did a survey and came to the same conclusion. Look for organic frozen raspberries at well-stocked supermarkets. If you prefer to use fresh raspberries, substitute two 6-ounce baskets. The recipe included here yields 1 cup, which is enough sauce to use 1 tablespoon for each serving. Double the recipe if you would like to serve more sauce.

Of all the produce that is treated with added pesticides and herbicides while the plants are growing, berries retain the highest percentage of residual chemicals after they are picked (page 41). I recommend buying organic berries. Cascadian Farms frozen organic berries are particularly good.

Superfine sugar dissolves more rapidly than traditional granulated sugar. To make your own superfine sugar, process granulated sugar in a food processor until it starts to become powdery. If you use granulated sugar in this recipe, grind the sugar in the food processor before adding the raspberries.

RECIPE SECRETS

There are two types of cocoa powder, natural and "Dutched." Both cake and frosting recipes call for natural, or non-alkalized, cocoa, which is lighter in color. Alkalized, or Dutch-processed, cocoa has been chemically treated to reduce harshness and acidity, and it typically has a milder taste.

To prevent overflow, be sure your 8-inch cake pans are 2 inches deep. If pans are 1½ inches deep, as many are, you'll have about 2 cups extra batter, which can be baked into cupcakes (at the same temperature, for less time).

DEVIL'S FOOD CAKE WITH DARK CHOCOLATE GANACHE OR CHOCOLATE FUDGE FROSTING

Everyone's heard of devil's food cake, the classic American chocolate layer cake, so named to distinguish it from its pure white cousin, angel food cake. But no one would ever guess that beets are the secret ingredient in this version. They contribute incomparable moistness to this tall, dark layer cake (as carrots do in carrot cake). This recipe features a choice of two toppings, a creamy, rich chocolate ganache (pronounced gah-*nosh*), adapted from a recipe from pastry chef Nick Malgieri, and a sweet, traditional American-style frosting, adapted from a recipe on the Hershey's cocoa box. If you prefer to use ganache, make it first, so it has time to set up while the cake layers bake and cool. If time is short, make the frosting while the cakes bake. Either way you frost this cake, a scoop of vanilla ice cream and a glass of cold milk would be perfect on the side.

Serves 12 to 16

Ganache

2 cups heavy (whipping) cream

4 tablespoons unsalted butter

1½ pounds semisweet or bittersweet chocolate, chopped

1 cup (2 sticks) unsalted butter, melted and cooled to room temperature

1 teaspoon pure vanilla extract

⅔ cup packed finely shredded raw beets

Cake

2 cups all-purpose flour

2 cups granulated sugar

1 cup natural unsweetened cocoa powder

2 teaspoons baking soda

¾ teaspoon baking powder

½ teaspoon fine sea salt

4 large eggs, room temperature

2 cups buttermilk

Chocolate Fudge Frosting

1 cup (2 sticks) unsalted butter, melted

⅛ teaspoon fine sea salt

⅔ cup hot brewed strong coffee, espresso, or hot milk, or a combination

1½ cups natural unsweetened cocoa powder, sifted

6 cups (1½ pounds) confectioners' sugar, sifted

1 teaspoon pure vanilla extract

1. *Prepare the ganache, if using:* In a 5-quart saucier or wide saucepan, combine the cream and butter and bring just to a boil over low heat. Turn off the heat and add the chocolate. Shake the pan to distribute the chocolate so it's covered with cream. Let stand for 5 minutes, undisturbed. Whisk until smooth and set aside on a rack to cool and set up. Do not stir or disturb. When the ganache cools to room temperature, in about 1 hour, refrigerate, if necessary, just until it thickens to a spreading consistency, 10 to 20 minutes. Whisk until smooth and set aside at room temperature until ready to ice the cake.

2. *Prepare the cake:* Position a rack in the lower third of the oven and preheat to 350 degrees F (or 325 degrees F on the convection setting). Butter and flour the sides and bottoms of two 8-inch round cake pans with 2-inch sides. Line the bottoms with parchment or waxed paper.

3. Sift together the flour, sugar, cocoa powder, baking soda, baking powder, and salt into a large bowl. Stir to combine. Make a well in the center. Set aside.

4. In a medium bowl, whisk the eggs to combine. Whisk in the buttermilk. Add to the dry ingredients all at once and stir to combine completely. Whisk in the butter slowly. Add the vanilla and stir to combine. Stir in the beets. Transfer to the prepared cake pans and spread evenly, using a ruubber spatula to pull the batter away from the center of the pans and out along the sides. (This ensures flat, rather than domed, layers.) Bake until the center of each cake springs back when lightly touched and the sides of each cake begin to pull away from the pan, 30 to 35 minutes.

/continued

RECIPE SECRETS

To prep ⅔ cup of finely shredded beets, start with about 5 ounces (2 small) raw beets (weigh without the stems). Beets stain, so I wear rubber or disposable gloves and work in a stainless-steel sink to contain any spray. Peel the beets with a swivel-blade vegetable peeler. The neatest shredding method utilizes a food processor with the shredding disk: trim off beet tails and tops, shred in the processor, and measure ⅔ cup. To use a box grater, trim off the tails, but leave the tops attached for a handle to protect knuckles. Shred into medium "strings" over the smaller teardrop holes of a box grater (see illustration, page 300). Use any leftover beets in "Roasted" Beets with Whole-Grain Mustard Sauce (page 268).

If you're nervous about splitting the layers, use dental floss. Wrap a long piece (about 3 feet) of clean floss around the outside edge of the cake, just at the point where you want to split it; cross the ends, and gently pull them in opposite directions to cut through the cake.

For the best results when making ganache, use good-quality chocolate and use a serrated knife to chop it. It's important to let ganache sit, undisturbed, as it sets up. Once it's almost firm, it's okay to stir with a whisk. If the ganache stiffens too much while frosting the cake, recipe tester Randall Hicks recommends placing the bowl of ganache over simmering water for 5 to 10 seconds; remove and stir well. Repeat as necessary, until you achieve a spreadable consistency.

When making the frosting, it's your choice whether to use hot coffee, espresso, or milk (or a combination). Hot liquid "wakes up" the flavor in cocoa powder and seems to help prevent sugar from clumping. Sift the sugar after measuring. If the frosting thickens as it sits, thin with a little hot water.

. . . .

This makes a tall 4-layer cake. If you prefer 2 layers, don't split the cakes. If you make 2 layers, store any extra ganache or frosting, covered, in the refrigerator for up to a month (or freeze the frosting for up to a month). Restore the frosting to spreading consistency by defrosting overnight in the refrigerator (do not microwave). Stir with a wooden spoon and, if necessary, drizzle in a little hot water until you achieve the desired consistency. Roll chilled leftover ganache into balls, then in cocoa powder for instant truffles.

5. Let cool on a wire rack for 10 minutes. Invert each cake onto another rack and remove the pans. Carefully peel off the paper and cool the cakes completely, upside down.

6. *Prepare the frosting, if using:* In a large bowl, whisk together the butter, salt, and hot coffee, espresso, and/or milk. Whisk in the cocoa. Add the sugar and stir with a wooden spoon to combine. Add the vanilla and stir to combine. Cover and set aside.

7. *Assemble the cake:* Split cakes in half horizontally with a serrated knife. Place 1 layer, cut side up, on a flat serving platter or cake pedestal. Using a metal icing spatula, spread with a scant 1 cup of the ganache or frosting. If necessary, to keep the frosting malleable as you spread, wipe off the spatula and dip in very hot water and shake or wipe dry. Top with the second layer, cut side down, and spread with a scant 1 cup ganache or frosting. Top with the third layer, cut side up, and spread with a scant 1 cup ganache or frosting. Top with the last layer, cut side down. Frost the top and sides with the remaining ganache or frosting. If using ganache and it seems loose, or if the kitchen is warmer than 70 degrees F, refrigerate the cake for about 15 minutes until the ganache firms up, then transfer the cake to a cool place until ready to serve.

BEETS MAKE YOU PREGNANT

One recipe tester was particularly candid in filling out her testing report for this recipe: "When I was about 7 years old, someone told me that beets make you pregnant. I believed it for a very long time. I have only eaten beets twice and after each time I became pregnant. As for last night, I will keep you posted . . ."

Box grater

LEMON MARZIPAN CAKE

I first ran across this compelling cake while editing recipes for a delightful little cookbook called *Cooking a Honker, Charring a Cheesecake and Other Kitchen Tales from the Livermore Valley Wine Country*. Juli Chouinard, former pastry chef–owner of Primrose Pastries in Castro Valley, California, and daughter-in-law of the owners of Chouinard Vineyards, contributed this recipe to the book. The first time I read it, I knew it had to be good. I usually sprinkle this tall Bundt cake with confectioners' sugar and place it on a pedestal plate. In spring and summer, I fill the center with fresh strawberries, arranging a few clusters of berries on the pedestal, also. A pool of raspberry coulis (page 295) or a dollop of lemon curd on each plate would complement it nicely. Primrose Pastries is now under new ownership, but thanks to Juli's generosity in sharing this recipe, many of her fans can still enjoy this moist, distinctive cake. I hope you will, too.

Serves 12 to 16

2¾ cups cake flour, sifted twice	6 large eggs, separated
¼ teaspoon baking soda	1 teaspoon pure vanilla extract, preferably Tahitian
¼ teaspoon fine sea salt	
4 ounces almond paste	1 cup sour cream
2¼ cups sugar	Grated or minced zest of 2 large lemons
1 cup (2 sticks) unsalted butter, at room temperature	Confectioners' sugar, for serving

---

/continued

RECIPE SECRETS

Fine-textured cake flour is lower in gluten than all-purpose flour, and can't be beat for ensuring a tender crumb in cakes such as this one. Look for cake flour in a box in your supermarket's baking goods aisle.

Pay attention to the location of the comma when you're sifting ingredients. In this recipe, because the comma comes before the word *sifted*, you should measure the flour before you sift it. Instead of using a traditional hand-cranked sifter, I find it's more efficient to use a medium-mesh sieve and to sift ingredients onto a sheet of parchment or waxed paper. It's much easier to funnel them back for a second sifting that way. If you do use a traditional sifter, be sure to keep it dry— don't wash it—to prevent rusting.

Despite its title, this recipe calls for almond paste, which is not quite as sweet as marzipan and has a coarser texture. Marzipan is generally rolled or shaped into decorative confections, although it could certainly be substituted for almond paste here. If buying almond paste in a tube (usually packed inside a long, narrow box), give it a good squeeze to be sure it's soft. It's harder to determine freshness if you buy almond paste in a can. But rest assured, having no alternative once, I made this cake with hard, crumbly almond paste. Instead of blending into the other ingredients as it normally does, it broke down into small, candy-like nibs, which no one seemed to mind a bit as we polished off the cake.

RECILE SECRETS

. . . .

Ideally, it's prudent to beat the egg whites separately, with dry, impeccably clean beaters or with the whip attachment in a separate bowl *after* the cake batter is mixed, just before you fold them into the batter. Such timing prevents the whites from deflating and works fine if you have two sets of beaters and bowls or both a stand mixer and a hand mixer. If you have just one mixer, beat the whites first and set aside. Use the same beaters (it's not necessary to clean them) to mix the batter in another bowl. Before you fold the beaten whites into the batter, refluff them by hand with a clean, dry whisk to restore any volume lost while sitting.

. . . .

In order to prevent the top and sides of the cake from becoming too dark before the inside of this dense cake is completely done, bake at a low temperature, 300 degrees F.

. . . .

This is the perfect cake for a fancy turban head mold or decorative Bundt pan. Be sure to butter every crevice and flour the pan very well, even if the pan has a nonstick coating. When the cake comes out of the oven, let it sit for just 5 minutes before removing the pan. Cakes come out perfectly every time. Here's how my colleague Charlene Vojtilla butters such decorative pans to be sure every surface is coated: Melt butter and brush it on the inside of the pan. Refrigerate the pan for about 5 minutes to harden the butter, enabling you to see any missed spots. Brush with another layer of butter and dust immediately with flour.

1. Preheat the oven to 300 degrees F. Generously butter and flour a 12-cup, 10-inch turban head mold, Bundt pan, or tube pan. Set aside.

2. Sift together the cake flour, baking soda, and salt onto a sheet of waxed paper or into a medium bowl. Set aside.

3. In a stand mixer with the paddle attachment, if available (or in a bowl with a handheld mixer), beat the almond paste on low speed until smooth. Add the granulated sugar and beat on low speed until completely combined. Add the butter and beat until fluffy, 3 to 5 minutes, stopping occasionally to scrape down the bowl. It's okay if you see a few small clumps of almond paste in the mixture. Add the egg yolks and vanilla extract and beat to combine completely.

4. Starting and ending with the dry ingredients, alternately add the sifted flour mixture in 3 increments and the sour cream in 2 increments, mixing well after each addition. Stir in the lemon zest.

5. In a clean, dry bowl, using clean beaters or the whip attachment, if available, beat the egg whites until stiff, but not dry. Add about one-third of the whites to the batter and mix on low speed just to combine. By hand, using a rubber spatula, gently fold the remaining whites into the cake batter. It's okay if a few white streaks remain.

6. Gently pour the batter into the prepared cake pan (it will come to within ½ inch of the rim of a 12-cup pan). Bake until a toothpick inserted in the center comes out clean and the cake begins to pull away from the pan sides, 1 to 1¼ hours. Transfer to a cooling rack and let cool in the pan for just 5 minutes. Place a rack on top of the cake, invert the cake and rack together, carefully remove the pan, and let the cake cool right side up. When completely cool, pour some confectioners' sugar into a fine-mesh strainer and dust the top of the cake.

ZUCCHINI–OLIVE OIL SNACK CAKE WITH LEMON ICING

I first tasted a version of this snack cake at a culinary event sponsored by Bertolli olive oil. It was love at first bite. Thanks to the olive oil in the batter, this cake is remarkably moist, and stays that way for days—a great boon, since this do-ahead recipe makes enough for leftovers. As a matter of fact, zucchini cake tastes even better the next day. It also freezes well. For a sturdy snack cake, bake the cake in a large, rimmed baking sheet and cut it into 36 or more bars. It's always welcome at potlucks, meetings, and sporting events. Whenever and wherever I serve it, someone asks for the recipe. While this cake is a great way to use zucchini that's proliferating in your summer garden, I wouldn't discourage you from making it all year long.

Serves 12 or more

Cake

1½ cups dark raisins

1½ cups sultanas (golden raisins)

About 2 cups apricot brandy, dark rum, orange-flavored liqueur, or hot water

3 cups all-purpose flour

2 teaspoons ground cinnamon

1 teaspoon baking powder

1 teaspoon baking soda

½ teaspoon fine sea salt

3 large eggs

1½ cups granulated sugar

1 cup mild-tasting extra-virgin olive oil

3 cups shredded, unpeeled zucchini, about 1¾ pounds

2 teaspoons pure vanilla extract

1 cup walnuts, toasted (page 89) and chopped

Icing

2 lemons

1 tablespoon mild-tasting extra-virgin olive oil

2 cups confectioners' sugar

RECIPE SECRETS

Soaking the raisins before adding them to the batter rehydrates and plumps them. Water would do the trick here, but to infuse them with great flavor, soak them in rum, whiskey, or a liqueur with a complementary flavor. My favorite is apricot brandy. For the best infusion, I begin soaking the raisins the day before I make the cake. Or, if time is short, warm the brandy and soak the raisins as you prep the other ingredients. After straining the raisins, I keep the apricot brandy, covered, in the refrigerator to use for my next zucchini cake.

When baking cakes with olive oil, use ¼ less olive oil than the amount of butter or shortening called for in the recipe. In addition to fewer fat grams, you'll also benefit from olive oil's legendary antioxidant properties. Because of the way it's extracted, extra-virgin olive oil has the best nutritional profile of any olive oil. You could certainly use a bold, fruity extra-virgin olive oil in this recipe, but I prefer to use a more delicately flavored oil, especially in the icing.

/continued

RECIPE SECRETS

Sifting dry ingredients results in a fluffier cake. When baking with olive oil, it's also important to sift the dry ingredients to prevent clumping.

For the sweetest flavor, choose the smallest zucchini.

To prevent the cake from doming in the center as it bakes, and to achieve an even, flat surface, spread the batter out from the center of the pan, up into each corner, and out along the sides. It's okay if the batter is concave in the center when you slide the pan into the oven; gravity will even things out as the cake bakes.

1. *Soak the raisins:* Measure the raisins and sultanas into a 4-cup liquid measure or bowl. Add enough brandy or other liquid to cover the raisins. Cover and set aside for at least 20 minutes or for up to 24 hours.

2. Preheat the oven to 350 degrees F (or 325 degrees F on the convection setting). For a thin snack cake (to eat out of hand), butter an 17-by-12-inch rimmed baking sheet. If you prefer a denser cake (more suitable if you plan to serve the cake for dessert on a plate), butter a 9-by-13-inch baking pan.

3. *Prepare the cake:* Sift together the flour, cinnamon, baking powder, baking soda, and salt into a large bowl. Set aside.

4. In a medium bowl, beat the eggs lightly. Add the granulated sugar and stir to combine. Whisk in the olive oil, zucchini, and vanilla extract. Add the egg mixture to the dry ingredients and stir to combine. Drain the raisins, reserving the soaking liquor for another use. Add the raisins and nuts to the batter and stir just to combine. Pour the batter into the prepared pan.

5. Bake until a toothpick inserted in the center comes out clean, the center springs back when lightly touched, and the edges begin to pull away from the pan sides, 40 to 45 minutes for an 17-by-12-inch pan (or 35 to 40 minutes, if using the convection setting) or 50 to 55 minutes for a 9-by-13-inch pan (or 45 to 50 minutes for convection). Transfer to a cooling rack and let the cake cool completely in the pan.

6. *Prepare the icing:* Using a Microplane zester or the small holes of a box grater, remove the zest from the lemons and measure out 2 teaspoons zest. Squeeze the lemons and measure out ¼ cup juice. Reserve any remaining zest and juice for another use. In a bowl, combine the lemon juice, olive oil, and lemon zest. Sift the confectioners' sugar into the bowl and stir to combine. Cover the icing with a piece of plastic wrap placed directly on the surface (to prevent a crust from forming), and set aside until the cake is cool.

7. *Ice the cake:* Leave the cake in the pan and spread the top with the icing. To prevent the icing from "cracking" when you cut the cake, score the cake into bars or squares before the icing hardens. After serving, cover any remaining cake with plastic wrap and store at cool room temperature for up to 3 days, refrigerate for up to 1 week, or freeze for up to 1 month.

ZABAGLIONE
WITH FRESH BERRIES AND PEACHES

According to legend, zabaglione (zah-ball-*yoh*-neh) was created by accident when a seventeenth-century chef from Turin fortuitously tipped over a bottle of fortified sweet wine into an egg custard. Since the unification of Italy, Sicilian Marsala has become the fortified sweet wine of choice for making zabaglione. In France, this egg-based sauce is called sabayon (sah-by-*own*), and—made without sugar—is also sometimes used in savory applications. Zabaglione is a quick, frothy dessert or snack to make for drop-in guests when there's "nothing" in the house. For a more delicate flavor, my Venetian cooking teacher colleague, Fulvia Sesani, prepares an ethereal zabaglione with Prosecco, the light sparkling wine from the Veneto, in place of the Marsala. For a do-ahead, chilled alternative in cooking classes, we sometimes prepare zabaglione as directed here, let it cool to room temperature in an ice-water bath, then fold in an equal amount of whipped heavy (whipping) cream. After dividing into individual servings, this "lighter" zabaglione mousse can be chilled for up to 6 hours before serving. This recipe features summer fruits, but don't hesitate to substitute perfectly ripe, juicy pears in fall or winter. They're a natural with Marsala.

Serves 4

1 cup or more mixed blueberries, strawberries, and blackberries

3 ripe peaches, peeled, pitted, and cut into bite-sized chunks

4 large egg yolks

¼ cup sugar

½ cup sweet Marsala, preferably imported

/continued

RECIPE SECRETS

Clean fragile berries gently, at the last minute: Place each variety separately in a colander and rinse under cool water. Immediately pat dry with paper towels.

When whipping egg yolks or whites in a copper bowl, a chemical reaction takes place between the copper and the egg, which increases the stability and structure of the resulting foam. Don't fret if you don't have a copper bowl. You can also make terrific zabaglione in a stainless-steel bowl.

A balloon whisk is shaped like a light bulb at the business end. It's the best whisk to use for incorporating air into a mixture such as zabaglione.

For the most successful results, I recommend improvising a double boiler—a heatproof bowl over a saucepan—to make zabaglione. To prevent the egg yolks from scrambling in the bowl, make sure the simmering water below doesn't touch the under-side of the bowl. And until you get the hang of it, keep the water no hotter than a bare simmer. It's safer to take a longer time whisking the yolks up into a creamy froth than to rush this step and scramble the eggs. Be sure to whisk constantly in a rotating figure-8 pattern, making contact with all inside surfaces of the bowl. Whisking all surfaces is more important than speed here.

1. Just before serving, hull (remove stems and leaves) the strawberries and cut them into pieces roughly the same size as the other berries. Save a few of the prettiest berries for garnish. Arrange the peaches and berries in 4 balloon-shaped wineglasses, large compote dishes, or parfait glasses. Set aside.

2. Half-fill a 4-quart Dutch oven or saucepan with water and bring to a simmer. Regulate the heat as necessary to maintain a constant, gentle simmer as you prepare the zabaglione.

3. Place the egg yolks in a broad, round-bottomed copper or stainless-steel bowl that will rest comfortably nestled on top of the pot. Whisk with a balloon whisk until the yolks turn light yellow. Whisk in the sugar, then the Marsala.

4. Rest the bowl on the pot of simmering water, making sure the water doesn't touch the underside of the bowl. Whisk the mixture constantly until the mixture is foamy, and then eventually soft and creamy, 10 to 15 minutes. Be sure to whisk the entire inner surface of the bowl. Don't hesitate to transfer the bowl (it's hot) to the countertop for a few moments if the mixture begins to separate. When done, the zabaglione should be the texture of lightly whipped heavy cream—light in texture, yet thick enough to coat a spoon heavily; it will register 170 degrees F on an instant-read thermometer. Immediately pour the zabaglione over the fruit and garnish with the reserved berries. Serve at once.

RICH CHOCOHOLIC PUDDING

For all you chocoholics, here's a double dose of heaven. If you'd like to dress this up a bit, pile alternating layers of dense, rich pudding and billows of softly whipped cream into tall, narrow parfait glasses (see the Secret for keeping the rims and sides clean). Top each with a few raspberries or a long-stemmed strawberry. Or serve in individual *pot de crème* cups. This makes about 5 cups of very rich pudding, enough for 4 copious to 8 respectable servings—it's your call. As for me, let's just say I know people who would eat any amount of this for breakfast.

Serves 4 to 8 (makes 5 cups)

3½ cups whole milk	¼ teaspoon fine sea salt
9 ounces semisweet chocolate, chopped	3 tablespoons crème de cacao
	1 teaspoon pure vanilla extract
10 large egg yolks, lightly beaten	Whipped cream, for serving (optional)
½ cup sugar	
½ cup all-purpose flour	

---

1. In a heavy 4-quart saucepan, combine the milk and chocolate and place over medium heat until the chocolate begins to melt. Remove from the heat and stir until the chocolate melts completely.

2. In a medium bowl or 2-quart liquid measure, whisk together the egg yolks and sugar. Add the flour and salt and whisk until no lumps remain. To temper the yolks, pour about 1 cup of the chocolate milk mixture into the yolks, whisking constantly. Place the saucepan with the remaining chocolate milk over medium heat and bring to a boil, stirring constantly with a wooden spoon. Remove from the heat.

/continued

RECIPE SECRETS

The two sources of chocolate flavor here are semisweet block chocolate and crème de cacao liqueur. You could certainly substitute bittersweet or milk chocolate for the semisweet, if you prefer. Just don't use chocolate chips, as they're formulated to retain their shape when heated, not to be used as melting chocolate. If you prefer the boozier flavor of rum, substitute dark rum for the crème de cacao.

If you have a choice, buy clear, rather than dark, crème de cacao. The clear variety is more versatile for brushing on sponge cake layers or adding to a drink. Both are inexpensive and last forever. One tester used Godiva liqueur instead of crème de cacao in this recipe; although quite different, it produced excellent results.

This recipe generates a fair amount of leftover egg whites. They'll keep for several days in the refrigerator, or for a few months in the freezer. For best longevity, store in as small a container as possible, so there's minimal headroom. Use egg whites to prepare macaroons, meringues, and angel food cakes.

To bump up the chocolate flavor, don't forget a little salt and pure vanilla extract. Each has a unique way of amplifying the flavor of chocolate.

RECIPE SECRETS

To steady the bowl so you can whisk with one hand while pouring with the other, twist a kitchen towel into a coil and place it on the counter with the two ends crossed. Rest the mixing bowl inside the coil, adjusting the coil as necessary to keep the bowl steady. In addition, you may want to have a damp sponge ready to wipe the edges of your pot and bowl as you transfer one vessel of hot chocolate mixture to the other, then back to the stove.

To transfer the pudding to narrow-mouthed parfait or wineglasses, use a retractable ice-cream scoop held a few inches above the glass. Aim and let the pudding fall from the scoop into the glass as you retract the spring-loaded handle.

3. Slowly pour all of the boiling chocolate milk into the yolk mixture, whisking constantly. Slowly pour the yolk mixture back into the saucepan, place over medium-high heat, and heat just until the mixture boils, about 1 minute, as you whisk constantly. Reduce the heat to medium-low and boil gently, stirring constantly with a wooden spoon, as the mixture thickens to the consistency of mayonnaise, about 2 minutes. Immediately remove from the heat.

4. If the pudding seems at all lumpy, uneven in texture, or has any bits of scrambled egg, strain through a medium- or large-mesh strainer (not a fine-mesh strainer) into a deep bowl. Rotate the back of a ladle over the mesh to coax the pudding through. Don't press too hard when you get to the bottom, and stop if and when you see any solid particles in the bottom of the strainer. Be sure to scrape the underside of the strainer, capturing as much pudding as possible. You should have about 5 cups.

5. Whisk in the crème de cacao and vanilla extract. If desired, transfer the pudding to individual dishes or ramekins. Let cool to room temperature. Cover with plastic wrap and refrigerate until cold or for up to 3 days. Garnish with whipped cream, if using, just before serving.

WHY SWITCH FROM A WHISK TO A WOODEN SPOON?

When making a flour- or egg-based sauce or pudding, use a straight (preferably not balloon) whisk to combine the ingredients efficiently. Switch to a wooden spoon or heatproof rubber spatula during cooking. The spoon or spatula makes contact with more surface area on the bottom of the pan, which helps prevent scorching, and wood or rubber is more likely to glide over the surface of any lumps that cook onto the bottom of the pan. A metal utensil would catch the lumps and drag them into the mixture. If there is any scorching, it's best to let those parts cling to the bottom. Such lumps are also a clue that you may want to strain the mixture after it's cooked, and that you should not scrape the pan bottom clean when emptying it.

STRAWBERRY GRANITA PARFAITS

Imagine the refreshing flavors of sweet, icy strawberries layered with softly whipped cream. This tastes like strawberry shortcake in a parfait glass. I have my Italian colleague, Nelly Capra, to thank for introducing my students and me to her version of this at a cooking class. When I serve timpano (page 126) in the summertime, I always serve this for dessert. Simple, yet special, it is the perfect finish for any rich or complicated meal.

Serves 6

Granita

2 pounds fresh or partially thawed, frozen strawberries

¾ cup sugar, or as needed

2 tablespoons rose jam or good-quality strawberry jam

1 tablespoon freshly squeezed lemon juice

2 teaspoons Triple Sec or other orange-flavored liqueur

1 teaspoon pure vanilla extract, preferably Tahitian

Parfaits

1½ cups heavy (whipping) cream

1 tablespoon sugar

2 teaspoons pure vanilla extract, preferably Tahitian

6 rolled "cigarette" cookies, for serving

---

1. *Prepare the granita:* If using fresh berries, select 6 small, perfect strawberries and set them aside for garnish (don't wash them yet).

2. Hull (remove the stems and leaves) the remaining fresh strawberries. Process the hulled berries in a food processor until smooth. Scrape down the sides of the work bowl and add the ¾ cup sugar, jam, lemon juice, liqueur, and vanilla extract. Process until smooth. Taste and add more sugar, if necessary. The mixture should taste very sweet (some of the sweetness mellows when frozen).

/continued

RECIPE SECRETS

This is the simplest technique I know to make granita without the constant stirring. Be sure to prepare the granita 8 to 48 hours before serving to be sure it's frozen solid. See the "cater-wrap" tip (page 310) on how to prevent the strawberry mixture from spilling from a 9-by-13-inch baking dish as you place it in the freezer. Or, use a rectangular plastic container with a secure lid.

Freeze granita in a rectangular (or square) container for ease in scraping when frozen. As you scrape the frozen granita, it will begin to melt. Trust me, it's much easier to scrape across the top of a melting rectangular surface than a round one.

For frozen desserts, especially sorbet and granita, be sure the liquid mixture tastes very sweet, since freezing mitigates some of the sweet sensation. The combination of jam and sugar here creates a very sweet purée, with rose jam adding a distinctive note of complexity. Look for rose-flavored or rose petal jam in Middle Eastern markets, specialty-food shops, or among the jams and jellies in upscale grocery stores. Or substitute good-quality strawberry jam.

A shot of lemon juice and a couple of teaspoons of Triple Sec brighten the flavor of the strawberries here. You can substitute Grand Marnier or Orange Curaçao for the Triple Sec, but don't add more liqueur than the recipe calls for, as too much alcohol impedes freezing.

To prevent the contents from spilling all over the freezer when making granita in a 9-by-13-inch baking dish, unroll a piece of plastic wrap almost three times the size of the baking dish. Don't cut the plastic wrap; just place the box on the counter. Place the filled pan lengthwise in the center of the outstretched plastic wrap. Bring the cut end of the wrap up and over the top of the dish and press the wrap firmly onto the sides. Lift the other end of the wrap, with box attached, across the top of the dish until the wrap extends beyond the end of the dish. Cut the wrap and press to form a completely sealed package. This is how caterers wrap trays of sandwiches—and other small items, such as cookies—to prevent sliding around in transit.

ORGANIC STRAWBERRIES

Of all the fruits and vegetables tested, sprayed strawberries retain the most pesticides and herbicides after harvest. If you don't usually purchase organic fruit, you may want to rethink this when it comes to strawberries.

3. Transfer the mixture to a 6-cup or larger rectangular or square plastic container with a lid or a 9-by-13-inch baking dish (porcelain and clay retain cold best). Cover securely with a lid or "cater-wrap" with plastic wrap (see right) and freeze until solid, at least 8 hours or overnight. Alternatively, freeze the granita in an ice-cream maker: Chill the puréed strawberry mixture in an ice-water bath (bowl filled with water and ice cubes) until it reaches 40 degrees F, about 45 minutes, then process in an ice-cream maker according to the manufacturer's directions. Transfer from the ice-cream maker to a prechilled 9-by-13-inch baking dish, spread evenly to compact the granita, and store in the freezer until the mixture is very firm and solid, about 2 hours.

4. *Prepare the whipped cream:* In a bowl, using an electric mixer, whip together the cream, sugar, and vanilla extract until soft peaks form. In the Italian tradition, this cream—called *panna*—shouldn't be too sweet. Cover and refrigerate until serving.

5. *Assemble the parfaits:* If the granita has been frozen for 8 or more hours, transfer to the refrigerator for 20 minutes before assembling the parfaits. If necessary, whisk the cream to restore any volume that may have been lost while resting. Place the container of granita on a damp kitchen towel on a flat surface. Use a retractable metal ice-cream scoop or large, heavy spoon to scrape across the surface of the granita to create shaved ice. Beginning and ending with a small scoop of whipped cream, alternately layer scoops of granita and whipped cream into parfait glasses or tall water goblets. Garnish with a reserved fresh strawberry and a cookie. Serve the parfaits at once, with long iced-tea spoons, if available.

ORANGE-MINT SORBET IN ORANGE SHELLS

This refreshing sorbet, inspired by a recipe in Anna Del Conte's out-of-print *Gastronomy of Italy*, is a perfect make-ahead dessert to serve after a rich meal. I was first introduced to this recipe by Mary Cramer, who worked at Linda Carucci's Kitchen as my assistant when I first started out. In winter, when citrus is in season, serve the sorbet in hollowed-out orange shells. You can fill the shells up to a week ahead and freeze them until serving time. Or, use this vibrant sorbet for an intermezzo. One year for our company Christmas party, I served small scoops of the sorbet in demitasse cups, a perfect palate cleanser between paella (page 158) and a cheese course. There was almost no sound as the guests devoured the sorbet. My typically talkative assistant, Meghan Wallingford, shot me a look as if I'd been holding out on her, keeping this recipe a big secret. I don't know what made her happier, second servings on sorbet or telling her that the recipe would appear in this book. For a quintessential flavor combination, serve the dessert sorbet with Dark Chocolate–Pistachio Wafers (page 313).

Serves 4

1¾ cups water

1¼ cups sugar

Zest of 1 orange, removed in long strips or with a Microplane

Zest of 1 lemon, removed in long strips or with a Microplane

1 bunch fresh mint, about 1 ounce, stems and leaves coarsely chopped, plus 1 sprig reserved for garnish

⅔ cup freshly squeezed orange juice

⅓ cup freshly squeezed lemon juice

· ·

4 frozen hollowed-out citrus shells (see page 312), for serving (optional)

Thin strips of orange zest, for garnish (optional)

---

1. In a 4-quart saucepan, combine the water and sugar and bring to a boil over high heat, stirring to dissolve the sugar. Reduce the heat to low and simmer gently, uncovered, for 5 minutes. Remove from the heat and add the orange zest, lemon zest, and chopped mint. Stir, cover, and set aside to steep for 1 hour.

2. Strain through a chinois or fine-mesh strainer into a nonreactive 4-cup container with a lid. Stir in the orange and lemon juices. Refrigerate the mixture for 4 hours or up to 8 hours.

/continued

RECIPE SECRETS

If you have a choice of several types, ask the produce manager which oranges are the sweetest for juicing.

· ·

Remove any inked-on grower stamps *before* washing citrus fruits. Rub the dry fruit with a dry kitchen towel until the ink is gone.

· ·

For the best texture and quickest freezing when making ice cream or sorbet in an electric or manual ice-cream maker, use an instant-read thermometer to be sure the liquid is no warmer than 40 degrees F when you add it to the machine. If possible, refrigerate the mixture for at least 4 hours before freezing. If time is short, place the mixture in an ice-water bath (bowl filled with water and ice cubes) and stir constantly until the temperature of the sorbet mixture drops to 40 degrees F.

· ·

Here's how to restore the fluffy, snowy texture to leftover, rock-hard sorbet: Transfer the container with the sorbet to the refrigerator for 10 minutes, then use an oyster knife or blunt table knife to break into roughly 2-inch chunks. Pulverize in a food processor until you achieve a fluffy, soft mass.

3. Freeze the chilled sorbet mixture in an ice-cream maker according to the manufacturer's directions. You should have about 3¼ cups sorbet. Transfer to a container with a tight-fitting lid or pack into citrus shells, if using. Freeze until ready to serve. (The texture of the sorbet is optimal if it is served within about 6 hours.) Garnish each serving with a mint leaf (from the reserved sprig) and a tangle of orange zest, if desired.

HOW TO CARVE OUT ORANGE SHELLS FOR SERVING SORBET

Wash and dry 4 or 5 perfect, small oranges, clementines, or tangerines. Use a dry kitchen towel to scrub off any ink marks. Cut a slice off the top of each fruit, creating an opening just large enough to insert a spoon for removing the inside pulp. Reserve the tops. If necessary, cut a small slice off the bottom of each fruit, so it will stand without rolling. Use a grapefruit knife or spoon to remove as much inside pulp as possible, keeping the skins intact. (Squeeze the removed pulp for juice to use in the sorbet recipe or for another purpose.) Line a plate or rimmed baking sheet with waxed paper. Place the hollowed-out shells and tops on it. Freeze until firm, at least 1 hour. Fill with the sorbet mixture as it comes out of the ice-cream maker, mounding it just over the tops. Place the tops on, slightly askew. Freeze until ready to serve, or for up to 1 week. Transfer to the refrigerator for about 20 minutes before serving to allow the sorbet to soften a bit. Serve on doily-lined saucers and garnish with a mint leaf or two.

THE DOILY LECTURE

Before the parents arrived for a kids' cooking camp final celebration one summer, my coteacher, Suzy Farnworth, and I were unexpectedly faced with ten extra minutes and a room full of pumped-up eight- to ten-year-olds. Realizing the danger inherent in idle time, I did what our chefs did in cooking school before all the guests arrived for each Friday's grand classical buffet. Looking out at the beautiful buffet the kids had just assembled, I began to praise them for their work. Feeling pressure to fill the time, I let myself get a little sidetracked. We had given the kids doilies to gussy up the large disposable catering platters they dutifully filled with hand-decorated cookies, cupcakes, and chocolate-dipped fruits. My mind jumped to a protocol I learned from my favorite baking and pastry chef-instructor, Robert Jorin, and I spontaneously launched into a ten-minute discourse on the proper use of, well, paper doilies. Suzy stood back, stunned, and let me go. For some strange reason, the class was mesmerized. I never knew I had such passion for the arcane, but the words just jumped out of my mouth. Here's the gist of what I told those spellbound children.

- **Do** use a small doily between a small plate and a ramekin of custard or crème brulée, or underneath any individual casserole that's served in the dish in which it was baked. Often these ramekins are unglazed on the bottom, and the doily protects the plate.

- **Do** use a doily under sticky or wet "natural" receptacles, such as orange shells for sorbet, or avocado shells for shrimp salad. The doily helps prevent these receptacles from sliding around.

- **Do** use doilies to line a platter of individual cookies and candies, both to set off the items on a uniform white background, and to prevent having to wash the platter if you're refilling it for a buffet. (If the candies or confections are sticky or if they tend to ooze, first place each in a crinkle-edged paper, similar to a small cupcake liner.)

- **Don't** use a doily directly under a cake or other moist food you'll be eating. The doily will stick to the food. To protect a cake platter, use a cake cardboard. (If you want to gussy up the cake platter, place the doily underneath the cake cardboard.)

DARK CHOCOLATE–PISTACHIO WAFERS

I'm grateful to my friend and colleague David McKey for sharing this recipe from his grandmother's repertoire. I've been making these thin, crisp refrigerator cookies for years. They're a big hit in cooking classes, especially when served with Orange-Mint Sorbet (page 311). For wafer cookies, shape the dough into a log and chill until firm, then roll in chopped pistachios, slice, and bake. If time is short, instead of making a log and chilling the dough, just stir in the nuts and bake these as drop cookies.

Makes 3 to 4 dozen, depending on size

2 ounces unsweetened chocolate	1 cup sugar
¾ cup all-purpose flour	1 large egg
½ teaspoon baking powder	1 teaspoon pure vanilla extract
¼ teaspoon fine sea salt	¾ cup pistachio nuts, chopped medium-fine
½ cup (1 stick) unsalted butter, at room temperature	

1. Place the chocolate in a microwave-safe bowl and melt in the microwave on medium for 2 to 4 minutes, stopping at 1-minute intervals to stir. Stop microwaving when you can stir the chocolate into a smooth mass. Alternatively, melt the chocolate in a double boiler over barely simmering water. Set aside.

2. In a bowl, stir together the flour, baking powder, and salt. Set aside.

3. In a stand mixer with the paddle attachment (or in a bowl with a handheld mixer), beat the butter and sugar together on low speed just until combined, about 1 minute. Add the egg and vanilla and mix on low until the egg is absorbed. Add the melted chocolate and mix on low speed just until blended. Add the dry ingredients and mix on low just to combine.

/continued

RECIPE SECRETS

Butter is the secret to making crisp cookies. I know it's popular, but I find that standard Plugra brand butter makes these cookies too greasy. I prefer to use European-style butter.

For the best texture, don't whip too much air into the dough when mixing, and shape it into a tight cylinder before chilling. Otherwise, the cookies will still be good, but they'll be lacy instead of firm, crisp wafers.

Be sure to use unsalted, unroasted shelled pistachio nuts. Chop them fine enough to adhere to the dough log when you slice it into thin wafers, but large enough to add color and texture.

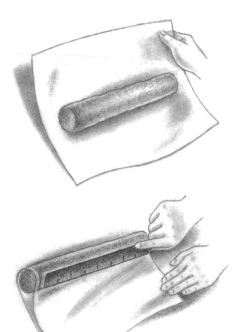

Cylinder of cookie dough inside a sheet of waxed paper, with a ruler coaxing it into a tight log

4. Transfer the dough to a 20-inch length of waxed paper and spread lengthwise into a roughly 12-inch log. Fold the paper lengthwise over the log and use a bench scraper, a nonrimmed edge of a cookie sheet, or other straight edge (I use a 16-inch ruler or a yardstick) to coax the dough into a tight cylinder about 16 inches long (see illustration). Compact the ends by pressing up against the waxed paper with the straight edge. Refrigerate until firm, at least 2 hours.

5. If the dough has been refrigerated for longer than 3 hours, bring to room temperature 15 minutes before proceeding. Position a rack in the middle of the oven and a second rack in the lower third and preheat to 325 degrees F (300 degrees F on the convection setting). Line 2 baking sheets with parchment paper or silicone baking liners. Set aside.

6. Place the pistachios in a 16-inch-long strip down the center of a cutting board. Unwrap the dough and roll the log in the nuts, pressing as necessary to coat the entire surface (not ends) evenly. Use a perforated cheese knife (see page 184) or a sharp knife with a very thin blade to cut the dough into slices. To keep the cookies round, roll the log a quarter turn after you slice off each cookie. Transfer the slices to the prepared baking sheets, placing them about 2 inches apart (the cookies will spread). If necessary, reshape them in to rounds as you transfer them. (Depending on the diameter of your cookies, you may need a third baking sheet.)

7. Place the pans in the oven and bake until the nuts just begin to turn golden brown, 12 to 15 minutes; bake for less time if using the convection setting, or longer for the conventional setting. Rotate the pans from front to back and switch them between the racks halfway through baking. Let the cookies cool on the pans on cooling racks for 2 minutes, then transfer them to the racks and let cool completely. Store in an airtight container with waxed paper between each layer for up to 1 week.

SEASONAL RECIPES, MENUS, AND SOURCES

PART THREE

SEASONAL RECIPES

You can prepare most recipes in this book with ingredients that are available year-round. Other recipes, listed below, are best when made "in season" with fresh fruits, vegetables, seafoods, and meats. Not discounting the benefits to farmers, anglers, and our environment, when you cook with the seasons, you'll be rewarded with vibrant flavors, ideal textures, more nutrients, and, often, a lower grocery bill. On top of that, you don't have to tinker much to make these raw ingredients sing. Typically, simple preparations bring out the best in seasonal foods.

Certainly, there is some variation across the United States as to when, or whether, certain seafoods come to market. Keep in mind that weather patterns and geographical locations affect the availability of all fresh foodstuffs. The suggestions here are guidelines for when to feature these ingredients. Generally, availability can vary as much as a month on either end of any season.

When you notice the same recipe listed here in more than one season, such as a salad with fresh figs, it's because figs have two crops. Also, since wild salmon spans more than a single season, you'll find salmon recipes listed in both spring and summer. Given our ever-increasing access to "fresh" foodstuffs from around the globe, you could prepare a perfectly respectable salad with fresh or dried figs any time of year. And certainly, wild salmon is always available frozen.

SPRING (APRIL, MAY, JUNE)

Figs and Arugula with Creamy Goat Cheese and Toasted Pecans — 90

Risotto Primavera with Wild Salmon — 102

Alaskan Halibut with Roasted Red Pepper Coulis — 148

Steamed Salmon and Creamer Potatoes with Sauce Verte — 150

Poached Salmon with Shortcut Hollandaise Sauce — 152

Honey-Mustard Glazed Ham with Grilled Pineapple Salsa — 220

Grilled Leg of Lamb with Pomegranate Marinade and Muhammara — 221

Rack of Lamb with Garlicky Bread Crumbs — 224

Braised Short Ribs with Frizzled Leeks — 237

Grilled Asparagus — 250

Fresh Fava Beans with Pecorino and Meyer Lemon Oil — 252

Zabaglione with Fresh Berries and Peaches — 305

Strawberry Granita Parfaits — 309

SUMMER (JULY, AUGUST, SEPTEMBER)

Red Bell Pepper Bisque with Crème Fraîche 66

White Corn Chowder 68

Tomato-Cheddar Soup 72

Heirloom Tomatoes with Bocconcini, Basil, and 86
White Balsamic Vinaigrette

Figs and Arugula with Creamy Goat Cheese and 90
Toasted Pecans

Baby Greens, Roasted Chicken, Stilton, and 91
Hazelnuts with Raspberry Vinaigrette

Risotto Primavera with Wild Salmon 102

Linguine Aglio e Olio 109

Braised Calamari in Red Sauce 144

Sautéed Fillet of Sole with Tartar Sauce 145

Alaskan Halibut with Roasted Red Pepper Coulis 148

Steamed Salmon and Creamer Potatoes with 150
Sauce Verte

Poached Salmon with Shortcut Hollandaise Sauce 152

Broiled Swordfish with Mango Salsa 155

Chicken Salad Véronique with Whole 168
Toasted Almonds

Thai-Style Minced Chicken with Basil and Chiles 170

Baked Portabello Mushrooms Stuffed with Turkey, 172
Eggplant, and Fresh Bread Crumbs

Grilled Stuffed Chicken Breasts with Prosciutto, 183
Taleggio, and Pesto

Italian Sausage Contadina with Roasted Sweet 215
Peppers, Potatoes, and Onions

Osso Buco with Sweet Red Peppers and Gremolata 234

Roasted Peppers 254

Savory Corn Pudding 256

Romano Beans 258

Eggplant Parmigiana 259

Braised Summer Squash with Sweet Peppers, 262
Tomatoes, and Basil

Roasted New Potatoes 271

Roasted Garlic Mashed Potatoes with Chives 281

Classic American Potato Salad 282

Orzo with Toybox Tomatoes and Fresh Mint 283

Grilled Peach Ice Cream Sundaes with Shortcut 289
Caramel Sauce

Zucchini–Olive Oil Snack Cake with Lemon Icing 303

Zabaglione with Fresh Berries and Peaches 305

Strawberry Granita Parfaits 309

FALL (OCTOBER, NOVEMBER, DECEMBER)

Red Bell Pepper Bisque with Crème Fraîche 66

French Onion Soup Gratinée 73

Shaved Celery with Medjool Dates, Feta, and Walnuts 88

Baby Greens, Roasted Chicken, Stilton, and Hazelnuts with Raspberry Vinaigrette 91

Butternut Squash Risotto with Parmigiano-Reggiano Rinds and Balsamic Drizzle 99

California Crab Gumbo with Chicken and Sausage 138

Cracker-Crusted Nubble Point Scallops 142

Paella with Shellfish, Sausage, and Chicken 158

Chicken Salad Véronique with Whole Toasted Almonds 168

Maple-Glazed Quail Stuffed with Wild Mushrooms, Sausage, and Sour Cherries 194

Italian Sausage Contadina with Roasted Sweet Peppers, Potatoes, and Onions 215

Vanilla-Scented Applesauce 217

Roasted Peppers 254

Butternut Squash with Maple Syrup and Allspice 273

Apple Crisp with Brandy and Sp'Ice Cream 291

WINTER (JANUARY, FEBRUARY, MARCH)

Three-Bean Minestrone with Sausage 75

Butter Lettuce with Ruby Grapefruit, Avocado, and Glazed Walnuts 82

Butternut Squash Risotto with Parmigiano-Reggiano Rinds and Balsamic Drizzle 99

California Crab Gumbo with Chicken and Sausage 138

Braised Calamari in Red Sauce 144

Paella with Shellfish, Sausage, and Chicken 158

Turkey Piccata 177

Herb-Crusted Chicken Potpies 198

Pork Loin Roast with Vanilla-Scented Applesauce 217

Slow-Roasted Beef Sirloin Tip with Pan Gravy or Creamy Horseradish Sauce 232

Braised Short Ribs with Frizzled Leeks 237

Pot Roast and Gravy with Peas and Carrots 241

Escarole with Garlic and Red Pepper Flakes 263

Braised Greens with Sausage and Onions 266

"Roasted" Beets with Whole-Grain Mustard Sauce 268

Roasted Root Vegetables 269

Butternut Squash with Maple Syrup and Allspice 273

Lemon Marzipan Cake 301

Orange-Mint Sorbet in Orange Shells 311

TWELVE SEASONAL MENUS FOR CASUAL AND SPECIAL OCCASIONS

Whether you're cooking for company or preparing a week-end family meal, here are some suggestions for how to combine the recipes in this book into complete menus. Use the Seasonal Recipes (pages 316–18) to make seasonal substitutions to suit your personal preferences. For more options, check the list of recipes by category at the beginning of each chapter. Each chapter recipe list has the Quick and Make-Ahead timing designations you see here.

While seasons are finite for when certain fish are allowed to be caught, they are much looser when it comes to fruits and vegetables. Geographical location and climate variations affect the availability of certain produce, especially at the beginning and end of their growing seasons. Take this into consideration and try to plan your menu with enough flexibility to incorporate early harbingers of the next season, as well as any vestiges from last season's bumper crops.

Please note that each recipe yields a particular number of servings, and that the yields vary from recipe to recipe. So, if you're making one recipe of gumbo (page 138), which serves 8 to 10 people, you'll have to double or triple the sorbet (page 311) recipe in order to serve the same number of people.

"PEOPLE MAY NOT REMEMBER WHAT YOU SERVED THEM, OR WHICH CHINA YOU SERVED IT ON, BUT THEY WILL ALWAYS REMEMBER HOW YOU MADE THEM FEEL AT YOUR TABLE."

—UNKNOWN

SPRING SPECIAL-OCCASION MENU (SUITABLE FOR MOTHER'S DAY)

	Q	Q2	MA	LM	Page
Poached Salmon with Shortcut Hollandaise Sauce				●	152
Wild Rice Pilaf			●		276
Fresh Fava Beans with Pecorino and Meyer Lemon Olive Oil				●	252
Figs and Arugula Salad with Creamy Goat Cheese and Toasted Pecans			●		90
Lemon Marzipan Cake				●	301

For a vegetarian menu, substitute My Grandmother's Baked Stuffed Manicotti (page 120) and 20-Minute Tomato Sauce (page 114) for Salmon with Hollandaise and Wild Rice; omit goat cheese from the salad.

SPRING CASUAL MENU

	Q	Q2	MA	LM	Page
Risotto Primavera with Wild Salmon				●	102
Weeknight Green Salad			●		81
Strawberry Granita Parfaits				●	309

For a vegetarian menu, omit the salmon and add 1 cup shelled edamame to the risotto.

Q = Quick—prep to table in 45 minutes.
Q2 = Prep time 30 minutes or less; may be prepared completely ahead with minimal last-minute attention required (tossing salad, reheating, and so on).
MA = Make ahead—part or all of the recipe can or must be made ahead.
LM = Last minute—advance prep plus *à la minute* cooking required.

SPRING SPECIAL OCCASION MENU (SUITABLE FOR FATHER'S DAY)

	Q	Q2	MA	LM	Page
French Onion Soup Gratinée				●	73
Rack of Lamb with Garlicky Bread Crumbs or			●	●	224
Grilled Leg of Lamb with Pomegranate Marinade and Muhammara			●	●	221
Roasted Root Vegetables	●				269
Grilled Asparagus				●	250
White Chocolate Cheesecake with Oreo Crust and Raspberry Coulis				●	295

For a vegetarian menu, use Vegetable Broth (page 63) in the soup; substitute Baked Portabello Mushrooms (page 172) made without turkey for the lamb and root vegetables.

SUMMER CASUAL MENU (CHOOSE 4 OR MORE)

	Q	Q2	MA	LM	Page
Grilled Marinated Flank Steak au Jus				●	230
Sautéed Mushrooms with Sherry and Garlic				●	271
Classic American Potato Salad			●		282
Heirloom Tomato Salad with Bocconcini, Basil, and White Balsamic Vinaigrette			●		86
Roasted Peppers			●		254
Grilled Peach Ice Cream Sundaes with Shortcut Caramel Sauce			●		289

For a vegetarian menu, substitute pasta with pesto or Linguine Aglio e Olio (page 109) for the steak, mushrooms, and potato salad.

SUMMER SPECIAL-OCCASION MENU

	Q	Q2	MA	LM	Page
White Corn Chowder			●		68
Grilled Stuffed Chicken Breasts with Prosciutto, Taleggio, and Pesto				●	183
Orzo with Toybox Tomatoes and Fresh Mint			●		283
Romano Beans			●		258
Zabaglione with Fresh Berries and Peaches				●	305

For a vegetarian menu, substitute Red Bell Pepper Bisque (page 66) made with Vegetable Broth (page 63) for the chowder; substitute Baked Macaroni with White Cheddar (page 110) for the chicken; omit the orzo.

SUMMER CASUAL MENU (CHOOSE 3 OR MORE)

	Q	Q2	MA	LM	Page
Alaskan Halibut with Roasted Red Pepper Coulis				●	148
Orzo with Toybox Tomatoes and Fresh Mint			●		283
Braised Summer Squash with Sweet Peppers, Tomatoes, and Basil			●		262
Figs and Arugula Salad with Creamy Goat Cheese and Toasted Pecans			●		90
Zucchini–Olive Oil Snack Cake with Lemon Icing			●		303

For a vegetarian menu, substitute Tomato-Cheddar Soup (page 72) made with Vegetable Broth (page 63) for the halibut.

Q = Quick—prep to table in 45 minutes.
Q2 = Prep time 30 minutes or less; may be prepared completely ahead with minimal last-minute attention required (tossing salad, reheating, and so on).
MA = Make ahead—part or all of the recipe can or must be made ahead.
LM = Last minute—advance prep plus *à la minute* cooking required.

FALL SPECIAL-OCCASION MENU (SUITABLE FOR THANKSGIVING)

	Q	Q2	MA	LM	Page
Shaved Celery with Medjool Dates, Feta, and Walnuts (as a first course, served in Belgian endive spears)			•		88
Roasted Stuffed Turkey with Pan Gravy			•		188
Butternut Squash with Maple Syrup and Allspice		•			273
Roasted Garlic Mashed Potatoes with Chives			•		281
Garlic Spinach with Currants, Pine Nuts, and Pecorino	•				265
Potluck Pies (have guests bring their favorite desserts)					N/A

For a vegetarian menu, substitute Butternut Squash Risotto (page 99) made with Vegetable Broth (page 63) for the turkey, butternut squash, and mashed potatoes.

FALL CASUAL MENU (CHOOSE 3 OR MORE)

	Q	Q2	MA	LM	Page
French Onion Soup Gratinée			•		73
Italian Sausage Contadina with Roasted Sweet Peppers, Potatoes, and Onions				•	215
Weeknight Green Salad		•			81
Apple Crisp with Brandy and Sp'Ice Cream			•		291

For a vegetarian menu, omit the soup; substitute Fettuccine Alfredo made without shrimp (page 113) for the Sausage Contadina.

FALL SPECIAL-OCCASION MENU (SUITABLE FOR CHRISTMAS)

	Q	Q2	MA	LM	Page
Red Bell Pepper Bisque with Crème Fraîche			•		66
Pork Loin Roast with Vanilla-Scented Applesauce			•		217
Roasted Root Vegetables	•				269
Escarole with Garlic and Red Pepper Flakes		•			263
White Chocolate Cheesecake with Oreo Crust and Raspberry Coulis			•		295

For a vegetarian menu, make the bisque with Vegetable Broth (page 63); substitute My Grandmother's Baked Stuffed Manicotti with 20-Minute Tomato Sauce (page 114) for the roast pork, applesauce, and root vegetables; substitute Lemon Marzipan Cake (page 301) for the cheesecake.

WINTER CASUAL MENU

	Q	Q2	MA	LM	Page
Butter Lettuce Salad with Ruby Grapefruit, Avocado, and Glazed Walnuts			•		82
California Crab Gumbo with Chicken and Sausage			•		138
Lemon Marzipan Cake			•		301

For a vegetarian menu, substitute French Onion Soup Gratinée (page 73) made with Vegetable Broth (page 63) for the gumbo.

Q = Quick—prep to table in 45 minutes.
Q2 = Prep time 30 minutes or less; may be prepared completely ahead with minimal last-minute attention required (tossing salad, reheating, and so on).
MA = Make ahead—part or all of the recipe can or must be made ahead.
LM = Last minute—advance prep plus *à la minute* cooking required.

WINTER SPECIAL-OCCASION MENU (SUITABLE FOR NEW YEAR'S EVE)

	Q	Q2	MA	LM	Page
Baby Greens, Roasted Chicken, Stilton, and Hazelnuts with Raspberry Vinaigrette			•		91
Osso Buco with Sweet Red Peppers and Gremolata			•		234
Risotto Milanese				•	98
Escarole with Garlic and Red Pepper Flakes			•		263
Orange-Mint Sorbet in Orange Shells				•	311

For a vegetarian menu, omit the chicken from the salad, substitute Butternut Squash Risotto (page 99) made with Vegetable Broth (page 63) for the Osso Buco and Risotto Milanese.

WINTER CASUAL MENU

	Q	Q2	MA	LM	Page
Braised Short Ribs with Frizzled Leeks or			•		237
Pot Roast and Gravy with Peas and Carrots			•		241
Horseradish Mashed Potatoes with Chives or			•		281
Creamy, Soft Polenta		•			274
"Roasted" Beets with Whole-Grain Mustard Sauce			•		268
Weeknight Green Salad		•			81
Bittersweet Chocolate Bread Pudding with Kahlúa Sauce			•		293

For a vegetarian menu, substitute Eggplant Parmigiana and Creamy, Soft Polenta made with Vegetable Broth (page 63) for the short ribs or pot roast and mashed potatoes.

SOURCES

Cookware & More
www.cookwarenmore.com
All-Clad seconds, Microplane graters, Scanpan seconds

EthnicGrocer.com
www.ethnicgrocer.com
Pomegranate molasses, porcini mushrooms, Aleppo peppers, white balsamic vinegar, *pimentón* (smoked paprika), Asian fish sauce, black soy sauce, ancho and guajillo chile peppers, rice vermicelli, cellophane noodles

Lotus Foods
www.lotusfoods.com
Kalijira rice, white and brown organic jasmine rice, Carnaroli rice from Argentina

Niman Ranch
www.NimanRanch.com
Natural, hormone- and antibiotic-free crown roast of pork, pork rib roasts

Shaw Guides
www.shawguides.com
The Guide to Cooking Schools
International listings of vocational and avocational cooking schools

The Spanish Table
Seattle, Berkeley, and Santa Fe
www.tablespan.com
Paelleras, pimentòn, piquillo peppers, saffron, Spanish condiments

Surfa's Chef's Paradise
www.surfasonline.com
Porcini mushrooms, stir-fry pans, Callebaut white chocolate, imported bay leaves, Madagascar Bourbon and Tahitian pure vanilla extract, Asian ingredients, dried cherries

Trader Joe's
Various locations across the U.S.
www.traderjoes.com (to find locations) or 1-800-SHOP-TJS
Non-irradiated granulated garlic powder, unsalted pistachios, dried cherries, braising greens, pure heavy (whipping) cream, long fusilli pasta, Arborio rice

Trudeau Corporation
www.trudeaucorp.com (to find retailer locations)
(888) 887-8332
Plastic cutting boards with gripper corners

Whole Foods Markets
Various locations across the U.S.
www.wholefoods.com
Organic granulated garlic powder, bulk spices, ghee, imported bay leaves, Diamond Crystal kosher salt, pure heavy (whipping) cream

BIBLIOGRAPHY

Aidells, Bruce, and Denis Kelly. *The Complete Meat Cookbook.* New York: Houghton Mifflin, 1998.

Barrett, Diane M. *Journal of Agriculture and Food Chemistry.* Bauman College Journal, February 26, 2003.

Bayless, Rick, with Deann Groen Bayless and Jean Marie Brownson. *Rick Bayless's Mexican Kitchen.* New York: Scribner, 1996.

Beard, James. *Theory & Practice of Good Cooking.* Philadelphia: Running Press, 1977.

Bloom, Carole. *The International Dictionary of Desserts, Pastries, and Confections.* New York: Hearst Books, 1995.

Bown, Deni. *The Herb Society of America Encyclopedia of Herbs & Their Uses.* New York: Dorling Kindersley, 1995.

Braker, Flo. *The Simple Art of Perfect Baking.* Shelburne, Vermont: Chapters, 1992.

Brenner, Barbara. "FAQ of the Month." *BCA e-newsletter.* San Francisco: Breast Cancer Action, November 2003.

Cook, Sandra, Sara Slavin, and Deborah Jones. *Salt & Pepper.* San Francisco: Chronicle Books, 2003.

Corriher, Shirley. *CookWise.* New York: William Morrow, 1997.

Davidson, Alan, and Charlotte Knox. *Fruit: A Connoisseur's Guide and Cookbook.* New York: Simon and Schuster, 1991.

Del Conte, Anna. *Gastronomy of Italy.* New York: Prentice Hall Press, 1987.

Evans, Matthew, and Gabriella Cossi. *World Food: Italy.* Victoria, Australia: Lonely Planet Publications, 2000.

Farrell-Kingsley, Kathy. *The Complete Vegetarian Handbook.* San Francisco: Chronicle Books, 2003.

Fletcher, Janet. *Fresh from the Farmers' Market.* San Francisco: Chronicle Books, 1997.

————"Sweet, Sour, Bitter, Salty—and Umami," *San Francisco Chronicle,* July 5, 2000.

Gage, Fran. *A Sweet Quartet.* New York: North Point Press, 2002.

Germain, Elizabeth. "Tuscan-Style Roast Pork Loin." *Cook's Illustrated,* September/October 2002, 10–12.

Grausman, Richard. *At Home with the French Classics.* New York: Workman, 1988.

Grigson, Jane. *Jane Grisgon's Vegetable Book.* London: Penguin Books, 1978.

Harlow, Jay. *West Coast Seafood.* Seattle: Sasquatch Books, 1999.

Herbst, Sharon Tyler. *The New Food Lover's Companion,* 3rd edition. New York: Barron's, 2001.

————*The New Food Lover's Tiptionary.* New York: William Morrow, 2002.

Hom, Ken, and Harvey Steiman. *Chinese Technique.* New York: Simon and Schuster, 1981.

Kasper, Lynne Rosetto. *The Italian Country Table.* New York: Scribner, 1999.

Kimball, Christopher. "Does Low-Salt Brining Work?" *Cook's Illustrated E-Notes,* April 2004.

Knickerbocker, Peggy. *Olive Oil from Tree to Table.* San Francisco: Chronicle Books, 1997.

Loha-unchit, Kasma. *It Rains Fishes.* San Francisco: Pomegranate Art Books, 1994.

Madison, Deborah. *Vegetarian Cooking for Everyone.* New York: Broadway Books, 1997.

Maii, Robynne L. "Label Watch," *Gourmet,* January 2003.

Malgieri, Nick. *Chocolate.* New York: HarperCollins, 1998.

Martin, Damiano, with Dana Bowen. *The da Fiore Cookbook.* New York: William Morrow, 2003.

McCullough, Fran. *The Good Fat Cookbook.* New York: Scribner, 2003.

Parvis, Sarah E. *The Quotable Feast.* Kansas City: Stonesong Press, 2001.

Peterson, James. *Fish & Shellfish.* New York: William Morrow, 1996.

Pham, Mai. *Pleasures of the Vietnamese Table.* New York: HarperCollins, 2001.

Piccolo, Jack. *Timing is Everything.* New York: Three Rivers Press, 2000.

Reinhart, Peter. *The Bread Baker's Apprentice.* Berkeley: Ten Speed Press, 2001.

Rodgers, Judy. *The Zuni Café Cookbook.* New York: Norton, 2002.

Schneider, Elizabeth. *Vegetables from Amaranth to Zucchini.* New York: William Morrow, 2001.

Severson, Kim. *The Trans Fat Solution.* Berkeley: Ten Speed Press, 2003.

Simmons, Marie. *The Amazing World of Rice.* New York: William Morrow, 2003.

Tropp, Barbara. *China Moon Cookbook.* New York: Workman, 1992.

————"Consider a Stir-Fry Pan Instead of a Wok." *Fine Cooking,* September 2001, 71-73.

Ubaldi, Jack, and Elizabeth Crossman. *Jack Ubaldi's Meat Book.* New York: Macmillan, 1987.

Wolke, Robert L. "Umami Dearest." *Washington Post,* September 4, 2002.

————*What Einstein Told His Cook.* New York: Norton, 2002.

Yan, Martin. *A Simple Guide to Chinese Ingredients and Other Asian Specialties.* Foster City, CA: Yan Can Cook, no date.

INDEX

A

Acid
  aluminum foil and, 108
  caramelizing onions and, 73
  flavor and, 38
  in marinades for meat, 208, 230
  nonreactive cookware for dishes
      containing, 108
  sautéing onions and, 72
  in tomatoes, baking soda to neutralize,
      72
Aidells, Bruce, 44
à la meunière style, 147
à la milanaise style, 146
à la minute sauces, sauté pans for
  preparing, 178
à l'anglaise style, 146, 147
à la parisienne style, 147
Alaskan Halibut with Roasted Red Pepper
  Coulis, 148–149
Albacore, 155
  substitution in Broiled Swordfish with
      Mango Salsa, 155–157
Alcohol. *See also specific alcoholic
      beverages*
  flavor and, 38
  hazard in broiling, 25
  in risotto, 95
al dente, 107, 110
Aleppo pepper
  Grilled Leg of Lamb with Pomegranate
      Marinade and Muhammara,
      221–223
Alkalized cocoa powder, 298
All-Clad pans
  saucepans, 15
  saucier pans, 96
  sauté pans, 16

Almond paste
  about, 301
  Lemon Marzipan Cake, 301–302
Almonds
  blanching, 169
  Chicken Salad Véronique with Whole
      Toasted Almonds, 168–169
  Grilled Skewered Shrimp with
      Romesco Sauce, 136–138
Al's Steamed White Rice, 279
Aluminum foil
  acid and, 108
  "tenting" poultry with, 165–166
Amaretti di Saronno cookies, 290
Ancho chiles, 204
Anglaise, à l' style, 146, 147
Annie's Naturals Organic Honey
  Mustard, 220
Antibiotics
  in farm-raised fish, 104
  poultry types and, 162
Apples
  Apple Crisp with Brandy and Sp'Ice
      Cream, 291–292
  choosing, 291
  color of applesauce, 217
  Pork Loin Roast with Vanilla-Scented
      Applesauce, 217–219
  varieties of, 291
Apricot brandy
  Zucchini-Olive Oil Snack Cake with
      Lemon Icing, 303–304
Arborio rice, 95
Arugula
  Figs and Arugula with Creamy Goat
      Cheese and Toasted Pecans, 90
  Rib-Eye Steaks with Arugula, Blue
      Cheese, and Grilled Red
      Onions, 228–229

Asiago cheese
  substitution in Garlic Spinach with
      Currants, Pine Nuts, and Pecorino, 265
Asian fish sauce, 71
  substitute for, 71
Asparagus
  blanching, 251
  caramelizing, 251
  choosing, 250
  Grilled Asparagus, 250–251
  keeping green, 102, 251
  peeling, 250
  Risotto Primavera with Wild Salmon,
      102–104
  Stir-Fried Velvet Chicken with
      Cashews, 174–175
Au jus, 230
Austin, Kay, 268
Autumn menus, 323–324
Autumn recipes, 318
Avocados
  Butter Lettuce with Ruby Grapefruit,
      Avocado, and Glazed Walnuts,
      82–84
  dicing, 85
  preventing browning of flesh of, 85

B

Baby basmati rice
  Kalijira Rice Pilaw, 277–278
Baby Greens, Roasted Chicken, Stilton,
      and Hazelnuts with Raspberry
      Vinaigrette, 91–92
Baileys Irish Cream
  substitution in Bittersweet Chocolate
      Bread Pudding with Kahlúa
      Sauce, 293
Bain-marie, 27, 296

Baked Macaroni with White Cheddar and
Buttered Bread Crumbs, 110–112
Baked Portabello Mushrooms Stuffed
with Turkey, Eggplant, and Fresh
Bread Crumbs, 172–173
Baked Rigatoni with Sausage and
Mushrooms, 119
Baking, 27
convection, 27
of savory foods, 26
temperatures for, 27
Baking dishes
for broiling, 25, 142
glass, 53
spraying with vegetable oil spray, 173
Baking pans, 53
for broiling, 142
dark, 27
decorative, buttering, 302
glass, 27
measuring size of, 16
metal, 53
springform, inverting bottom of, 105,
106(illus.)
Baking soda, to neutralize acid in
tomatoes, 72
Balloon whisks, 18, 305
for making pudding, 308
Balsamic vinegar, 80
authenticity of, 101
Butternut Squash Risotto with
Parmigiano-Reggiano Rinds
and Balsamic Drizzle, 99–101
everyday, 101
making syrup from, 101
White Balsamic Vinaigrette, 86–87
Bamboo skewers, soaking, 212
Bamboo steamers, storing, 32
Barilla pasta, 107
Basil
about, 187
Braised Summer Squash with Sweet
Peppers, Tomatoes, and Basil,
262–263
chiffonade of, cutting, 86(illus.)

chopping, 21
cut, keeping, 21
Grilled Skewered Shrimp with
Romesco Sauce, 136–138
Grilled Stuffed Chicken Breasts with
Prosciutto, Taleggio, and
Pesto, 183–185
Heirloom Tomatoes with Bocconcini,
Basil, and White Balsamic
Vinaigrette, 86–87
Pesto, 186–187
preserving color of, 186, 187
storing, 187
Thai-Style Minced Chicken with Basil
and Chiles, 170–171
Basting roasted turkey, 191, 192
Batonnet, 21, 22
Bay leaves, 58, 58(illus.)
Bayless, Rick, 204
Bay scallops, 142, 143(illus.)
Beans. See Cannellini beans; Fava beans;
Garbanzo beans; Green beans;
Kidney beans; White beans
Bean thread noodles
Chicken Soup with Glass Noodles,
70–71
Beard, James, 14
Béchamel sauce
about, 110
Béchamel Sauce, 123
Beef. See also Meat
au jus, 230
Braised Short Ribs with Frizzled Leeks,
237–241
cuts of, names for, 228
doneness of, 209
Double-Crusted Timpano with Fusilli,
Ricotta, and Tender Little
Meatballs, 126–130
Grilled Marinated Flank Steak au Jus,
230–231
Hamburgers, Italian Style, 226–227
internal doneness temperature for, 209
Pot Roast and Gravy with Peas and
Carrots, 241–244

reheating prime rib, 210
Rib-Eye Steaks with Arugula, Blue
Cheese, and Grilled Red
Onions, 228–229
short ribs, choosing, 238
Slow-Roasted Beef Sirloin Tip with
Pan Gravy or Creamy
Horseradish Sauce, 232–234
Spaghetti and Meatballs with
20-Minute Tomato Sauce,
114–117
Weeknight Chili, 245–246
Beets
choosing, 268
Devil's Food Cake with Dark
Chocolate Ganache or
Chocolate Fudge Frosting,
298–300
preventing staining by, 269
"Roasted" Beets and Whole-Grain
Mustard Sauce, 268–269
shredding, 299
variously sized, tips for cooking, 268
Bell peppers
Braised Summer Squash with Sweet
Peppers, Tomatoes, and Basil,
262–263
colors of, 139, 254
flavor of, 215
Osso Buco with Sweet Red Peppers
and Gremolata, 234–237
in Red Bell Pepper Bisque with Crème
Fraîche, 66–67
roasted. See Roasted peppers
skins of, 254
Bench scrapers, 17
Berries. See also Raspberries; Strawberries
choosing, 297
cleaning, 305
pesticides and herbicides on, 297
Zabaglione with Fresh Berries and
Peaches, 305–306
Best Foods mayonnaise, 168
Beurre manié
making, 200

storing, 198

Birds, caution regarding heating nonstick
pans and, 147

Bisques
about, 66
Red Bell Pepper Bisque with Crème
Fraîche, 66–67

Bitterness
of eggplant, leaching out, 259
of escarole, leaching out, 264
in nut skins, removing, 83

Bittersweet Chocolate Bread Pudding
with Kahlúa Sauce, 293–294

Blackberries
Zabaglione with Fresh Berries and
Peaches, 305–306

Black pepper
adding before cooking meat, 208
adding before grilling meat, 230
ground, coarseness of, 52

Black soy sauce, 170

Blanching foods, 24, 33
almonds, 169
asparagus, 251
texture and flavor and, 35
tomatoes, 261

Blenders, 18
puréeing sauces in, 235
puréeing soups in, 65

Blueberries
Zabaglione with Fresh Berries and
Peaches, 305–306

Blue cheese
Rib-Eye Steaks with Arugula, Blue
Cheese, and Grilled Red
Onions, 228–229

Bocconcini
about, 87
Heirloom Tomatoes with Bocconcini,
Basil, and White Balsamic
Vinaigrette, 86–87

Boiling, 34
texture and flavor of foods cooked by,
35

Bold tasting extra-virgin olive oil, 80

"Bolognese" Sauce, 124–126
in Lasagna Bolognese, 122–124
in Polenta with Bolognese Sauce, 275

Bones, removing from fish, 135

Boning knives, 17

Boston lettuce. See Butter lettuce

Bouquet garni, 56, 57

Bowls, 18

Box grater, 300(illus.)

Braised Calamari in Red Sauce, 144–145

Braised Greens with Sausage and Onions,
266–267

Braised Short Ribs with Frizzled Leeks,
237–241

Braised Summer Squash with Sweet
Peppers, Tomatoes, and Basil,
262–263

Braising, 24, 30–31
stewing versus, 30
texture and flavor of foods cooked by,
36

Braising pans
condensation on lid of, 246
size of, 242

Brandy
Apple Crisp with Brandy and Sp'Ice
Cream, 291–292
Zucchini-Olive Oil Snack Cake with
Lemon Icing, 303–304

Bread
Bittersweet Chocolate Bread Pudding
with Kahlúa Sauce, 293–294
Savory Baked Risotto Cake, 105–106

Bread crumbs
Baked Macaroni with White Cheddar
and Buttered Bread Crumbs,
110–112
Baked Portabello Mushrooms Stuffed
with Turkey, Eggplant, and
Fresh Bread Crumbs, 172–173
making, 106, 172
Maple-Glazed Quail Stuffed with Wild
Mushrooms, Sausage, and
Sour Cherries, 194–197

Rack of Lamb with Garlicky Bread
Crumbs, 224–225
Savory Baked Risotto Cake, 105–106
storing, 172

Breading, 28
keeping from becoming too thick, 180
before sautéing, 146, 147

Brining, 45–46
aromatic brines for, 46
salt-to-water ratios for, 46
of turkey, 189, 190, 191

Broiled Swordfish with Mango Salsa,
155–157

Broilers, 155

Broiling, 25
baking dishes/pans for, 25, 142
for browning before braising, 31
caramelization during, 24
of fish, preventing drying out during,
135
hazards with, 24

Broth
canned, 95
clarity of, 56
concentrating flavor of, 56
cooking time for, 57
flavor of, 57
ingredients for, 56
for risotto, 95
Shortcut Chicken Broth with a
Dividend, 61–62
simmering, 56
stocks versus, 57

Browning foods, 31. See also
Caramelizing foods
chicken, 202
in skillet, 31

Brown rice, long-grain, 279

Bun cha, 212–214

Bundt pans, buttering, 302

Burns, preventing while steaming, 32

Butter, 65
about, 288
beurre manié, 198, 200
burning of, preventing, 28

clarified. *See* Clarified butter; Ghee
for crisp cookies, 313
cultured organic, 288
European-style, 73, 288, 313
finishing with, 39–40, 272
monter au beurre, 39–40, 65, 272
organic, 73, 288
for risotto, 95
salted, 288
storing, 288
unsalted, 73, 288
Butterflying chicken breasts, 185,
    185(illus.)
Butter lettuce
    Butter Lettuce with Ruby Grapefruit,
        Avocado, and Glazed Walnuts,
        82–84
    cutting, 81
    Weeknight Green Salad, 81–82
Buttermilk, making crème fraîche from,
    67
Butternut squash
    Butternut Squash Risotto with
        Parmigiano-Reggiano Rinds
        and Balsamic Drizzle, 99–101
    Butternut Squash with Maple Syrup
        and Allspice, 273–274
    peeling and cutting, 100

C

Cabbage, Savoy
    choosing, 75
    Three-Bean Minestrone with Sausage,
        75–77
Caggiano, Biba, 95, 234
Cake flour, 301
Cakes. *See also* Cheesecake
    catering cut for, 106(illus.)
    Devil's Food Cake with Dark
        Chocolate Ganache or
        Chocolate Fudge Frosting,
        298–300
    Lemon Marzipan Cake, 301–302

preventing doming in center during
    baking, 304
splitting layers of, 299
Zucchini-Olive Oil Snack Cake with
    Lemon Icing, 303–304
Calamari. *See* Squid
Calcium silicate in salt, 43
California bay laurel, 58
California Crab Gumbo with Chicken
    and Sausage, 138–141
Callebaut white chocolate, 296
Cal-Riso rice, 95
Campiformio, Rosemary, 194
Canela, 205
Canned ingredients, 11
    broth, 95
    cannellini beans, 75
    tomatoes, 116, 126, 180
Cannellini beans
    canned, 75
    cooking, 75
    Three-Bean Minestrone with Sausage,
        75–77
Capers, 178
Capra, Nelly, 126
Capsaicin, 66, 170
Caramelizing foods
    about, 210
    asparagus, 251
    during braising, 31
    during broiling, 25
    deglazing pans and, 31
    garlic, 109
    glaçage, 135
    during grilling, 24, 25
    meat, 208, 238
    mushrooms, 118
    onions, 73, 267
    during roasting, 26
    during sautéing, 28
    in stir-frying, 29
    vegetables, 215, 270
Caramel sauce
    Grilled Peach Ice Cream Sundaes with

Shortcut Caramel Sauce, 289–290
storing, 289–290
usual method for making, 289–290
Carnaroli rice, 95
Carrots
    Chicken Cacciatore, 202–203
    Classic Chicken Stock, 60–61
    cutting for salads, 78
    cutting for stock, 56
    Herb-Crusted Chicken Potpies,
        198–201
    in mirepoix, 20
    Pot Roast and Gravy with Peas and
        Carrots, 241–244
    Roasted Root Vegetables, 269–271
    Vegetable Broth, 63
Carving
    of chuck roast during braising, 242
    letting meat rest before, 210
    of poultry, 166–167, 167(illus.)
Carving knives, Granton edge, 17, 220,
    232(illus.)
Cascadian Farms organic berries, 297
Cashews
    frying, 174
    Stir-Fried Velvet Chicken with
        Cashews, 174–175
Cassia, 205
Cast iron pots, 15
Cast iron stove-top grills, 16
Casual menus, seasonal, 320, 321, 322,
    323, 324, 325
Catering cut, 106(illus.)
"Cater-wrapping," 310
Cayenne pepper, amount of, 66
Celery
    Classic Chicken Stock, 60–61
    cutting for stock, 56
    in mirepoix, 20
    peeling, 78
    Shaved Celery with Medjool Dates,
        Feta, and Walnuts, 88
    shaving, 88
    Vegetable Broth, 63

Cellophane noodles
    Chicken Soup with Glass Noodles,
        70–71
Celsius scale, table of equivalents for, 329
Cèpes. See Porcini mushrooms
Chamomile teabag, in vegetable Broth, 63
Cheddar cheese
    Baked Macaroni with White Cheddar
        and Buttered Bread Crumbs,
        110–112
    grating, 111
    Macaroni and Cheese, 112
    Mornay Sauce, 110–111
    Tomato-Cheddar Soup, 72–73
    White Cheddar Polenta, 275
Cheese. See also specific types of cheese
    adding to hot soup, 72
    creamy, in salads, 78
    grated, measuring, 53, 96
    grating, 96, 111
    keeping white in salads, 78
Cheesecake
    preventing cracks in, 295
    White Chocolate Cheesecake with
        Oreo Crust and Raspberry
        Coulis, 295–297
Cheesecloth, use in roasting turkey, 191,
    192
Cheese knives, 17, 184(illus.)
Chef's knives, 17
Cherries
    Maple-Glazed Quail Stuffed with Wild
        Mushrooms, Sausage, and
        Sour Cherries, 194–197
Cherry tomatoes, 86
Chicken. See also Poultry
    Baby Greens, Roasted Chicken, Stilton,
        and Hazelnuts with Raspberry
        Vinaigrette, 91–92
    in Baked Portabello Mushrooms
        Stuffed with Turkey, Eggplant,
        and Fresh Bread Crumbs,
        172–173
    brining, 46
    broth, canned, 95

broth, recipes using, 59
browning, 202
butterflying boneless, skinless breasts
    of, 185, 185(illus.)
California Crab Gumbo with Chicken
    and Sausage, 138–141
carving, 166–167, 167(illus.)
Chicken Cacciatore, 202–203
Chicken Salad Véronique with Whole
    Toasted Almonds, 168–169
Chicken Soup with Glass Noodles,
    70–71
Chicken Thighs Parmigiana, 180–182
Classic Chicken Stock, 60–61
Classic Herb-Roasted Chicken,
    187–188
doneness of, 164, 165
fat of, in stock, 60
feet of, in stock, 60
fillet strip or tenderloin of, 176
flavor of, 180
Garlicky Chicken Breasts, 176–177
Grilled Stuffed Chicken Breasts with
    Prosciutto, Taleggio, and
    Pesto, 183–185
Herb-Crusted Chicken Potpies,
    198–201
internal doneness temperature for,
    164, 165
juices of, clear, as doneness test, 164
liver of, avoiding in stock, 61
Paella with Shellfish, Sausage, and
    Chicken, 158–161
poaching, 61–62
searing, 170
Shortcut Chicken Broth with a
    Dividend, 61–62
shredding, 62, 91
skin of, 60, 165, 202
Stir-Fried Velvet Chicken with
    Cashews, 174–175
stock, recipes using, 59
stopping cooking of, 63
substitution in Turkey Piccata, 179
Thai-Style Minced Chicken with Basil

and Chiles, 170–171
    thighs versus breasts of, 180
Chick peas
    Three-Bean Minestrone with Sausage,
        75–77
Chiffonade
    of basil, cutting, 86(illus.)
    cutting leaves into, 21, 22
Chiles, 157, 171(illus.)
    ancho, 204
    cutting, 170
    dried, 204
    handling, 157, 171
    heat of, 170, 171
    soothing hands after working with, 157
    Thai-Style Minced Chicken with Basil
        and Chiles, 170–171
    Turkey Mole, 204–207
Chinese strainers, 60(illus.)
Chinois, 61(illus.)
Chives
    mincing, 69
    Roasted Garlic Mashed Potatoes with
        Chives, 281
Chocolate
    Bittersweet Chocolate Bread Pudding
        with Kahlúa Sauce, 293–294
    Chocolate Fudge Frosting, 298, 300
    Dark Chocolate-Pistachio Wafers,
        313–314
    Devil's Food Cake with Dark
        Chocolate Ganache or
        Chocolate Fudge Frosting,
        298–300
    enhancing flavor of, 288
    Ganache, 298, 299
    Mexican, 205
    Rich Chocoholic Pudding, 307–308
    shaving instead of chopping, 288
Chopping foods, 19–20, 21, 22
    basil, 21
    onions, 19–20
Chouinard, Juli, 301
Chowders
    about, 68

White Corn Chowder, 68–69
Ciccarone-Nehls, Gloria, 194
Cilantro, unpleasant taste of, 157
Cinnamon
    Mexican, 205
    reusing cinnamon sticks, 273
Citrus fruit. *See also* Grapefruit; Lemons;
        Oranges
    Citrus Dressing, 83
    cutting into segments, 84
    removing inked-on stamps from, 78
    zest of, 53, 178
Clam juice
    Grilled Skewered Shrimp with
        Romesco Sauce, 136–138
    for thinning *romesco* sauce, 137
Clams
    cleaning, 134, 135
    Paella with Shellfish, Sausage, and
        Chicken, 158–161
Clarified butter, 155
    making, 155
    storing, 155
Clarity, of stocks and broths, 56
Classes, 47
Classic American Potato Salad, 282–283
Classic Chicken Stock, 60–61
Classic Herb-Roasted Chicken, 187–188
Cleaning equipment
    food processor blades, 138
    grill grates, 25
    paella pans, 160
    woks, 160
Cleaning foods
    berries, 305
    leeks, 56
    mushrooms, 119
    shellfish, 134, 135
    wild rice, 276
Cling peaches, 289–290
Cloves, ground, amount to use, 273
Cocoa powder, types of, 298
Coconut oil, 236
Cod

substitution in Cracker-Crusted
        Nubble Point Scallops, 143
Coffee
    Devil's Food Cake with Dark
        Chocolate Ganache or
        Chocolate Fudge Frosting,
        298–300
    to enhance chocolate flavor, 288
    Kahlúa Sauce, 293–294
Cold-pressed oils, 87
Color
    of applesauce, 217
    of basil, preserving, 186, 187
    of bell peppers, 139, 254
    dark and white meat of poultry, 165
    green on potatoes, 151
    pairing side dishes with main dishes
        and, 249
    of turkey after brining, 191
    of vegetables, 34, 80, 102, 258
    of white vegetables, preserving after
        cutting, 198
The Complete Vegetarian Handbook
        (Farrell-Kingsley), 41
Consistency, of soups, 65
Convection baking, 27
Convection ovens, for roasting meats,
        208, 225
Conventional produce, 41–42
Cookies
    Amaretti di Saronno cookies, 290
    Dark Chocolate-Pistachio Wafers,
        313–314
    making log to refrigerate, 314,
        314(illus.)
Cooking
    confidence for, 47, 48
    improving skills for, 47
    inspiration for, 48
*Cooking a Honker, Charring a Cheesecake,
        and Other Kitchen Tales from the
        Livermore Valley Wine Country*
        (Livermore Valley Winegrowers
        Association), 301
Cooking classes, 47

Cooking methods, 24–34
    dry-heat, 24–29
    flavor and, 35–36
    moist-heat, 30–34
    texture and, 35–36
Cooking spray, tips for using, 173
Cooking time, 57
Cookware, 15–17
    sources for, 326
CookWise (Corriher), 43, 170
Cooling foods
    blanched foods, 33
    stocks, 57–58
Copper bowls, whipping egg whites or
        yolks in, 305
Corn. *See also* Polenta
    cobs in Vegetable Broth, 63
    extracting flavor from cobs, 68
    "milk" of, 69
    removing kernels from cob, 69
    Savory Corn Pudding, 256–257
    White Corn Chowder, 68–69
Cornstarch, preventing lumps in, 174
Corriher, Shirley, 43, 170, 220
Coulis
    about, 148
    Raspberry Coulis, 295, 297
    Roasted Red Pepper Coulis, 148–149
Court bouillon, 152
    about, 154
Crab
    California Crab Gumbo with Chicken
        and Sausage, 138–141
    removing meat from shell, 141
Cracker-Crusted Nubble Point Scallops,
        142–143
Cracker meal, 147
Cramer, Mary, 311
Cream, 65
    about, 288
    heavy (whipping). *See* Heavy cream
    manufacturing, 113
    substitute for, in soups, 65
Cream cheese
    about, 295

White Chocolate Cheesecake with
Oreo Crust and Raspberry
Coulis, 295–297

Creamer potatoes
about, 150
Steamed Salmon and Creamer
Potatoes with Sauce Verte,
150–151

Creamy, Soft Polenta, 274–275

Creativity, 48

Crème de cacao
Rich Chocoholic Pudding, 307–308

Crème fraîche
to cool hot peppers, 66
homemade, 67
Horseradish Sauce, 232, 234
Red Bell Pepper Bisque with Crème
Fraîche, 66–67

Crepes
for My Grandmother's Baked Stuffed
Manicotti, 120–122

Crisps
Apple Crisp with Brandy and Sp'Ice
Cream, 291–292

Crookneck squash. See Yellow squash

Cross contamination, avoiding with
poultry, 163

Croutons, making, 73

Crown Roast of Pork, 219

Cruciferous vegetables
boiling, 34
odor of, 32, 34
steaming, 32
in stock, 63

Crumbling soft cheeses without
"melting," 91

Crusts
developing on meat or poultry during
roasting, 26
pastry. See Pastry crusts

Cucumbers, cutting, 78

Currants
Garlic Spinach with Currants, Pine
Nuts, and Pecorino, 265–266

Cutting boards, 17

D

Danger zone, 23

Dark Chocolate-Pistachio Wafers,
313–314

Dates
choosing, 88
Shaved Celery with Medjool Dates,
Feta, and Walnuts, 88
storing, 88
varieties of, 88

Dawson, Barbara, 194

DeCecco pasta, 107

Deep-frying foods, 29–30
texture and flavor and, 36

Deep-frying thermometers, 18

DeFeo, Patty, 226

Deglazing pans, 31

Del Conte, Anna, 96, 98, 311

Delmonico steaks, 228

Desserts, 285–314
ingredients for, 288
make ahead, 286
planning to fit menu, 287
quick, 286
tips for, 288

Devil's Food Cake with Dark Chocolate
Ganache or Chocolate Fudge
Frosting, 298–300

Diamond Crystal kosher salt, 43, 44, 52
preventing wilting of lettuce using, 78

Dicing foods, 21, 22
avocados, 85
onions, 20
tomatoes, 261

Dijon mustard, 268

di Lelio, Alfredo, 113

"Divided," use of term in recipes, 52

Doilies, uses for, 312

Doneness
of fish, 134, 156
instant-read thermometers to test for,
53
internal temperature for testing. See
Internal doneness temperature

of meat, 209, 211, 225
of poultry, 164, 165, 190
of risotto, 97

Double boilers, improvising, 305

Double-Crusted Timpano with Fusilli,
Ricotta, and Tender Little
Meatballs, 126–130

Dressings. See Mayonnaise; Salad
dressings

Dried mushrooms. See also Porcini
mushrooms
rehydrating, 195

Dry-heat cooking methods, 24–29
baking, 26
broiling, 25
deep-frying, 29–30
grilling, 25
roasting, 25
sautéing, 28
stir-frying, 29

Dry ingredients
for cakes, sifting, 304
measuring, 53

Dry measures, table of equivalents for,
329

"Dutched" cocoa powder, 298

Dutch ovens, 15
for braising, 31
for risotto, 96
for sautéing onions, 73

Dyes, in farm-raised fish, 104

E

Edamame, 102
Risotto Primavera with Wild Salmon,
102–104
substitution in Fresh Fava Beans with
Pecorino and Meyer Lemon
Olive Oil, 252

Eggplant
Baked Portabello Mushrooms Stuffed
with Turkey, Eggplant, and
Fresh Bread Crumbs, 172–173
cutting, 259

Eggplant Parmigiana, 259–261
leaching out bitterness of, 259
preventing from absorbing excessive
oil during cooking, 259
Turkey-Eggplant Casserole with Fresh
Bread Crumbs, 173
varieties of, 172
Eggs
Bittersweet Chocolate Bread Pudding
with Kahlúa Sauce, 293–294
Chicken Thighs Parmigiana, 180–182
Classic American Potato Salad,
282–283
Dark Chocolate-Pistachio Wafers,
313–314
Devil's Food Cake with Dark
Chocolate Ganache or
Chocolate Fudge Frosting,
298–300
Double-Crusted Timpano with Fusilli,
Ricotta, and Tender Little
Meatballs, 126–130
Eggplant Parmigiana, 259–261
Fettuccine Alfredo with Baby Shrimp
and Peas, 113–114
hard-cooked, shredding, 282
hard cooking, 129
Lemon Marzipan Cake, 301–302
My Grandmother's Baked Stuffed
Manicotti, 120–122
pasteurized, 113, 152
poaching, 33
Rich Chocoholic Pudding, 307–308
Sautéed Fillet of Sole with Tartar
Sauce, 145–147
Savory Corn Pudding, 256–257
White Chocolate Cheesecake with
Oreo Crust and Raspberry
Coulis, 295–297
Zabaglione with Fresh Berries and
Peaches, 305–306
Zucchini-Olive Oil Snack Cake with
Lemon Icing, 303–304
Egg whites
beating, 302

storing, 307
whipping in copper bowls, 305
Egg yolks, whipping in copper bowls, 305
Electrical appliances, small, 18
Electric deep-fryers, 29
Eliot, Steve, 39
Emile Henri baking pans, 17
Equipment, 15–21
cookware, 15–17
cutting boards, 17
knives, 17
price of, 19
small electrics, 18
small wares, 18–19
sources for, 326
thermometers, 18
Equivalents, table of, 352
Escarole
choosing, 264
Escarole with Garlic and Red Pepper
Flakes, 263–264
leaching out bitterness in, 264
in salads, 264
European-style butter, 113, 313
for risotto, 95
Evaporated milk
as cream substitute in soups, 65
in Savory Corn Pudding, 257
Expeller-pressed oils, 87
Extra-virgin olive oil, 80, 87
bold tasting, 80
for delicate sauces and vinaigrettes,
150
mild tasting, 80
for pesto, 186

F

Fahrenheit scale, table of equivalents for,
329
Fall menus, 323–324
Fallon, Sally, 67
Fall recipes, 318
Farm-raised fish, 104
Farnworth, Suzy, 312

Farrell-Kingsley, Kathy, 41
Fat
flavor and, 39–40
removing from cooled foods, 31
smoking of, 28
Fava beans
cautions about eating, 253
choosing, 252
Fresh Fava Beans with Pecorino and
Meyer Lemon Olive Oil,
252–253
removing skins from, 252
Risotto Primavera with Wild Salmon,
102–104
Fennel
Grilled Pork Chops with Garlic and
Fennel Rub, 211
Feta cheese
Shaved Celery with Medjool Dates,
Feta, and Walnuts, 88
Fettuccine Alfredo with Baby Shrimp and
Peas, 113–114
Fieler, Anna, 136
Fig Heaven (Simmons), 90
Figs
Black Mission, 90
Figs and Arugula with Creamy Goat
Cheese and Toasted Pecans, 90
storing, 90
Filberts. See Hazelnuts
Fillet knives, 17
Fillet strips, of poultry, 176, 178
Fine-mesh strainer, 67(illus.)
Fish. See also Clams; Cod; Haddock;
Halibut; Mussels; Salmon;
Scallops; Shellfish; Shrimp; Sole;
Squid; Swordfish; Tuna
buying, 134
cutting thin fillets of, 102, 103(illus.)
doneness of, 134, 156
farm-raised, 104
internal doneness temperature for, 134
odor of, 135
preventing drying out during broiling,
135

removing bones from, 135
removing skin from, 148(illus.), 149
rinsing, 135
sautéing, 146, 147
storing, 134
substitution in Cracker-Crusted
　　　Nubble Point Scallops, 143
sushi-grade, 134
Fish sauce, Asian, 71
substitute for, 71
Flat-leaf parsley, 117
Flat whisk, 112(illus.), 123(illus.)
Flavor. See also specific foods
acid and, 38
alcohol and, 38
cooking and, 35–36
factors influencing, 46–47
fat enhancement of, 39–40
in low-fat dishes, 40
pairing side dishes with main dishes
　　　and, 249
salt and. See Salting foods
umami and, 38–39
volatilizing, 38
Fleur de sel, 44
Flipping
pans for, 16
practicing, 28
in stir-frying, 29
Flour
cake, 301
sifting, 53, 301
Fond, 208
Fontina cheese
Creamy, Soft Polenta, 274–275
varieties of, 275
Food mills, 18
for puréeing soups, 65
Food processors, 18
chopping onions in, 20
cleaning blade of, 138
puréeing sauces in, 235
puréeing soups in, 65
scraping bowl of, 137
slicing onions in, 73

Food safety, 23
FoodSaver, 63
Fox, Phyllis, 142
Frangelico
substitution in Bittersweet Chocolate
　　　Bread Pudding with Kahlúa
　　　Sauce, 293
Free radicals, rancidity and, 87
Free-range poultry, 45, 162, 163
Freestone peaches, 289–290
Freezing foods
beurre manié, 198
meat, to cut thinly, 212
stocks, 58
Frenching bones
of pork roasts, 217
of rack of lamb, 224, 225(illus.)
French Onion Soup Gratinée, 73–75
Fresh Fava Beans with Pecorino and
　　　Meyer Lemon Olive Oil, 252–253
Fresh ingredients, 10–11
Frosting
Chocolate Fudge Frosting, 298, 300
storing, 300
Frozen desserts. See also Granita; Ice
　　　cream; Sorbet
sweetness of, 309
Fruit. See Citrus fruit; specific types of fruit

G

Galindo-Schnellbacher, Susan, 225
Ganache, storing, 300
Garbanzo beans
Three-Bean Minestrone with Sausage,
　　　75–77
Garde manger, 81
Garlic
about, 110
American, Italian, and Mexican, 110
burned, 208
caramelizing, 109
flavor of, 110, 208
Garlicky Chicken Breasts, 176–177

Garlic Spinach with Currants, Pine
　　　Nuts, and Pecorino, 265–266
green germ in, 110
Gremolata, 234, 235, 236–237
Grilled Pork Chops with Garlic and
　　　Fennel Rub, 211
Linguine Aglio e Olio, 109
poaching, 149
Rack of Lamb with Garlicky Bread
　　　Crumbs, 224–225
removing smell from hands, 110
Roasted Garlic Mashed Potatoes with
　　　Chives, 281
Garlic oil
to imbue fish with garlic flavor, 149
storing, 109
Garlic powder, 82
Garniture, 20, 21
Gas oven temperature, table of equiva-
　　　lents for, 329
Gastronomy of Italy (Del Conte), 96, 98,
　　　311
George Foreman grills, 16
Ghee
about, 155, 240
sautéing spices in, 278
storing, 240
Ginger, grating, 174
Glaçage, 135
Glass baking dishes, 53
Glass baking pans, 27
Glass noodles
about, 70
Chicken Soup with Glass Noodles,
　　　70–71
Global knives, 17
Glutamates, umami and, 39
Goat cheese
Figs and Arugula with Creamy Goat
　　　Cheese and Toasted Pecans, 90
Gobindavog rice
Kalijira Rice Pilaw, 277–278
Godiva liqueur
substitution in Rich Chocoholic
　　　Pudding, 307

Golden raisins
  Zucchini-Olive Oil Snack Cake with
    Lemon Icing, 303–304
The Good Egg (Simmons), 48
The Good Fat Cookbook (McCullough),
  30, 236
Grand Marnier, 309
Granita
  "cater-wrapping," 310
  scraping, 309
  Strawberry Granita Parfaits, 309–310
Granton edge knives, 17, 220, 232(illus.)
Grapefruit
  Butter Lettuce with Ruby Grapefruit,
    Avocado, and Glazed Walnuts,
    82–84
Grapes
  Baby Greens, Roasted Chicken, Stilton,
    and Hazelnuts with Raspberry
    Vinaigrette, 91–92
  Chicken Salad Véronique with Whole
    Toasted Almonds, 168–169
  cutting for salads, 78
Grapeseed oil, 146
Grated cheese, measuring, 53, 96
Graters
  box, 300(illus.)
  for semisoft cheeses, 111
Gratinée, 25
Grating foods
  cheese, 96, 111
  ginger, 174
  nutmeg, 273
Gravy
  pan drippings for, 208
  reheating, 191
  for Roasted Stuffed Turkey with Pan
    Gravy, 189, 190, 193
  seasoning, 233
  for Slow-Roasted Beef Sirloin Tip with
    Pan Gravy or Creamy
    Horseradish Sauce, 232, 233
  spoons for stirring, 233
  storing, 191
Gray sea salts, 44

Green beans
  Chicken Cacciatore, 202–203
  Romano Beans, 258
Green onions
  cutting into rings, 71
  shredding, 214, 214(illus.)
Greens. *See also* Salad greens; *specific
    greens*
  Braised Greens with Sausage and
    Onions, 266–267
Gremolata, 234, 235, 236–237
Grenadine syrup, 223
Grilled Asparagus, 250–251
Grilled Leg of Lamb with Pomegranate
    Marinade and Muhammara,
    221–223
Grilled Marinated Flank Steak au Jus,
    230–231
Grilled Peach Ice Cream Sundaes with
    Shortcut Caramel Sauce, 289–290
Grilled Pork Chops with Garlic and
    Fennel Rub, 211
Grilled Skewered Shrimp with Romesco
    Sauce, 136–138
Grilled Stuffed Chicken Breasts with
    Prosciutto, Taleggio, and Pesto,
    183–185
Grilling foods, 25
  texture and flavor and, 36
Grill marks, 25
Grill pans, 16
Grill racks, 25
Grills
  cleaning grates, 25
  indoor, 16
Gruyère cheese
  French Onion Soup Gratinée, 73–75

H

Haddock
  substitution in Cracker-Crusted
    Nubble Point Scallops, 143
Halibut

Alaskan Halibut with Roasted Red
    Pepper Coulis, 148–149
  Quick and Easy Roasted Red Pepper
    Sauce, 149
  removing skin from, 148(illus.), 149
  substitution in Cracker-Crusted
    Nubble Point Scallops, 143
Ham. *See also* Meat
  cooking, 220
  doneness of, 209
  Honey-Mustard Glazed Ham with
    Grilled Pineapple Salsa,
    220–221
  internal doneness temperature for, 209
Hamburgers
  Hamburgers, Italian Style, 226–227
  texture of, 226
Handheld mixers, 18
Hard-cooked eggs, shredding, 282
Hard cooking eggs, 129
Hazelnut oil, toasted, 91
Hazelnuts
  Baby Greens, Roasted Chicken, Stilton,
    and Hazelnuts with Raspberry
    Vinaigrette, 91–92
  toasting and skinning, 92
Health Valley Fat-Free Chicken Broth, 95
Heavy cream
  about, 288
  Fettuccine Alfredo with Baby Shrimp
    and Peas, 113–114
  Ganache, 298, 299
  making crème fraîche from, 67
Heirloom Tomatoes with Bocconcini,
    Basil, and White Balsamic
    Vinaigrette, 86–87
Hellman's mayonnaise, 168
Herb-Crusted Chicken Potpies, 198–201
Herbs. *See also specific herbs*
  bouquet garni, 57
  dried, bringing out flavor of, 172
Hicks, Randall, 299
Hollandaise sauce
  "broken," fixing, 153
  keeping warm, 152

Shortcut Hollandaise Sauce, 152, 153
Honey-Mustard Glazed Ham with Grilled
    Pineapple Salsa, 220–221
Horseradish
    Horseradish Mashed Potatoes, 281
    Horseradish Sauce, 232, 234
Hubbard squash
    substitution in Butternut Squash with
        Maple Syrup and Allspice,
        273–274
Hungarian paprika
    Grilled Leg of Lamb with Pomegranate
        Marinade and Muhammara,
        221–223
    Grilled Skewered Shrimp with
        Romesco Sauce, 136–138

I

Ibarra Mexican chocolate, 205
Ice cream
    Apple Crisp with Brandy and Sp'Ice
        Cream, 291–292
    Grilled Peach Ice Cream Sundaes with
        Shortcut Caramel Sauce,
        289–290
Ice water bath
    for moist chicken, 62
    to stop cooking of tomatoes, 261
Icing
    Lemon Icing, 303, 304
Ikeda, Kikunae, 38–39
Immersion blenders, 18
    for puréeing soups, 65
Indoor grills, 16
Ingredients, 10–11. *See also specific*
    ingredients
    dry, for cakes, sifting, 304
    measuring, 53
    seasonal, 40
    sources for, 326
Instant-read thermometers, 18
    for freezing ice-cream or sorbet, 311
    placement of, 53
    probe-type, 153(illus.)

Internal doneness temperature, 24
    for fish, 134
    for meat, 209, 211, 225
    for poultry, 164, 165, 190
    for stuffing for poultry, 164
Italian green beans
    Romano Beans, 258
Italian parsley, 117
Italian Sausage Contadina with Roasted
    Sweet Peppers, Potatoes, and
    Onions, 215–216

J

Jack Daniel's Honey Dijon mustard, 220
Jalapeño chiles, 157, 171(illus.)
Jones, Kimball, 241
Jorin, Robert, 10, 312
Juiciness of meat, letting meat rest before
    carving and, 210
Julienne, 21, 22
    cutting pancetta into, 125
Jus, au, 230

K

Kalijira Rice Pilaw, 277–278
Katzer, Matt, 194
Kidney beans
    Three-Bean Minestrone with Sausage,
        75–77
    Weeknight Chili, 245–246
King, Sam, 91
Knife skills and cuts, 19–22
    for batonnet, 21, 22
    for chiffonade, 21, 22
    for chopping, 19–20, 21, 22
    for dicing, 20, 21, 22
    for julienne, 21, 22
    for mincing, 22
    for mirepoix, 20
    for paysanne, 21, 21(illus.), 22
Knives
    boning, 17
    cheese, 17, 184(illus.)

chef's, 17
fillet, 17
Global, 17
Granton edge, 17, 220, 232(illus.)
paring, 17
serrated, 17
storing, 17
Knoff, Laura, 42
Kosher salt, 43–44, 52
    brands of, 43–44, 52
    sodium content of, 43
    substituting for Asian fish sauce, 71
Kronmark, Lars, 56

L

La Baleine sea salt, 43
Lamb. *See also* Meat
    butterflied leg of, cut into main muscle
        groups, 221(illus.), 222
    doneness of, 209, 225
    flavor of, 222
    frenching bones in rack of, 224,
        225(illus.)
    Grilled Leg of Lamb with Pomegranate
        Marinade and Muhammara,
        221–223
    internal doneness temperature for,
        209, 225
    rack of, frenched and not frenched,
        225(illus.)
    Rack of Lamb with Garlicky Bread
        Crumbs, 224–225
Lasagna Bolognese, 122–124
Latini pasta, 107
Lauric acid, in coconut oil, 236
Le Creuset cookware
    baking dishes, 142
    Dutch ovens, 73, 96
    pots, 15
    stove-top grills, 16
Lee, Ken, 277
Leeks
    Braised Short Ribs with Frizzled Leeks,
        237–241

Classic Chicken Stock, 60–61
cleaning, 56
in stocks and broths, 56
Vegetable Broth, 63
Lemon oil
Fresh Fava Beans with Pecorino and
Meyer Lemon Olive Oil,
252–253
making, 253
Lemons
Gremolata, 234, 235, 236–237
Lemon Icing, 303, 304
Lemon Marzipan Cake, 301–302
Turkey Piccata, 177–179
Length, table of equivalents for, 329
Lettuce. See also Butter lettuce; Romaine
lettuce
preventing wilting of, 78
Levine, Caryl, 277
Lids, for braising, 31
Light olive oil, 80
Lima French Atlantic sea salt, 43
Linguine Aglio e Olio, 109
Liquid, adding to braised dishes, 31
Liquid ingredients, measuring, 53
Liquid measures, table of equivalents for,
329
Liver, avoiding in chicken stock, 61
Long-grain brown rice, 279
Look cookware, 16
Low-fat cooking, flavor in, 40

M

Macaroni and Cheese, 112
Mahogany roux, 141
Maille Honey Mustard, 220
Maille mustard, 269
Main dishes, 131–246
make-ahead, 132–133
pairing side dishes with, 249
quick, 132–133
vegetarian, 132–133
Make ahead recipes
desserts, 286

main dishes, 132–133
pastas, 94
risottos, 94
salads, 55
side dishes, 248
soups, 55
stocks, 55
Malgieri, Nick, 295, 298
Mangos
choosing, 156
Mango Salsa, 156–157
Manicotti
My Grandmother's Baked Stuffed
Manicotti, 120–122
Manufacturing cream, 113
Maple syrup
Butternut Squash with Maple Syrup
and Allspice, 273–274
Maple-Glazed Quail Stuffed with Wild
Mushrooms, Sausage, and
Sour Cherries, 194–197
Marbling of meat, 213
Marconi, Thomas, 63
Marinades
acid in, 208, 230
omitting salt from, 222
Marsala wine
Zabaglione with Fresh Berries and
Peaches, 305–306
Marzipan, 301
Mashed Yukon Gold Potatoes, 280–281
Mayonnaise
commercial, 168
Tartar Sauce, 146
Maytag blue cheese
Rib-Eye Steaks with Arugula, Blue
Cheese, and Grilled Red
Onions, 228–229
McCullough, Fran, 30, 236
McKey, David, 126
Measuring cups, 18
Measuring ingredients, 53
Measuring spoons, 18
Meat, 208–246. See also Beef; Ham; Lamb;
Pork; Veal

caramelizing, 208, 238
cooking, 208
developing crust on, 26
doneness of, 209, 211, 225
freezing partially to cut thinly, 212
marbling of, 213
marinating, 208, 230
poaching, 33
pounding, 28, 177
rare or medium-rare, 208
removing silver skin from, 230
rubs for, 242
salting of, 44–45
sautéing, 172
seasoning, 208
shingle-stacking, 179
silver skin on, removing, 179,
179(illus.), 210, 230
temperature before roasting, 210
Meatballs
Double-Crusted Timpano with Fusilli,
Ricotta, and Tender Little
Meatballs, 126–130
Spaghetti and Meatballs with
20-Minute Tomato Sauce,
114–117
tender, secret to, 115
texture of, 114
Meat pounder, 181(illus.)
Meat tenderizer, 181(illus.)
Mediterranean bay laurel, 58, 58(illus.)
Medium-mesh strainer, 67(illus.)
Medium-rare meat, 208
Menu planning, 47
desserts and, 287
pairing side dishes with main dishes
for, 249
Menus, seasonal, 319–325
Metal baking pans, 53
Metric units, table of equivalents for, 329
meuniére, à la style, 147
Mexican chocolate, 205
Mexican cinnamon, 205
Meyer lemon oil

Fresh Fava Beans with Pecorino and
Meyer Lemon Olive Oil,
252–253
making, 253
Microplanes, 18, 53, 96
Milanaise, à la style, 146
Mild tasting extra-virgin olive oil, 80
Milk
Baked Macaroni with White Cheddar
and Buttered Bread Crumbs,
110–112
Béchamel Sauce, 123
Bittersweet Chocolate Bread Pudding
with Kahlúa Sauce, 293–294
evaporated. See Evaporated milk
Macaroni and Cheese, 112
Mornay Sauce, 110–111
Savory Corn Pudding, 256–257
Tomato-Cheddar Soup, 72–73
Mincing foods, 22
chives, 69
Mint, 284(illus.)
about, 283
Orange-Mint Sorbet in Orange Shells,
311–312
Orzo with Toybox Tomatoes and Fresh
Mint, 283–284
Minute, à la sauces, sauté pans for
preparing, 178
Mirepoix, 20
in poaching liquid, 33
in stocks and soups, 56
Mise en place, 22
for stir-frying, 29
Mixers, 18
Mixing bowls, 18
Moist-heat cooking methods, 30–34
blanching, 33
boiling, 34
braising, 30–31
poaching, 33
steaming, 32
Moisture, removing to encourage
caramelization, 24, 25
Mole with turkey, 204–207

Monter au beurre, 39–40, 272
in soups, 65
Monterey Jack cheese
Baked Portabello Mushrooms Stuffed
with Turkey, Eggplant, and
Fresh Bread Crumbs, 172–173
Turkey-Eggplant Casserole with Fresh
Bread Crumbs, 173
Mornay Sauce, 110–111
Morton kosher salt, 43, 52
Morton table salt, 43, 44
Mott, Weezie, 126
Mozzarella cheese
bocconcini, 87
Chicken Thighs Parmigiana, 180–182
Double-Crusted Timpano with Fusilli,
Ricotta, and Tender Little
Meatballs, 126–130
Eggplant Parmigiana, 259–261
Heirloom Tomatoes with Bocconcini,
Basil, and White Balsamic
Vinaigrette, 86–87
My Grandmother's Baked Stuffed
Manicotti, 120–122
types of, 180
Muhammara, 221, 222, 223
Mung bean noodles
Chicken Soup with Glass Noodles,
70–71
Mushrooms
Baked Portabello Mushrooms Stuffed
with Turkey, Eggplant, and
Fresh Bread Crumbs, 172–173
Baked Rigatoni with Sausage and
Mushrooms, 119
Braised Short Ribs with Frizzled Leeks,
237–241
caramelizing, 118
Chicken Soup with Glass Noodles,
70–71
choosing, 272
cleaning, 119
dried, 195. See also Porcini mushrooms
Herb-Crusted Chicken Potpies,
198–201

Maple-Glazed Quail Stuffed with Wild
Mushrooms, Sausage, and
Sour Cherries, 194–197
Pot Roast and Gravy with Peas and
Carrots, 241–244
Rigatoni with Sausage and Mushroom
Ragu, 118–119
Sautéed Mushrooms with Sherry and
Garlic, 271–272
sautéing, 118, 271
Vegetable Broth, 63
wild, 195
Mussels
cleaning, 134, 135
Paella with Shellfish, Sausage, and
Chicken, 158–161
Mustard
choosing, 220, 269
as emulsifier, 268
Honey-Mustard Glazed Ham with
Grilled Pineapple Salsa,
220–221
"Roasted" Beets and Whole-Grain
Mustard Sauce, 268–269
My Grandmother's Baked Stuffed
Manicotti, 120–122

N

Napé, 112
Natural cocoa powder, 298
Natural poultry, 162, 163
New potatoes
about, 150, 271
Mashed Yukon Gold Potatoes, 280–281
Roasted New Potatoes, 271
Steamed Salmon and Creamer
Potatoes with Sauce Verte,
150–151
Nielsen, Kara, 294
Niman Ranch, 45, 218
Nonfat milk, 65
Nonreactive cookware, 108
Nonstick pans
skillets, 16

toxicity to pet birds, 147

North American Salt Company kosher salt, 43, 44

Northern Italian Cooking (Caggiano), 234

Nourishing Traditions (Fallon), 67

Nutmeg, grating, 273

Nutrients, in organic versus conventional produce, 42

Nutrition, pairing side dishes with main dishes and, 249

Nuts. *See also* Almonds; Hazelnuts; Pecans; Pine nuts; Pistachios; Walnuts
   frying, 174
   removing bitterness from skins of, 83
   skinning, 92
   storing, 85
   toasting, 78, 89, 92

O

O brand Meyer lemon oil, 253

Odor
   of cruciferous vegetables, 32, 34
   of fish, 135
   of garlic, removing from hands, 110
   of onions, controlling, 73

Oils. *See also* Coconut oil; Grapeseed oil; Lemon oil; Olive oil
   avoiding in pasta cooking water, 107
   cold-pressed and expeller-pressed, 87
   garlic, 109, 149
   hazelnut, toasted, 91
   rancidity of, 30, 87
   refined, 30
   smoke point of, 30, 87
   storing, 87
   temperature for deep-frying, 29
   walnut, 91

Okra, in gumbo, 140

Olive oil, 73
   bold tasting extra-virgin, 80
   Braised Summer Squash with Sweet Peppers, Tomatoes, and Basil, 262–263

cold-pressed and expeller-pressed, 87

for delicate sauces and vinaigrettes, 150

emulsification in red sauce, 145

flavor of, 80

Fresh Fava Beans with Pecorino and Meyer Lemon Olive Oil, 252–253

as ingredient, 262

mild tasting extra-virgin, 80

for pesto, 186

types of, 80

Zucchini-Olive Oil Snack Cake with Lemon Icing, 303–304

Omega coconut oil, 236

Omega-3 fatty acids, in farm-raised fish, 104

Onions. *See also* Green onions; Leeks; Red onions; Shallots
   Braised Greens with Sausage and Onions, 266–267
   caramelizing, 73, 267
   chopping by hand, 19–20
   chopping in food processor, 20
   Classic Chicken Stock, 60–61
   controlling odor of, 73
   French Onion Soup Gratinée, 73–75
   grilling, 228
   Italian Sausage Contadina with Roasted Sweet Peppers, Potatoes, and Onions, 215–216
   in mirepoix, 20
   peeling and trimming, 215, 216(illus.)
   preventing tears when cutting, 73, 74
   for risotto, 95
   sautéing, 72, 73, 97
   shaving, 78
   slicing large volume of, 73
   storing, 74
   thickly sliced, grilling, 228
   unpeeled, for stock, 56
   Vegetable Broth, 63

Orange Curaçao, 309

Orange-flavored liqueur

Strawberry Granita Parfaits, 309–310

Zucchini-Olive Oil Snack Cake with Lemon Icing, 303–304

Oranges
   carving out orange shells, 312
   Orange-Mint Sorbet in Orange Shells, 311–312

Oregano, 145

Organic berries, 297, 310

Organic butter, 113
   for risotto, 95

Organic poultry, 162, 163

Organic produce, 41–42

Orzo with Toybox Tomatoes and Fresh Mint, 283–284

Osso Buco with Sweet Red Peppers and Gremolata, 234–237

Ovens
   cleanliness of, 26
   convection, 208, 225

Oven temperature
   for convection baking, 27
   with glass baking dishes, 27, 53
   for roasting, 26
   table of equivalents for, 352
   of warm oven, 53

Oven thermometers, 26

P

Pacific Free-Range Chicken Broth, 95

Paella pans *(paelleras)*
   cleaning, 160
   seasoning, 158

Paella with Shellfish, Sausage, and Chicken, 158–161

Pancetta, 75, 125
   julienning, 125

Pan drippings, 208

Pan-roasting, 26

Pans, 53
   All-Clad, 15, 16, 96
   baking. *See* Baking pans
   braising, 242, 246
   broiling, 25, 142

bundt, buttering, 302
Emile Henri, 17
grill, 16
measuring size of, 16
nonreactive, for pasta dishes with
        tomatoes, 108
nonstick, 16, 147
paella, 158, 160
for risotto, 96
roasting, 26, 191, 208
saucepans, 15
saucier, 15, 96, 104(illus.)
sauté, 16, 28, 53, 178
stir-fry, 16
Paprika. *See* Hungarian paprika;
        Pimentón dulce
Parchment paper
    hazard in broiling, 25
    during roasting, 26
Paring knives, 17
Parisienne, à la style, 147
Parmesan cheese. *See also* Parmigiano-
        Reggiano cheese
    Rigatoni with Sausage and Mushroom
            Ragu, 118–119
    substitution in Garlic Spinach with
            Currants, Pine Nuts, and
            Pecorino, 265
Parmigiano-Reggiano cheese. *See also*
        Parmesan cheese
    Butternut Squash Risotto with
            Parmigiano-Reggiano Rinds
            and Balsamic Drizzle, 99–101
    Fettuccine Alfredo with Baby Shrimp
            and Peas, 113–114
    Pesto, 186–187
    rinds of, 75, 100
    in risotto, 96
    Risotto Milanese, 98–99
    Risotto Primavera with Wild Salmon,
            102–104
    Savory Baked Risotto Cake, 105–106
    storing rinds, 100
    Three-Bean Minestrone with Sausage,
            75–77

Parsley
    flat-leaf (Italian), 117
    Gremolata, 234, 235, 236–237
    Sauce Verte, 150–151
    Shaved Celery with Medjool Dates,
            Feta, and Walnuts, 88
    Turkey Piccata, 177–179
Parsnips
    about, 198
    Herb-Crusted Chicken Potpies,
            198–201
    Roasted Root Vegetables, 269–271
Pasta, 107–130
    Baked Macaroni with White Cheddar
            and Buttered Bread Crumbs,
            110–112
    Baked Rigatoni with Sausage and
            Mushrooms, 119
    "Bolognese" Sauce for, 124–126
    brands of, 107
    cooking, 34, 107–108, 110, 111
    al dente, 107, 110
    Double-Crusted Timpano with Fusilli,
            Ricotta, and Tender Little
            Meatballs, 126–130
    dried, 107
    Fettuccine Alfredo with Baby Shrimp
            and Peas, 113–114
    Lasagna Bolognese, 122–124
    Linguine Aglio e Olio, 109
    Macaroni and Cheese, 112
    make ahead recipes, 94
    My Grandmother's Baked Stuffed
            Manicotti, 120–122
    Orzo with Toybox Tomatoes and Fresh
            Mint, 283–284
    quick recipes, 94
    Rigatoni with Sausage and Mushroom
            Ragu, 118–119
    semolina, 107
    Spaghetti and Meatballs with
            20-Minute Tomato Sauce,
            114–117
    vegetarian recipes, 94
Pasta serving spoon, 114(illus.)

Pasteurized eggs, 113, 152
Pastry crusts
    for Double-Crusted Timpano with
            Fusilli, Ricotta, and Tender
            Little Meatballs, 126, 127, 128,
            129, 130
    for pot pie, 198, 199–200
    tips for, 201
Paysanne, 21, 21(illus.), 22
Peaches
    about, 289–290
    Grilled Peach Ice Cream Sundaes with
            Shortcut Caramel Sauce,
            289–290
    Zabaglione with Fresh Berries and
            Peaches, 305–306
Peas
    Chicken Cacciatore, 202–203
    Double-Crusted Timpano with Fusilli,
            Ricotta, and Tender Little
            Meatballs, 126–130
    English, fresh, 113
    Fettuccine Alfredo with Baby Shrimp
            and Peas, 113–114
    Herb-Crusted Chicken Potpies,
            198–201
    Pot Roast and Gravy with Peas and
            Carrots, 241–244
    Risotto Primavera with Wild Salmon,
            102–104
    Three-Bean Minestrone with Sausage,
            75–77
Pecans
    Figs and Arugula with Creamy Goat
            Cheese and Toasted Pecans, 90
Pecorino romano cheese. *See also*
        Romano cheese
    Fresh Fava Beans with Pecorino and
            Meyer Lemon Olive Oil,
            252–253
    Garlic Spinach with Currants, Pine
            Nuts, and Pecorino, 265–266
    Pesto, 186–187
    rind of, in soup, 75
    in risotto, 96

Three-Bean Minestrone with Sausage, 75–77

Peeling foods
    asparagus, 250
    butternut squash, 100
    celery, 78
    onions, 215, 216(illus.)
    tomatoes, 261
    winter squash, 273

Pepper
    black. *See* Black pepper
    white, 198

Peppers. *See* Bell peppers; Chiles; *Piquillo* peppers; Roasted peppers

Pesticides, minimizing exposure to, 41

Pesto, 80, 186–187

Pet birds, caution regarding heating non-stick pans and, 147

Petti, Nicholas, 198

Pham, Mai, 70

Philadelphia brand cream cheese, 295

Pilaf
    Kalijira Rice Pilaw, 277–278
    Wild Rice Pilaf, 276–277

Pimentón dulce
    about, 138
    California Crab Gumbo with Chicken and Sausage, 138–141
    Grilled Skewered Shrimp with Romesco Sauce, 136–138

Pineapple Salsa, 220, 221

Pine nuts
    Pesto, 186–187

Piquillo peppers
    Grilled Skewered Shrimp with Romesco Sauce, 136–138

Pistachios
    Dark Chocolate-Pistachio Wafers, 313–314

Plantain
    about, 204
    Turkey Mole, 204–207

Plastic cutting boards, 17

Plate presentation, 49, 294

Pleasures of the Vietnamese Table (Pham), 70

Plugra butter, 313

Poached Salmon with Shortcut Hollandaise Sauce, 152–154

Poaching foods, 33
    court bouillon for, 152, 154
    eggs, 33
    fish, 152, 153
    garlic, 149
    texture and flavor and, 35

Polenta
    about, 274
    Creamy, Soft Polenta, 274–275
    keeping soft and flowing, 275
    Polenta with Bolognese Sauce, 275
    White Cheddar Polenta, 275

Polychlorinated biphenyls (PCBs), in farm-raised fish, 104

Pomace, 80

Pomegranate molasses (paste, concentrated juice)
    about, 221, 223
    Grilled Leg of Lamb with Pomegranate Marinade and Muhammara, 221–223

Pomi tomatoes, 126, 180

Porcini mushrooms
    about, 239
    Braised Short Ribs with Frizzled Leeks, 237–241
    Chicken Soup with Glass Noodles, 70–71
    Pot Roast and Gravy with Peas and Carrots, 241–244

Pork. *See also* Ham; Meat; Pancetta
    about, 212
    choosing loin roasts of, 217
    crown roast of, buying, 218
    Crown Roast of Pork, 219
    doneness of, 209, 211
    frenching bones in roast, 217
    Grilled Pork Chops with Garlic and Fennel Rub, 211

internal doneness temperature for, 209, 211
    "new white meat," 45
    ordering crown roasts of, 218
    Pork Loin Roast with Vanilla-Scented Applesauce, 217–219
    selecting chops, 211
    tender and juicy, 45
    in Turkey Piccata, 179
    Vietnamese-Style Honey-Glazed Pork Skewers with Rice Vermicelli, 212–214

Portabello mushrooms
    Baked Portabello Mushrooms Stuffed with Turkey, Eggplant, and Fresh Bread Crumbs, 172–173
    Turkey-Eggplant Casserole with Fresh Bread Crumbs, 173

Potatoes
    Classic American Potato Salad, 282–283
    cooking, 280
    "eyes" of, 151
    green color on, 151
    Herb-Crusted Chicken Potpies, 198–201
    Horseradish Mashed Potatoes, 281
    Italian Sausage Contadina with Roasted Sweet Peppers, Potatoes, and Onions, 215–216
    Mashed Yukon Gold Potatoes, 280–281
    for mashing, peeled versus unpeeled, 280
    new, about, 271
    Roasted Garlic Mashed Potatoes with Chives, 281
    Roasted New Potatoes, 271
    Roasted Root Vegetables, 269–271
    Steamed Salmon and Creamer Potatoes with Sauce Verte, 150–151
    storing, 74, 151
    tossing with dressings while hot, 282

Potpies
Herb-Crusted Chicken Potpies,
198–201
Pot Roast and Gravy with Peas and
Carrots, 241–244
Pots, 15
cast iron, 15
for deep-frying, 29
Le Creuset, 15
nonreactive, for pasta dishes with
tomatoes, 108
Revere Ware, 15
stockpots, 60, 63
Poultry, 162–207. *See also* Chicken; Quail;
Turkey
boneless versus bone-in, 165
dark and white meat of, 165
developing crust on, 26
doneness of, 164, 165, 190
fillet strip or tenderloin of, 176, 178
flavor of, 165
free-range, 162, 163
internal doneness temperature for,
164, 165, 190
juices of, clear, as doneness test, 164
natural, 162, 163
organic, 162, 163
pounding, 177
prices for, 162
safe handling of, 163
sautéing, 172
skin of, 165
"tenting" with foil, 165–166
trussing, 166, 166(illus.), 188
washing before cooking, 164
Pounding, of meat or poultry, 28, 177
Preheating
of broiler, 25
of grill, 25
of oven, 27
Presentation, 49, 294
Pressure test for doneness of meat, 209
Prime rib, reheating, 210
Probe-type instant thermometers, 18

Produce. *See also* Vegetables; *specific fruits
and vegetables*
organic versus conventional, 41–42
seasonal, 40
Prosciutto
about, 184
Grilled Stuffed Chicken Breasts with
Prosciutto, Taleggio, and
Pesto, 183–185
Proteins
braising of, 31
salting of meat and, 44–45
Pudding
Bittersweet Chocolate Bread Pudding
with Kahlúa Sauce, 293–294
Rich Chocoholic Pudding, 307–308
Savory Corn Pudding, 256–257
transferring to narrow-mouthed
glasses for serving, 308
Puréeing foods
soups, 65
tomatoes, 125
"Pure" olive oil, 87
Pyrex baking pans, 17, 27
breakage in broiling, 25
Pyrex liquid measures, 18

Q

Quail. *See also* Poultry
Maple-Glazed Quail Stuffed with Wild
Mushrooms, Sausage, and
Sour Cherries, 194–197
Quesadillas, 230
Quick and Easy Roasted Red Pepper
Sauce, 149
Quick recipes
desserts, 286
main dishes, 132–133
pastas, 94
risottos, 94
salads, 55
side dishes, 248
soups, 55
stocks, 55

R

Rack of Lamb with Garlicky Bread
Crumbs, 224–225
Raisins
soaking to plump, 303
Zucchini-Olive Oil Snack Cake with
Lemon Icing, 303–304
Rancid oil, 30, 87
Rare meat, 208
Raspberries
Raspberry Coulis, 295, 297
Raspberry Vinaigrette, 91, 92
Reboiling stocks, 58
Red Bell Pepper Bisque with Crème
Fraîche, 66–67
Red onions
Rib-Eye Steaks with Arugula, Blue
Cheese, and Grilled Red
Onions, 228–229
shaving, 78
soaking, 78
Reducing stocks, 56
Refined oils, 30
Reheating braised foods, 31
Rehydrating dried mushrooms, 195
Relish
Tartar Sauce, 146
Revere Ware pots, 15
Reverse osmosis, timing of salting and,
31, 44–45
Ribbons. *See* Chiffonade
Rib-Eye Steaks with Arugula, Blue
Cheese, and Grilled Red Onions,
228–229
Rice. *See also* Wild rice
Al's Steamed White Rice, 279
brown, long-grain, 279
Kalijira Rice Pilaw, 277–278
"new crop," 279
Paella with Shellfish, Sausage, and
Chicken, 158–161
preventing sticking and gumminess of,
96
for risotto, 95

in self-serve bulk containers, 95
serving, 277
texture of, 278
Rice vermicelli (rice sticks)
Vietnamese-Style Honey-Glazed Pork
Skewers with Rice Vermicelli,
212–214
Rice vinegar, 80
Rich Chocoholic Pudding, 307–308
Ricotta cheese
choosing, 121
Double-Crusted Timpano with Fusilli,
Ricotta, and Tender Little
Meatballs, 126–130
My Grandmother's Baked Stuffed
Manicotti, 120–122
Rigatoni with Sausage and Mushroom
Ragu, 118–119
Risotto, 95–106
Butternut Squash Risotto with
Parmigiano-Reggiano Rinds
and Balsamic Drizzle, 99–101
doneness of, 97
ingredients for, 95–96
make ahead recipes, 94
making ahead, 97
quick recipes, 94
Risotto Milanese, 98–99
Risotto Primavera with Wild Salmon,
102–104
Savory Baked Risotto Cake, 105–106
serving, 96
as side versus main dish, 97
stirring, 96
techniques for, 96
tips for, 95–97
vegetarian recipes, 94
"Roasted" Beets and Whole-Grain
Mustard Sauce, 268–269
Roasted Garlic Mashed Potatoes with
Chives, 281
Roasted New Potatoes, 271
Roasted peppers
Alaskan Halibut with Roasted Red
Pepper Coulis, 148–149

Grilled Skewered Shrimp with
Romesco Sauce, 136–138
Italian Sausage Contadina with
Roasted Sweet Peppers,
Potatoes, and Onions,
215–216
purchased, 149
Quick and Easy Roasted Red Pepper
Sauce, 149
in Red Bell Pepper Bisque with Crème
Fraîche, 67
Roasted Peppers, 254–255
Roasted Root Vegetables, 269–271
Roasted Stuffed Turkey with Pan Gravy,
188–193
Roasting foods, 26
texture and flavor of foods cooked by,
35
vegetables, 26
Roasting pans, 26
size of, 208
for turkey, 191
Rodgers, Judy, 44
Roll-cutting, 21, 22
Romaine lettuce
Chicken Soup with Glass Noodles,
70–71
reheating prime rib using, 210
tearing, 81
Weeknight Green Salad, 81–82
Romano beans, 258, 258(illus)
Romano Beans, 258
Romano cheese. See also Pecorino
romano cheese
Double-Crusted Timpano with Fusilli,
Ricotta, and Tender Little
Meatballs, 126–130
Rigatoni with Sausage and Mushroom
Ragu, 118–119
Room temperature, 53
side dishes that can be served at, 248
Root vegetables. See also specific vegetables
boiling of, 34
Roasted Root Vegetables, 269–271
Rose-flavored jam, 309

Rose petal jam, 309
Roux, mahogany, 141
Rubs, for meat, 242
Rum, dark
Zucchini-Olive Oil Snack Cake with
Lemon Icing, 303–304
Rustichella d'Abruzzo pasta, 107
Rutabaga
in chicken stock, 56
Vegetable Broth, 63

S

Sadaf pomegranate molasses, 223
Safety, 23
Saffron, 99
Paella with Shellfish, Sausage, and
Chicken, 158–161
Risotto Milanese, 98–99
steeping, 98, 99
storing, 99
Salad bowls, 79
Salad dressings
amount to use, 79
Citrus Dressing, 83
Raspberry Vinaigrette, 91, 92
Sauce Verte, 150–151
vinaigrette, separate versus combined
with salad, 79
White Balsamic Vinaigrette, 86–87
Salad greens. See also Lettuce; specific
types of greens
Baby Greens, Roasted Chicken, Stilton,
and Hazelnuts with Raspberry
Vinaigrette, 91–92
Figs and Arugula with Creamy Goat
Cheese and Toasted Pecans, 90
Salads
Baby Greens, Roasted Chicken, Stilton,
and Hazelnuts with Raspberry
Vinaigrette, 91–92
Butter Lettuce with Ruby Grapefruit,
Avocado, and Glazed Walnuts,
82–84

Chicken Salad Véronique with Whole
Toasted Almonds, 168–169
Classic American Potato Salad,
282–283
dressings for. *See* Salad dressings
escarole in, 264
Figs and Arugula with Creamy Goat
Cheese and Toasted Pecans, 90
Heirloom Tomatoes with Bocconcini,
Basil, and White Balsamic
Vinaigrette, 86–87
keeping cheese white in, 78
quick, 55
Shaved Celery with Medjool Dates,
Feta, and Walnuts, 88
tips for, 78–79
Vietnamese-Style Honey-Glazed Pork
Skewers with Rice Vermicelli,
212–214
Weeknight Green Salad, 81–82
Salivation, acid and, 38
Salmon
cutting fillets into slices, 102,
103(illus.)
doneness of, 134
Poached Salmon with Shortcut
Hollandaise Sauce, 152–154
removing pin bones from, 135
Risotto Primavera with Wild Salmon,
102–104
Steamed Salmon and Creamer
Potatoes with Sauce Verte,
150–151
Salmonella, 23, 162, 163
Salt
kosher. *See* Kosher salt
in making Hollandaise sauce, 152
omitting from marinades, 222
omitting from stocks, 56
sea. *See* Sea salt
table, 43, 44
Salting foods, 42–45
avoiding before deep-frying, 29
of blanching liquid, 33
before braising, 31

brining and, 45–46
gravy, 233
of ice-water bath for cooling foods,
33, 62
kosher salt and, 43–44
sea salt and, 44
soups, 65
tasting and, 42
timing of, 31, 44–45, 208, 230
types of salt and, 43
of water for boiling, 34
of water for cooking pasta, 107, 108,
109
San Marzano tomatoes, 116
Saucepans, 15
Sauces
Béchamel Sauce, 123
"Bolognese" Sauce, 124–126
caramel sauce, shortcut, 289–290
hollandaise sauce, shortcut, 152–154
Horseradish Sauce, 232, 234
Kahlúa Sauce, 293–294
Mango Salsa, 156–157
Mornay Sauce, 110–111
Mushroom Ragu, 118–119
napé and, 112
Pesto, 186–187
Pineapple Salsa, 220, 221
puréeing, 235
Raspberry Coulis, 295, 297
Romesco Sauce, 136–137
roux-based, 111
Sauce Verte, 150–151
spoons for stirring, 233
Tartar Sauce, 146
20-Minute Tomato Sauce, 115, 116
Velouté Sauce, 139, 140
Zabaglione with Fresh Berries and
Peaches, 305–306
Saucier pans, 15, 104(illus.)
for risotto, 96
Sausage
Baked Rigatoni with Sausage and
Mushrooms, 119
"Bolognese" Sauce, 124–126

Braised Greens with Sausage and
Onions, 266–267
California Crab Gumbo with Chicken
and Sausage, 138–141
cooking method for, 118
internal doneness temperature for, 164
Italian Sausage Contadina with
Roasted Sweet Peppers,
Potatoes, and Onions,
215–216
Maple-Glazed Quail Stuffed with Wild
Mushrooms, Sausage, and
Sour Cherries, 194–197
Paella with Shellfish, Sausage, and
Chicken, 158–161
removing casing from, 118
Rigatoni with Sausage and Mushroom
Ragu, 118–119
Three-Bean Minestrone with Sausage,
75–77
Sautéed Fillet of Sole with Tartar Sauce,
145–147
Sautéed Mushrooms with Sherry and
Garlic, 271–272
Sautéeing foods, 28
fish, 146
meat, 172
mushrooms, 118, 271
onions, 73, 97
poultry, 172
texture and flavor and, 35
Sauté pans, 16, 28, 53
for *à la minute* sauce preparation, 178
measuring size of, 16
Savoriness, 38–39, 70
Savory Baked Risotto Cake, 105–106
Savory Corn Pudding, 256–257
Savoy cabbage
choosing, 75
Three-Bean Minestrone with Sausage,
75–77
Scallions
cutting into rings, 71
shredding, 214, 214(illus.)

Scallops
    bay and sea, 142, 143(illus.)
    choosing, 143
    Cracker-Crusted Nubble Point
        Scallops, 142–143
    muscle of, 142
    Paella with Shellfish, Sausage, and
        Chicken, 158–161
    storing, 134
Scaloppine, 177
Scanpan cookware, 16
Schneider, Elizabeth, 268
Seafood. *See* Fish; Shellfish; *specific types*
    of fish and shellfish
Searing chicken, 170
Sea salt, 44
    in baked goods, 288
    sodium content of, 43
Sea scallops, 142, 143(illus.)
Seasonal ingredients, 40
Seasonal menus, 319–325
Seasonal recipes, 316–318
Seasoning to taste. *See also* Salting foods
    process of, 137
Seeding tomatoes, 261
Seeds, toasting, 78
Senses, using while cooking, 37
Serrano, Julian, 158
Serrano chiles, 157, 171(illus.)
Serrated knives, 17
Severson, Kim, 42
Shallots
    Roasted Root Vegetables, 269–271
Shaoxing (Shao Hsing) wine, 175
Shaved Celery with Medjool Dates, Feta,
    and Walnuts, 88
Shellfish. *See also* Clams; Mussels;
    Scallops; Shrimp; Squid
    cleaning, 134, 135
    Paella with Shellfish, Sausage, and
        Chicken, 158–161
    storing, 134
Sherry
    Sautéed Mushrooms with Sherry and
        Garlic, 271–272

Shingle-stacking meat, 179
Shortcut Chicken Broth with a Dividend,
    61–62
Shredding foods
    green onions, 214, 214(illus.)
    hard-cooked eggs, 282
Shrimp
    Fettuccine Alfredo with Baby Shrimp
        and Peas, 113–114
    Grilled Skewered Shrimp with
        Romesco Sauce, 136–138
    Paella with Shellfish, Sausage, and
        Chicken, 158–161
    removing shell and vein from, 136
    rinsing, 135
    size of, 159
    skewering, 136, 138, 138(illus.)
    storing, 134
Side dishes, 247–283
    make ahead, 248
    pairing with main dishes, 249
    quick, 248
    to serve at room temperature, 248
    vegetarian, 248
Sifting
    dry ingredients for cakes, 304
    flour, 53, 301
    strainer for, 288
Silicone baking liners, 26
Silver skin, 210
    removing, 179, 179(illus.), 210, 230
Simmer
    for braising, 31
    for clear stocks and broths, 56
    defined, 31
Simmons, Marie, 48, 90
Skewering
    shrimp, 136, 138, 138(illus.)
    using double skewers, 136
Skewers, bamboo, soaking, 136
Skillets, 16, 28, 53
    for browning foods, 31
    measuring size of, 16
Skimmers, 60(illus.)
Skimming stocks, 56

Skin
    of bell peppers, 254
    of chicken, 60, 165, 202
    peeling. *See* Peeling foods
    removing from fish, 148(illus.), 149
    removing from nuts, 92
    silver, 179, 179(illus.), 210, 230
Slicing onions, 73
Slotted spoons, 18
Slow-Roasted Beef Sirloin Tip with Pan
        Gravy or Creamy Horseradish
        Sauce, 232–234
Small electrics, 18
Small wares, 18–19
Smoke point, 30
    of clarified butter, 155
    of cold-pressed and expeller-pressed
        oils, 87
Smoking, of fat in pan, 28
Soft cheeses, crumbling without
    "melting," 91
Solanine, in potatoes, 151
Sole
    Sautéed Fillet of Sole with Tartar
        Sauce, 145–147
Sorbet
    Orange-Mint Sorbet in Orange Shells,
        311–312
Soups
    Chicken Soup with Glass Noodles,
        70–71
    consistency of, 65
    flavor of, 65
    French Onion Soup Gratinée, 73–75
    hot, adding cheese to, 72
    puréeing, 65
    quick, 55
    Red Bell Pepper Bisque with Crème
        Fraîche, 66–67
    seasoning to taste, 65
    Three-Bean Minestrone with Sausage,
        75–77
    tips for, 65
    Tomato-Cheddar Soup, 72–73
    White Corn Chowder, 68–69

Sources, 326

Soy sauce, black (sweet), 170

Spaghetti and Meatballs with 20-Minute
    Tomato Sauce, 114–117

Spaghetti server, 70(illus.), 114(illus.)

Special occasion menus, seasonal, 320,
    321, 322, 323, 324, 325

Spectrum coconut oil, 236

Spices. See also specific spices
    dried, bringing out flavor of, 172
    sautéing in ghee, 278

Spiders (strainers), 60(illus.)

Spinach
    Garlic Spinach with Currants, Pine
        Nuts, and Pecorino, 265–266

Spoons, 18, 19
    measuring, 18
    for serving pasta, 70(illus.), 114(illus.)
    slotted, 18
    wooden, 233, 308

Springform pans, inverting bottom of,
    105, 106(illus.)

Spring menus, 320–321

Spring recipes, 316

Squash. See Butternut squash; Winter
    squash; Yellow squash; Zucchini

Squid
    Braised Calamari in Red Sauce,
        144–145
    buying, 144
    cooking, 144
    cutting up, 144, 145(illus.)
    frozen, 144
    Paella with Shellfish, Sausage, and
        Chicken, 158–161
    storing, 134, 144

St. Ours clam juice, 137

Stand blenders, 18
    for puréeing soups, 65

Stand mixers, 18

Starchy foods, soaking pans used for, 34

Starchy ingredients, in braised dishes, 31

Steam burns, preventing, 32

Steamed Salmon and Creamer Potatoes
    with Sauce Verte, 150–151

Steamers
    bamboo, storing, 32
    improvising, 150

Steaming foods, 32
    texture and flavor and, 35

Stewing, braising versus, 30

Stick blenders, 18

Stilton cheese
    Baby Greens, Roasted Chicken, Stilton,
        and Hazelnuts with Raspberry
        Vinaigrette, 91–92
    crumbling without "melting," 91
    Rib-Eye Steaks with Arugula, Blue
        Cheese, and Grilled Red
        Onions, 228–229

Stir-Fried Velvet Chicken with Cashews,
    174–175

Stir-frying, 29

Stir-fry pans, 16

Stirring risotto, 96

Stock
    adding to risotto, 96, 97
    broth versus, 57
    clarity of, 56
    Classic Chicken Stock, 60–61
    concentrating flavor of, 56
    cooking time for, 57
    cooling, 57–58
    flavor of, 57
    heating for risotto, 96
    ingredients for, 56
    quick, 55
    for risotto, 95
    Shortcut Chicken Broth with a
        Dividend, 61–62
    simmering, 56
    skimming, 56
    storing, 58
    straining, 56
    Vegetable Broth, 63–64

Stockpots, 60, 63

Storing equipment
    bamboo steamers, 32
    knives, 17

Storing foods

basil, 187

bread crumbs, 172

butter, 288

caramel sauce, 289–290

clarified butter, 155

dates, 88

egg whites, 307

figs, 90

fish, 134

frosting, 300

ganache, 300

garlic oil, 109

ghee, 240

gravy, 191

nuts, 85

oils, 87

onions, 74

Parmigiano-Reggiano rinds, 100

potatoes, 74, 151

saffron, 99

squid, 144

stocks, 58

tomatoes, 78, 284

Strainers, 18, 67(illus.)
    for sifting, 288

Straining foods
    puréed soups, 65
    stocks, 56

Strawberries
    organic, 310
    Strawberry Granita Parfaits, 309–310
    Zabaglione with Fresh Berries and
        Peaches, 305–306

Stuffing
    for Maple-Glazed Quail Stuffed with
        Wild Mushrooms, Sausage,
        and Sour Cherries, 194–197
    for poultry, internal doneness temper-
        ature for, 164

Stuffing, for roasted turkey, 190, 191

Sugar, superfine, making, 297

Sultanas
    Zucchini-Olive Oil Snack Cake with
        Lemon Icing, 303–304

Summer menus, 321–322

Summer recipes, 316, 317

Superfine sugar, making, 297

Superfino rice, 95

Sushi-grade fish, 134

Sweating vegetables, 198

Sweet potatoes
Roasted Root Vegetables, 269–271

Sweet soy sauce, 170

Swivel-blade vegetable peelers, 19

Swordfish
availability of, 155
Broiled Swordfish with Mango Salsa, 155–157
doneness of, 134, 156

T

Tabasco sauce, 257

Table salt, 44
sodium content of, 43

Taleggio cheese
about, 184
Grilled Stuffed Chicken Breasts with Prosciutto, Taleggio, and Pesto, 183–185

Taste. *See* Flavor

Tears, when cutting onions, 73, 74

Temperature
danger zone for, 23
of food before cooking, 24, 33, 34
internal. *See* Internal doneness temperature
of meat before roasting, 210
of oven. *See* Oven temperature
room. *See* Room temperature

Tenderloin, of poultry, 176, 178

"Tenting" poultry with foil, 165–166

Texture of foods
cooking and, 35–36
hamburgers, 226
pairing side dishes with main dishes and, 249
of rice, 278

Thai-Style Minced Chicken with Basil and Chiles, 170–171

Thermometers, 18
instant-read, for freezing ice-cream or sorbet, 311
instant-read, probe-type, 153(illus.)
oven, 26

Three-Bean Minestrone with Sausage, 75–77

Thyme
branch of, 62(illus.)
between skin and breast meat of chicken, 188
sprig of, 62(illus.)
stripping off leaves from, 68

Timpano
Double-Crusted Timpano with Fusilli, Ricotta, and Tender Little Meatballs, 126–130

Toasting foods
nuts, 78, 89, 92
seeds, 78

Tomatoes, 284(illus.)
acid in, cookware and aluminum foil and, 108
acid in, onion and, 72
Baked Portabello Mushrooms Stuffed with Turkey, Eggplant, and Fresh Bread Crumbs, 172–173
Baked Rigatoni with Sausage and Mushrooms, 119
blanching, 261
"Bolognese" Sauce, 124–126
Braised Calamari in Red Sauce, 144–145
Braised Short Ribs with Frizzled Leeks, 237–241
Braised Summer Squash with Sweet Peppers, Tomatoes, and Basil, 262–263
California Crab Gumbo with Chicken and Sausage, 138–141
canned, 116, 126, 180
cherry, cutting, 78, 103
Chicken Cacciatore, 202–203
Chicken Thighs Parmigiana, 180–182
dicing, 261

Double-Crusted Timpano with Fusilli, Ricotta, and Tender Little Meatballs, 126–130
Eggplant Parmigiana, 259–261
heirloom, 86
Heirloom Tomatoes with Bocconcini, Basil, and White Balsamic Vinaigrette, 86–87
Mango Salsa, 156–157
My Grandmother's Baked Stuffed Manicotti, 120–122
Orzo with Toybox Tomatoes and Fresh Mint, 283–284
Osso Buco with Sweet Red Peppers and Gremolata, 234–237
peeling, 261
puréeing, 125
Rib-Eye Steaks with Arugula, Blue Cheese, and Grilled Red Onions, 228–229
Rigatoni with Sausage and Mushroom Ragu, 118–119
Risotto Primavera with Wild Salmon, 102–104
seeding, 261
Spaghetti and Meatballs with 20-Minute Tomato Sauce, 114–117
storing, 78, 284
Three-Bean Minestrone with Sausage, 75–77
Tomato-Cheddar Soup, 72–73
toybox, 86, 283
Turkey-Eggplant Casserole with Fresh Bread Crumbs, 173
20-Minute Tomato Sauce, 115, 116
Weeknight Chili, 245–246
Weeknight Green Salad, 81–82

Tomato paste, in tubes, 119

Tombo, 155

Tortillas, warming before serving, 205

The Trans-Fat Solution (Severson), 42

Trichinosis, 211

Triple Sec, 309

Tropical Traditions coconut oil, 236

Tropp, Barbara, 16, 174
Trudeau cutting boards, 17
Trussing poultry, 166, 166(illus.), 188
Tuna
    about, 155
    in Broiled Swordfish with Mango
        Salsa, 155–157
    doneness of, 156
Turban head molds, buttering, 302
Turkey. *See also* Poultry
    Baked Portabello Mushrooms Stuffed
        with Turkey, Eggplant, and
        Fresh Bread Crumbs, 172–173
    brining, 45, 46, 189, 190, 191
    carving, 166–167, 167(illus.)
    color of, after brining, 191
    cooking time for, 190
    doneness of, 164, 190
    fillet strip or tenderloin of, 178
    free-range, 45
    internal doneness temperature for,
        164, 190
    juices of, clear, as doneness test, 164
    resting before carving, 190
    roasted, basting, 191, 192
    Roasted Stuffed Turkey with Pan
        Gravy, 188–193
    size to buy, 165
    stuffing for, 190, 191
    Turkey-Eggplant Casserole with Fresh
        Bread Crumbs, 173
    Turkey Mole, 204–207
    Turkey Piccata, 177–179
Turkish bay leaves, 58, 58(illus.)
Turnips
    Roasted Root Vegetables, 269–271
20-Minute Tomato Sauce, 115, 116
    in My Grandmother's Baked Stuffed
        Manicotti, 120–122

U
Umami, 38–39, 70
United States measures, table of equiva-
    lents for, 352

V
Vanilla extract, 288
Veal. *See also* Meat
    doneness of, 209
    internal doneness temperature for, 209
    Osso Buco with Sweet Red Peppers
        and Gremolata, 234–237
    in Turkey Piccata, 179
Vegetable broth
    recipes using, 59
    Vegetable Broth, 63–64
Vegetable oil spray, tips for using, 173
Vegetable peelers, 19
Vegetables. *See also specific vegetables*
    boiling, 34
    braising, 31
    for broth, roasting, 63
    caramelizing, 270
    color of, 34, 80, 102, 258
    preventing leaching of chlorophyll
        from, 34
    Roasted Root Vegetables, 269–271
    roasting, 26, 63
    round, cutting, 78
    sweating, 198
    vinegar and color of, 80, 102, 258
    white, preventing browning of, 198
Vegetables from Amaranth to Zucchini
    (Schneider), 268
Vegetarian recipes
    main dishes, 132–133
    pastas, 94
    risottos, 94
    salads, 55
    side dishes, 248
    soups, 55
    stocks, 55
Velouté Sauce, 139, 140
Velveting, 174
Venison
    variation for Grilled Leg of Lamb with
        Pomegranate Marinade and
        Muhammara, 223
Ventilation, for grilling, 25

Vermicelli, 212–214
Vermouth
    French Onion Soup Gratinée, 73–75
    in risotto, 95
Vialone Nano rice, 95
Vietnamese-Style Honey-Glazed Pork
    Skewers with Rice Vermicelli,
    212–214
Vinaigrettes. *See* Salad dressings
Vinegar
    balsamic. *See* Balsamic vinegar
    color of vegetables and, 80, 258
    types of, 80
    white, 80, 87
Virgin Oil de Coco-Crème coconut oil,
    236
Vojtilla, Charlene, 58, 201, 302

W
Wallingford, Meghan, 311
Walnut oil, 91
    Baby Greens, Roasted Chicken, Stilton,
        and Hazelnuts with Raspberry
        Vinaigrette, 91–92
    Figs and Arugula with Creamy Goat
        Cheese and Toasted Pecans, 90
Walnuts
    Butter Lettuce with Ruby Grapefruit,
        Avocado, and Glazed Walnuts,
        82–84
    glazed, 83, 85
    Grilled Leg of Lamb with Pomegranate
        Marinade and Muhammara,
        221–223
    Shaved Celery with Medjool Dates,
        Feta, and Walnuts, 88
    Zucchini-Olive Oil Snack Cake with
        Lemon Icing, 303–304
Water, from cold and hot taps, 107
Watercress
    Sauce Verte, 150–151
Wearever skillets, 16
Weeknight Chili, 245–246
Weeknight Green Salad, 81–82

What Einstein Told His Cook (Wolke), 74

Whipping cream. *See* Heavy cream

Whisks
balloon, 18, 305, 308
flat, 112(illus.), 123(illus.)

White balsamic vinegar
White Balsamic Vinaigrette, 86–87

White beans
Three-Bean Minestrone with Sausage,
75–77

White Cheddar Polenta, 275

White chocolate
choosing, 296
White Chocolate Cheesecake with
Oreo Crust and Raspberry
Coulis, 295–297

White Corn Chowder, 68–69

White vinegar, 80, 87

White wine
adding to risotto, 96
French Onion Soup Gratinée, 73–75
for risotto, 95
Risotto Milanese, 98–99
Risotto Primavera with Wild Salmon,
102–104

Wild mushrooms
about, 195
Braised Short Ribs with Frizzled Leeks,
237–241
Chicken Soup with Glass Noodles,
70–71
dried, 195. *See also* Porcini mushrooms
Maple-Glazed Quail Stuffed with Wild
Mushrooms, Sausage, and
Sour Cherries, 194–197
Pot Roast and Gravy with Peas and
Carrots, 241–244

Wild rice
cleaning, 276
cooking, 276
Wild Rice Pilaf, 276–277

Williams, Chuck, 241

Willow-leaf bay, 58(illus.)

Wilting of lettuce, preventing, 78

Winchester, Michelle, 139, 141

Wine. *See also* Marsala wine; Sherry;
Vermouth; White wine
acid in, caramelizing onions and, 73
flavor and, 38
Shaoxing (Shao Hsing), 175

Wine vinegar, 80

Winter menus, 324–325

Winter recipes, 318

Winter squash. *See also* Butternut squash;
Hubbard squash
cutting up, 273
peeling, 273

Woks, 29
cleaning, 160
seasoning, 158

Wolke, Robert L., 74

Wooden salad bowls, 79

Wooden utensils, 19
spoons, 233, 308

Woods, Don, 48

Y

Yee, Rhoda, 61

Yellow Fingerling potatoes, 271

Yellow prussiate of soda, in Morton
kosher salt, 43

Yellow squash
Braised Summer Squash with Sweet
Peppers, Tomatoes, and Basil,
262–263
Three-Bean Minestrone with Sausage,
75–77

Yogurt, to soothe hands after working
with chiles, 157

Yukon Gold potatoes
about, 271
Mashed Yukon Gold Potatoes, 280–281

Z

Zabaglione with Fresh Berries and
Peaches, 305–306

Zest, 178
measuring, 53

Zucchini
Braised Summer Squash with Sweet
Peppers, Tomatoes, and Basil,
262–263
Three-Bean Minestrone with Sausage,
75–77
Zucchini-Olive Oil Snack Cake with
Lemon Icing, 303–304

The Zuni Café Cookbook (Rodgers), 44

TABLE OF EQUIVALENTS

The exact equivalents in the following table have been rounded for convenience.

Liquid/Dry Measures			Length		
U.S.	Metric		U.S.	Metric	
¼ teaspoon	1.25 milliliters		⅛ inch	3 millimeters	
½ teaspoon	2.5 milliliters		¼ inch	6 millimeters	
1 teaspoon	5 milliliters		½ inch	12 millimeters	
1 tablespoon (3 teaspoons)	15 milliliters		1 inch	2.5 centimeters	
1 fluid ounce (2 tablespoons)	30 milliliters		**Oven Temperature**		
¼ cup	60 milliliters		Fahrenheit	Celsius	Gas
⅓ cup	80 milliliters		250	120	½
½ cup	120 milliliters		275	140	1
1 cup	240 milliliters		300	150	2
1 pint (2 cups)	480 milliliters		325	160	3
1 quart (4 cups, 32 ounces)	960 milliliters		350	180	4
1 gallon (4 quarts)	3.84 liters		375	190	5
			400	200	6
1 ounce (by weight)	28 grams		425	220	7
1 pound	454 grams		450	230	8
2.2 pounds	1 kilogram		475	240	9
			500	260	10